Braga

SEEDS OF TRANSCENDENCE

ALSO BY JO ANN GARDNER

Old-Fashioned Fruit Garden

Heirloom Garden

Living With Herbs

Herbs in Bloom

Gardens of Use & Delight
with Jigs Gardner

Elegant Silvers
with Karen Bussolini

Seeds of Transcendence:

UNDERSTANDING THE
HEBREW BIBLE
THROUGH PLANTS

Jo Ann Gardner

DECALOGUE BOOKS
Mount Vernon, New York

Published in 2014 in the United States by

Decalogue Books
7 North MacQuesten Parkway
Mount Vernon, NY 10550
www.decaloguebooks.com
(914) 664-5930

Printed in the United States

Library of Congress Cataloguing-in Publication Data

Gardner, Jo Ann, 1935–
Seeds of Transcendence: Understanding the Hebrew Bible Through Plants
    p. cm
Includes bibliographical references and index.
ISBN: 978-0-915474-15-8 (softcover)
ISBN: 978-0-915474-14-1 (hardcover)
1. Bible. 2. Torah. 3. Botany. 4. Jo Ann Gardner. 5. Biblical Gardens. 6. Israel.

Cover and interior design by Rita Lascaro.

First Edition
May 2014

To Nogah Hareuveni, of blessed memory,
and to Avinoam Danin.
They showed and taught me the land.

PLANTS OF THE HEBREW BIBLE

This is a list of the major plants discussed in this book and is meant as a quick reference. For a more detailed listing with Latin plant names see *Common Names Cross Reference* on page 359.

Acacia Tree
Almond Tree
Anemone
Apple of Sodom
Balm of Gilead
Barley
Bitter Herbs
White Broom Bush
Bulrush
Burning Bush
Caper Bush
Carob Tree
Cassia
Cattail
Cedar of Lebanon
Cinnamon
Citron
Persian Crowfoot (Red Buttercup)
Cucumbers
Cypress
Date Palm
Fig Tree
Flax
Frankincense
Galbanum
Garlics
Golden Thistle
Wild Gourd
Grapevine
Gum
Golden Henbane

Hyssop
Juniper Tree
Ladanum
Leeks
Lentil
Mandrakes
Manna
Myrrh
Narcissus
Nightshade
Oak Tree
Olive Tree
Onions
Papyrus
Plane Tree
Poison Hemlock
Pomegranate
Poplar
Poppy
Reed
Sage
Squirting Cucumber
Stacte
Tamarisk Tree
Terebinth Tree
Thorny Burnet
Tulip
Watermelons
Wheat
Willow
Wormwood

CONTENTS

BOOK OF GENESIS
Bereshit

BOOK OF EXODUS
Shemot

BOOK OF DEUTERONOMY
Devarim

ACKNOWLEDGMENTS

I owe a great deal to my attentive readers: retired Jewish educator Paula Tobenfield; Michael and Elaine Solowey, Kibbutz Ketura, Israel; Reverend Matthew Borden in Ottawa, Canada; and publisher Bill Brandon, who wears many hats. I am grateful as ever to my husband, Jigs, my first literary editor, who always believed in this project and who labored on the Index. Any errors in this book are mine alone.

I am very thankful for the work of Rita Lascaro, a gem of a graphics editor and book designer.

The following people were helpful to me in various ways, all important: Gili Toper-Taieb at Neot Kedumim; Miriam Yekutiel, international plantswoman; Nell Gardner; Rabbi Chaim Strauchler of Shaarei Shomayim Synagogue, Toronto; Sara Spiegel, Volcani Center, Israel (ret.); Helen Tramte and Janeen Wright at the Herb Society of America; Sue Surkes, Director of Development at the Jerusalem Botanical Gardens; Helen Frenkley, retired Director, Neot Kedumim; Sharon Lieberman-Mintz, Curator of Jewish Art, Library of the Jewish Theological Seminary; Laurie Koretz in the Negev; and Shirley P. Sidell, Elie Weiss, Betty Clement, Eric Scheidker, Mary Ellen Angeletti, Mary Beth Colgan, Judy L. Moseley, Lois Rose, and Cheryl Blanchard at the Paine Memorial Library. And Dr. Jan Duus.

I am deeply indebted to those who contributed their photographs and patiently answered my questions.

Jackie Chambers, Ethnobotanist, Horticulturist, has worked at private and public gardens around the world, worked and studied at the Jerusalem Botanical Gardens (2005–6) as the recipient of a scholarship from the British Friends of JBG.

Avinoam Danin, Professor Emeritus of Botany, Department of Ecology, Evolution, and Behavior, The Hebrew University of Jerusalem.

Ori Fragman-Sapir, Head Scientist, Jerusalem Botanical Gardens.

Nell Gardner, Flower Fields Farm, and Horticulturist at the Frank Lloyd Wright Darwin Martin House.

Joshua D. Klein, Israel Ministry of Agriculture, Volcani Center, Unit for Agriculture according to the Torah.

John Lytton Musselman, Mary Hogan Professor of Botany, Old Dominion University.

Shirley P. Sidell, founder of www.biblicalgardens.com.

Elaine Solowey, Director of the Center for Sustainable Agriculture at the Arava Institute, Kibbutz Ketura.

Place names in the photographs are all in Israel unless otherwise noted.

PREFACE

Seeds of Transcendence: Understanding the Hebrew Bible through Plants of the Holy Land

In 1971 my husband and I and our four children moved to Cape Breton Island at the tip of Nova Scotia in Canada to restore a back country farm. It was then that my husband transferred his herb collection to me, since he no longer had time for it. When these plants were the only ones that survived my first foray into ornamental gardening, I took a closer look at them. I was attracted to exploring their useful and esthetic properties and I was drawn to their Old World histories. At the time I had only a vague notion of the group of plants known as Holy Land flora, the wild plants of the Land of Israel, among which, I later learned, are many species renowned for their uses as well as for their associations with the Bible. I had assumed the subject was irrelevant, remote from my life. While my interest in plants was burgeoning, what could such exotica offer me?

But life takes surprising turns, and so one raw spring day in the early 1980s I found myself looking through drifts of snow in our still-frozen garden for something green and bitter to fulfill the role of bitter herbs at our Passover Seder, for it was through these plants that I was taking my first steps back to Judaism after a lapse of many years.

It had surprised me to learn that the bitter herbs of Passover, referred to in the Bible as *merorim* and individually named in the Talmud (the post-biblical compendium of rabbinic commentaries, teachings, and laws interpreted from the Bible) are simply five common, edible weeds, one of which, chicory, I grew in my garden for its roots as a coffee substitute. The rabbis, apparently keen observers of the natural world (an even greater surprise to me), associated these weeds with the Israelites' experience in Egypt of being welcomed at first, then enslaved, because the plants themselves mirror this experience in their appearance around the time of Passover: in winter in the Middle East they sprout from the ground and grow as soft-stemmed plants whose plentiful bittersweet leaves are gathered for food, but months later, as they mature, their foliage becomes sparse and very bitter, growing now on hard stems. Participants in the Passover ritual would be unlikely to forget their shared history as a people when they saw and tasted this symbolic reminder of their past.

I felt strongly drawn to what has been called teaching Torah in the field: the Bible and Talmud's ongoing effort to drive home the values of ethical monotheism through imagery inspired by the familiar plants of the everyday biblical landscape. A new and exciting world was opening for me to explore, one that combined my passion for a deeper understanding of Judaism with my growing interest in Israel's native flora.

It was inevitable that I would feel the need to see and touch, and even taste, the plants I had read about, and so one cold mid-February morning in1988 my husband Jigs hitched up our team of horses to the bobsled and took me over the ice-covered road to the railroad tracks a mile from the farm, where we hailed the train for the initial leg of my first trip to Israel.

In the bright light of morning in Jerusalem I was struck by lush Mediterranean growth. Whatever I had imagined about the Land of Israel, it wasn't characterized by a breathtaking floral carpet, a low patchwork of annual reds, yellows, pinks and vivid blues. On a later trip I accompanied students to Mount Gilboa to see the stunning native iris: large, fluted upper petals veined and blushed burgundy with darker lower petals, the whole head about five inches across, the plant itself about two and half feet tall, a magnificent flower in nature that

Photograph © Jackie Chambers

Meadow mix of sorrel (*Rumex* sp.), chamomile (*Anthemis* sp.), and poppy (*Papaver umbonatum*) near Ashdod.

would be hard to improve. Our leader mused that the Almighty must have stopped here for a moment, and while He wasn't paying attention, His pockets spilled open with all these wonderful things. Perhaps this explains the almond tree's cloud of white bloom in late winter, the sheets of lilac, pink, and yellow flowers that cover bare desert slopes in wet years, menorah-shaped salvia, shimmering from high cliffs, and the succession of reds— tulips, anemones, buttercups, poppies—blooming in fallow fields and on rocky outcrops. Although dazzling, they inspired the prophet's admonition that their beauty is only transient: their flowers fade while the word of God lives forever (Isaiah 40:6-8).

On successive trips I was bowled over not only by the exuberance and variety of Israel's native plants in their short season of bloom (March–April), but by the ability of so many different types to grow in seemingly inhospitable terrain. From the Negev desert to the hill country in the Galilee, I saw hyssop, *Majorana syriaca*, growing between rocks as described in the Bible (I Kings 5:13), and its symbolic meaning of humility could not be denied.

Many plants find nourishment near or between rocks, or like the caper bush (a symbol of Jewish survival in Talmudic literature), flourish between the cracks of walls or large boulders in otherwise barren places. It is not difficult to imagine how such plants

Photograph © Avinoam Danin

Iris haynei. Haynei's iris, Mount Gilboa.

Photograph © Jackie Chambers

Anemone coronaria. Carpet of anemone flowers, Alumin near Gaza.

Capparis zoharyi. Caper bush, Judean Desert.

Lotz Cisterns landscape, Negev Highlands.

Iris-regis uzziae. Uzzia's iris's emerging foliage, Lotz Cisterns, near the Ramon Crater/Makhtesh Ramon.

Iris-regis uzziae. Uzzia's iris in bloom.

assumed meanings suggested by their outstanding characteristics and ecological place in the landscape. In the central Negev Highlands to the south, for instance, a landscape of immense and forbidding limestone and chalk cliffs and mountains, smooth-faced rocks, acres of gravelly or dry and cracked soil, of deep valleys, occasional wadis (temporary river beds), a surprising number of diverse, useful, and quite often beautiful plants find the means to survive. In wadis, green with vegetation, an occasional tamarisk or pistachio tree, hundreds of years old, provides welcome shade in treeless surroundings. Such is the land and its flora with which our forbears were intimately familiar.

Even considering that in biblical times the Land of Israel encompassed both sides of the Jordan River and part of Syria, the variety of plant life in present-day Israel is remarkable: nearly three thousand species grow in a country that today is no more than two-hundred and seventy-three miles long and seventy-four miles wide, about the size of New Jersey. This number is even more impressive when measured against countries much larger than Israel. In the British Isles, for instance, an area ten times that of Israel, there are less than two thousand plant species. The explanation for this floral abundance lies in the land's strategic geographical position as a transitional zone wedged between extreme desert in the southern and eastern parts of the region and the relatively moist, cooler areas to the north. Differences in climate, soil, and rainfall ranging from as much as forty inches annually in the Mediterranean parts of the country, to as little as two inches or less in the south, create conditions for many different types of plants to thrive within a small geographic area. Within a day's drive, a visitor can see poppies on the Golan and date palms in Dead Sea Valley oases.

It was thrilling to think that the plants I had seen were direct descendants of those that shepherds, farmers, poets, prophets, and kings in biblical times, and later, rabbis in Talmudic times, saw as they went about their lives and work. For just as the country's topographical features—rock formations, mountains, valleys, plains, and rivers—have remained unchanged despite an extraordinarily long history of human activity that includes the cutting down of forests, fires, wars, overgrazing, neglect, and abandonment, the native plants, too, have remained unchanged over millennia.

Photo courtesy Neot Kedumin, Israel's Biblical Landscape Reserve

Nogah Hareuveni.

At Neot Kedumim, the 650-acre Biblical Landscape Reserve that he founded, I met Nogah Hareuveni of blessed memory, whose work had inspired me, had started me down a path I might never have taken. A slim, humble, intense man, then in his sixties, he seemed to grow from the soil of Israel like the caper bush—the symbol of Neot Kedumim—a plant that finds nourishment in difficult places as I had seen with my own eyes. After years of struggle, his revelation that nature is an integral part of Judaism (a continuation of his parents' pioneering work) was becoming accepted. It was the self-evident truth of his vision that had drawn me from thousands of miles away to see the landscape in which this point of view was born. I felt very grateful that much of my adult life living close to the land had prepared me to be so receptive to Nogah's brilliant interpretations of the Land of Israel's influence on its sacred texts and traditions as reflected in the Hebrew Bible and Talmud, and in the idea that a small handful of bitter-tasting weeds could embody so vividly the Exodus experience. The land and its flora is of inescapable significance in Judaism.

As I built up a body of my own work, I realized that the conventional format of a book about plants of the Bible, where the focus is on the plants with minimal references to the text, was inadequate. I was more interested in focusing on the biblical text itself to find out how knowledge of the wild plants of Israel and of the land itself illuminates the text. When, for instance, we realize what shepherding means in a semi-arid land, then Abram/Abraham's movements from Shechem to Bethel and "by stages" south to the Negev, as we read in Genesis 12:9, are no longer just words on a page that we may read and pass over, but full of meaning, for this is still the way semi-nomadic shepherds, today as in the past, move about to find grazing ground for their sheep. The narrative takes for granted that its audience would understand the significance of Abraham's journeys, but we, who are far removed from such a life, need the details filled in for us. When they are, the text comes alive and the characters seem to stand forth, as we read about them engaged in their work as shepherds or farmers.

On another level, it is crucial for our understanding of the most important ideas in the Bible to know that the land, then as now, experiences only two important seasons, winter and summer, rain and drought. Then we can understand the significance of God's promise to bless the people with "the rain for your land in season, the early [winter] rain and the late [summer] rain that you may gather in your grain, your wine, and your oil." These words from Deuteronomy 11:13-14, proclaimed from the thresholds of Jewish homes for millennia and inscribed on mezuzahs, express the essence of Jewish faith, a belief in the oneness of God: the God of history Who brought forth the children of Israel from Egypt and made a covenant or pact with them at Sinai to obey His laws, is the same God Who rules the universe, Who gives the rain in its season for the grain (barley and wheat), wine (grapes), and oil (olive trees), the basic foods without which life, in biblical terms, cannot survive. The plants which give these products, when grouped together with figs, pomegranates, and dates, are known as the Seven Species, *Shivat Haminim*. They are not only representative of the bounty with which God blesses the people of Israel, they exemplify the dangers inherent in farming in a difficult land where the right conditions for growing and ripening such crops cannot be taken for granted. Faced with such problems, farmers might be lured away to propitiate the various pagan gods of nature as their neighbors did. In this sense, the Seven Species are infused with meaning far beyond their earthly significance. They become a floral symbol of Israel's call to be faithful to the belief in the oneness of God.

When viewed in this light, the material and spiritual world of the Bible are inseparable. We cannot hope to understand one without the other.

I have organized the book around the annual cycle of weekly Sabbath readings (portions or *parashat*) from the Torah, for the benefit of those interested in gaining insights into them. This means that the scope of my exploration of the bond between plants and text is necessarily confined to the first five books of the Hebrew Bible, the Pentateuch (from the Greek for five books), or in Jewish terms, the Torah, literally, "the teaching." The informed reader will note that while there are fifty-four readings in the annual cycle, here there are but thirty-six chapters. That is because not every portion mentions plants or the land in a significant way. I have also drawn on some of the *Haftarah* readings from the Prophets, which follow the Torah readings and are linked to them thematically. These are a source of memorable plant references—there is the hyssop that grows 'in the rock' (I Kings 5:13) just prefacing the reading, and Jeremiah's sheltering broom tree (I Kings 19:4)—which bring the history of the people of Israel forward in time (Deuteronomy, the last of the five books, leaves them on the plains of Moab across from Jericho, about to enter the Promised Land), so the reader gets a sense of the movement of the text from the relative simplicity of semi-nomadic shepherd life in Canaan to the complexities of farming life and its consequences in the Land of Israel.

Bible plant buffs will also note that although roughly one-hundred and ten plants are mentioned in the Bible (the Hebrew and Christian Bibles combined), only sixty-five or so major plants (or plant groups) are discussed here. But these are some of the most important plants of the Hebrew Bible and some of them, like hyssop, are rarely discussed in detail (and not always correctly identified), or like the salvias (thought to be a model for the first menorah), are not discussed at all. I have relied primarily on the New Jewish Publication Society translation (NJPS) of the Hebrew Bible, *Tanakh*

(1985), except where noted if other translations differ significantly (these references are in the Bibliography). KJV refers to King James Version; RSV is the Revised Standard Version.

Each chapter is divided into two sections: the first is devoted to the context in which the plant reference appears; the second part discusses the plant (or plants) in detail: its physical description, habitat, uses, and its symbolic role in the text. Lentils, the plant reference in Chapter Four, *Fateful Stew*, are in themselves nothing but a common food of the place and time, but when they are set in the context of the vivid story of Jacob and Esau and the relationship between them, and the birthright scene in which Esau sells his inheritance for nothing more than a mess of Jacob's pottage, then they have great significance.

I have written *Seeds of Transcendence* to fulfill the need for an accessible work about understanding the Hebrew Bible through the plants of the Holy Land for an English-speaking audience, for Jews, non-Jews, believers, non-believers, for those knowledgeable about the Torah or about plants, as well as those who know little about either but are curious. I know I will have succeeded in this aim when someone who was never interested in the Bible, picks up this book, reads a chapter or two, feels compelled to read on, and then to read in the Bible itself. I, myself, am neither a Bible scholar nor a botanist (I have a rudimentary knowledge of Hebrew, have studied biblical matters for many years, and have observed plants and written extensively about them), so the reader needn't be daunted by an academic text. Still, I have provided the more scholarly reader with stimulating material (the Endnotes just grew as the text moved on to more complexities). I have no interest in burdening the reader with Higher Criticism, which I believe takes away from the power of the biblical text and does little to enlighten us. The Hebrew Bible is an absorbing, powerful work on its own terms.

The book's focus on the marvelous stories of Genesis, Exodus, and Numbers, on the characters' imperfections, struggles, and achievements, helps us to appreciate how far a rough shepherd culture—driven, by the conditions of its semi-nomadic existence to mistrust strangers (the shameful Dinah episode in Genesis 34 unsparingly shows its rough edges)—must transcend its origins in order to reach the heights of moral and ethical behavior spelled out in Leviticus and elaborated in Deuteronomy. Through the books of the Torah, and against the vivid background of the land and its flora, we follow this transformation, as each succeeding generation, led by the example of Abraham, who first answered God's call, manages through thick and thin, to pass on God's blessing and promise of a nation. Abraham's offspring, as we read in the Bible, are his 'seed,' who, God promises, will be "as numerous as the stars of heaven and as the sand that is on the seashore" (Genesis 22:17). They, the carriers of the blessing, are the very seeds of transcendence, an apt metaphor for a book about the plants of the Hebrew Bible.

Introduction

THE BOOK OF GENESIS

Bereshit

The Book of Genesis/*Bereshit* is the first of the five books that comprise the Pentateuch (Greek for "five"), known in Jewish tradition as the Torah (literally "teaching").[1] "Genesis" comes from the Greek and means "beginning" or "origin." The Hebrew name for the first book of the Torah is *Bereshit*, after the opening words of the text, "In the beginning."[2] Genesis/*Bereshit* is divided into two parts: the first is concerned with the creation of the world and the origins of the human family; the second centers on the beginning of the Israelite people and their early history according to the well-known stories of the Patriarchs (their wives, too), concluding with the descent of the children of Israel into Egypt.

ENDNOTES

1. In a broad sense, Torah encompasses not only the first five books of Moses (called in Hebrew *Humash*, from the Hebrew for five, *hamesh*), but the entire Hebrew Bible, *Tanakh*, after the initial letters of each section: *Torah* (Pentateuch), *Neviim* (Prophets), *Ketuvim* (Writings); the Talmud; and Rabbinic literature.
2. Most translations. *NJPS*'s preferred translation is "When God began to create" after Rashi (11th century Rabbi Solomon ben Isaac) in his commentary on the Torah. Nahum Sarna explains the reasoning behind both translations in his *Genesis*, JPS Torah Commentary, 5.

Ficus carica. Fig leaves, Ein Almin near Katzrin, Golan.

Chapter One

IN THE GARDEN

Portion-*Bereshit* / In the beginning (Genesis 1:1-6:8)

*The Lord God planted a garden in Eden in the east, and placed there
the man whom He had formed. And from the ground the Lord God
caused to grow every tree that was pleasing to the sight and good for
food, with the tree of life in the middle of the garden, and the tree of
knowledge of good and bad.* (Genesis 2:8-9)

*When the woman saw that the tree [of knowledge] was good to eat
and a delight to the eyes, and that the tree was desirable as a source of
wisdom, she took of its fruit and ate. She also gave some to her husband and he ate. Then the eyes of both of them were opened and they
perceived that they were naked; and they sewed together fig leaves and
made themselves loincloths.* (Genesis 3:6-7)

The Hebrew Bible's story of creation in the opening chapters of
Genesis, while drawing on Near Eastern motifs, is set apart from
them by its uncompromising emphasis on God as the sole creator of
the world and every living thing in it, and the importance of man's
relationship with God. The expulsion of Adam and Eve from the
Garden of Eden that follows can be viewed as an allegory about
humankind's place in the universe. With the eating of forbidden fruit
the first couple acquires a sense of morality (knowing the distinction
between good and evil) and are now responsible for choosing their
own destiny, rather than to remain in a place of perfection—but also
limitation. It is clear that man (*Adam*), fashioned from the earth's
dust (*adamah*) will be forever bound to the soil and all the practical

work that necessarily follows from it. Nevertheless, even after he and his wife Eve (*Hava*, life) have been expelled from the garden for disobeying God's injunction not to eat of the Tree of Knowledge, they and their descendants will have an all-consuming interest in God and He in them. These biblical themes of the interrelationship between God and humankind—first presented in Chapters Two and Three—will be pursued throughout the Hebrew Bible. The land and its flora are always present in the text, whether implicitly or explicitly, sometimes referred to in a metaphorical or figurative sense; at other times in their plain or more literal meaning, as they are an integral part of everyday ancient Israelite life as well as a source of general admiration.

This garden where God put Adam is a setting of ideal beauty and fruitfulness, but that is not mentioned in the initial description of creation because, as we learn in Chapter Two, "when the Lord God made earth and heaven, no shrub of the field was yet on the earth and no grasses of the field had yet sprouted." Why? Because "the Lord God had not yet sent rain upon the earth [to make the plants grow] and there was no man to till the soil" (Genesis 2:5). Man, Adam, will be more than a fixture in Paradise (*Gan Eden*, the Garden of Eden), he will be a co-worker with God in turning the earth into a garden, assisting plants to reach their maximum fruitfulness, in contrast with untended plants that yield little. The rabbis noted this with satisfaction: "See what a great thing is work! The first man was not to taste of anything until he had contributed some work. Only after God told him to cultivate and keep the garden, did He give him permission to eat of its fruits." (*Avot D'Rabbi Nathan*).

"Eden" (variously translated from the Hebrew as derived from "delight" or referring to steppe country to the east)[1] is translated as "Paradise" in the Septuagint or Greek translation of the Hebrew Bible, based on the Persian word for an enclosed area or pleasure ground of orderly design (from which the Hebrew word for orchard, *pardes*, is derived). Both names, "Garden of Eden" and "Paradise," have become synonymous with a comforting, attractive oasis from the distractions and complications of the outside world.

A vast literature of speculation places this garden in Armenia, in Southern Arabia, in Babylon, or near Damascus, among other sites. Only two of the four rivers that are said to feed it—the Euphrates and Tigris—are known, leading to further speculation about the identity of the other waters. Current work on the natural history of the Bible suggests that the writing in Genesis may have been inspired by a Mesopotamian tradition that plantations were watered by a system of canals.[2] Being able to pinpoint Eden or the rivers that form the garden's irrigation system, however, is immaterial to the picture we envision from the Genesis description: this is a beautiful, lush garden full of good things to eat, that is well-watered, and easy to maintain (suggested by the phrase "dress it and keep it" or "till it and tend it" (Genesis 2:15).

The layout of the garden is impressive, with two fruit-bearing trees as central features: one is the Tree of Life, the other the Tree of Knowledge of Good and Evil. Throughout the Hebrew Bible a variety of trees—olive, oak, date palm, cedar, for instance—plays a significant role as symbols, metaphors, sources of protection, for food, and inspiration: "There is hope for a tree; if it is cut down it will renew itself; Its shoots will not cease . . . But mortals languish and die; Man expires; where is he?"(Job 14:7-10). In a sense, this insight shows that the growth cycle and regenerative powers of many trees exemplify, or suggest, immortality, as in the garden's Tree of Life. In Proverbs the phrase is used figuratively to exemplify righteousness, "The fruit of the righteous is a tree of life" (Proverbs 11:30), and wisdom, "Happy he who has found wisdom for it is the tree of life to all who grasp it, and those who hold fast to it are happy" (Proverbs 3:13-18). The Tree of Life, *Etz Haim*, is a Jewish symbol associated with the study of Torah, as in the rabbinic saying "The Torah is the Tree of Life to those who cleave to it," sung at the Sabbath synagogue service after the Torah is placed back in the Ark.

The Tree of Knowledge, on the other hand, has acquired a physical identity. The 'Temptation' scene, depicted in Western Christian art since the Middle Ages and Renaissance, most often featured Eve plucking and eating a luscious red apple from a heavily laden idealized tree. A well-tended apple tree is esthetically pleasing in every way: its thick trunk, spreading branches, and round crown are in perfect proportion, its branches easily supporting the load of fragrant fruits in rosy clusters. Other less convincing candidates for the Tree of Knowledge include pomegranate, citron, mountain ash, quince, apricot, and tamarind, but none of them, including the apple, have any basis in the text. One theory for the prominence of the apple as the forbidden fruit is said to be the similarity between the Latin word for evil (*malum*) and the Latin for apple (*malus*). A more likely reason for the dominance of the apple motif in Western art is the habit of taking license with the text by substituting or, in this case, inserting, familiar plants for the unknown, as has been the case in Bible translations into European languages.[3] Apples are not native to Israel, but may have been introduced from Iran or Armenia around 4,000 BCE.[4]

The rabbis or Sages of the Talmudic era (ca. 200 CE to 560 CE) favored the fig tree as the Tree of Knowledge, reasoning that "with that which they sinned they repaired their misdeed." (*Berakhot* 40a): "Then the eyes of both of them were opened and they perceived that they were naked; and they sewed together fig leaves and made themselves loincloths" (Genesis 3:7). While there is no basis for regarding the Tree of Knowledge as a fig tree, it is the only plant, or rather the leaves from it, that are specifically mentioned by name in the description of the Garden of Eden, and immediately after Adam and Eve ate from the forbidden fruit.

—〜〜—

THE FIG TREE, *Ficus carica* (*te'enah*), has been cultivated so long in the Land of Israel that it is regarded as indigenous, although its exact origins are in dispute.[5] The returning scouts whom Moses sent to Canaan to explore the land, returned with heavy clusters of grapes, as well as pomegranates and figs (Numbers 13:23). Thereafter these and other fruits and grains (the Seven Species) were forever associated with the bounty of the land (Deuteronomy 8:8). In Israel, wild fig trees grow near springs along the Jordan Rift and Dead Sea Valleys; fossils of leaves have been found at Ein Gedi in the sediment of very ancient springs.[6] Untended trees may grow from nine to fifteen feet tall with spreading crowns of thick branches and twigs, and may bear fruit, but not reliably. In biblical times, fig trees, which have an unusually long harvest season in Israel from May to September, were cultivated to increase the tree's production of fruit, so vital to the economy of everyday life. Excavations near Jericho in the lower Jordan Valley and at the ancient city of Gezer in the Judean mountains have turned up preserved figs from thousands of years ago.

When grown for use, especially near water or by the side wall of a dwelling where they are protected, fig trees may reach forty feet tall, their large lobed foliage a welcome umbrella of shelter from the hot sun. 'To sit in the shade of the [cultivated] fig tree' became a Biblical metaphor for peace and prosperity: "In that day [of peace] you will be inviting each other to the shade of vine and fig trees" (Zechariah 3:10). Conversely, the destruction of fig trees is a prophetic symbol of destruction of the land: "[a nation from afar] will devour your vines and your fig trees" (Jeremiah 5:17). The pairing of the vine and fig tree in numerous images in the Hebrew Bible attests to their central importance both in agriculture and daily life. The fig, along with olives, dates, grapes, pomegranates, barley and wheat, is one of the Seven Species, arguably the most important crops of the land (Deuteronomy 8:8).[7]

Photograph © Ori Fragman

Ficus carica. Figs and foliage, Israel.

There is little doubt from which tree's leaves the first couple would cover themselves, for they were, presumably, the largest in the garden. Those from the fig tree are prominently veined, palmately lobed with wavy margins, and rough to the touch. Latex, present in all the tree's parts, can be a skin irritant, so Adam and Eve may have received their first lesson in what was in store for them in the real world outside Paradise when "they sewed together fig leaves to make themselves loin cloths (Genesis 3:7)." The tree's tiny flowers are hidden inside a pear-shaped fleshy container, syconium, where they are fertilized by the tiny female fig wasp which enters the enclosure through a small hole.

Figs were valued as a widely available source of food, high in sugar and therefore quick energy, much as they are today. They were available year round as fresh, green unripe figs or as dried fruit, easily carried on a journey, pressed and squeezed into a cake to refresh the traveler. The Amalekite who reports the death of King Saul to David ate part of a cake of pressed figs and "was revived" (I Samuel 30:12). Medicinally, figs were regarded as a laxative, tonic, and for poultices to treat infections. Sap from the tree was used to curdle milk for cheese-making.

The closely related species, the sycomore fig, *Ficus sycomorus* (not to be confused with the "sycamore," a common name for the American plane tree, *Platanus occidentalis*, and the Scottish maple, *Acer pseudoplatanus*) is also fertilized by wasps, but it is dependent on piercing or dressing to produce edible fruit, without which fruit turns into inedible galls. The prophet Amos describes himself as "a herdsman and a dresser of sycomore fruit" (Amos 7:14). To visualize this procedure imagine that the dresser had to climb the tree (which could reach fifty feet or more with a very wide canopy) and pierce every unripe fruit with a long knife, then wipe the cut with oil. The ancient practice of piercing unripe sycomore figs speeded ripening, but how? Original research into the life cycle of the sycomore reveals that cutting the unripe fruit releases ethylene gas, used today as a ripening agent for various stored unripe fruits such as bananas and oranges. Within three days after cutting, the immature figs greatly increase in size.[8] The hand labor needed to ensure a good crop of figs is no longer economically viable in Israel, although piercing is still carried out in other Middle Eastern countries. Today sycomores are planted as shade trees in Israel. In ancient times, the tree's wood was considered far more important than its fruit (inferior in taste to true figs and thus regarded as food for the poor), and techniques were developed to get as much usable wood from the trees as possible. The many references in the Mishna to rules concerning planting and harvesting wood from sycomores attests to its role as a popular building material. Trees were encouraged to produce a thick straight trunk by removing side branches. The stems that sprouted and then grew up from the base of the cut trunk were used for building material, as well as those from the re-cut trunk. The sycomore's incredible regenerative powers are preserved in its Hebrew name *shikma*, related to *shikum*, meaning "rejuvenation."[9]

Viewed philosophically, the Garden of Eden story has a surprisingly hopeful ending. Even as God expels the pair and tells them in devastating detail what hardships are in store—rather than sprouting all the good and beautiful plants as in Paradise, the land will bring forth only "thorns and thistles"[10]—God takes pity on the pair and clothes them with animal skins (Genesis 3:21), far more substantial and comfortable than their flimsy fig leaves. In this compassionate act, the rabbis saw the Jewish ideal of *Imitatio Dei*, the duty to imitate God's ways of loving kindness and pity: "... at the beginning of the Torah, God clothes Adam; at the end He buries Moses."[11]

ENDNOTES

1. E. A. Speiser in *The Anchor Bible Genesis*, 16, associates "eden" with plain or steppe country from the Akkadian *edinu*. The term, he says, was used as a geographical destination which came to be associated with the unrelated Hebrew noun for "enjoyment."
2. Daniel Hillel, *The Natural History of the Bible*, 41.
3. The idea for connecting evil (*malum*) with the apple (*malus*) may have been inspired by the Latin or Vulgate translation of the Bible by St. Jerome in the 4th century CE.
4. Goor and Asaph, *The Fruits of the Holy Land*, 185.
5. Goor discusses the possible origin of cultivated figs. He concludes that "The consensus today [1960s] inclines to Western Asia and migration thence to the Mediterranean." Michael Zohary in *Plants of the Bible*, 58, states that "Although its origin is disputed, it is now reliably believed that the fig growing in the jungles of the Caspian foreshore, northwest Turkey, and probably elsewhere in these surroundings, is the ancestor of the one domesticated by man." His source for the origin of figs and other plants in Israel is Daniel Zohary, Maria Hopf, *Domestication of Plants in the Old World: The Origin and Spread of Cultivated Plants in Western Asia, Europe and the Nile Valley*, a very important work on a complex subject.
6. Avinoam Danin, *Distribution Atlas of Plants in the Flora Palaestina Area*, 24.
7. In Chapter 10, *Shepherd and Farmer*, I discuss another aspect of the Seven Species based on the work of Nogah Hareuveni in *Nature in Our Biblical Heritage* (the English translation of "*minim*" meaning "species" is translated as "varieties" in his work; I use "species" throughout). Usually linked to the bounty of the Promised Land, Hareuveni suggests an alternative meaning. In the Deuteronomy passage the Seven Varieties as a group emphasize that God alone is responsible for their successful ripening. Inherent in the selection is a warning against worshiping pagan gods, a natural impulse to farmers, since each of the seven requires different natural conditions to flourish.
8. Research into the origin and life cycle of the sycomore and how the fig dressing was carried out was extensively researched by Jacov Galil of Tel-Aviv University. The results were published in 1966 in *Teva V'aretz* vol. 5, booklets 9, 10, 11, as well as in various academic journals.
9. Nogah Hareuveni, *Tree and Shrub in Our Biblical Heritage*, 87. For a comprehensive overview of the fascinating sycomore, which includes

Professor Galil's research, see Nogah Hareuveni, 89–92; at "Flora of Israel Online" (see Bibliography for Internet address), edited by Avinoam Danin, go to Table of Contents, *Plant Stories*, Chapter G, Parts 1 and 2, "Trees that fail to live up to the equality test." Also Nigel Hepper's *Illustrated Encylopedia of Bible Plants*, 112–114. Each of these sources widens our knowledge of the sycomore from a biological, botanical, or biblical perspective, or a combination of them. For anyone interested in following up the rabbinic references cited in Hareuveni see: *Shiv'it* 4,5 (regarding whether in a sabbatical year one can cut down a 'virgin' sycomore—a tree that has never been cut down); *Baba Metzia* 9,9 (how to deal with sycomore when renting a field); *Tosefta Menakhot* 13,20; *Tosefta Zevakhim* 11,17 (on the importance of sycomore trunks); *Pesahim* 4,8; *Tosefta Pesahim* 2,22 (on the permissibility of eating sycomore fruit); and *Shvi'it* 2,5 (on piercing sycomore fruit).

10. These are the detested, thorny field weeds, the bane of farmers everywhere. As we shall see the Land of Israel produces some of the most dramatic specimens. The pairing of "thorns and thistles" throughout the text is a shorthand for the desolation of the land. See Chapter Twenty-Eight, *Warning of the Thorns*.

11. Cited in J. H. Hertz, *The Pentateuch and Haftorahs*, 13.

Chapter Two

Noah's Ark and the Olive Branch

Portion-*Noach* / Noah (Genesis 6:9-11.32)

Make yourself an ark of gopher wood. (Genesis 6:14)

The dove came back to him toward evening, and there in its bill was a plucked-off olive leaf! Then Noah knew that the waters had decreased on the earth. (Genesis 8:11)

The history of humanity continues with an account of its shortcomings, moral failures, and family strife. The influence of the land in all its physical character—its very soil—and the plants that grow from it are evident throughout the biblical text where the struggle to

Photograph © Ori Fragman

Cupressus sempervirens/Cupressus sempervirens var. horizontalis. Wild cypress, White Mountains in western Crete.

attain a moral and ethical life is often expressed through the imagery and symbolism of nature and agriculture, as in the riveting story of the brothers Cain and Abel, the first sibling rivalry in *Genesis* (Ishmael and Isaac, Jacob and Esau, and Joseph and his brothers follow). A biblical audience would understand the distinction between farmer Cain and shepherd Abel as the universal enmity and distrust between those who grow crops from productive soil and those who graze their flocks on poorer adjacent or outlying areas unsuitable for farming. In Jewish tradition, shaped by the people's origin as shepherds and their later farming experience in hill country, the desert shepherd represented purity of spirit [1] like the leader David who leads his flock beside the still waters in the paths of righteousness (Psalms 23:2-3), while tillers of the soil such as Cain, suggest corruption because in their anxiety for a good harvest they resorted to the worship of idols.[2] The prophets saw in God the ideal shepherd: "Like a shepherd He pastures His flock: He gathers the lambs in His arms, And carries them in His bosom" (Isaiah 40:11). Cain kills his brother out of jealousy when God prefers Abel's offering of "the choicest of the firstlings of his flock" to his offering "from the fruit of the soil" (Genesis 4:3, 4). Cain is banished to the land of Nod (wandering) where, God tells him, "the soil will not yield to you," (Genesis 4:12) thus compounding his daily struggles.

Later, Noah is born, his name derived from *niham*, to comfort, for "This one will provide us relief from our work and from the toil of our hands, out of the very soil which the Lord placed under a curse" after Cain's sin (Genesis 5:29). And "Noah found favor with the Lord" (Genesis 6:8). But events move swiftly, as they do in biblical narrative, and God is angered by the state of the world He created, appalled by its wantonness, licentiousness, and general unrestraint in the pursuit of pleasure, and rather than merely punishing the sinners, as he did by banishing Adam and Eve from Eden, He plans a wholesale destruction of "all flesh under sky in which there is breath of life . . . " (Genesis 6:17) by means of a great flood.

The parallels between the biblical flood and Near Eastern flood myths is based on the actual periodic flooding experienced in Mesopotamia, only explicable to the ancient pagan mind as the whim of the gods. Flooding occurred annually and could become so violent that it was impossible to control. Explained in ecological terms, soil degradation occurred when water was diverted from the Tigris and Euphrates rivers to irrigate valley agriculture. Gradually these upland watersheds were overgrazed and deforested, resulting in severe erosion. Silt carried along during seasonal rains to the valley was deposited along the riverbanks, thus elevating them above the plains and creating the unstable conditions for uncontrolled flooding.[3] It is this phenomenon that is preserved in Mesopotamian myths and echoed in the Genesis account (Genesis 7:11): "All the fountains of the great deep burst apart—the rush of water over land—and the floodgates of the sky broke open"—annual rain—as if the separation from heaven and earth that God created had been torn asunder. But the Bible's account is driven by a moral vision entirely lacking in other Near Eastern stories such as the Epic of Gilgamesh account.

—⁂—

BECAUSE NOAH WAS A RIGHTEOUS MAN God saved him, instructing him to take all his family and pairs of animals into an ark of *gopher* wood so they would be safe from the Great Flood. The Hebrew word *"gopher"* remains untranslated in many Bibles because its identity is uncertain. Among the candidates are pine, cedar, oleander, and cypress,[4] the last being the most popular (although its Hebrew name is *brosh*). While the nomenclature can be confusing, the two forms of common or Mediterranean cypress, *Cupressus sempervirens*, are apparent: there is the wild form with wide spreading horizontal branches, *Cupressus sempervirens* var. *horizontalis*, native to the eastern Mediterranean, and the narrow, erect form, *Cupressus sempervirens* var. *sempervirens*. It has been cultivated from early historic or prehistoric times and is unknown in the wild. Wild cypress occurs spontaneously in the

Photograph © Ori Fragman

Cupressus sempervirens/Cupressus sempervirens var. *sempervirens*. Common or Mediterranean cypress, Tel-Aviv.

Galilee, also in Gilead (east of the Jordan River), and more often in the highlands of Edom (south of the Dead Sea in Jordan) where it grows from cliffs in extremely forbidding conditions, but it is very often cultivated, too. Growing to a height of eighty feet or more, its leaves are aromatic and scale-like, tightly overlapping to create a rope effect, unlike the needle-like leaves of other conifers; the tree's cones, of overlapping woody scales, are knobby. Cypress trees can be very long-lived and are said to have a beneficial effect on the soil. In this sense, the cypress has been called an "earth healer."[5] If true, what better wood for an ark intended to save a remnant of humanity and the animal kingdom during the long days of the Great Flood? More important, cypress wood is unsurpassed for building boats since its wood is impervious to rot. Wooden furniture and building parts, as well as cypress pollen, have been discovered in archeological digs in the Judean mountains, where wild cypress was once common.[6] Its oil has been used in cosmetics and its medicinal effect is antiseptic. The cultivated cypress, now planted and naturalized across the Mediterranean region and in many areas of the world, is also called funeral cypress after the tradition of planting it in graveyards. Seldom reaching eighty feet, its slender, upright growth is the one we associate with the Mediterranean landscape. In Israel it is extensively planted and also grows spontaneously on very disturbed sites such as quarries and roadsides.

Photograph © Jackie Chambers

Olea europaea. Olive branch with silvery leaves and fruit near Luzit caves in the Jewish National Fund Britannia Park in the Judean Plains area west of Jerusalem.

One of the most memorable scenes from the Flood story, a brilliant and significant addition to the Gilgamesh chronicle, is of the dove returning to the ark with a freshly plucked olive leaf in her mouth, signifying to Noah and his family that it was now safe to leave the ark because the waters have receded enough to reveal the olive tree; of relatively small stature, it grows from about sixteen to twenty-six feet tall, and only at lower altitudes (under three thousand feet). In a sense, the dove carried more weight than all the ark with the animals in it, for the leaf contained a new and safe green world.[7] How often we have seen this image of the pure white dove carrying a leafy olive twig depicted as a universal symbol of peace and reconciliation. But there is more to it than that in Jewish tradition, for through long association these representatives of Israelite flora and fauna have acquired additional layers of meaning. The olive tree, its fruit, oil, or the tree itself are mentioned at least fifty times in the Bible. The dove, among all fauna, was regarded as a symbol of purity and chastity. "If the Torah had not been given to us we should have learned the virtue of chastity from the dove" (*Eruvin* 100b). This should give us hope that mankind can mend its wicked ways.

Photograph © Jackie Chambers

Olea europaea. Silhouette of olive tree, Garden of Gethsemane.

It is the silhouette of the wide-spreading silvery crown of the olive tree, *Olea europaea* (*zayit*), one of the Seven Species with which the Land of Israel is identified (Deuteronomy 8:8), that we most associate with the landscape of the Holy Land. Self-planted trees grow among the rocks of limestone cliffs and *maquis* (characteristic dense Mediterranean growth of tall evergreen shrubs and short or stunted trees) on scattered mountain slopes in the Galilee, Samaria, Judea, and on hard sandstone hills of the Coastal Plain. The familiar population of cultivated olive trees on the Mount of Olives in Jerusalem is maintained by trimming and cutting off large branches to encourage rejuvenation, a technique probably used in earlier times as well. As the Israelites gained experience as farmers and learned to grow trees and grapevines on slopes by transforming them into terraces built into hillsides (still apparent today), olive groves were established. Slow-growing to a venerable age from a very wide-spreading root system—trees over a thousand years old are possible[8]—the olive tree's gnarled gray trunk eventually becomes hollow, while new shoots spring from its base even as the old tree continues to bear fruit, from which habit the olive tree

Photograph © Ori Fragman

Olea europaea. Aged olive tree, Israel.

was associated with the virtues of righteousness, constancy and continuity: "I am like a thriving olive tree in God's house; I trust in the faithfulness of God forever and ever" (Psalms 52:10).

The tree's graceful branches are crowned with long tapering silver-green leaves, among which inconspicuous flower buds open to small white flowers in May. Fruits turn from green to black and are harvested in the fall. It is the leaves which most arrest the eye. These are green above and silvery-gray underneath from the minute, closely pressed silvery hairs or scales that protect the foliage from drying out in drought conditions. The least rustle of wind turns up the leaves' undersides sending out dramatic waves of silvery shimmers that light up the landscape. It is this phenomenon that suggested the olive tree and its leaves as a symbol of light in the sense of spreading righteousness. The rabbis drew inspiration from this association: "Israel was called 'an olive tree, leafy and fair' (Jeremiah 11:16), because [Israel] shed light on all." (*Shmot Raba* 36,1). The sacred and profane were inseparably intertwined in the olive tree's symbolism and its everyday use: Olives were an important feature on the biblical menu, the first-pressed and purest pressed oil from olives was used to light the Temple Menorah, olive oil was used to anoint kings and priests (I Samuel 10:1; Exodus 29:7), to treat the sick, light the home, and as a solvent in concocting perfumes and cosmetics. Its wood was turned into ornaments and household utensils.

With the ark safely landed, its occupants dispatched, and sacrifices offered to God, "the Lord said to Himself: Never again will I doom the earth because of man, since the devising of man's mind is evil from his youth; nor will I ever again destroy every living being, as I have done" (Genesis 8:21). In stirring terms drawn from the seasons and cycles of the agricultural year, God declares,

> *"So long as the earth endures,*
> *Seedtime and harvest,*
> *Cold and heat,*
> *Summer and winter,*
> *Day and night*
> *Shall not cease,"* (Genesis 8:22)

and sends a rainbow in the clouds as a sign of His covenant (Genesis 9:13).

Following this lofty declaration it is a letdown to learn that the righteous Noah, a tiller of the soil, planted a vineyard, "drank of the wine and became drunk and he uncovered himself within his tent" (Genesis 9:21), presumably in a drunken stupor. His nakedness becomes the source of a sin—we are not told precisely what it is. Ancient audiences would have understood the broken taboo—perhaps of a son seeing his father naked and bragging about it—or an implied sexual misconduct. We are back where we started, with moral failings and family strife, as Noah curses Canaan, the descendants of his son, Ham, who had seen him naked. Why is the grapevine chosen for its ignominious role in this episode? Rashi[9] comments that Noah should have planted anything but the vine because it is the source of so much sin and crime among the children of men.[10] Perhaps the vine was chosen because of its antiquity of cultivation, to prove the antiquity, also, of this story. We shall have more opportunity to see how the grapevine, *Vitis vinifera*, was an integral part of daily and religious Israelite life and how its culture and fruitfulness suggested parables, metaphors, and images that span human expression from joy to despair, from blessing to curse, in the pursuit of teaching ethical monotheism from the land.

ENDNOTES

1. For more on this theme see Nogah Hareuveni *Desert and Shepherd in Our Biblical Heritage* 15, 47 and throughout.

2. For a full discussion of the temptation on the part of farmers to "serve other gods" because of the difficult agricultural realties in the Land of Israel (lack of water, for instance), see Nogah Hareuveni *Nature in Our Biblical Heritage*, 27, "Hills and Valleys—The Water Problem": "the Israelites are instructed to remind themselves several times a day that there is only One God Who controls all phenomena of nature. **Recognizing this continuous war against polytheism is the key to understanding one of the major threads woven throughout our Biblical heritage.**" [Emphasis in the original.]

3. See Daniel Hillel, *The Natural History of the Bible*, 49–52, "The First Riverine Domain, Influence of Mesopotamia," for a discussion of the flood phenomenon in Mesopotamian agriculture and the Epic of Gilgamesh.

4. Harold N. and Alma L. Moldenke, *Plants of the Bible*, 60. Common cypress is also a candidate for the wood, along with cedar, that King Hiram of Tyre supplied Solomon (I Kings 9:11).

5. Referred to in Irene Jacob, *Biblical Plants: A Guide to the Rodef Shalom Biblical Botanical Garden*, 36.

6. Michael Zohary, *Plants of the Bible*, 106.

7. Paraphrase of an insight by Isak Dinesen in *Out of Africa*, 122. Reader Paula Tobenfeld, pointed out that "If you consider that the mountains in Utah are approximately 10,000 feet high, and the Himalayas are often twice that height, it is easy to understand why Noah and his family felt it was safe to leave the ark when they saw the bird carrying a branch from the low-altitude loving olive tree."

8. Zohary, 106; See Yehuda Feliks, *Nature and Man in the Bible*, 215. He discovered an ancient olive tree in the Negev from the time of Nabatean agriculture (early centuries of the common era) in that area.

9. Acronym for Rabbi Shlomo ben Isaac (1040–1105), author of commentaries on the whole Bible and most of the Talmud that became (and still are) very popular.

10. Cited in J. H. Hertz edition, *The Pentatuech and Haftorahs*, 34.

Chapter Three

ABRAHAM'S TREES

Portion-*Lech Lecha* / Go forth (Genesis 12:1-17:27)
Abram passed through the land as far as the site of Shechem, at the terebinth of Moreh. And Abram moved his tent, and came to dwell at the terebinths of Mamre, which are in Hebron. (Genesis 12:6, 13:18)

Portion-*Vayyera*/And the Lord appeared to him. (Genesis 18:1-22:24)
The Lord appeared to him by the terebinths of Mamre . . . [Abraham] *planted a tamarisk at Beer Sheva, and invoked there the name of the Lord.* (Genesis 18:1, 21:33)

Photograph © Jackie Chambers

Tamarix aphylla. Large tamarisk near Luzit caves in the Jewish National Fund Britannia Park in the Judean Plains area west of Jerusalem.

The biblical narrative moves from a general story about human-kind (Adam and Eve, Cain and Abel, and Noah) to the lively, fast-paced stories of the Israelite Patriarchs and God's promises to them and their descendants. The obstacles and struggles that intervene in transferring these promises from generation to generation provide the rich details of the Patriarchal sagas—mostly shepherd-based before the period of settlement farming—beginning with Abram (later renamed Abraham). In language drawn from the natural world and expressed in beautifully graphic images, God says to Abram:

> Raise your eyes and look out from where you are, to the north and south, to the east and west, for I give all the land that you see to you and your offspring forever. I will make your offspring as the dust of the earth, so that if one can count the dust of the earth, then your offspring too can be counted. (Genesis 13:14-16)

Abram's story unfolds as he travels with his father Terah and family from Ur northwestwards along the arc of the Fertile Crescent, settling in Haran (between northeastern Syria and southeastern Turkey). When Terah dies, Abram leaves Haran as instructed by God to begin a new journey to an undesignated place, "to a land that I will show you" (Genesis 12:1-6). This is a momentous undertaking—to leave the familiar world he knows for the unknown—but he obeys without hesitation, thereby launching a remarkable and difficult odyssey of geographic and spiritual dimensions. His first stop in Canaan is at Shechem (near Nablus) to the terebinth of Moreh (Genesis 12:6); from there he goes to Bethel, literally "House of God," [near Ramallah], and "by stages" south to the Negev (Genesis 12:9), then down to Egypt because of famine, then back to the Negev, from where he proceeds "by stages" back to Bethel (Genesis 13:3). After God's blessing of the land, he "moved his tent, and came to dwell at the terebinths of Mamre, which are in Hebron," where he "built an altar [of thanksgiving] there to the Lord" (Genesis 13:18), then he traveled south to Beer Sheva and planted a tamarisk tree.

What do these journeys mean? Are they aimless wanderings? When viewed against the background of the land in its physical detail, we see how Abram/Abraham's movements fit the pattern for semi-nomadic Bedouin clans in semi-arid areas, as true today as it has been for millennia.[1] When he moves his tent from one place to another he knows what he is doing. Since Abram/Abraham was "very rich in cattle" (Genesis 13:2), we can assume he and his retinue occupied non-farming semi-arid hills and plains with less than twelve inches of rain a year, enough moisture to encourage the growth of sparse trees and shrubs and a mixture of perennial and annual grasses and green plants for grazing. Even such areas, however, cannot be counted on to provide enough grazing and water resources for long since the climate is unstable, drought always a possibility. It takes an experienced shepherd to guide his immediate and extended family, servants, and flocks of sheep and goats successfully on terrain like this. Other tribes compete for grazing land and springs, wells and cisterns. When the area can no longer sustain the shepherd way of life the group moves on, as recorded in Genesis 13:6-10 Abram/Abraham realized that "the land could not support them staying together" so he urged Lot, his nephew, to choose another place, giving him first choice: "Let there be no strife between you and me, between my herdsmen and yours . . . " Rather than just take the best land for himself, he generously urges Lot to choose which land he wants, telling him "if you go north, I will go south; and if you go south I will go north." Lot looks around and chooses the well-watered flood plain to the north, "like the garden of of the Lord, like the land of Egypt (Genesis 13:10)," a more favorable place in the physical sense but morally corrupt (near the wicked city of Sodom).

Abraham deals more shrewdly in a different setting when he is securing the all-important water rights from Abimelech (who has claimed the well for his own). Abraham sets aside seven female lambs for Abimelech whom he tells in straight terms: "You are to accept these seven ewes from me as proof that I dug this well" (Genesis 21:30), from which agreement the Negev city of Beer Sheva or Beersheba ("Well of the Seven" or "Well of the Oaths") derived its name.

Once we understand the land's influence on the text through the physical world of the shepherd Abraham and his daily reality, the ancient words come to life for us, even though we are far removed from them in time and in life experience. Through the narrative we come to know Abram/Abraham as a real person, whose character and moral development match his skills as a successful leader-shepherd, setting the standard for the archetypal leader-shepherds to follow: Jacob, Moses, and David. When Abram learns that Lot has been captured he becomes a decisive military leader who rescues his nephew and his entire entourage (Genesis 14:16). When three strangers visit Abraham by the terebinths of Mamre, he "ran from the entrance of the tent to greet them" (Genesis 18:2), responding with hospitality characteristically without hesitation,[2] while Lot, when two angels call on him, merely "rose to greet them" (Genesis 19:1). It is when God promises him an heir (at the age of 100!) from his ninety-year-old wife Sarai (henceforth known as Sarah-Princess), that God changes his name to Abraham, "father of a multitude" (Genesis 17:5).

What is significant about the places where Abram/Abraham stops and the trees that mark them? These were already well-established sites whose tall trees, easily seen on the horizon, were not only welcome for shade but were probably also venerated by the tree-worshiping Canaanites,[3] a practice Abram/Abraham must have known from his past. It is not surprising that Abram/Abraham stopped at these places, and for his own purposes "built an altar there [Shechem] to the Lord who had appeared to him" (Genesis 12:7), at Bethel "where he built an altar to the Lord and invoked the Lord by name (Genesis 12:8), at Hebron, where he "built an altar there to the Lord" (Genesis 13:18), and at Beer Sheva. The Talmud fills in the nature of Abraham's worship at these sites: "Do not read this as he [Abram/Abraham] called on the name of the Lord; rather that he caused others to call on the name of the Lord. This teaches us that the Patriarch Abraham caused the name of the Holy One, blessed be He, to be uttered by every passerby" (*Sota* 10a-b).[4] Trees, as we have already seen in the Garden and Flood stories, have a significant role in the Bible. This is astonishing considering that of the great number of plant species in Israel (2,825) only about five percent are trees. But those that were especially tall, long-lived, and capable of remarkable powers of regeneration (like the sycomore)[5] were bound to be noticed and made the subject of innumerable metaphors, images, and symbols in the Bible. In everyday life such trees were places of worship and an honored burial site.[6] Since the trees mentioned in the text are drought-tolerant species they are just the sort to be expected in semi-arid country, and if there was a source of water these places would recommend themselves as campsites. At Beer Sheva where Abraham himself dug the well, he must have judged this to be an ideal site, though surrounded by arid desert land, for he stays here quite a while: "And Abraham resided in the land of the Philistines a long time" or many days (Genesis 21:34).

—⁓—

ATLANTIC TEREBINTH, *Pistacia atlantica* (*elah*), is mainly a dry-land tree that establishes itself in niches between evergreen woodland and steppe-like (semi-arid) and desert (very dry) conditions where Abraham must have encountered them; some populations also grow in the humid climate zones of Samaria, the Golan, Mount Carmel, and some coastal areas. According to conditions this species can grow from thirteen to over sixty feet tall from a short trunk that yet supports many wide-spreading branches; it sheds its deciduous leaves in autumn. *P. atlantica* is also called the turpentine tree from the smell of its fruits (nuts) which have been used mostly for dyeing and tanning; in the old Jerusalem market they are sold for making a spice for cakes.[7] Although the fruits are bitter when raw, they become edible when roasted and have been known as a source for food since time immemorial; they should not be confused with commercial pistachio

Photograph © Avinoam Danin

Pistacia atlantica. Atlantic terebinth, Negev Highlands.

nuts from *P. vera*, cultivated in a few places in Israel.[8] Resin from *P. atlantica* is used in folk medicine as an astringent. The revered ancient oak tree near Hebron, known as "Abraham's Oak" or "the oaks of Mamre," based on the passage in Genesis 13:18, has a history of its own going back about two thousand years, but according to some commentators, it would appear that originally a terebinth had stood there, and that only later was an oak planted in its place.[9]

The terebinth, as well as the Tabor oak, *Quercus ithaburensis*, were revered as sacred trees (pre-dating biblical times). Preserved specimens or groves were recognized sites for both worship and burials, especially of distinguished or important people: Saul and his sons, for instance, were buried under a terebinth (I Chronicles 10:12). The terebinth also suggested place names as in the Valley of Elah, where David killed Goliath (I Samuel 17:2).

The Palestine terebinth, *Pistacia palaestina*, grows with the Kermes oak, *Quercus calliprinos*, in Mediterranean *maquis* areas and is a slight tree compared to the dry-land species. Its deciduous leaves are not only shed in the fall in common with Atlantic terebinth, but turn flaming red before they drop, as does the fall foliage of certain species of hardwood trees in the colder parts of North America. It is probably this terebinth that the prophet Isaiah had in mind when he linked it with the oak in an extended metaphor describing ruin for the degenerating Kingdom of Judah. Like the terebinth in its fall colors, Judah only *appears* to be in its glory, but it, like the foliage itself, is on its way to dying. The kingdom, Isaiah prophesies, will collapse from corruption and the oppression of its people. "And even if a tenth part yet remains in it, it too shall be consumed, like the terebinth and the [Tabor] oak in their season" (Isaiah 6:11-13, based on RSV). But as we have seen elsewhere, 'there is hope for a tree,' and that is Isaiah's message. The "holy seed within the dead

Photograph © Ori Fragman

Quercus ithaburensis. The large acorn of the Tabor oak.

trunk" suggests that seeds (acorns) dropped on the ground by the oak may sprout in the coming rainy season to bring forth a sapling that will grow into a tree, suggesting the idea that a new society may arise, built on a better moral foundation. New leaf buds that form in the axils of the dying oak leaves reinforce the image of hope and renewal.[10] A biblical audience, familiar with these natural phenomena, would have understood the powerful metaphorical images derived from the world they knew.

Abraham made a wise choice when he planted the tamarisk, *Tamarix aphylla*, the *eshel* of the Bible, at Beer Sheva, since it is both drought and heat resistant, grows well in the dry, sandy soils of the Negev and in the hot desert regions of the Dead Sea and Arava Valley, where its roots penetrate deep into the soil to find water. In planting this particular tree, perhaps Abraham was following a long-established custom to plant tamarisk near wells;[11] there's no missing it in a desert landscape where it can reach thirty feet or more in height and can be seen from afar. Its pointed sheath-like foliage is pressed onto the plant's stem, from which characteristic the tree is called "leafless tamarisk" (the Latin epithet *aphylla*, means "no leaves"). The many stems together have a feathery silvery-gray appearance and form a thick crown that provides cooling shade, a blessing in hot desert regions. So esteemed was the tamarisk in ancient Israel that for the Sages the term "large tamarisk" referred to an especially learned rabbi.[12] Nogah Hareuveni recounts that his father, Ephraim, then a botanical adviser to the British Mandate, successfully advised planting tamarisk trees to prevent the spread of sand dunes that threatened to cover railroad ties between Rafiah and El Arish in the Sinai desert.[13] Tamarisk trees are planted as shade trees in Israel especially along the coast. Its wood has been used to make ploughs as well as bowls for milking (camels), and its bark, high in tannin, has been used for dyeing; the stems are edible for fodder.

As we have seen in the stories of the Garden and the Flood, the Bible's narrative is laid over the well-established conventions of the pagan world where tall trees were deified and were sites for worship and burial. In Abram/Abraham's trees, embedded in a text driven by a moral purpose, this convention is turned toward the pursuit of ethical monotheism. As we leave him planting a tamarisk in Beer Sheva, we know that he is about to face his most strenuous test in the binding-of-Isaac episode, whose unanticipated outcome must have seemed thrilling as well as revolutionary in the context of child sacrifice in the surrounding pagan world.

ENDNOTES

1. Daniel Hillel, *The Natural History of the Bible*, 60.
2. Extending hospitality to strangers is an important feature of the shepherd code, shaped by living in a harsh land where sources of food and water are uncertain. See Hillel, 77–81 for a detailed discussion of this phenomenon. Rebekah, too, fulfills this pastoral custom with great generosity (Genesis 24: 17-20). Perhaps the Leviticus laws to love your fellow and the stranger (19:18,34) grew out of this well established part of desert life.
3. In Everett Fox's translation of *The Five Books of Moses*, 46, he translates the NJPS's "the site of Shechem (Genesis 12:6) as 'Place of Shechem,'" "implying a sacred place." J. H. Hertz in *The Pentateuch and Haftorah* notes that some translate "the terebinth of Moreh" (Genesis 12:6) as 'the directing terebinth,' i.e., the oracular tree held sacred by the tree-worshiping Canannites."
4. Cited in Nogah Hareuveni, *Tree and Shrub in Our Biblical Heritage*, 23, as part of *midrashim* that connect Abraham's youthful criticism of pagan tree worship to his old age when he entertained his guests beneath the tamarisk tree he had planted, teaching them to give thanks to God for the food He provided. *Midrashim* (singular, *midrash*), are interpretations of the biblical text, in this case meant to drive home a moral point.
5. See discussion of the sycomore tree in Chapter One, "In the Garden."
6. Michael Zohary *Plants of the Bible*, 110.
7. Avinoam Danin.
8. According to Zohary, 65, it was the nuts from *P. vera*, introduced from Syria or Persia, that Jacob sent down to Egypt as "choice fruits of the land" (Genesis 43:11).
9. Yehuda Feliks, *Nature and Man in the Bible*, 83.
10. Nogah Hareuveni discusses the imagery of the terebinth and oak in Isaiah in *Tree and Shrub in Our Biblical Heritage*, 112.
11. "Deep wells dug by inhabitants throughout the ages exist at various points in the deserts of Sinai and Israel. Large *Tamarix aphylla* trees are often found near deep wells in northern Sinai and the Negev." Avinoam Danin, *Desert Vegetation of Israel and Sinai*, 123.
12. Hareuveni, 25.
13. Ibid.

Chapter Four

FATEFUL STEW

Portion-*Toledot* / Generations (Genesis 25:19-28:9)

Once when Jacob was cooking a stew, Esau came in from the open, famished. And Esau said to Jacob, "Give me some of that red, red stuff to gulp down, for I am famished"—which is why he was named Edom [red]. Jacob said, "First sell me your birthright." And Esau said, "I am at the point of death, so of what use is my birthright to me?" But Jacob said, "Swear to me first." So he swore to him, and sold his birthright to Jacob. Jacob then gave Esau bread and lentil stew; he ate and drank, and he rose and went away. Thus did Esau spurn the birthright. (Genesis 25:29-34)

In this graphically sketched vignette the narrator overdraws Esau as an impetuous and coarse fellow who cares more for satisfying his immediate appetite than for his birthright— what is due him as first-born son—to emphasize that he is wholly unfit for the role for which he should be destined; God's favoring the younger son, however, is already familiar in the story of Cain and Abel (Genesis 4:3-16). Jacob and Esau are the twin brothers conceived by Rebekah after her husband Isaac's successful intercession with God to end her barrenness (Genesis

Photograph © Joshua D. Klein

Lens culinaris. Split and whole lentils for stew, all available in the Israeli *shuk* (open air market).

25:21). The offspring from such barren women in biblical narrative are regarded as special, a gift from God for the fulfillment of His purposes.[1] When we consider the story of Jacob and Esau as part of God's plan for the passing of His spiritual, as well as material blessing, we see how masterfully this riveting story of sibling rivalry drives to its logical conclusion, by brilliantly using all too human characters, rooted in the imagery of the land, to forward what God wills. It is the characters' imperfections, their flawed natures and struggles as well as achievements towards that goal that gives the plain text its life, a life that still speaks to us today as it did in biblical times.

Watch for the signposts along the way, most obviously in the children's symbolic names—Esau ("rough one"), Jacob ("heel-holder," "may God protect you"), in the contrasts of their occupations—Esau the hunter, Jacob the tent-dweller—and in the carefully built characters of their father and mother who also play distinctive roles in the ensuing drama.

The boy's father, Isaac, the coddled son of Abraham and Sarah in their dotage, is often regarded by critics as almost a non-entity, the second generation that is bound merely to live in the shadow of its famous forebears (in Isaac's case sandwiched between Abraham and Jacob) and maintain the status quo.[2] But is this entirely true? When we look at the text we see that Isaac is not only a shepherd, but unlike his ancestors, also a farmer (Genesis 26:12). This first known effort at settled agriculture foreshadows the future, when a nation of shepherds is transformed into a nation of farmers in the Land of Israel. In this sense Isaac is an innovator, yet he is often accused of metaphorically 'digging his father's wells' or doing nothing new. His combined farming/grazing, however, is no mean feat because he lives precariously on the frontier between the sown land and the desert. This is a risky proposition because farmers are not happy to compete for water and land with those who farm as well as graze their flocks. This puts the increased struggles over water sources and the stopping up of Abraham's wells (Genesis 26:18-21) in perspective. Again the figure of Abimelech comes forth to express the farmers' general dissatisfaction: "Go away from us, because you have become far too big for us." (Genesis 26:16). Isaac, it seems, has done very well, carefully guiding his family and flocks, sowing land, and finding water. "Now at last," he says, "the Lord has granted us ample space to increase in the land" (Genesis 26:22). When famine occurred, as it had in Abraham's time, and God had commanded Isaac not to go down to Egypt (the usual solution to prolonged drought and consequent diminished food and fodder), he had obeyed the command: "Reside in this land, and I will be with you and bless you; I will assign all these lands to you and your offspring, fulfilling the oath that I swore to your father Abraham. I will make your descendants as numerous as the stars of heaven inasmuch as Abraham obeyed Me and kept My charge: My commandments, My laws, and My teachings" (Genesis 26:3-5). Isaac's main contribution to the passing on of this blessing to the next generation—a great responsibility—is to remain in the land, a command he has faithfully fulfilled, even with flair.

Rebekah (possibly "fatling," a term used for the choicest or best animals in a herd or flock) is described as young and beautiful. She is chosen by Abraham's senior servant who has been sent on the quest of finding Isaac a wife from among Abraham's other family branch in Mesopotamia. Unlike Isaac, Rebekah has been raised in a rough environment (Jacob will find out how rough when he works for her brother Laban)[3] and learned from her experiences to act for herself, to make sharp decisions, as in her quick generosity in drawing water not only for Abraham's servant Eliezer, but for his ten camels (not a light job),[4] in her agreeing at once to marry Isaac, sight unseen, in her leaving her family at once, rather than dallying, and most movingly, in her love for Isaac as she sees him for the first time in his field (Genesis 24:64-65); the love is returned, in the first real love story of the Bible, one that passes so quickly we might miss it. Her grounding education in a rough school makes her all the more attuned to the vagaries of the real world—in contrast to the protected upbringing of Isaac—so she is ready to act when needed to further God's plan. This has been revealed to her when, after she has conceived and the boys are already struggling in her womb, she asks God, "Why do I exist?" God answers: "Two nations are in your womb, Two separate peoples shall issue from your body; One people shall be mightier than the other, And the older shall serve the younger" (Genesis 25:22-23).

The boys' birth is described in the briefest but most telling way: "The first one emerged red, like a hairy mantle all over, so they named him Esau. Then his brother emerged, holding on to the heel of Esau, so they named him Jacob" (Genesis 25:25-26). As the boys grow up, the contrasts between them and their parents' attitude toward them are further signposts on the way to the birthright scene. Esau is described as a skillful hunter, a man of the [wild] outdoors, while Jacob is "a mild man who stayed in camp." To Isaac, the exploits of his older son are appealing, especially because Esau brings him wild venison, a change from probably eating the culled sheep or goats of his own herd, and so he favors his elder son. Rebekah loves Jacob— no reason given in the text, and so all the more eloquent a declaration (Genesis 25:27-28).

The birthright scene hits hard, infused as it is with the brownish red of the earth, the color of lentil soup, the color of ruddy Esau himself. He is so consumed with a passion to eat that he can barely get the words out, and so eager to eat that he "gulps" his food, a vernacular verb in the Hebrew usually associated with the feeding of animals.[5] If the text is colored red, it is delivered in hard-driving prose: "Jacob then gave Esau bread and lentil stew; he ate and drank, and he rose and went away. Thus did Esau spurn the birthright." Jacob shows more audacity than one would expect from a mild man of the tents, and even more so later, when at Rebekah's urging, he fools his now blind father Isaac (blind physically as well as spiritually) into giving him the first-son's blessing. The first part of this blessing, the one Esau later receives after bitterly sobbing and pleading with his father, bestows the same material benefits on both sons: "...the dew of heaven [life-giving moisture] and the fat of the earth," but in addition, Jacob receives the all-important spiritual blessing of the chosen leader; the superior status of the shepherd life over that of the hunter has been established: "And nations bow to you; Be master over your brothers, And let your mother's sons bow to you..." (Genesis 27:29).

But Jacob must earn this blessing and develop the necessary character for his new name, Israel ("one who strives [or "struggles"] with God"), which he does throughout the episodes of conflict and courage ahead.

—⚬—

THE FATEFUL STEW was made from simmering lentils (*adashim*), the small, round greenish-brown or reddish seeds of the plant *Lens culinaris*, in water until they reached the consistency of porridge, hence the expression "a mess of pottage" (a thickened soup). The plant itself is a dainty branched annual which grows to a height of eighteen inches, its seeds (lentils) growing in pods that hang down from wispy tendrils along the plant's weak stems. Lentils, along with other nutrient-rich pulses or legumes such as chickpeas, *Cicer arietinum*, and broad beans, *Vicia faba*, have been cultivated for millennia as relatively easily grown garden crops that can be gathered by hand (from which characteristic the word "legumes," from the French for "bean," is derived). High in protein and with a savory, satisfying flavor, lentils have been known as "the poor man's meat" throughout history, and were the second most important component of the biblical diet after grain.[6] Prepared either from fresh or dried seed, lentils were valued in the

Photograph © Avinoam Danin

Lens culinaris. Lentil plant, Mount Scopus Botanical Garden, Jerusalem.

biblical kitchen and on the road for their versatility. In addition to using them in nutritious stews, lentils could be mashed into pastes and purées, or ground like a flour and combined with other grains to produce cakes. Lentils were included in the list of foods, such as wheat, barley, parched grain, beans, honey, curds (clabbered milk), and cheese that Barzillai and others brought David and his followers, for they knew that "the troops must have grown hungry ...in the wilderness" (II Samuel 17:29). According to Jewish legend, lentils are mourners' food because they resemble death: "As the lentil rolls, so death, sorrow, and mourning constantly roll about among men, from one to the other."[7] In everyday biblical and post-biblical life, however, lentils were just common fare. To know that Esau sold his birthright, his very soul, for nothing more than a common food, sheds light on his character.

ENDNOTES

1. J. H. Hertz, *The Pentateuch and Haftoras*, 93 n. 21.
2. See Everett Fox *The Five Books of Moses*, 111 on the Yaakov Cycle and Isaac's function as the second generation, and Adin Steinsaltz in *Biblical Images: Men and Women of the Book*, 31 on Isaac's "non-action" life.
3. For an analysis of Rebekah's background and character see Steinsaltz, 41–47.
4. A biblical audience would have understood just how much labor was involved in drawing water for ten camels "until they finish drinking" [want no more] (Genesis 24:19) and would have been greatly impressed by Rebekah's character. Since the animals had been traveling for weeks in the desert and were thirsty, each would require about twenty-six gallons of water. Estimated in Neot Kedumim's *Self-guided Tour* booklet for Trail A, Station 3 B: "Water," 16–17.
5. Robert Alter, *The Five Books of Moses*, 131. The genius of the biblical narrative is the way it portrays the human character in all its complexity, for as reader Matthew Borden points out, to be fair to Esau, according to some interpretations, the later reconciliation scene with Jacob (Genesis 34) shows that by then he has grown beyond the stage of immediate self-gratification.
6. Miriam Feinberg Vamosh, *Food at the Time of the Bible*, 54.
7. Louis Ginzberg, *Legends of the Bible, 152*.

Chapter Five

RACHEL'S MANDRAKES

❦

Portion-*Vayyetze* / And [Jacob] went out (Genesis 28:10-32:3)

Once, at the time of the wheat harvest, Reuben came upon some mandrakes in the field and brought them to his mother Leah. Rachel said to Leah, "Please give me some of your son's mandrakes." But she said to her, "Was it not enough for you to take away my husband, that you would also take my son's mandrakes?" Rachel replied, "I promise, he shall lie with you tonight, in return for your son's mandrakes." (Genesis 30:14-15)

The sibling rivalries in Genesis continue with the bitter antagonism between two sisters, Leah and Rachel (the third and fourth matriarchs).[1] Their struggles are associated with a plant whose miraculous powers are deeply embedded in folklore. It is not surprising that the Hebrew Bible, whose moral thrust is opposed to such superstition, gives prominence to a folk motif since the text is a many-layered narrative that draws on familiar Near Eastern myths of all sorts (as in its depiction of the Garden of Eden) and a rich folk tradition, but uses them for its own purpose to drive home lessons of ethical monotheism.

Photograph © Jackie Chambers

Mandragora autumnalis. Mandrake fruits, Jerusalem Botanical Gardens.

This is especially true of the mandrake, a plant linked to fertility and love in the Middle Eastern pharmacopeias.

Jacob's story continues. When he comes "to the land of the Easterners" to find a wife among his uncle Laban's people, we are at once involved in a heightened meeting at a well, the favored place among nomadic and semi-nomadic shepherds for social encounters, exchange of gossip and information, and in the biblical narrative, finding suitable brides for the patriarchs (this is where Abraham's servant Eliezer noticed Rebekah). Jacob approaches the well and while he is still being told by the shepherds there that it is too early to remove the huge stone that blocks the well's mouth because "It is still broad daylight, too early to round up the animals; water the flock and take them to pasture" (Genesis 29:7), he sees Rachel ("ewe"—signifying her shepherdess origin) approaching the well with a flock, and it is love at first sight. How a biblical audience would have relished the scene, skillfully drawn from the realities of shepherd life combined with the heroic actions of a traditional folk tale! Jacob, 'the mild man of the tents,' is transformed into a super hero: "And when Jacob saw Rachel, the daughter of his uncle Laban, and the flock of his uncle Laban, Jacob went up and rolled the stone off the mouth of the well [a feat usually requiring all the shepherds present] and watered the flock of his uncle Laban.[2] Then Jacob kissed Rachel, and broke into tears" (Genesis 29:10-11). This melodramatic first encounter, compressed into a few words, gives us insight into the relationship between Jacob and Rachel. Jacob makes the first move; Rachel, so sure of his love, need not do anything to encourage him. Theirs will prove to be a tension-filled and ultimately tragic love.

The narrative with its underlying folk motifs continues with the struggle between the hero Jacob and the wily Laban, for whom he has worked for over a month without pay. When his employer asks him what he wants for wages, Jacob answers without hesitation that he will serve Laban seven years for Rachel, "and they seemed to him but a few days because of his love for her" (Genesis 29:20). Jacob (the deceiver of the first son's blessing) is himself deceived, however, for on the wedding night the older sister Leah of the "weak eyes" (aptly, her name means "weary") was substituted for the "shapely and beautiful" Rachel, the justification being that Laban was obligated to marry off the elder daughter first.[3] Laban drives a hard bargain with Jacob for another seven years' servitude for Rachel. He will now have worked fourteen years as Laban's unpaid herdsman, but this experience will prove its worth, not only in his gaining Rachel but in becoming a superior shepherd.

To compensate the unloved Leah (or less loved, tradition suggests[4]), God "opened her womb [to conceive]," but Rachel was barren. Over time an explosive situation develops with Leah producing son after son (six of Jacob's twelve sons)—and hoping, always in vain, that this will win Jacob's heart—while Rachel, the beloved, remains infertile. Rachel demands of Jacob, "Give me children or I shall die" (Genesis 30:1). Most uncharacteristically, mild Jacob is incensed and retorts, "Can I take the place of God, who has denied you fruit of the womb?" Jacob's utter dismissal of any other power than God's to effect a change in Rachel's barren state points toward future events. The intense sibling rivalry between the sisters—Leah, jealous of Jacob's preference for her younger, beautiful sister, and Rachel, jealous of her sister's fruitfulness—comes to a head when Leah's son, Reuben, brings her mandrakes from the remnants of a just-harvested field of wheat (we are in a land of mixed farming/grazing) because Leah has stopped conceiving and thinks the plants would help her. With its fabled reputation as a fertility drug and an aphrodisiac, she can't lose.

The acquiring of mandrakes at the wheat harvest is significant because by this time (late May to early June) their fragrant fruits would have already ripened and been eaten by birds and wild animals. Thus the ones Reuben brings to her are especially prized by Leah who is outraged when Rachel asks for some of the mandrakes for herself: "Was it not enough for you to take away my husband," Leah retorts, releasing years of simmering resentment, "that you would also take my son's mandrakes?" The bargain motif, a favorite folk theme, between the two sisters reveals the depths to which Leah will sink to gain favor with Jacob, and Rachel's desperation. Rachel arranges that in return for some of the mandrakes she will allow Leah to sleep with Jacob ("he shall lie with you tonight"), a statement that reflects Rachel's status as the favored wife at the expense of Leah. Meeting Jacob coming in from the field, Leah has to explain that she has hired him for the night with her son's mandrakes!

Leah conceives after this night, and later, bears her sixth son. Rachel, too, conceives at last. But mandrakes, according to the plain text, have nothing to do with either sister's fertility. A biblical audience would have expected the mandrakes to work according to superstitious belief, but having God intervene upsets expectations and effectively drives home the moral lesson that *it is God, as Jacob has proclaimed, who is responsible for the blessing of fertility.* After Jacob "lay with her that night God heeded Leah and she conceived" (Genesis 30:17), then "God remembered Rachel; God heeded her and opened her womb. She conceived and bore a son, and said 'God has taken away my disgrace.' So she named him Joseph, which is to say, 'May the Lord add another son for me.'" (Genesis 30:22-24). The tragedy of Rachel's life is that in demanding sons to carry on God's blessings, she forfeits her own life, dying as she gives birth to Benjamin ("son of the right hand" or favorite)[5] shortly after Jacob and his entourage return, at last, to Canaan (Genesis 35:18-19); Jacob's unwitting curse that the stealer of Laban's household idols (Rachel) would die is thus fulfilled in his wife (Genesis 31:32). In Jewish tradition, the tragic figure of Rachel became a metaphor, among other things, for the Jewish people, as in the image of "Rachel weeping for her [exiled] children. She refuses to be comforted for her children who are gone" (Jeremiah 31:15), her weeping prefiguring later exile, suffering, and ultimate return. Rachel's tomb became a place of pilgrimage, especially for women in need of consolation for barrenness.

—m—

WHAT IS THE MANDRAKE PLANT, and is it really a fertility drug? Mandrakes (*dudaim*), *Mandragora autumnalis*, belong to the deadly nightshade family (Solanaceae), the Latin genus name "mandragora" indicating that the plant is deadly to cattle. These grow up from fleshy, thick forked roots that may reach three to four feet downward in the earth and weigh more than four pounds. A rosette of large dark green leaves, heavily wrinkled and veined with an unpleasant odor when rubbed, flatten to the ground when mature, surrounding a bunch of nearly stemless, small bell-shaped flowers tinged with purple that bloom from January to March. The mature pulpy fruits are smooth, about the size of a large plum, and deep yellow with the strong fragrance of apple or pineapple. Under certain conditions at night, chemical substances in the fruit react with dew to produce a phosphorescent effect, as recorded by first century CE Josephus Flavius, the Jewish general and historian.[6] In Israel, mandrakes occur frequently in Mediterranean and semi-steppe *batha*, a term of biblical origin that describes areas dominated by dwarf shrubs, usually in poor, lean soil, as well as in wheat fields and fallow lands in the center and north of the country. Since the wheat harvest occurs in late May or early June it would be unusual to find a mandrake plant in the field still with fruit; thus Reuben's find is especially lucky.

Photograph © Jackie Chambers

Mandragora autumnalis. Blooming mandrake, Jerusalem Botanical Gardens.

Because the harvested plant with its two-pronged "legs" resembles the human figure, mandrake acquired a great reputation for healing all parts of the body, for witchcraft (warding off evil), and as a fertility drug, especially in the Middle East where carvings, bracelets, and necklaces made from the roots were worn or held by infertile women in the hope that they would conceive.[7] What are the plant's actual properties? In common with other members of the nightshade family, mandrake root contains the powerful alkaloids scopolamine, hyoscine, and atropine which affect the relaxation of smooth muscles, dilate pupils of the eyes, and accelerate heart activity. If used in small quantities, these potentially lethal properties can be beneficial. A preparation of the shaved root steeped in wine was an early anesthetic and tranquilizer. In modern medicine, hyoscine from mandrakes is still used in preoperative preparations to soothe patients and reduce bronchial secretions, and to control motion sickness.[8] Experiments are supposed to have shown that the mandrake contains both sedatives and aphrodisiacs, but because the sedatives are in larger quantity, the small number of stimulating hormones probably do not produce an aphrodisiac effect.[9]

The mandrake's entrenched position throughout the biblical world as a plant associated with fruitfulness and love is reflected in the rich erotic imagery of the *Song of Songs* drawn from the ripening world of nature: "Let us see if the vine has flowered, if its blossoms have opened, if the pomegranates are in bloom. There I will give my love to you. The mandrakes yield their fragrance, at our doors are all the choice fruits; both freshly picked and long-stored, have I kept my beloved for you" (7:13-14). For Leah and Rachel it is God who intervenes to bless them with fertility, but in the poet's song about his beloved, we feel their heightened attraction through the context of plants, like mandrake, whose heady fragrance brings thoughts of love in the season of fruitfulness.

ENDNOTES

1. The reader should be aware that Jewish tradition offers a more nuanced interpretation of the Jacob-Leah-Rachel relationships than is here presented. Rachel, for instance, is said to have compassion for her sister, whom she sees as an extension of herself.

2. The rolling away of the well stone parallels his mother's feat in hauling up twenty buckets of water (twenty-six gallons) for each of Eliezer's ten thirsty camels, and "The drawing of water after encountering a maiden at a well in a foreign land signals to the audience that a betrothal type-scene is unfolding." See Robert Alter *The Five Books of Moses*, 153 n.10.

3. The story of the switched brides has been recognized since late antiquity as a meting out of poetic justice to Jacob, the deceiver. See Alter, 155 n. 26. The switched brides story, according to one traditional Jewish interpretation, shows Rachel's compassion for Leah who, if Rachel had married first, would have been ostracized for being the unmarried eldest daughter. This insight from reader Paula Tobenfeld.

4. *Bereshit* 29:30. For an analysis of the character of the two sisters, their relationship with Jacob, and their ultimate meaning in Judaism, see Adin Steinsaltz, *Biblical Images*, 49–61.

5. Or connoting strength. Among other explanations of "Benjamin" are "son of days," referring to Jacob having a child in his old age, and "son of the south," referring to his birth in Canaan.

6. Josephus Flavius *Jewish Wars* (Book VII, 6:3).

7. D. Palevitch & Zohara Yaniv *Medicinal Plants of the Holy Land*, 181. In the Pesach, 2006 edition of Neot Kedumim's newsletter, Paula Tobenfeld writes: "The root is disproportionately large in relation to the visible plant and bears a striking resemblance to the human male anatomy. The mandrake's Hebrew name, *duda'im*, shares a root with the word for 'beloved,' *dodi*."

8. Roger Phillips & Nicky Foy, *The Random House Book of Herbs*, 159.

9. Michael Zohary, *Plants of the Bible*, 189.

Chapter Six

JACOB'S RODS

Portion-*Vayetze* / And [Jacob] went out (Genesis 28:10-32:3)

Jacob then got fresh shoots of poplar, and of almond and plane, and peeled white stripes in them, laying bare the white of the shoots. The rods that he had peeled he set up in front of the goats in the troughs, the water receptacles, that the goats came to drink from. Their mating occurred when they came to drink, and since the goats mated by the rods, the goats brought forth streaked, speckled, and spotted young. (Genesis 30:37-39)

Photograph © Avinoam Danin

Platanus orientalis. Oriental plane trees growing by the spring water of Nahl Kziv Upper Galilee. Small willow trees grow below them.

Bargains, deceptions, and magic are folk themes woven throughout the fascinating episode of Jacob's rods, all under the watchful eye of God. Magic-possessing rods or divining rods, a Near Eastern motif, turns up in Exodus 7:8-9 and Numbers 17:16-26, but seldom are the trees from which the rods are fashioned given specific species names (Aaron's almond blossoming rod in Numbers 17:23 is an exception). The idea behind Jacob's rods is deeply rooted in folk wisdom: when fresh shoots of certain trees are prepared to look streaked by cutting strips in the bark to reveal the white pith beneath, and these shoots or (magic) rods are then laid in the troughs where the all-white or all-black sheep and goats see them when they mate, then the females would produce "streaked, speckled, and spotted young" as described above. This would be to Jacob's advantage based on the bargain he makes with his father-in-law. Is this really how Jacob increased his flock?[1] As we shall see, the folk motif is there, up front, but as we already know from his life's work as a shepherd, Jacob has built up years of experience, is a smart shepherd, and is blessed by God.

When Jacob, after more than twelve years, implores Laban to release him from servitude and allow him to return to his homeland in Canaan, he asks only for sheep that are not all white and goats that are not all black (Genesis 30:32), the dominant colors for these animals in that region. To Laban this is a good deal since spotted and streaked animals would be in the minority. Laban acknowledges that his flocks have flourished under Jacob's care but the wheeler-and-dealer cannot resist cheating Jacob even out of his modest request. "But that same day he [Laban] removed the streaked and spotted he-goats and all the speckled and spotted she-goats—every one that had white on it—and all the dark-colored sheep and left them in the charge of his sons. And he put a distance of three day's journey between himself and Jacob, while Jacob was pasturing the rest of Laban's flock [of all-white sheep and all-black goats]. (Genesis 30:35-36)

While Jacob used the time-honored folk tradition of increasing the probabilities for streaked and spotted offspring by placing peeled rods before the mating animals, he also knew from careful observation over many years of shepherding that a proportion of the monochrome animals would produce spotted and streaked offspring (since some of them carried the gene for different coloring). Jacob further refined the breeding process to increase his chances of more spotted animals by selecting for hybrid vigor in the next generation, a phenomenon well known in the biblical world and later described in the Mendelian laws of heredity. The biblical text uses the term *mekusharot* (the stronger) to describe hybrid sheep and goats that conceived earlier than others and were generally more vigorous. These were the ones he used for breeding to build up his own flock over a period of six years. In the narrative Jacob's astuteness is ascribed to his dream in which an angel of God told him, "Note well that all the he-goats which are mating with the flock are streaked, speckled and mottled; for I have noted all that Laban has been doing to you" (Genesis 31:12-13). As the text tells us, at breeding time Jacob placed the rods only in front of the most vigorous animals; he didn't place them before the less vigorous ones. "Thus the feeble ones ['*atufim*, late-breeding sheep or goats] went to Laban and the sturdy [early breeding sheep or goats] to Jacob. So the man grew exceedingly prosperous, and came to own large flocks, maidservants and menservants, and camels and asses" (Genesis 30:43) in the earliest known example of selective animal breeding.[2] This feat was achieved ostensibly through the rods (and modern research suggests this may have been possible), but as shepherds of the day would also appreciate, Jacob outwitted Laban by his sharp observation of the animals under his care (knowledge which Laban lacked), aided by an angel of God.

—◊◊◊—

SUITABLE RODS FOR JACOB'S PURPOSES could have come from the branches of poplar, almond, and the oriental plane tree, all of which grew in the region and would have produced enough pliant fresh or green branches to peel at breeding time. In some translations of the Bible (the King James and others) the almond and plane tree are translated as "hazel" and "chestnut," tree species unknown in the Middle East but familiar in the West. This tendency to translate Hebrew names into more familiar flora because of inadequate knowledge of the native plants of the biblical region accounts for much confusion over centuries about their significance in the text.

The white poplar, *Populus alba*, is a riverbank tree. Its scientific and common name refer to its whitish-gray bark and woolly leaves. Native to most Middle Eastern countries, including Syria and Lebanon, it thrives in wet places. Mentioned only twice in the Bible, *"livneh"* is regarded as *Populus alba* in the Jacob story, but as styrax, *Styrax officinalis*, in Hosea's description of sacrifices made on the tops of mountains in a shady grove "under oak, poplar [styrax], and terebinth, because their shade is so pleasant" (Hosea:4:13).[3] The Euphrates poplar *(P. euphratica)* is the *"tzaftzafah"* in the famous passage "By the rivers of Babylon, there we sat, and sat and wept, as we thought of Zion. There on the poplars we hung up our lyres..." (Psalms 137:1-2).

The almond tree, *Amygdalus communis* (*Prunus dulcis*) (*shaked* or *luz*), discussed in Chapter Nineteen, *The Blooming Menorah*, and Chapter Twenty-Six, *The Blooming Rod*, is a prominent harbinger of spring in the landscape, with its sudden and dramatic burst of profuse bloom at the end of winter. Oriental plane tree, *Platanus orientalis*, the *armon* of Genesis 30:37, grows by riverbanks and springs, mainly in the north. Aged specimens grow to sixty feet or more with huge branches

Photograph © Ori Fragman

Amydaglus communis. Almond trees in bloom west of Jerusalem.

and a vast trunk as much as forty feet wide. Its flaking bark peels off in sheets giving the trunk a pale, naked look. Perhaps the derivation of *armon* is from the Hebrew *erom* meaning naked.[4] The plane tree's size was used along with other trees to illustrate Ezekiel's prophecy against Egypt: "Cedars in the garden of God could not compare with it; cypresses could not match its boughs, and plane trees could not vie with its branches. Now you know who is comparable to you in glory and greatness among the trees of Eden. And you, too, shall be brought down with the trees of Eden to the lowest part of the netherworld" (Ezekiel 31:8-18).

ENDNOTES

1. With the recent advent of epigenetics, Joshua Backon points to the intriguing idea that there may be a scientific basis to the folklore based on amino acids released into the water from the peeled rods and this could affect the coat color of Jacob's sheep, an idea that violates Mendelian principles. "Jacob and the Spotted Sheep: The Role of Prenatal Nutrition On Epigenetics of Fur Color," *Jewish Bible Quarterly*, 36:4, Oct–Dec, 2008, 263–264.
2. See Yehuda Feliks *Nature and Man in the Bible*, 9–13 for the traditional explanation of how the Mendelian laws of heredity worked in Jacob's breeding program.
3. Michael Zohary, *Plants of the Bible*, 118.
4. Zohary, 129.

Chapter Seven

OAK OF THE WEEPING

Portion-*Vayyishlach* / And Jacob sent (Genesis 32:4-36:43)
And Deborah, Rebekah's nurse, died, and she was buried under an oak below Bethel; so the name of it was called Allon-bacuth, oak of the weeping. (Genesis 35:8)

Photograph © Ori Fragman

Quercus ithaburensis. Tabor oak, North Hula Valley.

This obituary notice in the midst of Jacob's saga seems almost arbitrary. Yet is it? Rebekah's nurse, briefly mentioned and unnamed in the text when accompanying Rebekah at the time she left her family in Mesopotamia to marry Isaac (Genesis 24:59), is now named and given a dignified burial under a landmark oak tree in *Allon-bacuth,* a biblical place name identified with a well-known oak. Deborah may have accompanied Jacob and his entourage hundreds of miles from Mesopotamia to the land of Canaan when Jacob fled Laban's oppression, or met him there. The text does not say. We must assume she was an esteemed and beloved figure, particularly for her association with Jacob's mother, Rebekah, so it was fitting to bury her under a grand oak tree. Significant trees in the landscape such as oaks were revered and deified by ancient peoples, and among the early Hebrews such grand specimens were regarded as appropriate burial sites for an honored person.[1]

Nurse Deborah, who had merely a walk-on part in the previous narrative, has been promoted to center stage to prepare us for the other deaths to follow: Rachel in childbirth on the way to Bethlehem (Genesis 35:18), and Isaac, the old Patriarch, in Hebron (Genesis 35:28-29). The nurse's death gains impact because it is wedged between Jacob's order to his household to bury their pagan idols under a terebinth tree (sacred in pagan culture) as he prepares himself to receive God's word at Bethel, and the event itself at Bethel (Genesis 35:9). We feel, as a biblical audience must have felt, that in ordering his household to bury their pagan gods, and in burying the old nurse, he was himself burying his Aram (Mesopotamian) past, his links to the pagan culture in which he had sojourned for twenty years in the service of his father-in-law. Tragically, Rachel's death is associated with that past, too, since it was she who stole her father's pagan gods to ensure the well-being of Jacob's household. Jacob unwittingly hastened her death when he swore to Laban that whoever stole Laban's gods would die, not realizing that the thief was his beloved Rachel (Genesis 31:32; 34).

Jacob's audience with God at Bethel is a return visit (Genesis 28:13-17)—now representing the culmination and successful resolution of his struggles, beginning in his mother's womb when he tried to overtake his older brother by "holding on to the heel of Esau" (Genesis 25:26). They continue with his brother Esau over Jacob's theft of the first-born blessing, and after he fled his ancestral home, carry over in his contentious relationship with his Mesopotamian father-in-law, Laban: first about Rachel (for whom he labors fourteen years), then over his release from servitude (add another six years). After his flight from Laban (Genesis 31:21) he is very anxious over a reunion with Esau, fraught with foreboding, followed by his encounter with a mysterious stranger at the Jabbok gorge whom he wrestles to a stalemate (Genesis 32:24-33). Perhaps, as has been suggested, the meeting and struggle originated in existing folkore of a hero fighting a river god, but as with other borrowings (such as the Flood story), it has been re-shaped and transformed into something much broader.[2] As we shall see, this event marks the beginning of Jacob's recognition as a carrier of God's blessing to Israel. Borrowings from the surrounding pagan cultures are not so surprising, but what sets them off from their origins, is their radical departure in the service of ethical monotheism. Following the occurrence at Jabbok gorge, Jacob's actual reunion with Esau—approached with caution and diplomacy—is succeeded by the horrific actions after the rape of his daughter, Dinah (Genesis 34:25-29).

In terms of compressed biblical narrative, these developments represent several years in which Jacob has continued to live by his shepherd wits, ever maturing, gaining in material and spiritual power. His story is told within the context of shepherd life in the semi-arid regions of the Fertile Crescent (Laban country), and afterwards in Canaan, thus bringing Jacob's story vividly to life for a biblical audience, for whom the details would be familiar. It is the land itself, the basis of existence, which shapes the story, providing the important framework in which Jacob acts. In this sense, the land is inseparable from the new spiritual vision and should be given its due. If we are to understand Jacob and his development, we must see it in terms of unsettled shepherd life and its semi-nomadic culture, built up from living on the edge (literally the edge of rainfed and semi-arid regions), its fierce loyalty to its own clan, and its traditional mistrust of the outside world.[3]

These preoccupations are all present in the troubling episode of the rape of Dinah, a simple shepherdess (probably not much older than thirteen[4]) and sister to Simeon and Levi (they are all offspring of the same mother, Leah), who "went out to see the daughters of the land" (Genesis 34:1) after Jacob settled temporarily on the outskirts of Shechem (Genesis 33:18). Among similar shepherd groups, this free and easy style would have been natural. The honor code among clans would have protected her from molestation, but in the city of Shechem this was not the case, and it is this difference—the contrast between the pastoralist and city culture—that drives the story to its logical and disturbing conclusion. Hamor, the father of young Shechem (the same name as the city) who raped Dinah and who wants to marry her, proposes that the clan of Jacob intermarry with the people of the city. Jacob's sons plan a deceit: they propose that this can only occur if all the men of Shechem become circumcised, the sign of the Hebrews' covenant with God. After the Shechemites agree and while they are still weak, Simeon and Levi slay all the males of the city (Genesis 34:25) in accord with rough clan justice, with its obsession with the clan's honor and its fierce group solidarity against the outside, alien world. Jacob and his clan could never have assimilated into this pagan city since that would have run counter to Jacob's mission, one that had been passed on to him by Abraham and Isaac, of fulfilling God's promise to make the Patriarchs' descendants a people in their own land following God's laws and teachings (Genesis 13:14-16; 26:3-5). Significantly, Jacob had neither ordered nor approved the onslaught by his rebellious sons against the city of Shechem. His passivity in this episode signals his future diminished role in his family's life.

This glimpse into the raw edges of shepherd culture makes us appreciate how far the Israelites' spiritual and moral vision had evolved beyond the shepherd tradition from which it grew, to insist that the individual, not the clan or group, is responsible for his behavior (Deuteronomy 24:16), that strangers must be treated with loving kindness (Leviticus 19:18), and that God is merciful (Exodus 34:6),[5] as indeed He shows Himself to be repeatedly toward the wayward Israelites. The *mitzvot* (laws) given in Exodus and Leviticus, and repeated in Deuteronomy, all reflect a striving toward an ideal "to make a holy nation" (Exodus 19:6), one that is much different from what we see in shepherd clan culture where actions are guided by a different set of rules. The beginnings of the nation Israel as told in the stories of the Patriarchs do not shy away from moral ambiguity and human weakness (similar themes are pursued throughout the Hebrew Bible), causing us to understand that life, wherever it is lived, poses problems of behavior for which the later laws fulfill an obvious need. Yet as soon as Abram answered God's call to "Go forth from your native land and from your father's house to the land that I will show you. I will make of you a great nation . . . " (Genesis 12:1-2), the seeds were planted for transcending shepherd culture toward a new moral vision. The thrilling aspect of Genesis is that the problematic humans we meet along the journey unfailingly manage to carry the torch forward toward a new order, borne in the heart of pagan culture.

It is just after the darkness of Shechem, when Jacob needs counsel, that "God said to Jacob, 'Arise, go up to Bethel and remain there; and build an altar there to the God who appeared to you when you were fleeing from your brother Esau'" (Genesis 35:1). And we are where our exploration of the text began, with his household burying their pagan idols and Deborah, the nurse, under the landmark oak tree.

When Jacob wrestled the stranger to a stalemate, his opponent stranger told him "your name shall no longer be Jacob, but Israel, for you have striven with beings divine and human, and have prevailed" (Genesis 32:29), but it is only now at Bethel when God, for the first time, speaks directly to him (not in a dream) that he is officially named Israel, achieves the status of Patriarch, and receives the blessing and promise of a nation in its own land. "The land that I assigned to Abraham and Isaac I assign to you; And to your offspring to come will I assign the land" (Genesis 35:12). Jacob has passed through his ordeals to enter a new, more passive, phase of his life. Jacob's displacement as leader, already challenged by his restive sons in the Dinah affair, comes, ironically, as he assumes his mantle of revered Patriarch. But he has performed his role in the biblical scheme and is now ready to give way to his sons, waiting none too peacefully in the wings. His diminished power is later confirmed when Jacob/Israel found out that his son Reuben "went and lay with Bilhah, his father's [Jacob's] concubine" (Genesis 35:22)—a traditional challenge to parental or chieftan authority[6]—and did nothing about it. He will now retire from active duty, as it were, but his favoring of Joseph, first-born of beloved Rachel, suggests continuing family strife.

THE PAGAN WORLD from which the new vision of God evolved is clearly evident in the recurring theme of pagan traditions associated with sacred trees: Jacob's household buries their idols under a terebinth tree near the pagan city of Shechem, and Jacob buries Rebekah's nurse, Deborah, under the oak of the weeping near Bethel, an indication that it is an acknowledged burial site. This suggests a wealth of trees in the landscape. Although perhaps true in Jacob's time, deforestation of the land began millennia ago, as soon as people needed to clear trees to plant food crops. Over-harvesting, in addition to over-grazing, wars, fire, and finally neglect and abandonment, eventually led to the destruction of once abundant forests and woodlands (maquis).[7]

Of the three species of oak present in Israel, the two most dominant are the common oak, *Quercus calliprinos* (*alon matsui*), and the Tabor oak, *Quercus ithaburensis* (*alon hatabor*). The generic name, *alon*, derived from *el*, meaning God, suggests that oaks were regarded as sacred trees. Throughout the Hebrew Bible they are synonymous with power, longevity, and rejuvenation: Even as Isaiah prophesies about destroying the wicked population of the Kingdom of Judah, he holds out hope for rejuvenation through the image of Israel as the holy oak seed, capable of sprouting from the dead tree stump (Isaiah 6:13). Strength, associated symbolically with the oak, is referred to by another prophet: "Yet I destroyed the Amorite before them, whose height was like the height of the cedars, and who was stout as the oak" (Amos 2:9).

The common oak is a shrubby-like Mediterranean tree of upland *maquis* thickets in the Galilee, Judea and Samaria. If protected from grazing, as in Upper Galilee, it may reach about ten feet in height. Under certain conditions, however, a single specimen can grow as an impressive single-trunk tree to thirty to fifty feet tall with wide spreading top growth. It's not difficult to imagine how such specimens came to be symbolically associated with strength and power. Such tall oaks still exist in Judea and elsewhere as markers for tombs or as remnant Arab sacred groves, but where goats are allowed

Photograph © Ori Fragman

Quercus calliprinos. Common oak, Mount Carmel.

Photograph © Ori Fragman

Quercus calliprinos. Common oak acorn, Mount Carmel.

to graze freely among them, they are so stunted, dwarfed, and badly formed that they hardly appear to belong to the same species. The common oak has small leathery leaves with very prickly margins. Old leaves only begin to fall in the spring, by which time they have been replaced by fresh fully developed leaves, so the tree is never without leaves. In March or April the common oak bears catkins, hundreds of inconspicuous male flowers that hang erect under sparsely-flowered staminate female blossoms. Aided by wind pollination the tiny pistillate female flowers are fertilized by pollen from the staminate male blossoms, from which acorns of variable size and shape develop. These are held in a bristly cup and will be shed by wind and rain later in the fall-winter season; they lose their viability within a few weeks. This is a tough tree, tolerating dry conditions and able to regenerate when cut down, or even burned. In biblical times, the Israelites pulverized the female insect which infests the common oak, *Kermes ilicis,* to produce a scarlet dye for priestly garments (Exodus 35:23).[8] In Arab folk medicine acorns are boiled and the decoction is drunk to alleviate ulcers, reduce blood pressure, and treat diarrhea, among other ailments.[9]

The Tabor oak, *Q. ithaburensis (alon hatabor)*, is largely confined to lower altitudes where growing conditions are warmer. Forest stands once spread throughout the Coastal Plain, Lower Galilee, Dan Valley, Hulah Plain and the Golan Heights. Undisturbed specimens, such as the one traditionally associated with Abraham's oak in Hebron, can live hundreds of years or more, growing to over eighty feet tall and spreading sixty-five feet in crown circumference. In places where pure stands of tall oaks remain, they support the assumption that they are remnants of forests decimated when they were cut down by the Turkish army during World War I for locomotive fuel.[10] The Tabor oak usually grows up to about thirty-one feet, with wide-spreading branches and a round crown. Leaves are variable in size with toothed margins and woolly undergrowth (making them drought-tolerant). These are shed in late winter, but may hang on longer where temperatures are mild. Like the common oak, the Tabor oak bears male and female flowers on the same tree and also bears distinctive acorns. They are larger than those from the common oak and held in a distinctive bristly cup. In biblical times the acorns and bark were boiled to obtain a tannin-rich solution in which prepared hides were immersed to turn them into supple leather.[11]

ENDNOTES

1. Michael Zohary, *Plants of the Bible*, 110.
2. Suggested in Everett Fox, *The Five Books of Moses*, 154.
3. For his insights into the clan outlook and moral code referred to here and throughout the Dinah episode, I am indebted to Daniel Hillel, *The Natural History of the Bible*, 76–77.
4. Leon Kass in *The Beginning of Wisdom*. See 477–478 n.8 for his calculations.
5. Daniel Hillel *The Natural History of the Bible*, 80.
6. *The Jewish Study Bible*, 72 n.22a.
7. The botanical term *maquis* is of Corsican origin, but was adopted as the name for the French resistance movement during World War II when members hid in its thick growth. The gradual destruction of the original forests and woodlands is discussed in Zohary, 33 and Nigel Hepper *Illustrated Encyclopedia of Bible Plants*, 23.
8. Hepper, 170.
9. D. Palevitch and Zohara Yaniv *Medicinal Plants of the Holy Land*, 199.
10. Hepper, 23.
11. Hepper, 172.

Chapter Eight

THE TRADE ROUTE

Portion-*Vayeshev* / And he lived (Genesis 37:1-40:23)
Then they sat down to a meal. Looking up, they saw a caravan of Ishmaelites coming from Gilead, their camels bearing gum, balm, and ladanum [myrrh] to be taken to Egypt. (Genesis 37:25)

The biblical narrative from now until the end of Genesis constitutes an uninterrupted story centering on the figure of Joseph, Jacob's next-to-youngest-son, and the apple of his father's eye as the first-born son of Jacob's beloved Rachel. It is Joseph's fantastic adventures that move the story in a new and startling direction, one that leads us away from the familiar territory of semi-nomadic shepherd culture in Canaan based on the constant search for grazing and water rights, to exotic Egypt, a highly developed agricultural-based urban society founded on the annual flooding of the Nile River.[1] The brilliant means by which the story literally progresses on

Photograph © Elaine Solowey

Commiphora gileadensis. Balm of Gilead in new trial orchard at Moshav Beer Tuvia on the southern Coastal Plain.

the ground are the dusty caravans that traverse well-established trade routes from Babylon, through Gilead and Canaan, down to Egypt, carrying precious plant products highly prized for medicine, perfume, and embalming. One of these caravans will carry Joseph into exile away from his family. Although God is not evident as He has been in the patriarchal narratives, He is, nevertheless, powerfully behind the scenes, guiding the course of human events in certain directions for the fulfillment of His plans for the Israelite nation.

As the chapter opens we find Jacob finally settled in his ancestral home in Hebron after his own exile and travails. For anyone who has followed the saga of the Patriarchs with their all-important mission to keep alive God's blessing and promise, the question is, who shall lead, who shall carry on the work that began with Abraham to transform ordinary shepherds into a mighty, blessed nation in the land of Canaan, whose offspring will be counted as numerous as the dust of the earth and the stars of heaven, who will follow the new way, observing God's commandments, laws, and teachings? We have already observed that Jacob is in semi-retirement, that his sons Simeon and Levi (at Shechem), and Reuben (consorting with his father's concubine) have challenged his leadership.

Two developments push Joseph's brothers' jealousy over the edge into the realm of hatred, a simmering one that must have release: Jacob's flagrant bestowal on his favorite son of an "ornamented tunic" (the "coat of many colors"), and Joseph's insistence on relating his dreams to his brothers. Dressing Joseph in a special tunic is a sign that his father, Jacob, not only favors him but considers Joseph to be his heir, chief of the clan.[2] To Leah's sons, already jockeying for position as leader, this is an insupportable affront: "When his brothers saw that their father loved him more than any of his brothers, they hated him so that they could not speak a friendly word to him" (Genesis 37:4).

Joseph subjects his older brothers to accounts of his dreams, not because he wants to torment them, but because he is so supremely self-confident and self-absorbed. How could they *not* want to know of his great future? "Hear this dream" he demands of them about his first dream in which "we were binding [wheat] sheaves in the field, when suddenly my sheaf stood up and remained upright; then your sheaves gathered around and bowed low to my sheaf" (Genesis 37:6-7). Never mind that it is improbable—Jacob's clan leads a pastoral shepherd existence on the fringes of agriculture where wheat is not cultivated. What could this upstart mean by elevating himself above them? "And they hated him even more for his talk about his dreams" (Genesis 37:8).

The second dream is even wilder: "Look," he again demands of them, "...this time the sun, the moon, and eleven stars were bowing down to me" (Genesis 37:9). Not only do the brothers bow down to him in this dream, but so does the entire universe! Joseph reigns supreme. Joseph's brothers, the text tells us, were "wrought up" but "his father kept the matter in mind," meaning he mulled it over. Maybe there was something to these dreams. In the Joseph story dreams in pairs come true,[3] as we shall see.

The scene is now set for the resolution of the conflict between Joseph and his brothers. His doting father sends Joseph out to Shechem where Leah's sons are grazing their flocks. Perhaps they have moved to a better spot? Jacob wants a report. Indeed, they have moved, as Joseph learns, to Dothan, a richer source of grazing than Shechem, now a wild field after its devastation following the rape of Dinah. Even before Joseph reached them in Dothan, when they only "saw him from afar," a small figure in an ornamented tunic, their rage was rekindled and they "conspired to kill him" (Genesis 37:18). But how? Their chilling proposals reflect how far they have sunk into moral depravity. The first idea is to kill him outright, then throw him in an empty water cistern, "one of the pits," covering their deed by reporting that 'a savage beast devoured him' (Genesis 37:20). Reuben tries to dissuade them, not from a horror of killing his own brother, although he cynically uses the argument against the shedding of blood, but to promote his self-interest. Just throw him into the pit without killing him, he counsels, thinking that he will return later, drag Joseph from the cistern and restore him to his father, thereby improving his, Reuben's standing, with Jacob (Genesis 37:21-22). Thus is the brothers' rage against Joseph discharged: "When Joseph came up to his brothers, they stripped Joseph of his tunic, the ornamented tunic that he was wearing, and they took him and cast him into the pit. The pit was empty; there was no water in it" (Genesis 37:23-24). Although well aware that the opening of the cistern's mouth is so narrow that Joseph will die if he is not helped out, they "then sat down to a meal." How far will these brothers have to travel in moral terms to make up for their degradation?

When the brothers note an Ishmaelite caravan coming from Gilead, Judah puts forth the idea that they should sell him as a slave to the passing traders, thereby absolving themselves of the crime of murder. He persuasively counsels, "let us not do away with him ourselves" (Genesis 37:27), so "They sold Joseph for twenty pieces of silver to the Ishmaelites, who brought Joseph to Egypt" (Genesis 37:28). In Egypt, another group of traders, the Midianites, sell Joseph to Potiphar, Pharaoh's chief steward (Genesis 37:36), thus placing him deep within Egypt's ruling establishment. The pastoral semi-arid landscape of the founding patriarchs is left far behind, but not before the hated tunic, a material symbol of Joseph's ascendance and all that stands between the brothers and their father, is dipped in the blood of a slaughtered kid to convince the grieving Jacob that his beloved son was truly "torn by a beast" (Genesis 37:33). Yet despite the brothers' success in separating Joseph from the blessing inherent in the special garment, Joseph survives his ordeal to fulfill his dreams, because, as we will learn, "the Lord was with him" (Genesis 39:2).

The Higher Critics point to discrepancies in the text: After agreeing to sell Joseph to the Ishmaelites, "Midianite traders passed by, they pulled Joseph up out of the pit. They sold Joseph for twenty pieces of silver to the Ishmaelites, who brought Joseph to Egypt" (Genesis 37:28). Where was Reuben when Judah's plan was put into action? Who are the "they" who pulled Joseph out of the pit, and who sold Joseph to the Ishmaelites? Are the Ishmaelites and Midianite traders synonymous? Are there two different texts pasted together, one called the E version, the other the J version?[4] Are, in fact, camels, domesticated in the time of the Joseph story or is this a later bit of poetic license to move the narrative along?[5]

But does any of this matter to our enjoyment and understanding of Joseph's thrilling story? The broad outlines of the text are plain: the seventeen-year-old son of Jacob, named Joseph, indulged and favored by his father, is blessed with extraordinary powers of prophesying the future through his uncanny dreams. He is hated by his jealous older brothers who sell him into slavery. As in any successful narrative, the reader (or listener) wants to know, what next? what happens to Joseph now? This is a page-turning introduction to Joseph's story.

BIBLE CRITICS, biblical botanists, and naturalists through the centuries have struggled to learn the precise identity of the plants whose extracted resins and saps are preserved in the magical names "gum, balm, and ladanum," without success. Although the Bible and Talmudic literature mention names of plants and the fragrances and sap extracted from them, we cannot be sure to what these Hebrew or Aramaic names refer. Later translations only add to the confusion for they are not based on any sound knowledge of the plants or plant products mentioned in Scripture. What we do know is that certain plants earned a widespread reputation throughout the Middle East for healing, scent, and industrial processes based on long experience, and that even today they are still favored for their unique properties. In biblical times it was essential to reduce plants to their essence in the form of ointments, oils, and gums so they could travel long distances without losing their potency. It is in these very valuable forms that they were carried down to Egypt along with Joseph.

Notwithstanding controversies surrounding their identity, certain plants according to tradition fulfill the role ascribed to them in Joseph's story.[6]

"Gum," translated from the Hebrew *nekot*, is more properly gum tragacanth, used since ancient times in medicines, industrial processes, and in the manufacture of confections. The flakes of gum are even today collected by shepherds from several species of *Astragalus* such as *A. gummifer* and *A. bethlehemiticus,* both of which grow in Israel. Although there are over a thousand species in this genus, only six of them yield gum. The plant itself is a spiny shrublet cushion adapted to dry climates and resistant to grazing. The roots of the plants are tapped by making a couple of longitudinal cuts usually in June and continuing until the rains begin in the fall or early winter. Nowadays, demand for gum tragacanth, used extensively in foods, toiletries, and textiles, outstrips supply and continues to be harvested from wild plants.

"Balm" or *tzori* appears six times in the Bible, three times in association with Gilead, presumed by some (Zohary, for instance) to be a center for producing the gum or resin that was extracted from the bark of a tree. Others consider this to be *Liquidambar orientalis,* perhaps synonymous with *"tzori"* as well as *nataf* meaning drops, the latter translated into the Greek as *"stacte."* *Stacte* is one of the ingredients mentioned in the preparation of holy annointing oil in Exodus 30:34. It has been suggested that "balm" and *"stacte"* refer to *Styrax officinalis,* styrax or storax, but this has been discounted on the grounds that while the tree has grown in Israel since biblical times, it does not yield gum. Others say that *"tzori"* is a generic term for any healing plant. But current research[7] makes a very good case for *Commiphora gileadensis* and the improved variety developed from it, the famous Balm of Gilead, *tzori gilead,* named for the place through which it was transported down to Egypt on the spice route. Introduced from the Arabian deserts, it shares the characteristics of other drought tolerant plants in the *Commiphora* genus such as myrrh: small trees from seven to fourteen feet tall with stout green trunks and thin, papery, peeling bark; their spineless branches yield a fragrant liquid or resin known as "opobalsamum," shortened to "balsam" or "balm." At the time of the Joseph story, there was already a brisk trade in the resin extracted from the wild type. Later, the now extinct improved variety known as "Judean balm" became famous throughout the region for its high quality and healing properties. The Bible does not go out of its way to celebrate healing from plants since this would be regarded as idolatry. The ultimate healer, the Bible teaches, is God: "The Lord sustains him on his sickbed; in his illness thou healest all his infirmities" (Psalms 41:3, RSV). Nevertheless, the prophet Jeremiah cries out, "Is there no balm in Gilead? Is there no physician there? Why then has the health of the daughter of my people not been restored?" (Jeremiah 8:22, RSV). Based on the many medicinal properties which the Judean balm was thought to possess,[8] Jeremiah's cry is a well founded metaphor.

Most scholars translate the Hebrew *lot* as ladanum or labdanum (not to be confused with laudanum, a tincture of opium derived from *Papaver somniferum*). Ladanum is a resinous substance exuded on the branches of *Cistus* species (*lotem*), shrubs up to three feet tall. In Israel, two *Cistus* species grow among *batha* and *maquis,* both shrubs resembling an overgrown rugosa rose; their common name is "rockrose." They bear similar wide open and crinkly single-petaled flowers surrounding bushy golden stamens and attract bees

Photograph © Jackie Chambers

Photograph © Jackie Chambers

Cistus creticus. Pink-flowered rockrose near Ashdod.

Cistus salviifolius. White-flowered rockrose near Ashdod.

during their season of bloom, from March to June. The more common is the pink-flowered *C. creticus (C. incanus, Cistus villosus)*; the Latin epithet, "*incanus*," refers to the plant's gray, hairy foliage. White-flowered *C. salviifolius*, has more sage-like pebbly-textured foliage, as preserved in its Latin epithet, "sage-like." Resin from *Cistus* species' sticky leaves was once harvested by combing it out of goats' beards and coats after they had grazed in an area where rock rose was prominent. Another method, described by first century CE Greek naturalist Dioscorides, was to beat the bushes with rake-like leather thongs, then collect the resin that stuck to them.[9] Resin can also be extracted by boiling the branches in water. Ladanum is marketed today in spiral pieces with a penetrating balsamic aroma. Once used primarily as a medicinal for healing coughs and treating dysentery, it is now used primarily in the perfume industry and for incense in Eastern churches.

ENDNOTES
1. For a full discussion of the impact of the Nile's seasonal flooding see Daniel Hillel, *The Natural History of the Bible*, 88–89.
2. See Leon Kass *The Beginning of Wisdom*, 514, for a discussion of Joseph's garment as "the garb of rule."
3. Robert Alter *The Five Books of Moses* 208 n.9.

4. See *The Jewish Study Bible*, 76 n.28 for a general discussion of these issues.
5. See Daniel Hillel, *The Natural History of the Bible*, 295 n.3 for two different views.
6. For a general discussion of biblical ointments and balms, see F. Nigel Hepper, *Illustrated Encyclopedia of Bible Plants*, 146–148. For a discussion of what he considers to be the appropriate plants see Michael Zohary *Plants of the Bible*, 192–195.
7. Current research here is based on a paper by Shimshon Ben Yehoshua, Bar Ilan University: "Judean Balsam, In Hebrew 'Afarsemon' or 'Tzorey Gilead'—Balm of Gilead."
8. Ben Yehoshua, 3; David Lluz, Miri Hoffman, Nechama Gilboa-Garber and Zohar Amar, "Medicinal properties of *Commiphora gileadensis*," *African Journal of Pharmacy and Pharmacology*, Vol 4(8), pp. 516–520, August 2010. In this later paper, the authors review the entire history of medicinal uses from ancient times and conclude that its healing powers [from extracts using all parts of the plant, including bark, seeds, and resin] were "claimed to have been used for the treatment of almost all human diseases," among them curing headaches, early-state cataract, hearing disorders, paralysis, mending fractures, respiratory diseases, and as a snake-bite antidote. Rabbinic literature mentions a tonic, "aluntis," composed of old wine mixed with clear water and balsam, which was drunk in the bathhouse after bathing as a cooling beverage or to anoint and strengthen the body (*Talmud Bavli*). From their own research into its effectiveness, the authors conclude that *C. gileadensis* does possess antibacterial activities "that validate its usage in the local treatment of wound infections" and suggest that further research is required to expand their findings.
9. Hepper, 147.

Chapter Nine

DREAMS OF THE LAND

Portion-*Mikketz* / And it came to pass (Genesis 41:1-44:17)

He [Pharaoh] fell asleep and dreamed a second time: Seven ears of grain, solid and healthy, grew on a single stalk. But close behind them sprouted seven ears, thin and scorched by the east wind. And the thin ears swallowed up the seven solid and full ears. Then Pharaoh awoke: it was a dream! (Genesis 41:5-7)

Photograph © Joshua D. Klein

Triticum aestivum. Bread wheat, Moshav Mevo Horon in the foothills of Jerusalem.

Pharaoh's first disturbing dream is about cows standing by the Nile, the seven "ugly and gaunt" cows who consume seven "handsome and sturdy cows" (Genesis 41:2-4). His second dream is about the scorched wheat consuming the good wheat. Since a successful wheat crop was the source of all Pharaoh's wealth and power, these were not dreams to brush aside. They were so deeply disturbing to Pharaoh that his "spirit was agitated," and despite the wealth of dream interpreters in Egypt, "none could interpret them for Pharaoh" (Genesis 41:8). It is then that his chief cupbearer belatedly recalls his former prison-mate Joseph, "a Hebrew youth," who had successfully interpreted his dream when he was in prison. In a dramatic turn-around Joseph "was rushed from the dungeon. He had his hair cut and changed his clothes, and he appeared before Pharaoh" (Genesis 41:14). A new Joseph for whom at age thirty a fresh chapter in his turbulent life is about to open.

Joseph's imminent rise to power in Egypt, his position as second only to the great Pharaoh himself, has been slow in coming. He has languished in prison for twelve years, wrongfully accused of attempting to seduce his master Potiphar's wife, when, in fact, it was she who made the advances. We are told that "the Lord blessed his [Potiphar's] house for Joseph's sake" (Genesis 39:5) and even at Joseph's lowest point, in prison, "the Lord was with him": "The chief jailer did not supervise anything that was in Joseph's charge, because the Lord was with him, and whatever he did the Lord made successful" (Genesis 39:23). In the best folkloric tradition—the rise of the hero against great odds—we anticipate great things ahead for Joseph and we will not be disappointed.

Joseph's interpretation of Pharaoh's dreams is firmly based on the agricultural realities of the land of Egypt. Both dreams, Joseph tells Pharaoh, are the same. The gaunt cows of the first dream and the scorched wheat of the second represent the famine years associated with the failure of the Nile to flood, while the "handsome and sturdy cows" of the first dream and the "solid, healthy" wheat stalks of the second, represent other years of great harvests when the Nile floods, bringing life-giving water and nutrient-rich silt. Not to worry. Joseph has a contingency plan whereby the excess grain of abundant years is stored against bad times. All grain storage shall be centralized in the cities, and as it worked out in practice, taxation and the acquisition of the destitute farmers' land increased the concentration of power in Pharaoh's hands (Genesis 47:13-20).[1] Why should not Pharaoh favor Joseph when Joseph has not only given him a workable plan of action, but increased his wealth and power, and made it seem as if he, Pharaoh, was the savior of his people?

The question is, how did Joseph understand the dynamics of the annual flooding of the Nile, bringing in its wake humus-rich silt and moisture to nourish the wheat crop? How did he know that sometimes the Nile failed to rise, the rains did not come, and that even when the wheat did successfully grow it could be ruined by the hot, dry desert wind if it occurred when the grain had reached a third of its ripening, before the kernels were filled with starch?[2] How could Joseph, the product of a semi-arid shepherd culture based on grazing, not cultivation, know enough about the intricacies of Egyptian agriculture to be able to offer his comprehensive plan for the lean years? No matter how observant, it is unlikely that he could have gleaned the information during his years in prison. This is Joseph's explanation: "I have heard it said of you that for you to hear a dream is to tell its meaning," Pharaoh tells Joseph. "Joseph answered Pharaoh, saying, 'Not I! God will see to Pharaoh's welfare.'" (Genesis 41:16). If God is silently behind the scenes pushing the narrative forward to its goal—the confrontation between Joseph and his brothers and its resolution—it is the land itself that provides the impetus.

The famine, we are told, spread to all the lands, "So all the world came to Joseph in Egypt to procure rations," since Egypt was the traditional source throughout the Near East of famine relief. At Jacob's prodding, Joseph's brothers, too, take this route, the same one that Abram had taken during famine times (Genesis 12:10). "Go down and procure rations for us there," Jacob tells his sons, "that we may live and not die" (Genesis 42:2). Thus the scene is set for an encounter, not only between Joseph and his brothers, but between Egyptian and Israelite culture, between Joseph the thoroughly assimilated Egyptian and all that he has left behind—his family and tribal ties. Does he still belong to these people, or is he glad to be shed of his family and his cruel brothers who sold him into slavery? We know that Joseph looks and acts every inch an Egyptian, thinking only of executing his contingency plan, working to give ever more power to Pharaoh, hardly the sort of life's work that recommends itself to God's blessing and plan for the Israelites. Joseph now has an Egyptian name and an Egyptian wife. Yet his two sons are given Hebrew names: "*Manasseh,*" meaning "God has made me forget completely my hardship and my parental home" and "*Ephraim,*" "meaning God has made me fertile in the land of my affliction" (Genesis 41:51-52). Whatever their meaning, they tie him to his past. They represent a tenuous association with his origins.

When the brothers appear before Joseph, the vizier or chief dispenser of supplies, they "bowed low to him, with their faces to the ground" just as predicted in Joseph's boyhood dream, as, indeed, "all the world came to Joseph" in severe famine times [and bowed down] (Genesis 41:57). Joseph recognizes his brothers at once but does not show it. This gives him the opportunity to find out about his family. Have they changed? Are they still the coarse brothers who thought nothing of stripping and abandoning their younger sibling in a cistern? Joseph, acting like a stranger, accuses them of being spies rather than suppliants for Egypt's grain. They deny this and tell him their antecedents: "We your servants were twelve brothers, sons of a certain man in the land of Canaan; the youngest, however, is now with our father, and one is no more" (Genesis 42:13). Joseph, we can imagine, is touched to hear of his only true brother, son of their beloved mother Rachel. He is being drawn further into the affairs of his family. To prove their honesty, he tells them, he requires that they bring the young Benjamin to Egypt to verify their story while he holds Simeon as hostage.

It is at this point, when the destiny of Benjamin is in their hands, that the brothers are struck with guilt over what they had done to Joseph. "They said to one another, 'Alas, we are being punished on account of our brother, because we looked on at his anguish, yet paid no heed as he pleaded with us. That is why this distress has come upon us'" (Genesis 42:21). And Joseph, understanding, yet not admitting to them that he understood what they said, "turned away from them and wept" (Genesis 42:24).

This marks the beginning of the brothers' redemption for their crime against Joseph, and the beginning, too, of Joseph's reconciliation not only with the brothers but with Israelite destiny. He cannot be aloof. He is bound to his people, he cannot turn away from them. He will use his great power to save his family and, as we shall see, establish them in a favorable grazing area in Goshen "where you will be near me" (Genesis 45:10). He cares about the welfare of his family, he is still sympathetic to shepherd culture. Meanwhile, there will be more testing: Benjamin will be brought to Egypt, and eventually Jacob and his clan will join the brothers. Only then can the Israelite covenant with God move forward. The land of Egypt in its famine years has served its purpose, acting not just as a background to momentous events, but as a player in its own right.

—w—

TO FULLY APPRECIATE HOW PHARAOH FELT threatened by his dreams, it is helpful to understand the scope of farming activities in Egypt and the nature of the land in which they occurred. Little or no rain falls in Egypt even in winter, so it was entirely dependent for its fortunes on the seasonal rising of the Nile and the rich silt deposits that accompanied it. The silt was virtual fertilizer, and so famous for its beneficial properties that it gave the land one of its ancient Egyptian names, "*khami*." The Greeks considered this nutrient-rich soil to be the mother lode of all substances and named the study of all materials, "*khimia*," after it. Ultimately the name provides the basis for the study of "alchemy," from which the English word "chemistry" is derived. Egypt's reputation throughout the Near East as the land of great harvests was based on what the Greek historian Herodotus called this 'gift of the Nile.'[3] All this would have been Pharaoh's to lose if he had not discovered Joseph and his contingency plan!

The productive land of Egypt is divided naturally by the Nile River into two sections, Upper and Lower Egypt. In Upper Egypt to the south is a well-watered flood plain (the water coming from the Nile's source), hundreds of miles long and very narrow, bordered by deserts on both sides. It is from this characteristic that the Hebrew word for Egypt, "*Mitzrayim*," meaning a narrow place, is based. Lower Egypt to the north is a broad, marshy delta from the branching of the Nile River into many tributaries, the river ultimately opening to the Mediterranean Sea. In biblical times this area represented more than half of Egypt's arable land, but only after it was drained and regulated with canals. This must have taken place after a long period of experimentation as farmers came to understand that they could have a hand in directing the Nile's potential.

The main grain crop was wheat, *Triticum* sp., sometimes translated as "corn" (KJV) according to the European tradition of describing wheat or any small grain as corn (corn itself is known as "maize"). The most common type grown in Egypt until later times was emmer wheat *T. dicoccum* (*kussemet*), the ancient cultivated wheat descended from the wild wheat, *T. dicoccoides* (*khitta*), native to Israel and neighboring countries.[4] Unlike wild wheat, the kernels of emmer wheat do not shatter and fall to the ground when ripe (leaving straw), but remain on the plant to be harvested. By a process of mutation and selection over a long period, curious and observant farmers in each generation helped to advance civilization by the introduction of a nutritious crop that vastly improved the lives of the people. Emmer wheat was eventually replaced by durum wheat (*T. durum*), whose hard, high-gluten 'naked' grains, unlike those of the older hulled or enclosed grains, are easier to thresh. This was a great improvement because emmer wheat requires further processing before being milled into flour or consumed. Durum wheat, which gives a characteristic texture and flavor to Mediterrean flat breads like pita, is still widely cultivated in the Middle East, but is being replaced by modern bread wheats,[5] such as *T. aestivum*.

Photograph © Ori Fragman

Triticum dicoccoides. Wild wheat, Jerusalem Botanical Gardens.

Wheat is an annual member of the grass family with ears of spikelets along the central axis of the stem. Each spikelet has three to seven flowers of which only a few produce grains. The seeds, or fruit, are capable of storing seventy percent of starch and about ten percent of proteins. The outer layer of the seed is bran, useful for cattle and poultry feed as well as human consumption. The fantastic "seven-headed" wheat that Pharaoh saw in his dream is unusual but still known in Egypt as a variety of rivet wheat, *T. turgidum*,[6] very similar to durum wheat.

Before the development of sophisticated canal systems (earthen dikes fashioned to trap or let out excess water as needed to water the crops, as well as to preserve the nutrient-rich silt), farmers probably sowed their wheat in the wet mud after the annual flooding of the Nile; but when the Nile failed to rise, drought and famine ensued. In Deuteronomy, the Israelites compared their own growing conditions, almost wholly dependent on God favoring them with the early and late rains, to Egypt's good years, where a farmer could use his bare feet to easily direct excess water from one channel to another channel in the dike system: "For the land that you are entering to possess: It is not like the land of Egypt from which you went out, where you sow your seed and water it with your foot like a garden of greens" (Deuteronomy 11:10, Everett Fox translation).

The biblical narrative reflects an intimate and profound knowledge of Nile-based Egyptian agriculture in all of its detail as well as of the tradition of Semitic pastoralists seeking relief from the famine. Pictorial records on tombs and reliefs record this event as well as showing a master overseeing the grain harvest, from threshing and winnowing to carrying the grain for storage,[7] knowledge that stands behind the biblical narrative. It has been suggested that this intimacy with Egyptian practices among the Israelites bespeaks a collective memory of the Israelites' sojourn in Egypt.[8]

ENDNOTES

1. "Once the great famine is under way, Joseph institutes a twenty percent tax on the produce of the lands that have been made over to Pharaoh." Robert Alter, *The Five Books of Moses*, 234 n.34. Gradually, the farmers became virtual serfs of Pharaoh as he acquired first their animals, then their land.

2. This phenomenon occurs also in the Land of Israel and was commented on in the Jerusalem Talmud (*Shkalim* 5:1): "Once the whole world was scorched and they did not know from where to bring the grain offering." The Jerusalem Talmud mostly reflects Israelite traditions of the third and fourth centuries BCE, as distinct from the more comprehensive Babylonian Talmud.

3. These insights regarding silt are discussed in Daniel Hillel, *The Natural History of the Bible*, 88.

4. Agronomist Aaron Aaronson discovered wild wheat, the 'Mother of wheat" (*eim hakhitta*), growing in Rosh Pinnah in 1906. Commenting on the domestication of wild wheat, Michael Zohary writes that it

"took place about eight thousand years ago in one or more of the most primitive agricultural villages of the Assyrian mountains (Jarmo in Iraq), and probably in the Land of Israel as well where the culture is even older and the wheat ancestor more abundant." Michael Zohary, *Plants of the Bible*, 76. Nogah Hareuveni's father, Ephraim, discovered wild wheat on the outskirts of Jerusalem about twenty years later. He recounts how his father, in the 1920–30s, learned from Kurdish friends that they knew this 'Mother of wheat,' wild wheat, in Iraq where it is called "*jadassah*." They explained that "it was special in that it grows even during drought years: "The Mother of Wheat," *Neot Kedumim Newsletter*, Pesach 2007, p. 3. This may shed light on the type of wheat that could be harvested in Egypt at the time of Joseph during the seven lean years.

5. Nigel Hepper, *Illustrated History of Bible Plants*, 85.
6. Ibid.
7. Wall painting from the tomb of Mena, fourteenth century BCE, is "reminiscent of the description of Joseph's supervision of grain production and storage throughout Egypt." Hillel, 100.
8. "Ultimately, the saga of the Israelites' sojourn in Egypt became so deeply imprinted in the collective consciousness of their descendants as to be considered a defining event in their birth and subsequent development of their nationhood and religion." Hillel, 103.

Chapter Ten

SHEPHERD AND FARMER

Portion-*Vayehi* / And it came to pass (Genesis 47:28-50:26)

He [Judah] *tethers his ass to a vine. His ass's foal to a choice* [extra sweet] *vine. He washes his garment in wine. (Genesis 49:11)*

As the Book of Genesis draws to a close, it is fitting that the patriarch Jacob, now dying, takes center stage once more. In the famous deathbed scene (Genesis 49:1-33) he bestows his final blessings on his twelve sons, addressing them not as they are but as they (or their

Photograph © Ori Fragman

Vitis vinifera. Ripening grapes, Cyprus.

descendants) will be in the Promised Land. Judah, the fourth son of Jacob and Leah, is a late bloomer, who throughout the ordeal with Joseph over Benjamin's fate, has shown remarkable qualities of leadership. It was he, after all, who had convinced his brothers not to kill Joseph but to sell him to passing traders (Genesis 37:26-28), a hint that Judah might be capable of developing a more refined morality. It is he, rather than the first-born Reuben (obviously ill-equipped to assume a leadership role)[1], whom Jacob brings to the fore as the acknowledged future leader, bestowing on him a blessing of national dimensions: "The scepter shall not depart from Judah" (Genesis 49:10). While commentators agree that the deathbed scene is textually difficult,[2] it is clear that the Tribe of Judah is marked for great things. Biblical history bears out Jacob's vision for Judah: His tribe was the largest and most important in the Promised Land, and through his son, Peretz, he was an ancestor of David and the Royal line. After the death of Solomon and the splitting of the kingdom in two parts, north and south, in 933 BCE, the Kingdom of Judah (surviving until the Babylonian conquest in 586 BCE) was established in the southern section of ancient Israel. Now its land, beyond that originally given to the Tribe of Judah, encompassed most of the territory originally given to Benjamin and that of the Tribe of Simeon. It was from Judah's name that the appellation *Jew* was derived.

Judah's success as a leader is metaphorically tied to the cultivation of the grapevine, a symbol of bounty and of God's blessing throughout the Bible. So strong are the vines grown by the farmers of Judah's tribe that Judah will be able to use them like tree trunks to tether his ass and his ass's foal.[3] The vines will produce (red) wine in such abundance that Judah "washes his garment in wine," as if it were water. This blessing gives us a glimpse into the future when former shepherds will be, over time, transformed into successful farmers.

As we recall, God has already told Abraham that "your offspring shall be strangers in a land [Egypt] not theirs, and they shall be enslaved and oppressed 400 years" (Genesis 15:13), so even as Jacob performs his blessings we understand that the settling of the Promised Land is far into the future. For now, Jacob's entire clan has been saved from starvation by the intervention of Joseph, who, after his reconciliation with his brothers, has arranged for them to leave Canaan and settle in Egypt's best pasturage to pursue their lives as shepherds, the only way of life they have ever known. Even though Joseph enjoys the Pharaoh's favor, in applying for permission for them to stay in the land he carefully plots what the brothers are to say to the supreme ruler, to put their case to him in the most favorable light. They are, after all, simple shepherds, considered by most Egyptians to be coarse, primitive, and uncivilized, living unsettled lives at the edges of organized society. The area Joseph has in mind is Goshen, rich pasture land on the eastern fringes of the Nile Delta, an area traditionally granted to nomads in times of famine. Close to the Sinai border, it was far enough away from settled agriculture and the major Egyptian population centers in the cities to avoid conflict. Pastoral nomads such as Jacob's clan, whose survival was based on the need to move in the constant search for new grazing areas and sources of water, who passed on their inheritance from generation to generation through family and tribal associations, represented a way of life that sharply differed from highly organized Egyptian society with its rigidly imposed political and economic structures. Shepherds were traditionally regarded as aliens, not to be trusted. This geographical separation ensured that Jacob's clan would not be assimilated into Egyptian culture, that it would retain its unique characteristics, and would continue to follow its own spiritual vision.

Joseph carefully rehearses the brothers' audience with Pharaoh, a reflection of Joseph's concern that they be well received. Joseph understands that his brothers are in a tenuous position, that their case must be put in the best light. He decides that full disclosure is the best path, but being Joseph, he cleverly tilts his description of their occupation, suggesting a higher value: "The men are shepherds; *they have always been breeders of livestock*" [emphasis added]. He adds, "they have brought with them their flocks and herds and all that is theirs" (Genesis 46:32), suggesting that the Egyptians have nothing to lose in the bargain. In addressing Pharaoh, the brothers restate their case. "We have come to sojourn in this land," they say, explaining the dire conditions in Canaan (Genesis 47:4). What do they mean by "sojourn"? To stay until the famine is over and then return to the land of their ancestors? Or do they mean to settle in Egypt? It would seem the latter, for at the time of Jacob's death, they have already been in Egypt seventeen years, past the time of the famine. In Egypt they have enjoyed a more secure life than they would have had in Canaan where they remembered hunger, struggles over water rights, and an unsettled climate—a striking contrast with Egypt. Why should they want to return? From the time of their entry into Egypt, even during the famine while others starved, they enjoyed a secure life: "Joseph sustained his father, and his brothers, and all his father's household with bread, down to the little ones" (Genesis 47:12). In the verse that immediately follows we learn that "Now there was no bread in all the world, for the famine was very severe; both the land of Egypt and the land of Canaan languished because of the famine" (Genesis 47:13). The Israelite shepherds continued to prosper in their new home: "Thus Israel settled in the country of Egypt, in the region of Goshen; they acquired holdings in it, and were fertile and increased greatly" (Genesis 47:27). The growing resentment at their prosperity, as we will learn in the Book of Exodus, will eventually result in their enslavement after their protectors, Joseph and Pharaoh, have died, leaving them exposed and vulnerable.

Jacob's blessings return the brothers to their unique destiny in the Promised Land. Jacob has never doubted this, for before leaving Canaan, God had counseled him: "Fear not to go down to Egypt, for I will make you there into a great nation. I Myself will go down with you to Egypt and I Myself will also bring you back" (Genesis 46:2-4). These are stirring words, clearly and unequivocally setting forth the divine plan. Evidently, the Israelites must undergo severe hardship and testing, and must accept willingly the strictures of a new moral code before a future generation is deemed worthy to enter the Promised Land.

WHEN THE TRIBE OF JUDAH entered the Promised Land it originally occupied the hill country between the vicinity of Jerusalem and Hebron, an area that became famous for the production of grapes (*anavim*) from the grapevine, *Vitis vinifera* (*gefen*). Miles of steep, terraced hillsides, now mostly abandoned, and the presence of wine presses (even grape seeds) attest to the importance of grape growing throughout most of Israel where the climate—rainy in winter, hot and dry in summer—is ideal for grape cultivation. The vines, dormant in winter, sprout new leaves that elongate in spring

Photograph © Joshua D. Klein

Vitis vinifera. Fruit clusters on a young grapevine at the Volcani Center of Argicultural Research, Bet Dagan, near Tel-Aviv.

(March–April) from slender branches that trail along the ground or climb by tendrils. Fruit clusters develop under the leaves. The hot, dry southern *hamsin* wind, which can ruin wheat, helps to open the small greenish flower clusters so that they can be pollinated by bees to form fruit. Floating aroma, *smadar*, helps to paint an evocative scene of fruiting and flowering, a time for love, as in Song of Songs 2:13: "The green figs form on the fig tree, The vines in blossom give off fragrance. Arise, my darling; my fair one, come away!" Good grape crops are assured between July and October if the weather remains hot and dry, but can be ruined by sudden winds and rain. Vines were commonly pruned to produce short, erect trunks often propped up on piles of stones. It may have been this phenomenon which suggested the image of Judah tethering his ass to a vine.

The cultivation of the grapevine was well known in Canaan even before the Israelites settled in the Promised Land (Noah planted a vine—the first plant to go in the ground—after the flood, Genesis 9:20). The incident of the scouts reported in Numbers (13:23) sheds light on the vine's prominence in Canaanite agriculture. Who has not been impressed by the well-known depiction of the scouts (sent by Moses to look over the land before they entered it), carrying between them a huge bunch of oversized cultivated grapes slung on a pole. These had been brought back from Nahal Eshkol (*nahal*, usually a flowing river or creek; *eshkol*, cluster of grapes) in Canaan to show Moses what impressive crops the land produces. To the scouts, living a bare life in the desert, the grapes must have seemed especially magnificent. But later, when the Israelites entered the Promised Land they did not have suitable land at hand as the Canaanites did for grape cultivation. To make maximum use of the hill country for agriculture they had to construct flat terraces on the slopes to prevent erosion and water run-off. This technique bespeaks a high level of agricultural savvy and was quite outside the knowledge of shepherds, so it must have taken some time to figure out a successful growing strategy, one that involved the backbreaking work referred to in Isaiah's famous parable of the vineyard:

> "He [the Israelite farmer] broke the ground, cleared it of stones and planted it with choice vines. He built a watchtower inside it; he even hewed a wine press in it; for he hoped it would yield grapes. Instead it yielded wild [stunted] grapes"[4] (Isaiah 5:2).

Here the grapevine, usually a symbol of bounty and blessing, is a symbol of Israel's destruction for turning away from God toward idolatry. Why did the Israelite farmer still worship pagan gods? At some point, as agriculture developed and mostly superceded shepherding as the basis for life (although the line between shepherd and farmer was not strictly divided),[5] it became apparent to farmers that successful crops depended on contrasting physical conditions:[6] What's good for the grapevine, for instance, spoils the wheat. To counter such effects, it was not uncommon for Israelite farmers to take out insurance, as it were, by worshiping the Canaanite gods (the rain god, Baal, and the goddess of fertility, Ashera) instead of tying their fate exclusively to the One God of the new monotheism: "Hear, O Israel: The Lord our God, The Lord is One" (Deuteronomy 6:4).[7] Railing over Israel's moral backsliding, in the context of a nation of farmers dependent on natural forces, is a major biblical theme,[8] and one which the prophet Isaiah pursues in powerful imagery drawn from the real world of grape cultivation:

"Now I am going to tell you / What I will do to My vineyard. / I will remove its [protective] hedge, / That it may be ravaged [by grazing goats and other animals]; / I will break down its wall, That it may be trampled. / And I will make it a desolation; / It shall not be pruned or hoed, / And it shall be overgrown with briers and thistles. / And I will command the clouds / To drop no rain on it" (Isaiah 5:5-6).

The imagery associated with the grapevines' destruction must have been especially telling for an Israelite farmer intimately familiar with every step in the work of establishing productive grapevines that might not produce significant crops for several years. To a farmer, and to a biblical audience, this catalog of destruction, topped by drought, must have been devastating and sobering.

The grapevine is one of the Bible's Seven Species, the most prominent crops with which the Promised Land is blessed (Deuteronomy 8:7-8), and is the most frequently mentioned plant in the Bible. Many words in the Bible are associated with place names derived from the plant as in *gefen* (vine), *kerem* (vineyard), *soreq* (choice vine), and Nahal Eshkol where the scouts found grapes growing in abundance. Although not necessary for survival in the same way as olives and wheat, fresh grape juice, *tirosh*, functioned in making the last, precious-yet-muddy, cistern water of the dry season palatable. In these conditions, wine may have worked as a purifier.[9] The grapevine became synonymous with God's blessing to Israel, and synonymous with Israel itself. Its image was firmly implanted on Israelite consciousness: the grapevine design appeared on mosaic floors, murals, on synagogues, pottery, furniture, coins, and tombs. Wine, fresh grapes and raisins preserved from grapes were a feature of daily life; wine was one of the offerings brought daily to the altar (Exodus 29:41), and was drunk at festival times and on celebratory or special occasions: Nehemiah and Ezra told the people to drink "sweet drinks" (as opposed to diluted or vinegar-wine, the drink of the people) to celebrate the rediscovery of the law after the return from the Babylonian Exile—597 BCE–538 BCE (Nehemiah 8:10).[10] The Bible warns, however, against overindulgence: "Those who guzzle wine will be impoverished." (Proverbs 23:20).

Even in exile, the indissoluble link between a people and its land was preserved in the grapevine's symbolic representation on the

Sabbath table by wine, as olives and wheat are represented by candles (light from olive oil) and two loaves of *hallah,* over which the traditional blessings are recited to welcome the Sabbath.[11] Thus the crops of ancient Israel, important in themselves and as symbols of God's blessing to the people of Israel, are still present at this commemoration of the Seventh Day of Creation (Genesis 2:1-3), which also recalls the saga of the Exodus: "Remember that you were a slave in the land of Egypt, and the Lord your God freed you from there with a mighty hand and an outstretched arm; therefore the Lord your God commanded you to observe the sabbath day" (Deuteronomy 5:15).

ENDNOTES

1. Reuben's natural rights as first born have been forfeited by his want of character, which Jacob characterizes as "unstable as water" (Genesis 49:4). In dealing with Reuben in the deathbed scene, Jacob is still smarting over Reuben's breach of etiquette in having had intercourse with Jacob's concubine (Genesis 35:22), a clear challenge to Jacob's leadership. None of Reuben's suggestions to save Joseph (Genesis 37:21-22) or Benjamin (Genesis 42:37), to win back his father's favor, have been effectual. With the triumph of Judah over Reuben in Jacob's blessings, the Bible makes clear the principle that moral character is more important than hereditary right (think of the story of Jacob and Esau).

2. "The chapter [49] is textually among the most difficult in the Torah. Many passages are simply obscure, leaving the translator to make at best educated guesses." Everett Fox, *The Five Books of Moses,* 228.

3. An alternative translation: "Harnessing his foal [for the produce of one vine], And his ass's colt [for the produce of] one choice vine," i.e., one ass is required to carry away the produce of just one vine. See J. H. Hertz, *The Pentateuch and Haftorahs,* 185.

4. Nogah Hareuveni explains "sour grapes" or bad grapes (Hebrew, *beushim*) based on the Jerusalem Talmud's discussion of Mishna (*Ma'asrot* 1, 2). These are stunted grapes afflicted with a disease that prevents them from developing, hence by analogy the Israelites remain "in the stunted stage of 'worshiping at both altars' (I Kings 18:21)." That is, they "did not perceive the full meaning of the belief in One God." See Hareuveni, *Tree and Shrub in Our Biblical Heritage,* 73.

5. Shepherds, for instance, sowed crops, as did Isaac (Genesis 26:12); the prophet Jeremiah came from the village of Anatot (Jeremiah 1:1), an area used for grazing because it was unsuitable for agriculture. See Chapter Twenty-Three, *Tree of Desolation, Tree of Hope.*

6. Hareuveni explores the idea of agricultural realities in the Land of Israel as tempters to farmers to serve other gods: "These realities [opposing

forces of nature necessary for the health of various crops] were a great temptation to believe in various deities, each controlling opposing forces of nature." See *Nature in Our Biblical Heritage*, 27–42.

7. Hareuveni, 43, explores the meaning of this whole verse from Deuteronomy (6:4-9) in the context of the opposing forces of nature and what this means to the farmer in the Land of Israel: "The Bible underscores that only *through a true understanding of the concept of the One Unifying God is it possible to comprehend the balance between the opposing forces which seem to determine the fate of the grain, wine and olive crops.*" Emphasis in the original text.

8. Hareuveni, 29: "*Recognizing this continuous war against polytheism is the key to understanding one of the major threads woven throughout our Biblical heritage.*" Emphasis in the original text.

9. Personal communication from Paula Tobenfeld. The idea came originally from Nogah Hareuveni. On the possible function of wine as a purifier: "The mixing of water with wine, common in Bible days, may have also had the effect of killing off bacteria in water stored over a long period": Miriam Feinberg Vamosh, *Food at the Time of the Bible*, 36. Our family lived for many years with a water cistern supplied by irregular rainfall. I can attest to the problems of keeping the water clean.

10. Diluted or substitute wines for the poor could be made from pressed grape skins. The harvesters in Ruth 2:14 drank vinegar, diluted with water. An old New England haying drink, switchel, is based on the same combination, sometimes with the addition of sugar and ginger. The injunction in Nehemiah to drink "sweet drinks," i.e., pure wine, thus underscores the momentous occasion when the people stood for hours in awe re-learning the law: " . . . the Levites explained the Teaching to the people, while the people stood in their places" (Nehemiah 8:7).

11. See Hareuveni, 44–45, "The Altar and the 'Table of Man.'"

Introduction

THE BOOK OF EXODUS

Shemot

The Greek name for the second book of the Torah, Exodus, means "the departure" [of the children of Israel out of Egypt]. The Hebrew name, *Shemot*, means "names," based on the opening line, "And these are the names [of the sons of Israel who came to Egypt with Jacob]." Exodus vividly reflects the struggle within a rough shepherd culture to become a holy nation. It continues the story of Jacob's descendants, now led by Moses, in their journey from Egypt through the desert to the Promised Land, and has four prominent themes: the Israelites' deliverance from bondage in Egypt; their journey to Sinai and acceptance of the Ten Commandments; the spelling out of their obligations in terms of laws, statutes, and institutions; and the building of the Tabernacle, a portable sanctuary symbolizing God's presence among them.

Photograph © Ori Fragman

Cyperus papyrus. Papyrus growing in the Hula swamps with east Galilee slopes in the background.

Chapter 11

AMONG THE REEDS

Portion-*Shemot* / Names (Exodus 1:1-6.1)

When she could hide him [Moses] no longer, she got a wicker basket for him and caulked it with bitumen and pitch. She put the child into it and placed it among the reeds by the bank of the Nile. (Exodus 2:3)

A little basket or ark (*teva*) floats on the Nile River among the reeds, an Egyptian princess (daughter of the cruel Pharaoh) sees it while bathing, discovers therein a crying baby and rescues it, while the baby's sister (Miriam, we later learn) hides nearby to see what will happen to her little brother. Miriam approaches the princess to ask whether she would like her (Miriam) to find a wet nurse for the baby; the princess accepts the offer, and so the infant is raised by his own mother, despite the decree that all Hebrew males should be killed at birth to destroy their too numerous population. When the child "grew up" (Exodus 2:10) Miriam returns him to the princess who adopts him, inferring that he was welcomed into the royal family. No comment is made in the text concerning this amazing circumstance.

Thus the second chapter of Exodus opens with the unforgettable, fairytale-like story about the origins of Moses (*Mosheh*),[1] "the one who is born," the great leader who will bring his people out from bondage in Egypt, lead them across the Red Sea, or more appropriately, Sea of Reeds (*yam suf*) into the wilderness, on their arduous journey to the Promised Land. Drawing heavily on Near Eastern folk motifs, but always with its own twist, the biblical narrative is, as ever, condensed but rich in graphic images and telling detail. The little ark reminds us of another ark (*teva*) in the flood story from Genesis. Just as Noah saved humanity by sheltering a remnant in the ark (Genesis 6:14), so Moses, saved from destruction because his mother hid him in a (little) ark, eventually becomes the means of rescuing his people from slavery and massacre.

Throughout his life Moses is associated with water:[2] he floats among the reeds in his basket/ark, later crosses the Reed Sea with the fleeing Israelites (Exodus 14:21-23), and in the desert wilderness produces water for the thirsty Israelites (Exodus 17:3-7). On the other hand, the land, with its features, not only shapes the story of the Israelites in their journey to the Promised Land, it also shapes Moses himself. Raised as an Egyptian prince and very much a product of its culture in his name, looks, and bearing, in his heart he knows he belongs to the suffering Israelites he sees enduring harsh labor (as Joseph, an assimilated Egyptian to his fingertips, ultimately acknowledges his bond to his suffering father Jacob and his brothers). After young Moses kills an Egyptian he sees beating an Israelite slave (Exodus 2:11-12), he flees to the desert in the land of Midian, and it is here, in the semi-arid open spaces reminiscent of his ancestors' origins, that he becomes a shepherd and recovers the shepherd roots of his people.

In his escape from Egypt to the desert, Moses stops by a well to rest, the signal to a biblical audience that an important event is about to take place: according to tradition a betrothal scene. Remember that Abraham's servant finds a wife for Isaac at a well (Genesis 24:18-27) and Jacob falls in love with Rachel by a well (Genesis 29:10-11). And just as Jacob defies the shepherds who prevented Rachel from watering her father Laban's flock by refusing to roll away the huge stone blocking up the well, Moses now goes to the defense of Reuel's (a priest of Midian) seven daughters who are prevented from watering their father's flock by violent shepherds. The narrative tells it very simply: "Moses rose to their defense, and he watered their flock." (Exodus 2:17). Suddenly we feel we are back in time among the events of Genesis centering around simple shepherd life. Subtly, the biblical narrative prepares us for the change of scene to come when the Israelites will leave the land of Egypt forever—and the culture it represents—and wander forty years in the desert as they look forward to a new physical and spiritual space in the Promised Land.

For Moses' good deed in watering Reuel's flock, the father gives his daughter Zipporah to Moses as his wife. She bears him a son, Gershom ("a stranger there"; traditionally, "a stranger in a strange land").

In Egypt the enslaved Israelites are greatly suffering "with harsh labor at mortar and bricks and with all sorts of tasks in the field" (Exodus 1:14). "God heard their moaning, and God remembered His covenant with Abraham and Isaac and Jacob. God looked upon the Israelites, and God took notice of them" (Exodus 2:25). It is not as if God had forgotten them and suddenly recalled them. On the contrary, He chose His time to actively intervene for the first time in the lives of the Israelites, in the momentous events to follow. Recall that God had foretold Israel's destiny—as well as Abraham's: "Know well that your offspring shall be strangers in a land not theirs, and they shall be enslaved and oppressed four-hundred years; but I will execute judgment on the nation they shall serve, and in the end they shall go free with great wealth" (Genesis 15:13-14).

—⁊⁊⁊—

DEPENDING ON THE TRANSLATION of the phrase "*tevat gomeh*" (Exodus 2:3), baby Moses was placed in "an ark of bulrushes" (KJV); "a wicker basket" (NJPS); or "a little-ark of papyrus" (Fox), which was placed "among the flags [*suf*]" (KJV) or "among the reeds [*suf*]" (NJPS) (Exodus 2:3, 5). Is it crucial to our understanding of the text to know precisely from which plant the baby's ark or basket was made? Does it matter if we visualize "a wicker basket" or "a wicker ark," rather than "a little ark of papyrus" set afloat among "flags" or "reeds"? The story line is clear: the baby is in some sort of little cradle-boat placed among water plants near the edge of the Nile. But what we miss when we know nothing about these plants or their uses is a loss of color, the kind that brings the biblical narrative vividly to life, helping us to envision the characters living and acting among real flora growing in a real land.

While we have become used to associating baby Moses with bulrushes, baby Moses was hidden in a basket generally accepted to be made from papyrus,[3] *gomeh*, a lightweight material that floats, from the fiber-filled stems of *Cyperus papyrus*. In common usage, the name "bulrush" is often used to describe cattails, quite another plant.

True bulrush or lake rush, *Scirpus lacustris* belongs to the sedge family and is common in marshes and along riverbanks. Like all sedges, it is grass-like but with solid stems, and grows to about three feet tall from creeping roots; it bears clustered heads of minute greenish flowers. True bulrush may be the "*agmon*" of Isaiah who compares a man bowing down his head "like a bulrush" (Isaiah 58:5) after the way the mature flower heads bend down.[4] True bulrush was used for making baskets and mats, ropes, cords, and fishnets, among other useful things. At least six species of bulrush grow in Israel.

Papyrus is also a member of the large sedge family. It grows to over ten feet in height on a rigid, triangular green stalk with short scale-like leaves at its base. At its top it bears a mop-like head of brown scaly flowers. Papyrus' rhizomatous or stem-like shallow roots thrive and spread in muddy conditions, as on the banks of the Nile, creating dense thickets of papyrus stems. The papyrus plant was so dominant in the Nile Delta that it became the floral symbol of Lower Egypt. It was from such numerous wild (and later, cultivated) stands that legions of products were made from the plants' stems and inner pith, including boats, made by tying bundles of stems together. The advantage of making baby Moses' boat or basket from papyrus was not only that it floated and was lightweight, but also that it could easily be made watertight by caulking it with a thick tar-like substance; wicker baskets, woven from supple tree stems, were seldom made in ancient Egypt, and would be more difficult to seal.[5] The best substance for sealing the little boat is said to be conifer pitch from a tree, rather than bitumen, a mineral substance from naturally occurring evaporated petroleum or other matter,[6] although the text refers to caulking the "wicker basket with bitumen and pitch" (NJPS; Exodus 2:3). In Israel papyrus grows at the northern limit of its distribution, in swamps, water, near springs, and riverbanks on the Coastal Plain, but mainly in the Upper Jordan Valley.

Of all the uses for papyrus (ropes, boxes, mats, cords; edible roots) it is most associated with the ancient paper-like product made from the plant, also called "papyrus." To make paper from the plant, the outer rind of the stalk was pared away, the pith was cut into strips laid together horizontally, and then a second layer was placed on top of them laid vertically to form a sheet. Sections would be glued together, pressed, and finally dried, then sheets of papyrus could be used separately or glued together to make scrolls. The resulting material represented a great advance over writing on hard surfaces such as stone, pieces of pottery, or clay tablets. Egypt dominated the production of papyrus paper in the Near East because of the ideal conditions that existed along the banks of the Nile for the growth of wild and cultivated populations. When papyrus was superseded by parchment made from animal skins, production declined. Gradually the papyrus plant population itself declined from over-harvesting as well as the altering of its habitat. In common with other wild plants, the papyrus plant's need is quite specific: a constant supply of fresh, shallow water. Silting and the diversion of the Nile's tributaries, as well as the influx of sea water (intolerable to the papyrus plant) finally led to its near extinction in Egypt. Its impact lives on in our vocabulary in the word "paper," derived from "papyrus," and in the very word "Bible," derived from "byblos," the Greek word for the papyrus plant's pith. The paper we are familiar with today is manu-factured from wood pulp.

What are "flags" and "reeds," the English rendering of the Hebrew, "*suf*," among which Moses' cradle floated? "Flag," an older common plant name derived from the Middle English, "flagge," is based on the Scandinavian for "reed." The name describes any of several water-loving plants with long, sword-shaped leaves and blue, white, or yellow flowers, such as "blue flag," *Iris versicolor*, "yellow flag," *Iris pseudacorus*, and "sweet flag," *Acorus calamus*.[7] True reeds are hollow-stemmed plants of the grass family, among them *Phragmites australis*, common reed or *kaneh*, from which the English word "cane" is derived. It grows in swamps and marshes worldwide (it is common in wet places in Israel), and is a hardy perennial grass found in damp areas along highways in the north-eastern United States, where winter temperatures may dip to minus 20 degrees F for two weeks. An imposing plant from ten to eighteen feet tall, it forms great colonies from its spreading rootstalks. The tall, jointed stems, covered with bluish green foliage, are topped by tassel-like flowers. In the Bible *kaneh* is associated with weak-ness because of its easily broken stem, as in the phrase "a broken reed": "Behold you are relying now on Egypt, that broken reed of a staff" (II Kings 18:21, RSV); "He shall not break even a bruised reed" (Isaiah 42:3). *Kaneh* could also be a collective term in biblical parlance to cover various aquatic grasses or reeds such as the giant reed, *Arundo donax*, which grows not in the water itself, but, as in Israel, near water and along riverbanks. Growing up to sixteen feet in height on thick stems, its flowers bloom in fluffy plumes. Both reeds had many uses in the biblical world including the making of mats, baskets, scales, pens, small boxes, and even flutes. In ancient Israel the reed was cut as a measuring rod to equal six cubits (approximately eight feet, nine inches), the cubit itself measured by two handspans. (Ezekiel 40:5; 42:15-20). "Canon," as in a collection of authoritative books, is ultimately derived from *kaneh*, as is the metaphorical use of "rod" for a rule or standard of excellence.[8] All this from a swamp plant!

Like "*kaneh*," "*suf*" may be a collective term for water plants, but a good case can be made for cattail or reed-mace as the "reed" of Exodus 2:3-5.[9] Cattail, as it is known in North America, is a universally familiar swamp and marsh grass of the genus *Typha*. *Typha domingensis* (*Typha australis*) is common in ditches and tributaries of the Nile River, where it forms large colonies in wet conditions, often competing with common reed. Cattails grow six to ten feet tall, their straight stems clothed with flat-bladed leaves. A long dark brown cigar-shaped flower head, composed of tiny flowers, tops each stem. When massed, as they usually are, cattails are very impressive and synonymous with swampy areas. Unlike papyrus, cattails grow in salt water, as in the Sea of Reeds (*yam suf*). Perhaps the Israelites hid among these crowded 'reeds,' then escaped to safety when pursued by the Egyptians who, with their cumbersome machinery, got bogged down in the muddy marsh (Exodus 14:25).[10] In Israel, *T. domingensis* grows in many parts of the country along riverbanks and in ponds, lakes, springs, and wet ditches.

By becoming familiar with the specific water flora of the Nile Delta—about which the biblical text seems to be extraordinarily informative—we become more aware and attuned to the actual physical world in which Moses' story begins. The words on the page spring to life and we are able to imagine a down-to-earth scene in which a little papyrus ark floats among stands of papyrus, bulrush, reeds, and cattails near the banks of the river, bearing the future leader of the Israelite people and nation.

Photograph © Ori Fragman

Typha domingensis. Cattails, Einot Zukim in the Dead Sea area.

Photograph © Avinoam Danin

Cyperus papyrus. Papyrus at sunset, Hula Plain.

ENDNOTES

1. In *Chumash with Rashi* (Judaica Press translation), Exodus 2:10, the French medieval commentator, Rashi (Rabbi Shlomo ben Isaac, 1040–1105), explains that "It [the name Moses] is derived from the Hebrew root m-sh-h, and it means taking out and similarly, He drew me out of many waters (II Samuel 22:17)." Alternatively, "Moses" is an authentic Egyptian name meaning "the one who is born" or "gave birth," a shortened form of Egyptian names compounded with deities, as in "Thutmose." "The folk etymology relates it to the Hebrew verb *mashah*, 'to draw out from the water.' Perhaps the active form of the verb used for the name *mosheh*, 'he who draws out,' is meant to align the naming with Moses's future destiny of rescuing his people from the water of the Sea of Reeds." Robert Alter, *The Five Books of Moses*, 313–314; similarly interpreted in Everett Fox, *The Five Books of Moses*, 264.

2. Rev. Matthew Borden commented on the interesting contrast between Moses and Reuben with regard to association with water, in Jacob's unflattering description of his son Reuben as "unstable as water" (Genesis 49:4), and pointed out that in Chagall's Jerusalem Windows depicting the Twelve Sons of Jacob (the Twelve Tribes of Israel) the painter employs a blue (water) color to represent Reuben.

3. See Nigel Hepper, *Illustrated Encyclopedia of Bible Plants*, 175; *Michael Zohary Plants of the Bible, 137.*

4. Zohary, 135.

5. Hepper, 174. Coiled rather than wicker baskets were woven in ancient Egypt.

6. Ibid., 175. Hepper also discusses discoveries of an entire Babylonian basket made of plaited plant leaves which survived in damp conditions because it had been dipped in melted bitumen, and cites a Babylonian legend "in which a baby was hidden in a basket water-proofed with bitumen." In *Chumash with Rashi*, Exodus 2:3, Rashi suggests that the correct translation of the text is "clay and pitch," with "pitch on the outside and clay on the inside so that the righteous person [Moses] should not smell the foul odor of pitch."

7. See *Webster's New World Dictionary*, or any standard dictionary, under "flag."

8. Zohary, 134.

9. Ibid., 136; Hepper 71. For differing opinions about the identity of "reeds," see Harold N. and Alma L. Moldenke, *Plants of the Bible*, under these names: *Arundo donax*, 50–51; *Phragmites communis*, 172–173; *Typha angustata*, 235–236.

10. For a naturalistic explanation for the Israelites' crossing of the Sea of Reeds, see Daniel Hillel, *The Natural History of the Bible*, 115.

Chapter Twelve

AT THE BURNING BUSH

Portion-*Shemot* / Names (Exodus 1:1-6.1)

An angel of the Lord appeared to him [Moses] *in a blazing fire from within the bush.*[1] *He gazed, and there was a bush all aflame, yet the bush was not consumed.* (Exodus 3:2)

Now an experienced shepherd, Moses knows all the surrounding grazing areas and every feature in them, every rock, every source of water, and every plant. Why, then, did he drive his father-in-law's flock [of goats and sheep] "into the wilderness to Mount Horeb/Sinai, the mountain of God" (Exodus 3:1)?[2] Was Moses in search of a new

Photograph © Ori Fragman

Rubus sanguineus. Holy bramble or burning bush, Hula Valley.

grazing area or was he irresistibly drawn for some other reason? This is dry desert, poor for grazing, although plants, even trees, grow in its cliffs, between rocks, in its valleys and in dry wadis. It is the bush, *sneh*, which he sees from afar and cannot ignore. Unlike other desert shrubs with which he is intimately familiar, this one produces flames of fire but is never destroyed. He must go nearer to get a better look. Then he is caught. First "the angel of the Lord," God's messenger, gets his attention with "the blazing fire from within the bush," then God Himself speaks to him (Exodus 3:4), announcing who He is: "I am the God of your father, the God of Abraham, the God of Isaac, and the God of Jacob" (Exodus 3:6). It seems that nothing less than this dramatic stratagem—God appearing in a burning bush—would have caught the attention of Moses, who already recognized every desert plant and would have no need to view any of them more closely.

God tells Moses His plan: He has "marked" His people's suffering and he has "come down" to rescue them, appointing Moses as the one who will confront Pharaoh, lead the people out of Egypt to freedom, then return with them to this now holy ground in the desert to worship God on their way to the Promised Land, "a good and spacious land, a land flowing with milk and honey"[3] (Exodus 3:8). In biblical parlance, Moses has been called.

For contemporary readers, Moses' role as a shepherd may seem relatively unimportant, an interlude before he is called to greater things. A biblical audience, however, would understand the importance of shepherding in prophetic tradition as a trial period for future leaders (such as David). From ancient Jewish sources, beginning with the Bible, elaborated in the Talmud and collected in legends,[4] the good shepherd is the model and synonym for extraordinary leadership, the idea being that the shepherd who protects his flock from danger (wild predators, robbers, difficult terrain) provides it with sufficient water and pasture under the difficult conditions of prolonged drought, and who understands each animal's needs, also possesses the qualities to lead God's "flock," Israel: "He who knows how to look after sheep, bestowing upon each the care it deserves, shall come and tend My people" (*Shemot Rabbah* 2,2).

Except that Moses wants nothing to do with God's plan. He refuses His call with different excuses, among them that he is "slow of speech and slow of tongue" (Exodus 4:10), not a good talker, finally refusing outright God's mission for him: "Please, O Lord, make someone else Your agent" (Exodus 4:10-13); perhaps, as tradition interprets, he has his older brother Aaron, in mind.[5] It is an extraordinary scene: Moses, the reluctant prophet, arguing with God in the formidable desert at a mysterious burning bush about momentous issues that will determine the fate of the Israelite people, the Israelite nation. God rejects Moses' special pleading and sends him on his way, reminding him to take his shepherd's rod, "with which you shall perform the signs" [of God's powers] (Exodus 4:17). God has shown Moses how He can turn Moses' rod or shepherd's staff into a snake, then back again to a rod, "that they [the Israelites] may believe that the Lord, the God of their fathers, the God of Abraham, the God of Isaac, and the God of Jacob, did appear to you" (Exodus 4:2-5). This miracle presages God's power to release the Ten Plagues against Pharaoh.[6]

God reassures Moses that his brother Aaron, whom we have not previously met, will be Moses' spokesman, first to the Israelite elders who must endorse him, then to Pharaoh himself. However much he is helped, all Moses' leadership skills, earned while shepherding his father-in-law's considerable flock, must serve him now in a different and more difficult cause, the freedom of his people. And just as he had used his wooden shepherd's crook,[7] a simple but effective all-purpose tool, to protect and control his flock, so he will use it now for the benefit of the Israelites, to protect and guide them. Transformed into "the rod of God" (Exodus 4:20) it is endowed with divine power. Long after most Israelites are no longer shepherds, images and symbols drawn from shepherd life will continue to have an impact on the way Israelites think of themselves and their relation to God, as in the idea that it is God Himself who is a shepherd to His people (Isaiah 40:11), an image most beautifully preserved in the well-known Psalm of David, "The Lord is my shepherd": "Though I walk through a valley of deepest darkness, I fear no harm, for You are with me; Your rod and Your staff—they comfort me" (23:4).[8]

—⏑⏑⏑—

IS THE BURNING BUSH, *sneh*, a real plant, or is it a vision, a sign of God's presence? The word *sneh* is found only once more in the Torah, in the phrase "the Presence [or "dweller"] in the Bush" (Deuteronomy 33:16).

The mistaken belief that every plant reference in the Bible can be nailed down, and that every reference has a natural basis, is apparent in the many candidates for the burning bush that have been advanced over the centuries by biblical scholars.[9] Among these is *Dictamnus albus*, native to Europe and Asia and a familiar garden ornamental in the West. It is commonly called gas plant because it gives off vapors which under warm and humid conditions can be ignited. The Asian, *Euonymus alatus*, also a familiar garden ornamental in the West with brilliant scarlet fall foliage, is called "burning bush." Other plants such as thorny *Acacia nilotica*, native to the Middle East, but not the Sinai, are suggested. Candidates native to the Sinai include *Loranthus acaciae* (*Plicasepalus acaciae*), a spectacularly crimson-flowered semi-parasitic mistletoe that lives on acacias, and when in bloom has the appearance of being ablaze; *Crataegus sinaica*, a hawthorn bush whose crimson fruits are said "to recall a flame"; yellow-flowered *Colutea istria*, bladder senna, densely covered with yellow flowers in spring. The late botanist Michael Zohary opts for *Cassia senna* (*Senna alexandrina*), senna bush, because it is linguistically supported by its Arabic name, *sene*. It grows up to three feet tall, is covered with large yellow flowers, and grows in the Sinai in stony wadis.

Photograph © Avinoam Danin

Rubus sanguineus. Holy bramble in bloom, Beit Shean Valley.

The most popular candidate for the burning bush is *Rubus sanguineus* or holy bramble (*petel kadosh*), a thorny relative of the blackberry. It was discussed at length in the post-biblical period by the rabbis of the Talmud, who assumed the *sneh* of the Bible was a thorny bush or bramble.[10] This shrub, with which they were very familiar, grows in Israel, mainly in the north, forming dense thickets up to three feet tall near springs and swamps, by streams and damp places, and along roadsides, recognized by its pink petaled rose-like flowers and red, then black, fruits. The rabbis drew from its form—relatively low compared with a tree—and hooked prickles, a wealth of interpretations.

Why, for instance, did the Lord appear in a lowly plant? "In order to teach that there is no place where the Divine Presence is not to be found, even in a lowly bush" (*Shemot Rabbah* 2,5), and as they observed, "Just as in the case of the *sneh* one can insert one's hand into it with impunity, and it is only when he withdraws it that the thorns scratch him, so the children of Israel entered Egypt in peace, and only when they had to emerge did they have to have recourse to signs, wonders and battles."[11] The rabbis were not interested in natural history, and their interpretation was understood to be metaphorical. They were more interested in the moral and ethical lessons that could be drawn from nature. In this sense, why not the bramble?

The problem with this identification is that no native *Rubus* occurs in Sinai or Egypt or even in southern Israel; it grows in the Sinai Desert only where cultivated. Also called *Rubus sanctus*, holy bramble, because of its association with the Bible, it was established over a thousand years ago at St. Catherine's Monastery at the foot of Mt. Sinai to reinforce the tradition that the burning bush had grown there since the revelation.[12]

It is fruitless to search for the identity of the burning bush in physical phenomena (even a mirage has been suggested) since its meaning is drawn from the Israelite's vision of God, not from a nature guide.[13] A 'lowly' desert shrub aflame in the vast reaches of the mostly barren Sinai is a spectacularly impressive image of God's power, one that can be felt even in deep wilderness (the rabbis had noted a similar phenomenon in their midrash). In this sense, the shrub, *sneh*, is not a material shrub, but a means of bringing forth the divine spirit. A biblical audience would not be surprised that God Himself should speak out of a burning bush to Moses, since God's presence is marked repeatedly in the Hebrew Bible in such phrases as "a flaming torch" (Genesis 15:17), "consuming fire" (Deuteronomy 4:24), and "fiery flames" (Psalms 104:4). It is that same divine presence in fire that follows the Israelites out of Egypt as they travel in the wilderness. "The Lord went before them in a pillar of cloud by day, to guide them along the way, and in a pillar of fire by night, to give them light, that they might travel day and night. The pillar of cloud by day and the pillar of fire by night did not depart from before the people" (Exodus 13:21-22). And at Mount Horeb/Sinai God spoke to the people "out of the fire" (Deuteronomy 4:11-12), in the very image of the burning bush.

ENDNOTES

1. NJPS translates this phrase, "out of a bush;" KJV and others, "out of the midst of a bush." Paula Tobenfeld has pointed out that the phrase in Hebrew, *mitokh hasneh*, means simply "from within the bush," which seems most graphic.

2. Robert Alter's loose translation of *horeb* is 'Parched Mountain,' from the probable root of *harev*, meaning dryness. See *The Five Books of Moses*, 318.

3. The phrase, repeated many times in the Bible, has become a common metaphor to describe a fruitful land. Nogah Hareuveni offers an alternative and convincing interpretation regarding the different way it is used in the Bible, depending on context. To shepherds, "A land of milk and honey" describes limitless grazing ground for their flocks [therefore they produce more milk], the honey is wild honey from prolific wild flowers in their season. After the Israelites settled the land and became mainly farmers, however, the same phrase brought vividly to mind the wild vegetation and forests that spring up in the wake of the destruction of carefully cultivated ground: "I will lay waste her vines and fig trees . . . I will turn them into brushwood" (Hosea 2:14). For a detailed discussion see Nogah Hareuveni, *Nature in Our Biblical Heritage*, 11–22.

4. As in Louis Ginzburg, *Legends of the Bible* "The Faithful Shepherd," 309.

5. According to which Moses considers his older brother Aaron (the first-born) more deserving of this honor. Aaron has, moreover, been fulfilling this role as prophet for many years. See *Chumash with Rashi* (Judaica Press), Exodus 4:10.

6. Robert Alter, *The Five Books of Moses*, 325.

7. Bill Brandon relates, "Interestingly, it is said that the Hebrew letter *l* is in the shape of a shepherd's crook because "*lamed*," the name of the Hebrew letter, comes from the root word *l-m-d* meaning to teach; in essence, the shepherd is teaching his flock to follow instructions by utilizing his crook." Paula Tobenfeld has pointed out, *l-m-d* is also the root of "to learn," a vital quality of any leader, who should also learn from those he leads.

8. In the psalm, "rod" and "staff" have two different meanings: "rod" (*shevet*) means a weapon; while "staff" (*mishenet*) is something to lean on. Moses' "rod," on the other hand, is "*mateh*," as in the heads of the tribes, with a connotation of "command." In modern Hebrew military terminology it means "staff" (a group of senior officers). Thanks to Michael Solowey for pointing out these differences.

9. Harold N. and Alma L. Moldenke review the literature in *Plants of the Bible*, 23. Also see Michael Zohary, *Plants of the Bible*, 140–141.

10. For possible connections between *sneh*, sharp-toothed rock (*seneh*) and Sinai (related to *shen*, meaning tooth), see Nogah Hareuveni, *Tree and Shrub in Our Biblical Heritage*, 40.

11. Cited in Louis I. Rabinowitz, *Torah and Flora*, 29.
12. Zohary, 140.
13. For example, Hareuveni, 39 discusses the well-known phenomena of mirages in the desert as a possible explanation of what Moses saw, but concludes that the low probability that refracted light rays could transmit an image of a flame onto the *sneh*, "puts it [the burning bush] in the category of a miracle."

Chapter Thirteen

THE SEVENTH PLAGUE

Portion-*Va'eira* / And I appeared (Exodus 6:2-9:35)
   Now the flax and barley were ruined, for the barley was in the ear and the flax was in the bud; but the wheat and emmer were not hurt, for they ripen late. (Exodus 9:31-32)

Photograph © Joshua D. Klein

Hordeum vulgare. Barley growing near Shoham in the Coastal Plan.

Moses and Aaron, as directed by God, ask permission from Pharaoh to let the Israelites hold a feast to "the Lord God of Israel" at a distance of three days' journey into the desert (Exodus 5:1-3). Not only does Pharaoh refuse because, as he says, he does not "know the Lord," he is so incensed by the idea of losing three days' slave labor in 'idling' that he charges his taskmasters (Egyptians) and foremen (Israelites who enforce Pharaoh's orders) to lay an even heavier burden on the Israelites. "You shall no longer provide the people with straw for making bricks as heretofore; let them go and gather straw for themselves. But impose upon them the same quota of bricks as they have been making heretofore" (Exodus 5:7-8). Pharaoh's extreme cruelty and the people's increased misery is vividly conveyed in the compressed scenes or vignettes that follow one another in quick succession: the taskmasters and foremen repeat Pharaoh's orders: "I will not give you any straw. You must go and get the straw yourselves wherever you can find it" (Exodus 5:10-11); the scattering of the people over the countryside to scavenge for stubble (Exodus 5:12), the substance without which bricks cannot be made;[1] the hounding of the slaves by the taskmasters, reminding them that they must complete the same work assignment each day as when they had been given straw (Exodus 5:13); the taskmasters beating of the foremen, who are held responsible for the slaves' inability to meet their brick quota (Exodus 5:14). We are a world away from the pastoral shepherd life depicted in Genesis even with its family strife. The descendants of Jacob have lost everything. Where is God's blessing and promise of a life in their own land?

In the unfolding drama of the plagues launched by God against Pharaoh (and by extension against the entire structure of Egyptian paganism), following His renewed pledge to rescue the Israelites (Exodus 6:1), the Seventh Plague of hail is significant for its differences from the previous six (blood, frogs, insects, gnats, pestilence and boils). There is the new depth of ferocity, destroying everything in its wake: "Moses held out his rod toward the sky, and the Lord sent thunder and hail, and fire streamed down to the ground, as the Lord rained down hail upon the land of Egypt . . . Throughout the land of Egypt the hail struck down all that were in the open, man and beast; the hail also struck down all the grasses of the field and shattered all the trees of the field" (Exodus 9:23, 25). Also, this is the first time that God had warned about the imminent plague of hail, and those who feared Him, among them some of Pharaoh's courtiers, heeded His warning, securing themselves and their livestock indoors, thus escaping destruction (Exodus 9:20, 21). The action marks the first crack in Egyptian solidarity, suggesting its eventual collapse. This is the first time, too, that a plague affects the land itself and all growing things, and specific plants are named: flax, barley, wheat and emmer, sometimes translated as "spelt."[2]

In the Seventh Plague, flax (from which fine linen, the pride of Egypt, was made) and barley (to make beer and food for animals and the poor), were ruined by a freak hail storm as they were nearly ready to harvest. "Very heavy hail" (Exodus 9:18), driving hard down upon the fields, would bend and crush the stiff-stemmed flax and heavy-headed barley (their spikes filled with kernels of grain). Both wheat and emmer were not all destroyed by hail because they "ripen late" (Exodus 9:32), were in early growth and might recover. But they and any other growing thing, Moses and Aaron promise Pharaoh, will be finished off in the next plague of locusts (about a month later when the wheat has matured), unless Pharaoh gives in to their demand to let the Israelites go. There is no longer any mention of a leave of absence for the Israelites. God has instructed Moses and Aaron to say in His name, "Let My people go to worship Me" (Exodus 9:1). In the Eighth Plague, "They [locusts] shall devour the surviving remnant that was left to you after the hail; and they shall eat away all your trees that grow in the field" (Exodus 10:5). In other words, expect total and irreversible destruction of everything that grows from the land. Unlike the other plagues, reversed in accord with Pharaoh's pleading, the hail, and later, locusts, will have destroyed Egypt's most important crops and there is no way they can be restored.

Pharaoh once again pleads for mercy ("The Lord is right, and I and my people are in the wrong" (Exodus 9:27), although he will once again reverse himself when the plague is withdrawn (Exodus 9:35). Recognizing this pattern of behavior, when Moses causes the hail to cease he spells out God's universal powers for the first time, perhaps as a final warning to Pharaoh that he is up against a superior force: "As I go out of the city, I shall spread out my hands to the Lord; the thunder will cease and the hail will fall no more, so that you may know that the earth is the Lord's" (Exodus 9:29). This is a new theme, one that will be of major concern throughout the Hebrew Bible, directed as much to wayward Israelites as to the surrounding pagan culture.[3] While there may have been a naturalistic basis for nine of the ten plagues[4] (the last is the death of every first-born among both humans and animals), the plagues are, like the entire Torah, *whether in its narrative or laws, a means of teaching ethical monotheism.*[5] The plagues' lesson, directed to an Israelite audience, as to the Egyptians, is that God's power is not restricted to one people, one land, or one crop. The entire earth "is the Lord's."

—ᴍ—

THE JUXTAPOSITION OF TWO FIELD CROPS, flax and barley, one associated with making linen, the other with the feeding of animals and the poor, emphasizes the extent of God's powers to punish Pharaoh for refusing to let his Israelite slaves go. Fleshing out the destruction by actually naming the plants that were destroyed in the Seventh Plague brings the landscape vividly to life, as it surely did to a biblical audience familiar with flax and barley as essential food and fiber.

Photograph © Avinoam Danin

Linum usitatissimum. Flax in bud and bloom, roadside in the Shefela (foothills of the Judean Mountains) in central Israel near Moshav Tal Shahar.

Flax, *Linum usitatissimum* (*pish-tah*), is one of the oldest known textile plants, cultivated since 5000 BCE in the Middle East, and probably originating in Israel where its wild progenitor, *L. bienne*, still occurs;[6] *L. usitatissimum* grows as a wildflower in parts of North America. In Egypt, the center of linen production in the Near East, seeds were sown in late October to avoid scorching heat, and harvested the following April or May.[7] A fully grown plant reaches three feet tall, its erect, narrow-leaved stems branching near the top, bearing pretty blue five-petalled flowers. To produce fibers for making fine thread to weave into fine linen, plants were grown close together to encourage tall, less branching stems. The cultivation of flax, the harvesting of the plants and the processing of the stems to produce fibers was a well-understood craft, fine-tuned for making a range of products from the finest to the coarsest of linens as well as things of everyday use such as rope and lamp wicks.

After the flax plants bloomed and quickly formed seed heads—but before the seeds ripened—the entire plant was pulled up by its roots and bundled for processing. In the Gezer Calendar, a limestone plaque dating from the time of Solomon that lists the agricultural seasons and the work associated with them, the March–April task is "hoeing up the flax" (or "pulling up").[8] This record, suggesting that flax in parts of Israel was already harvested when in Egypt it was still "in the bud," is confirmed in the *Book of Joshua*. Two of Joshua's spies sent to Jericho were hidden in "the stalks of flax which were laid out on the flat roof of the house" [to dry] (Joshua 2:6). Six days later when Joshua crossed the Jordan river, on the tenth of *Nisan* (March–April), the Jordan overflowed its banks "throughout the [barley] harvest" (Joshua 4:19; 3:15), indicating that these crops—flax and barley—were closely tied together in their time of harvest as described in the Seventh Plague.[9]

After flax plants were harvested, their stems were soaked in stagnant, usually muddy, water in a process called *retting*. Bacterial action from the mud separated soft tissue from the stem's tough fibers, then they were removed and dried. As suggested in *Joshua*, a roof would do. The next step, *scutching*, involved gently beating or rolling the fibers to separate them, followed by *hacking* (combing them), and finally spinning them into thread. Depending on the grade of thread, different qualities of linen could be produced. Rougher thread produced linen for ordinary clothes, wrappings, sails, and rope. Broken fibers, or tow [as in "towels"][10] could be used for lamp wicks, as recorded in *Isaiah*: "The strong shall become tow, and his work a spark" (Isaiah 1:31, Soncino).

Flax (and linen), mentioned many times in the Bible, was the only fiber plant cultivated in ancient Israel; sheep provided wool. Fine linen was a quality product, reserved for the wealthy or to be worn on special occasions, as for religious observances. The curtain for

Photograph © Ori Fragman

Hordeum spontaneum. Wild barley with anemones, Northern Negev.

the Tabernacle, the portable sanctuary constructed at Sinai, was to be made of "blue, purple, and crimson yarns [of wool][11], and fine twisted linen" (Exodus 26:31), and the "sacral vestments for your brother Aaron and his sons, for priestly service to Me" are to be made "of blue, purple and crimson yarns and the fine linen" (Exodus 28:4-5). The exception to the commandment against mixing wool and linen, known as *shatnez*, was confined to garments of wool and linen for sacred use alone, thus separating the holy from the profane.[12]

Barley, *Hordeum vulgare* (*seorah*), one of the Seven Species with which the Promised Land was blessed (Deuteronomy 8:8)[13] has probably been grown since time immemorial. Widely cultivated because, unlike wheat, it is adaptable to difficult growing conditions such as poor soil and prolonged heat and drought, it was developed through a long process of selection and mutation of wild barley, *H. spontaneum*, common in the eastern Mediterranean region. An erect, shallow-rooted annual grass growing to about thirty-two inches, its grain-bearing 'ears,' surrounded by long whiskery hairs or awns (a characteristic preserved in *seorah*, associated with long hairs or hairiness) are produced atop stems which emerge from the plants' foliage. Maturing barley kernels are packed in spikelets arranged in rows on either side of the ear (ranging from two to six rows), and when the kernels are ripe the 'ear' nods. This was when the barley of the Seventh Plague was ready to harvest. The wheat, on the other hand, was just sprouting.

Both wheat and barley (mentioned many times in the Bible, often together) were the staple cereal crops in Egypt and ancient Israel. Barley was cheaper than wheat—easier to grow and more abundant—and was used mainly to feed cattle (especially horses) and provide sustenance for the poor to make a coarse bread; unlike wheat, barley retains its chaff. Barley, rather than wheat, would most likely have been used by the Israelites to make *matza* at the first Passover in Egypt.

The process of producing bread from wheat or barley, the 'staff of life,' is preserved in a passage in the Talmud that looks backward to bread production in earlier times: "Ben Zoma [a contemporary of first century CE Rabbi Akiva] said: 'What labors Adam had to carry out before he obtained bread to eat! He had to plow, sow, reap, bind the sheaves, thresh, winnow, sieve the grain, grind, sift [the flour], knead, and bake, and only then could he eat; whereas I get up and find all these things prepared for me,'" (*Brakhot* 58a), as we do today. He failed to mention that it would be Eve, or the woman of the household, who had the job of grinding the grain on a special stone. It is estimated that it took a housewife in biblical times three hours to produce enough flour to feed a household of five to six people.[14] This procedure would be repeated every day in addition to other chores.

Because barley ripened before wheat, it was used as the first grain offering, the *omer*, at Passover, cut for this purpose when the barley was 'in the ear' or *aviv* (through a connection to *nevov*, meaning "to hollow out," a reference to the hollow grain stalk when it matures); in modern Hebrew *aviv* means "spring." Directions for this ritual are very clear: The Israelites were commanded to begin their Passover on the eve of the fourteenth day of the biblical month, *Aviv*, to coincide with the ripening grain in Israel, and on the fifteenth, the following day, they are to "bring the first sheaf [*omer*] of your harvest to the priest" (Leviticus 23:5-11). Since climate and growing conditions vary considerably throughout the Land of Israel, experienced farmers adjusted their sowing and harvesting dates to accord with the law. Farmers in warmer areas such as Jericho harvested and stacked their barley before the *omer*, since it ripened earlier there and would have deteriorated or been ruined by rain if left in the field until the fourteenth of *Aviv* (later *Nisan*). In cooler areas, farmers chose south facing slopes to grow barley, banking on increased heat to speed ripening. The commandment to bring the *omer* to Jerusalem at the same time from throughout the country, despite differences in growing conditions, was a unifying force among the people as they gathered to remember their shared history in the first Passover in Egypt when God redeemed their ancestors "in the month of *Aviv*" (Exodus 13:4).[15] So was the inseparable connection between the land and the people's spiritual vision institutionalized.

ENDNOTES

1. "This substance played a crucial role in the brickmaking process. Its function was not just to act as a binding element. Through the action of the acid in the vegetable matter [chopped straw] that was released in the course of chemical decay, the strength and plasticity of the bricks were greatly enhanced. Without the addition of the chopped straw, the bricks would shrink, develop cracks, and lose their shape." Nahum Sarna, *Exploring Exodus*, 65. See 22–23 for the importance of brick-making in Egyptian building programs and details about the process. Here Sarna also gives an idea of the daily brick quota the Israelite slaves would be expected to meet: "A leather scroll from the fifth year of Rameses II tells of forty men who were each assigned a quota of two thousand bricks [with chopped straw supplied], making a total supply of eighty thousand. The text shows that the target was rarely reached by any of them." As the author points out, a practiced contemporary Egyptian artisan, using the same techniques, could turn out about three thousand bricks in the course of a seven-to-eight-hour working day, but "such a quota imposed on raw slaves would constitute an intolerable burden." Sarna, 23.

2. Spelt is a wheat variety, *Triticum aestivum* var. *spelta*, and like emmer wheat, remains hulled after threshing.

3. "The object of the plagues is not only to teach Egyptians but Israel, too, 'that I am the Lord.' For that it is desirable that the series be drawn out in a crescendo that will leave an indelible impression on Israel for all time." Moshe Greenberg, *Understanding Exodus*, 162.

4. See discussion in Sarna, 68–78.

5. Suggested in Greenberg, 182. My emphasis.

6. Michael Zohary, *Plants of the Bible*, 78.

7. Nigel Hepper, *Illustrated History of Bible Plants*, 166. For the account of linen-making from time of harvest through processing into thread, see 167.

8. Hepper suggests that "pulling up" is the more accurate translation.

9. Louis Rabinowitz cites these passages from the *Book of Joshua* to connect the ripening of flax with the barley harvest in *Torah and Flora*, 30–31.

10. The ancient art of producing fiber from flax was still within living memory in Cape Breton Island, Nova Scotia in the 1980s when I interviewed three brothers and their sister, then in their seventies and eighties, who recalled their family making towels from broken flax fibers, from plants they had raised.

11. In biblical times, wool, unlike linen, could be dyed. See *The Jewish Study Bible*, 168. Scarlet dyes could be obtained from the pulverized female kermes or karmil insect that infests the Kermes oak (see Chapter Seven, *Oak of the Weeping*). Purple and crimson "were obtained solely from the shellfish (bivale) *Murex* and *Purpura*," Hepper, 170. He goes on to say that blue, purple and crimson dyes are considered variants of the same dye.

12. "Livestock, like the inhabited land, received the blessing of God. Both land and livestock were fertile by the blessing, both were drawn into the divine order [as outlined in Genesis in its classifications: heaven and earth; the waters and firmament]." The farmer's duty was to preserve the order of creation, thus no hybrids either in fields or clothing. The dietary laws would follow along the same lines of divine order. Mary Douglas, *Purity and Danger: An Analysis of Pollution and Taboo*, 55.

13. See Endnote 6, Chapter One, for an interpretation of the Seven Species.

14. Miriam Feinberg Vamosh, *Food At The Time Of The Bible*, 26–27.

15. I am indebted to Nogah Hareuveni's brilliant analysis of the significance of bringing the *omer* to Jerusalem during the biblical month of *Aviv* and how it was achieved; i.e., that the fifteenth of *Nisan* always occurs during the time when the barley is 'in the ear.' See Nogah Hareuveni, *Nature in Our Biblical Heritage*, 46–55.

Chapter Fourteen

TEACHING TORAH IN THE FIELD

Portion-*Bo* / Go [to Pharaoh] (Exodus 10:1-13:16)
They shall eat the flesh [of lamb or kid] *that same night; they shall eat it roasted over the fire, with unleavened bread and with bitter herbs.* (Exodus 12:8)

Take a bunch of hyssop, dip it in the blood that is in the basin, and apply some of the blood that is in the basin to the lintel and to the two doorposts. (Exodus 12:22)

Photograph © Avinoam Danin

Photograph © Avinoam Danin

Majorana syriaca. Flavorful oregano-like hyssop leaves, Kiryat Anavim, Judean Mountains.

Majorana syriaca. Hyssop, flowering stem, Mount Herzl, Jerusalem.

As promised, Moses releases the Eighth Plague of locusts which arrive in terrifying swarms, darkening the land, devouring everything on the ground. Imagine how a biblical audience, familiar with this natural phenomenon, would identify with such a scene of devastation, and with the following Ninth Plague of darkness, perhaps drawn, as some have speculated, from the natural phenomenon of *hamsin* dust storms.[1] But however we may find parallels in nature, the plagues God releases against Egypt are of another order, one that reflects His divine power and reaches far beyond the natural world.

In the increasingly heated exchanges between Moses and Pharaoh concerning Moses' requests to let the Israelites go (followed by Pharaoh's repeated refusals despite the escalating plagues), Moses comes to the fore as a developing character who vigorously champions his mission to free the Israelites, no longer scripted entirely by God's instructions. When Pharaoh, thinking he can strike a bargain, asks, 'Who's going?' Moses replies, without hesitation, "We will all go, young and old: we will go with our sons and daughters, our flocks and herds..." (Exodus 10:9). When Pharaoh doesn't allow the children and flocks to go, multitudes of locusts are released upon the land, then, darkness, as Pharaoh, with one last proviso, agrees to let all the Israelites go, but "your flocks and herds shall be left behind" (Exodus 10:24). The tension between the two comes to a climax after Moses explicitly defies Pharaoh's seeming beneficence ("even your children may go with you"). "Our own livestock, too," Moses bluntly tells Pharaoh, "shall go along with us—not a hoof shall remain behind" (Exodus 10:26), an incredibly strong, graphic image.

The scene is now set for the terrifying Tenth Plague, the one that will finally persuade Pharaoh to free his slaves. "Indeed," says God, "when he lets you go, he will drive you out of here one and all" (Exodus 11:1). Moses relays to Pharaoh what God has told him: "Toward midnight I will go forth among Egyptians, and every first-born in the land of Egypt shall die, from the first-born of Pharaoh who sits on his throne to the first-born of the slave girl who is behind the millstones" (Exodus 11:4-5). Not waiting for a bargaining session this time, Moses "left Pharaoh's presence in hot anger" (Exodus 11:8). This is a different Moses from the shy shepherd who pleaded with God to find someone else to undertake His mission to free the Israelites. Moses has found his voice and his courage.

The high drama of Moses and Pharaoh's last confrontation, spelling out impending doom for Egypt and the imminent exodus of the Israelites, is interrupted by a set of instructions from God for the Israelites to follow before they depart. These are anything but perfunctory for they mark a decisive break from Egyptian culture by reconnecting the Israelites to their pastoral roots and their future as farmers in the Promised Land. Everything is to be different from now on. Freedom means a wholly new life as a nation with distinctive institutions.

Some scholars believe that the sacrificial meal described in Exodus Chapter Twelve is based on a very ancient pre-Exodus lambing festival associated with renewing bonds among kindred and community by partaking of a communal meal meant to give protection to the shepherds' animals at the beginning of the new season.[2] Purity, essential in such an undertaking, expressed the common will to propitiate the various gods thought to rule at that season: the sacrificial animal must be perfect and unblemished, the meal must be eaten in haste lest putrescence occur, and only hastily prepared unleavened or unfermented, hence, pure, bread must be eaten for as long as the festival lasted.

The central celebration is the same as the one described as the Feast of Unleavened Bread[3] (Exodus 12:3-17), except that in the Exodus story these rituals take on an entirely new meaning, now associated with God's spiritual and physical redemption of the Israelites from the pagan culture of Egypt. Their freedom, we begin to learn, comes with obligations, the first one being to remember the Passover (*Pesah*) as it will be known, because God passed over[4] their houses, marked with a brush of hyssop stems dipped in blood, when He struck the land of Egypt with the Tenth Plague (Exodus 12:12). Remembering the Passover is central to the Israelite's new life: "This day shall be to you one of remembrance: you shall celebrate it as a festival to the Lord throughout the ages; you shall celebrate it as an institution for all time" (Exodus 12:14, 17). The mandated recitation of *mikra bikkurim* (declaration of the offering of first fruits at *Shavuot* based on Deuteronomy 26:5) drives home the same point, which emphasizes the Oneness of the God Who brought the people out of Egypt, the same God Who gives the fruit growing in the Promised Land. The pagan bonding ceremony has been transformed into a key element in Israel's declaration of monotheism.

Even before their dramatic departure from Egypt, the Israelites had begun to forge a nation entirely independent from the alien culture in which they sojourned for 430 years (or according to another tradition, 210 years, in accord with the genealogies in Exodus 6:14-26). The severing of all ties is reflected in their new calendar, reckoned not by the Egyptian system, but linked to the future agricultural realities of the Land of Israel.[5] "This month [*Aviv*] shall mark for you the beginning of the months; it shall be the first of the months of the year for you" (Exodus 12:2). "You go free on this day, in the month of *Aviv*" (Exodus 13:4), the time of the barley harvest in Israel. Just as the *omer*, the first-cut sheaf of barley, was a sanctified offering of first-ripening grain to God, so the Israelites saw themselves as "holy to the Lord, the first fruits of His harvest" (Jeremiah 2:3). The Israelites' new beginning is thus bound to its land as well *as to its spiritual history*, a pattern repeated in its other Pilgrimage Festivals:[6] *Shavuot*, seven weeks later, celebrates both the wheat harvest and the giving of the Torah; and *Sukkot* (Feast of Tabernacles), the fall festival of late ripening harvest and first rains that inaugurate the new growing season, remembers the years of its desert wandering. In this sense, Israel's redemption is at the heart of its history, the signal event that marks it as a nation and launches it on the road to the Promised Land.

—⚏—

WHY EAT BITTER HERBS with unleavened bread on Passover? Why use hyssop to mark the doorposts and lintels with blood?

Various plants have been eaten from time immemorial to ensure ritual purity and to ward off evil or repel the demons believed to be rampant at certain times of the year.[7] The biblical text, however, does not indicate the plants to be eaten at the pre-Exodus festival except to suggest that they are bitter (*merorim*, singular *maror*) and can be hastily gathered from the wild, haste being the central motif of the paschal meal in anticipation of the Israelites' quick departure from Egypt. Perhaps these plants were so well known that no further description was necessary.

The long established tradition of eating bitter herbs at Passover was codified in the Mishna (the older orally transmitted Talmud), filling in what the Bible leaves out—the identity of the plants according to their Hebrew common names and the reason for eating them. "These are the vegetables [plants] with which a man fulfills his obligations on Passover: *hazeret, olshin, tamcha, harhavina, maror.* Bitter herbs because the Egyptians made the lives of our ancestors bitter in Egypt" (*Pesachim* 2,6). Later in the Gemara (the Talmud's interpretative commentary on the Mishna), the reason for eating these particular plants is spelled out: "See this bitter herb whose beginning is soft [sweet] and whose end is hard [bitter]—thus were the Egyptians" (*Pesachim* 39a). In this interpretation *appearance* is added to *taste* in the meaning of eating bitter herbs at Passover, suggesting that the plants somehow mimicked the Israelites' experience in Egypt: they had entered the land as free shepherds, then they were enslaved, as the plants themselves change in both taste and appearance as they mature. But we still do not know which plants were meant by *hazeret, olshin, tamcha, harhavina,* and *maror.* What do they have in common and how are they different from other edible wild greens that in a general way change from sweet to bitter-tasting as the season advances? What is so special about the bitter herbs, *merorim*?

It was not until the early twentieth century that the probable identity of the five bitter herbs was offered by pioneer biblical botanists Ephraim and Hannah Hareuveni. Through their knowledge of botany, the Bible, Talmud, folklore and field research, they determined that *merorim* belong to a group of wild, bittersweet weeds whose growth pattern most closely matches the one described by the Talmud, 'whose beginning is sweet [soft] and whose end is bitter [hard].' Among the possible candidates, they suggested *Lactuca serriola*, compass lettuce (*hazeret*); *Cichorium pumilum* (now *C. endivia*), chicory (*olshin*); *Sonchus oleraceus*, sow-thistle (*tamcha*); *Eryngium creticum*, eryngo (*harhavina*); and *Centaurea* sp., centary, (*maror*), as in *C. iberica*, star thistle. At the Passover Seder, the bitter herbs are known collectively as *maror*, after the last-named plant, the first one to turn bitter.[8]

The rabbis of the Talmud closely observed the natural world around them and were familiar with all growing things, including edible wild greens. Gathering wild greens to augment the limited

Photograph © Avinoam Danin

Centaurea iberica. Star thistle (*dardar, maror*), early growth in August, Mount Hermon.

Photograph © Avinoam Danin

Centaurea iberica. Star thistle (*dardar, maror*), late growth in April, Jerusalem.

diet of the times was well known among the entire population. In Israel in the fall or early winter, *merorim* emerge from the cool, soaked ground of the early rains after the hot, dry summer. This is the time when their soft green leaves, lying close to the ground, are gathered and eaten raw as salad in the same way that the tender bittersweet leaves of dandelions and other greens have been picked and eaten in the spring by people in the West, eager for something fresh in their diet. By Passover the *merorim* are nearly at the end of their growth cycle and have changed dramatically in appearance. A hard stalk has developed from the center of each plant, from which sprout very small, very bitter leaves, edible only when cooked (in the West, this season approximates late summer, long past Passover). The Mishnaic injunction against cooking the bitter herbs, however, ensures that even the small amount eaten raw at Passover (equal in amount to the bulk of a small Mediterranean olive) will remind celebrants of the bitter life of their ancestors. The distinguishing characteristic of the *merorim* is in their growth habit. Other wild greens (like dandelions) are bitter, too, at maturity, but they do not develop the necessary hard central stalk suggestive of transformation. The rabbis used natural phenomena, as in the distinctive ripening of *merorim*, to teach what has been called Torah in the field. 'Go out to the field,' the rabbis seemed to be saying, 'and pick the leaves that are now too bitter to eat fresh, but eat them anyway and you will not soon forget your eternal bond to your ancestors' sojourn in Egypt, nor their (and your) redemption by God.'

By summer and early fall the leaves of *merorim* are dried up and the stems hard, and some species, like *harhavina* and *maror*, develop long, sharp thorns, quite formidable in appearance. Bible plant scholars and enthusiasts over centuries, who have offered up numbers of inappropriate plants as the bitter herbs, have missed the point of the Talmud's lesson that the plants must mirror the Exodus experience in their change from sweet to bitter, from soft to hard, to coincide with Passover *in the Land of Israel;* that is, at a specific time of the year in a specific place.[9] The solving of this particular botanical puzzle reinforces the idea of the land itself as teacher, pressed into service for ethical monotheism. No plant was too humble to convey the message of Israel's spiritual vision, as we shall see in the story of the lowly hyssop.

Lettuce (*hazeret*) was the only one of the wild bitter greens to be widely domesticated and available in the early spring. The tradition was kept alive by Sephardic Jews living in the more southerly climates of Europe and by Jews living in Arab lands, where Romaine or similar lettuce was the bitter herb of choice (and remains so today) for the Passover Seder. For Ashkenazim, circumstances were quite different. Living in the colder areas of Europe, where lettuce was not always available in the early spring, the custom arose of using a familiar and virtually indestructible vegetable root, horseradish (alien to the Middle East), as a substitute for *maror*. By the fourteenth century this custom, already well-established, was rabbinically sanctioned.[10]

Hyssop or Syrian hyssop (*ezov*), like other biblical names, could be a collective term for closely related members of the mint family with a similar growth habit, scent, and uses. The most prominent candidate is *Majorana syriaca* (*Origanum syriacum, O. maru*), a wide-spreading shrubby herb about eighteen to twenty-four inches tall, with downy, heart-shaped, highly aromatic leaves that are most similar in design, scent, and flavor to various species of *Origanum* (some of which are known as "oregano"), to which it is closely related. By mid-summer it produces small white flowers in dense clusters atop twiggy stems. The whole plant, especially from a distance, has a grayish cast from the many hairs on its stems and leaves which help protect it from burning sun and summer drought. Modest in its growth requirements, it flourishes now as it did in the past, in dry rocky land throughout Israel from north to south, from Mediterranean areas to wadis and rocky outcrops of the Negev desert, and even in the Sinai. Near at hand for daily use as kindling, flavoring, and in folk medicine (where its uses are legion),[11] hyssop gradually acquired symbolic meanings in Israel's religious life, as did many other common plants (such as the bitter herbs). First mentioned as a brush to mark the Israelites' houses with blood in the Exodus story (its stems are easily bundled together), it was later to be used in the purification ceremony of the afflicted *metsora*—leper or someone afflicted with a skin disorder—"with cedar wood and crimson stuff [red dye from the bivalve *Murex* and *Purpura*]" (Leviticus 14:4). The bundled stems along with a live bird are dipped into the blood of a slaughtered bird, then the resulting mixture is diluted with water and sprinkled over the leper, the idea being that when the live bird is released, it will carry away the disease's impurities.[12] The link between hyssop and purification is further strengthened in the ritual of the red heifer described in detail in Numbers 19:6, 18. Contamination by contact with a corpse is nullified by burning the dead cow with "cedar wood, hyssop and crimson stuff," then sprinkling these ashes, mixed with water, on the contaminated person, in the belief that this mixture absorbs the taint from the dead.[13]

In ruling on the permissibility of substituting other woods such as *brosh* (perhaps the cedar-like juniper, *Juniperus excelsa*), for the cedar in the ceremony of the leper (Leviticus 14:1-5)[14] the rabbis were not so lenient when it came to hyssop, perhaps because, unlike cedar, it was widely available: "Hyssop, and not Greek hyssop [*Teucrium capitatum*], not blue hyssop [*Lavandula stoechas*], not Roman hyssop [*Satureja thymbra*], and not 'wild' hyssop [*Micromeria fruticosa*, tea hyssop] and not any other hyssop that has a descriptive name"[15] should be used. Perhaps hyssop's use as a purgative for dealing with intestinal worms, recorded in the Talmud (*Shabbat*, 109b), suggested its association with cleansing and purification, and when combined

Photograph © Jo Ann Gardner

Micromeria fruticosa. Wild or tea hyssop growing in a pot with marigolds in the background. Gardner farm, Cape Breton, Nova Scotia, Canada.

with its use as a brush, indicated its symbolic presence in these rituals. Hyssop's well-established symbolism is felt in David's ringing cry to God, begging for forgiveness for his adulterous episode with Bathsheba: "Purge me with hyssop till I am pure; wash me till I am whiter than snow" (Psalms 51:9).

In common with true hyssop, the 'false hyssops' belong to a group of shrubby plants that grow in *batha*, the soil of which has been impoverished from millennia of overgrazing, over-harvesting of forests, burning, and other human activities.[16] The erosion of topsoil reveals rocks of all sizes, and it is among and between them that such plants flourish. They have evolved to cope well under these conditions—the hotter and drier the better—by the shape and size of their foliage (usually short and narrow) and on some species, by the growth of tiny protective hairs on their stems, leaves, even on their buds and flowers, often giving them a glowing, silvery appearance.[17] All the hyssops are members of the mint family known for their ability to attract wild bees and as a source for gathering kindling (the latter being a very important attribute in a country where wood is at a premium). Their strong aromas, indicating the presence of thymol, menthol, camphor, and carvacrol in their etheric oils, recommend them for healing or preventing infections. But only true hyssop, *ezov*, is, in the words of the Talmud, "crushed by all," suggesting its popular use among the entire population. Over time, such a plant stands out from others and acquires associations formed over centuries by daily encounters in everyday life. In the *Haftarah* reading in Chapter Seventeen, we will explore hyssop's important role as a symbol of modesty.

ENDNOTES

1. *Hamsin*, from the Arabic, is based on the Hebrew word for fifty (*hamishim*), the days between the transition from winter to summer,

during which a hot, dry wind periodically blows in from the desert and "may dessicate vegetation and blanket the land with so much desert dust as to obscure the sun." Daniel Hillel, *The Natural History of the Bible*, 113–114. The corresponding Hebrew word is *sharav*.

2. Theodore H. Gaster, *Festivals of the Jewish Year*, 33–35.

3. Sarna and others consider that the paschal sacrifice and the Feast of Unleavened Bread originally referred to two distinct festivals. See Nahum Sarna, *Exploring Exodus*, 87.

4. The Hebrew verb *p-s-h* combines the idea of passing over and sparing. It has been translated as "I [God] will spare you," (Targum) and "I will protect you," (Septuagint), cited in J. H. Hertz, *The Pentateuch and Haftorahs*, 256.

5. In the Israelites' lunar calendar the year was to begin in the spring (*aviv*), while the Egyptian solar calendar was reckoned according to the rise and fall of the Nile and the agricultural activities it influenced. When the Israelites became farmers in Israel, the shepherd's lunar calendar gave way to a lunisolar calendar to reflect new realities. "A people that was once nomadic and became agricultural may adhere to the ancient tradition of lunar months, but must adjust it to serve the need of farmers to schedule their annual tasks to accord with the expectable onset of the rainy and dry seasons. The Israelites adjusted their lunar calendar [making it lunisolar] by adding an extra lunar month just before *Nisan* (the Passover month *Adar II*) in seven years out of nineteen." Daniel Hillel, *The Natural History of the Bible,* 145. Without this adjusted 'leap year' calendar Passover would occur at varying times, not always in accord with the barley harvest. Later, Tishrei became the first month of the year to reflect the season of late harvest and first rain (new growth). For more insights on the evolution of the Hebrew calendar see Sarna, 81–85; Hareuveni, *Nature in Our Biblical Heritage*, 46–50; Daniel Hillel, 144–145.

6. This idea is worked out in Hareuveni, 50: "The linking, by means of the leap month, of the historical event of the exodus from Egypt with the [biblical] agricultural month of *Aviv* is rooted in the inculcation of the monotheistic belief that the success of crops is dependent on the same God Who brought the people out of Egypt, the same 'Lord (Who) is our God, the Lord (Who) is One.'" [Deuteronomy 6:4], as expressed in the *Sh'ma*, the Jewish credo.

7. A common notion preserved in the ancient herbals and collected by Mrs. M. Grieve in *A Modern Herbal*. In Grieve, 695 see Rue (*Ruta graveolens*), considered a powerful defense against witches in the Middle Ages; Theodore H. Gaster, *Customs and Folkways of Jewish Life,* cites a Greek custom of chewing leaves of laurel and bay [probably the same plant, *Laurus nobilis*] at the Annual Feast of the Dead to prevent attacks from ghosts.

8. I am indebted to the teachings of Nogah Hareuveni for understanding the significance of the bitter herbs according to his parents' identification. See Nogah Hareuveni, *Nature in our Biblical Heritage*, 46–47 and Neot Kedumim's educational materials: "Pesach," *Guide to Filmstrip NKF-10*, pp. 10–14.

9. See Jo Ann Gardner, "A Quest for the Bitter Herbs of Passover," 62–65, *The Herbarist*, Issue 71, 2005: "Summing up the scholarship on the subject [of the bitter herbs] that was then available, the Moldenkes, in their authoritative *Plants of the Bible*, dismiss mints (a favorite with many writers) as well as horseradish (because it is not native to the area). They agreed with the opinion that the original bitter herbs were from plants like lettuce, endive, the young leaves of chicory, dandelion, and sorrel: weedy plants that were common in Egypt and western Asia. Mrs. Grieve cites coriander, nettle and tansy, as well as horseradish, horehound, and lettuce." Other possibilities mentioned in herbal literature are rue and nasturtium, and so on to the current time. It should be noted that in the discussion in the Gemara on the identity of the plants mentioned in the Mishna, are some of the 'bitter herbs' mentioned in herbal literature such as horehound, the latter identified by Rashi from the Hebrew *arkablin*. This may explain how horehound (a species of *Marrubium*) came to be associated with the bitter herbs. Although bitter in taste, it does not change dramatically in appearance in maturity as prescribed in the Gemara.

10. In his popular *Jerusalem Post* column, "Torah and Flora" of March, 1983, Louis Rabinowitz cited the work of Arthur Schaffer's "The History of Horse-radish as the Bitter Herb of Passover," from *Gesher*, Vol. VIII, 1981, from which he learned that R. Alexander Suslin of Frankfurt, who died in 1349, was the first to permit substituting horse-radish for the bitter herbs in the Seder, 'where lettuce is not available.' For the evolution of the *maror* ritual see Gardner, "In Search of Maror," 45–47, *Midstream* April 1996.

11. Among the contemporary uses of hyssop (*ezov*) cited in D. Palevitch and Zohara Yaniv, *Medicinal Plants of the Holy Land*, based on a comprehensive survey of local Arabs and Jews, are teas to relieve colds and stomachaches, headaches, earaches, and labor pains. The authors attribute its healing powers, especially when applied to the treatment of diseases caused by fungi and microbes, to the plant's essential oils, thymol and carvacrol. See 264–265. Reader Elaine Solowey reports that *Origanum dayi*, a close relative of *Majorana syriaca* that grows in the Negev, Judean Desert, and Jerusalem, is a powerful antiviral; she has domesticated some and grown it for use at Hadassah Hospital.

12. *The Jewish Study Bible*, 238; also source for interpretation of biblical "leprosy" as a scale disease, 235.

13. Ibid., 321, notes on Numbers 19:1-22 "Ritual of purification with the ashes of a red cow." Why red cow? The commentary notes parallels in

ancient Near Eastern literature, "and may be understood using anthropological understandings of how rituals function." Based on the principle of sympathetic magic, the red of the cow's ashes, which include a red dye, is symbolic of blood, thereby ensuring the efficacy of the rite.

14. *Safra Metzora*, chapter 1, 12–13. Nogah Hareuveni discusses the Talmud's reference to permissible substitutions for true cedar in *Trees in Our Biblical Heritage*, 122.

15. The identity of what I call the 'false hyssops' are according to Ephraim Hareuveni, cited in Nogah Hareuveni, *Tree and Shrub in Our Biblical Heritage*, 122. See further discussion of 'hyssops' in Chapter 17, *Mighty Cedar, Lowly Hyssop.*

16. Michael Zohary, *Plants of the Bible*, 33, discusses the biblical term *batha* as the establishment of dwarf shrubs on bare ground created by deforestation or abandonment.

17. See Jo Ann Gardner and Karen Bussolini, *Elegant Silvers*, 35–40 for an easy-to-follow discussion of the biology of silver plants.

Chapter Fifteen

HEAVENLY GRAIN

Portion-*Be-shallah* / When he [Pharaoh] sent (Exodus 13:17-17:16)
And the Lord said to Moses, "I will rain down bread for you from the sky." (Exodus 16:4)

The house of Israel named it manna; it was like coriander seed, white, and it tasted like wafers in honey. (Exodus 16:31)

And the Israelites ate manna forty years, until they came to a settled land; they ate manna until they came to the border of the land of Canaan. (Exodus 16:35)

The Israelites are freed, but are they free? In fleeing Egypt, God has them take a circuitous wilderness route to Canaan (see map, page 376), fearful that if they take the straight, easy way His children will not be toughened up sufficiently to do battle with the Canaanites. Perhaps they would rather remain slaves than fight for their Promised Land. When the Israelites see the Egyptians advancing on them, they panic. "Was it for want of graves in Egypt that you brought us to die in the wilderness?" (Exodus 14:11) They remind Moses that they had already told him, even before they were freed, that they would prefer the known to the unknown, "for it

Photograph © Avinoam Danin

Tamarix nilotica. Ants eating honey-dew excreted by a species of aphid on Nile tamarisk, Enot Tzukim, Dead Sea Valley.

is better for us to serve the Egyptians than to die in the wilderness" (Exodus 14:12). It is a wonder that God did not then give up on them, but His compassion is infinite when it comes to His errant children.

In the thrilling scenes that follow, Moses holds out his arm with raised rod and splits the reed-filled sea, the Israelites cross over on dry land while God, looking down from His pillar of fire and cloud, observes the action of the Egyptians and locks the wheels of their chariots so they cannot follow, the sea fills in (Moses, as instructed, reverses the water) and the entire Egyptian army drowns. Euphoria follows, with the "Song of the Sea" (Exodus 15:1-18) to the Lord who has delivered Israel. Its physical redemption complete, Israel's spiritual redemption lies ahead.

The wilderness journey is especially daunting for a people unused to its rugged and bleak terrain. The lack of water, edible plants and grazing ground for their sheep and goats, taken for granted in Egypt, utterly destroy the Israelites' sense of triumph at the Reed Sea. With no inner resources the realities of desert life undo them and they loudly complain. After three days without water, they cry out to Moses when the water they do find at Marrah is bitter: "What shall we drink?" Moses, following God's instructions, throws a piece of wood into the water and it is made sweet (Exodus 15:23-25); perhaps he remembers this trick from his shepherd days.[1] It is at this point that God lays down His "fixed rule": "If you heed the Lord your God diligently, doing what is upright in His sight, giving ear to His commandments and keeping His laws [aside from the institution of Passover, they have not yet received any],[2] then I will not bring upon you any of the diseases that I brought upon the Egyptians, for I the Lord am your healer" (Exodus 15:26). We begin to appreciate how the formidable desert landscape provides the opportunity for God to prove His ability to meet the Israelites' material needs, and for the Israelites to learn to trust Him. Are they mature enough to accept God's guidance and learn to walk in His image, doing what is upright, or would it have been better to remain slaves in Egypt, serving pagan masters?

When the people's grievances reach a crisis, they complain loudly and bitterly to Moses, "If only we had died by the hand of the Lord in the land of Egypt, where we ate our fill of bread! For you have brought us out into this wilderness to starve this whole congregation to death" (Exodus 16:3). Forgotten is their bitter labor of scavenging the countryside for straw to make bricks for Pharaoh's grand enterprises, dismissed is the cruelty of their taskmasters in forcing them to work harder. Egypt is now regarded with nostalgia as the place of plenty, in sharp contrast to the emptiness of the desert. There are no words of reproach from God Who freed them, only the astonishing news that He will rain down bread for them from the sky. Every day the people will gather that day's portion (an *omer*, about two quarts, only enough food for the day's needs), but on the sixth day, although they will bring in their portion as usual, it will be doubled, no reason given. The only stipulation, explained by Moses, is that they should not leave any trace of unused grain until the next morning. God regards these simple directions as a test of the people's trust in Him. Are they up to it? Can they pass this exercise when more difficult ones lie ahead?

The hungry Israelites pay no attention to the directions from Moses about only harvesting a day's worth of bread and not leaving any leftovers, with the result that these "became infested with maggots and stank" by the following morning (Exodus 16:20). It is clear that the people do not yet trust in God; perhaps, they think, there will be no more "manna" from heaven (as the bread is later called) so they'd better store some for the future. Even after they have seemingly repented and followed Moses' instructions regarding gathering only enough for a single day's needs, and even when they have been told that the meaning of the double portion on the sixth day is because the seventh day will be a day of rest, "a holy sabbath of the Lord" (Exodus 16:23)—a cessation of activity modeled on God's own rest from His labors in creation—and that leftover grain on this occasion will *not* decompose as it does on other days, *still* they do not trust in God to provide for them: "Some of the people went out on the seventh day to gather, but they found nothing" (Exodus 16:27). Learning from experience that God fulfills His promises if they fulfill their obligations, the Israelites finally obey Him. In this way Sabbath observance was instituted, using the story of manna as an example of what it means to work (gather manna) and rest (no gathering),[3] but it has been a struggle. To drive home the lesson of how God nurtured His children in need when they obeyed Him, He instructs Moses to preserve an *omer* of manna in a jar as witness for future generations to see that "I fed you in the wilderness when I brought you out from the land of Egypt"(Exodus 16:32).

WHAT IS MANNA? Generations of scholars and Bible plant enthusiasts have asked the same question as did the Israelites when, after the dew had lifted, they saw a fine and flaky substance, as fine as frost, on the ground, and asked each other, "What is this?"/ *"Mahn hu"* [4] (Exodus 16:15)? "The House of Israel," we are told, "called its name *mahn* (English, "manna"), or the English equivalent of the slang "whatsitsname." [5] In other words, they had never seen the substance before, had no idea of its proper name, and so incorporated their question into its name, *mahn*, thought to be an archaic form of the Hebrew *mah*, meaning "what." [6]

Are there clues in the text as to the 'bread's' identity? We learn that it resembles coriander seed (the round, whitish fruit of *Coriandrum sativum*, an annual herb used for seasoning not found in the desert) and tastes like wafers in honey. It sounds delicious, but where is the bread? We find out later that "The people would go about and gather manna, grind it between millstones or pound it in a mortar, boil it in a pot, and make it into cakes" and it tasted like "rich cream" (Numbers 11:8).

Scholars looking for a natural basis for this phenomenon have advanced several plants as candidates for producing manna. For some time the leading contender has been *Tamarix nilotica*, the Nile tamarisk, a many-branched shrub that grows to about fifteen feet, existing in limited numbers in the Sinai. Beginning in early June and lasting no longer than six weeks, small scaly insects (aphids) suck the tree's carbohydrate-rich sap, then excrete the surplus onto the plant's twigs in the form of droplets that crystalize and fall to the ground. These are sweet and sticky and must be harvested quickly before ants eat them. Known to the Bedouins by the biblical name, *mahn*, this substance is gathered and stored, like honey, to use as a sweetener. Estimates of the average annual yield in the entire Sinai Peninsula are said to range from five or six-hundred pounds to as much as thirteen-hundred pounds in a good rainy year. [7]

Other plants in the Sinai exhibit a similar phenomenon, among them a prominent shrub, *Haloxylon salicornicum* (*Hammada salicornia*). Much more numerous than the Nile tamarisk, it grows in wadis in fine-grained sand and during the summer months exudes sweet droplets on its bare, jointed stems, excreted by insects. When the liquid hardens, it, too, is gathered and used by Bedouins as a sweetener, in the same way as *mahn*. The Bedouins call it *mann rimth* to distinguish it from the sweet droplets from the tamarisk.[8] It has been suggested that the name *mann*, or its derivatives, came to be associated with any food miraculously produced in times of scarcity or in barren deserts.[9]

References to a number of plants, as well as to the gummy or sweet substances exuded from them or from the insects that attack them, are found in the vast, often heated, literature on the subject of biblical "manna" collected by the Moldenkes.[10] Some of the plants do not grow in the Sinai, none of the substances are especially nutritious, and none appear regularly and in enough quantity to feed the Israelites every day during their forty-year journey to the Promised Land (according to the biblical account in Exodus 12:37 the Israelites numbered 600,000 males above the age of twenty when they left Egypt). As the text tells us, "And the Israelites ate manna forty years, until they came to a settled land; they ate the manna until they came to the border of the land of Canaan" (Exodus 16:35). The origin of this manna is explained in the Book of Psalms: "He [God] commanded the skies above, He opened the doors of heaven, and rained manna upon them for food, giving them heavenly grain" (Psalms 78:24). A biblical audience, listening to the story of how God fed the hungry Israelites in the desert, would comprehend "manna" as a symbol of God's compassion and of the Israelites' trust in Him. In other words, manna, like the burning bush, is, we must assume, a substance beyond the realm of nature.

According to Jewish legend, "Centuries later the prophet Jeremiah exhorted his contemporaries to study the Torah, and they answered his exhortations, saying, 'How shall we then maintain ourselves?' The prophet brought forth the vessel with manna, and spoke to them, saying: 'O generation, see ye the word of the Lord; see what it was that served your fathers as food when they applied themselves to the study of Torah. You, too, will God support in the same way, if you will but devote yourselves to the study of Torah.'"[11]

ENDNOTES

1. Daniel Hillel in *The Natural History of the Bible*, 128, offers several explanations for Moses' feat in turning the bitter waters of Marrah into sweet water, one of which is that the wood or branch that Moses cast into the water, being a desert plant, exuded salt from its leaves, as

does tamarisk. "If so, the tree may have been salty enough to cause the suspended matter in the water to coagulate and settle, thereby rendering the water clear of the offensive turbidity." He adds that "Moses may have known how to clarify fouled waters from his earlier experience as a shepherd in the semi-arid domain, at the desert's edge." Reader Elaine Solowey gives such evidence in her observation that an old shepherd's trick is to sweeten water with the tropical Marrah tree, *Moringa peregrina* which grows near warm climate springs in places in the Sinai and in Israel, especially in the area of Ein Gedi. The Marrah tree is pruned, its branches are split and stripped and the raw wood and bark is dropped into an alkaline spring. The salts are precipitated out and then the water is drinkable. Elaine points out that its tropical cousin, *Moringa oliefera*, is used in all kinds of places to purify water today. In Nogah Hareuveni's *Desert and Shepherd in Our Biblical Heritage*, the author looks at the sweetening of the bitter waters from the rabbinical point of view. "Clearly in their search for the tree that Moses used, the Sages were not looking for a plant that could really sweeten bitter water. They asked themselves which plant was used *for the miracle*," as discussed in *Yalkut Shimoni* 1, 256, and elsewhere. The one suggested by Rabbi Yehoshua ben Korha (fourth generation of *tannaim*, sages of the Mishnaic period from about 20 CE to 200 CE) of the beautiful but poisonous oleander (*Nerium oleander*), may have been based on the well known concept that 'like cures like' (as in homeopathy where a small amount of poisonous substance is said to be curative) and that the oleander always grows near water. See Hareuveni, 56–57.

2. Unless retrospectively, the Noahide Laws which are included in the Laws given to the children of Israel at Sinai, and which, according to tradition, are derived from Genesis 2:16, 9:4-6.

3. Several Sabbath customs are derived from the manna story: the presence of two loaves of *hallah*, traditionally present on the Sabbath table (among other interpretations), are said to be derived from the double portion of manna the Israelites received on the sixth day (Exodus 16:5); the napkin or embroidered cloth that traditionally covers the two Sabbath loaves is based on the manna the Israelites saw covered with "a fine and flaky substance, as fine as frost on the ground" (Exodus 16:14). See T. H. Gaster's chapter on the Sabbath, *Festivals of the Jewish Year*, 263–286. The rule that cooked food for the Sabbath must be prepared before the Sabbath comes from the rabbinic interpretation of "apportion," which according to Halakhic exegesis means "prepare": "But on the sixth day when they apportion what they have brought in . . ." (Exodus 16:5). See *The Jewish Study Bible*, 139.

4. This is the NJPS rendering of the phrase. Others, including Rashi, translate it as "It is manna."

5. Suggested as a playful rendering by Everett Fox, *The Five Books of Moses*, 348.
6. For the origin of *mahn* see Fox; Nahum Sarna, *Exploring Exodus*, 117.
7. Sarna, 118, cites the lower number. Yehuda Feliks in *Nature & Man in the Bible*, 17, cites the much higher figure for years of plentiful rain.
8. Avinoam Danin describes this plant in detail in *Desert Vegetation of Israel & Sinai*, 95. The information on Sinai vegetation is based on the work of a research team, of which the author was a member, of the Department of Botany from The Hebrew University, Jerusalem, during the time Israel held the Sinai, from 1967–1982. A section includes details on edible and medicinal plants, how to find sources of water, make mattresses, ignite a fire, and even how to make rope from desert flora, knowledge about which experienced shepherds, such as the Bedouins, acquired from necessity.
9. Harold N. Moldenke and Alma L. Moldenke, *Plants of the Bible*, 127.
10. Moldenke, 31–32;125–128.
11. Louis Ginzberg, *Legends of the Bible*, 367.

Chapter Sixteen

HOLY WOOD

Portion-*Terumah* / Offering (Exodus 25:1-27:19)
> *They shall make an ark of acacia wood . . .* (Exodus 25:10)
> *You shall make a table of acacia wood . . .* (Exodus 25:23)
> *You shall make the planks for the Tabernacle of acacia wood, upright . . .* (Exodus 26:15)
> *You shall make bars of acacia wood, upright . . .* (Exodus 26:26)
> *Hang* [the curtains] *upon four posts of acacia wood . . .* (Exodus 26:32)
> *Make five posts of acacia wood for the screen . . .* (Exodus 26:37)
> *You shall make the altar of acacia wood . . .* (Exodus 27:1)
> *Make poles for the altar, poles of acacia wood . . .* (Exodus 27:6)

Photograph © Avinoam Danin

Acacia raddiana. Acacia trees, east Sinai.

The Israelites have reached the foot of Mount Sinai on their journey to the Promised Land. This is where their leader Moses, then a simple shepherd, had received his mission from God to rescue them from their travail in Egypt. We expect that something momentous will occur at this holy place in the wilderness where, stripped of all distractions, heaven and earth seem to meet. We are not disappointed. God called down to Moses from the mountain and told him to tell the people: "... if you will obey Me faithfully and keep My covenant, you shall be My treasured possession among all the peoples. Indeed, all the earth is Mine, but you shall be to Me a kingdom of priests and a holy nation" (Exodus 19:5). The challenge is thus thrown down to the Israelites to establish a new covenant (*brit*) with God,[1] to forge a wholly new way of life. From mainly passive recipients of His compassion, they are given the chance to become active participants in a divinely ordained order, one that is far more complex and demanding than anything they have ever known.[2] When Moses descends from the mountain and reports the new covenant to the elders, "All the people answered as one, saying, 'All that the Lord has spoken we will do!'" (Exodus 19:8) Then God Himself descends to the top of Mount Sinai in a thick cloud to meet Moses and declare the Ten Commandments to him in the hearing of the people gathered at the foot of the mountain below, so they all, every one of them, will hear the words directly from God to Moses and will forever trust Moses' words as His prophet (Exodus 19:9). This occasion is declared by the signs one would expect: "Now Mount Sinai was all in smoke, for the Lord had come down upon it in fire; the smoke rose like the smoke of a kiln, and the whole mountain trembled violently" (Exodus 19:18). So powerful was this evocation of God's presence that the people themselves trembled.

From a casual reading, the rest of the Book of Exodus is a disappointment, seemingly obsessed with relentless details for building a moveable sanctuary, *mikdash* (holy place), where the Israelites can worship God during their desert travels. The directions come directly from God to Moses (Exodus 25:10-31:11), are repeated by Moses to the people (Exodus 35:5-36:7), and are then carried out (Exodus 36:8-39:31), interrupted once by the sorry episode of the Golden Calf.[3] These details include not only a listing of the building materials ordered by God for the people to offer as gifts (Exodus 25:3-7), but how they are put together, where the articles are placed, and who will make them. As someone once remarked, "Now we go to the hardware store." But is this so?

When we understand that the Architect's design is inspired by the idea of erecting a structure where His presence will be felt, then we begin to appreciate the supreme importance of this undertaking. Distinctions between what we consider spiritual and holy and what we regard as earthly and common disappear: "Make Me a sanctuary," God tells Moses (to relate to the people), "that I may dwell among them. Exactly as I show you—the pattern of the Tabernacle and the pattern of all its furnishings—so shall you make it" (Exodus 25:8-9). In this divinely ordered construction, the covenant is to be placed within the Ark, the most important article within the Tabernacle, the "Tent of Meeting."[4] God is not conceived as actually being *in* the Ark as a corporeal form or in any part of the sanctuary (as would a pagan god), or even in the cloud by day and fire by night that covered the Tabernacle in the Israelites' journeys, but He was felt to be a presence, a force, that accompanied them. By carrying the entire structure with them in their travels they are continually reminded of God's claims on them and their obligations to Him. They are, in essence, taking God with them wherever they go.[5]

Viewed in this way, details count because they are invested with a meaning that transforms their physical being. We see that the gifts the people offer range from the most precious (gold and silver) to the most ordinary, "tanned ram and *tachash* skins" (the latter perhaps dyed sheep or goat leather), and in the building of the sanctuary we see this same principle of descending value at work.[6] While the Ark is made of ordinary wood (*shittim*), it is covered not only outside, but within, with pure gold, as a sign of its holiness or sanctity. The text proceeds from a description of the inner sanctum where the Ark is housed, the "Holy of Holies," to an antechamber occupied by a table and lampstand for ritual purposes (these, too, are covered or made with gold), followed by a description of the elaborate tent that covers them and creates the Tabernacle (*mishkan*, the abode for God). The lowest layer of the tent's cover is made from the finest linen, the secondary cover, from goat's hair, and the topmost layer, furthest from the Ark, is made from the least precious, but perhaps most practical (tough and waterproof) material, tanned ram and other animal skins. The principle of descending value, which is applied to the entire design of the sanctuary, tells us that the value placed on the covenant is the highest order of all and is meant to be the supreme center of Israelite life. In its careful layout, ordering of priorities, and construction, the sanctuary represents a striving not only to reach God, but to imitate His own work in Creation.[7]

The undertaking's importance gains impact as its details are meticulously repeated. Extreme care and planning has gone into this project, as it would with any attempt to create a sense of sacred space. We will see this attention to detail in the building of Solomon's grand Temple, but there it is strictly a human endeavor, not commanded by God. In this sense, the construction of a sanctuary in the desert, especially its Tabernacle, embodies a greater sense of the holy. The range of crafts involved is extraordinary, especially for a desert people. Work in silver, gold and copper, the cutting of stones and carving of wood, the designing and elaborate embroidering of the priestly garments (the women themselves had already woven the linen and dyed the wool) is impressive. That this work is undertaken by real artisans, to whom we are finally introduced, gives color to the whole enterprise. Who are these extraordinarily gifted people? They are Bezalel, endowed by God with special gifts (Exodus 31:1-3) and his helper Oholiab, "and all the skilled persons whom the Lord has endowed with skills and ability to perform expertly all the tasks connected with the service of the sanctuary" (Exodus 36:1).

This great divinely inspired plan and its execution, the introduction of the artisans who do the actual work, and Moses' apparent satisfaction in a job so splendidly carried out (he blesses the workers), is a moving testimonial to the Israelites' growing spiritual awareness. All that energy devoted to an undertaking beyond their material needs, and of such magnitude, has profound implications. Descended from semi-nomadic shepherds of rude culture who, nevertheless, succeeded in passing on God's blessing and promise for them, enslaved for hundreds of years in a strictly pagan culture which must have rubbed off on them, then emerging from this experience still slavish in their mentality, they have begun to learn that they must earn God's protection by their own exertion and by His rules. In imitation of God, they, too, will rest on the seventh day from their labors (Exodus 31:15-17; 35:1-3).[8] The successful construction of the sanctuary and Tabernacle, when understood within this context, is a thrilling accomplishment.

THE ONLY WOOD MENTIONED throughout the description of the sanctuary is *shittim*, and there is no dispute among commentators that this is from the acacia tree (*shittah*). But which one? Several tropical species grow in the Sinai Desert and in Israel. The two most common acacias in the Sinai Desert are *Acacia raddiana* and *A. tortilis* (the latter named after the twisty pea-like seed pods which both species bear). They are able to grow even without rain by absorbing moisture from wadis in gravel plains, in alluvial fans (gravelly soil collected at the base of hills), and in oases.[9] Their feathery foliage is borne on very spiny twigs, an adaptation to repel grazing animals. Small pale yellow flowers shaped like little round balls, bloom in spring and late summer, in accord with the trees' African origin rather than in response to the climatic conditions of their home in the Sinai.[10] *A. raddiana*, a striking form in extreme desert where other trees are scarce, is regarded as the acacia most likely to have been used for building the sanctuary; it grows in Israel, too, but is confined to the Negev Desert and Arava Valley, where temperatures are warmer than in the rest of Israel. Unlike the shorter, more shrubby *A. tortilis*, *A. raddiana* can reach twenty feet or more in height under favorable conditions (enough moisture), has a more or less erect trunk from which straight "upright" planks to strengthen the Tabernacle might have been harvested (although their trunks are often twisted), and its wood is very dense and durable. Yet for Bedouins who live *in* and *from* the Sinai Desert, it is the tree's leaves, flowers, and fruits, useful as animal fodder, that are regarded as having more value than the tree's wood for fuel.[11] *Acacia pachyceras*, known as "straight-boled acacia," is another desert species, found in the Sinai and Negev, whose wood could have been made into good lumber.

Are there other acacia candidates for biblical *shittim*?

Rabbinic literature and contemporary research are suggestive. In one legend, the wood came from the Patriarch Jacob who took it with him to Egypt from a place called Migdal Zav'aya (*Genesis Raba* 94). In a ruling recorded in the Jerusalem Talmud regarding acacias that were growing at that time at Migdal Zav'aya (first century BCE), a question was submitted to R. Hanina: "Is it permissible to do work with them? He replied: 'Seeing that your ancestors forbade work to be done with them, do not digress from the custom of your ancestors'" (*Shir Hashirim Raba* 1, 12). Evidently these acacias were traditionally regarded as holy trees, not allowed to be cut because of their association with making the Ark as described in Exodus. Bible plant authority Yehuda Feliks questioned the identity of *shittim* as *A. raddiana*, a desert species. "The main problem which arises is whether it was at all possible to make boards from the acacia trees that are so profuse in the wadis of the Arava and of the Sinai Peninsula, 'Ten cubits [fifteen feet] shall be the length of a board, and a cubit and a half shall be the breadth of the board'[twenty-seven inches] (Exodus 26:16)." He reports that his close examination of thousands of *A. raddiana* growing in the desert wadis showed that not one would yield straight boards of such dimensions. "The trees have short, thin and tortuous trunks."[12] Feliks located the village of Migdal Zav'aya on the eastern banks of the Jordan River and found there a small grove of *A. albida*, a non-desert acacia species, still regarded as holy by the town's local Arabs. Could this be the *shittim* of the Tabernacle?

Faidherbia albida, as it is now called, seems like an ideal candidate, although it does not grow in the Sinai Desert. It, too, is a tropical tree, but grows best in cooler temperatures than either of the Sinai species. In Israel it is found in many areas, from the Dead Sea Valley in the south to the Hula Valley in the north, it can reach up to thirty feet in height on a thick, straight trunk, its wood is reported to be light, yet hard, and is impervious to moisture. As we learn later, the entire traveling sanctuary, with its pillars, planks, tent, and Ark, had to fit into six wagons, each one pulled by a yoke of oxen (Numbers 7:3), so it should not be surprising that the narrator might have had in mind the light and durable wood of this moisture-loving tree. Perhaps it was chosen for its role in the text simply because it was familiar and admirably suited for the work at hand. Feliks suggests, too, that this species may be the one that the prophet Isaiah had in mind when God promises to redeem Israel, the poor and needy nation returning from exile, by causing the desert to bloom with trees that do not normally grow there: "I will plant cedars in the wilderness, acacias and myrtles and oleasters . . . That men may see and know, Consider and comprehend, That the Lord's hand has done this, That the Holy One of Israel has wrought it" (Isaiah 41:18-20).

1. In previous covenants God promised to make Abraham and his descendants fruitful in their Promised Land (Genesis 17:4-8); now God makes the covenant conditional on the people's obeying His moral laws: the Ten Commandments and the legislation that fleshes it out. "From the Creator God we have moved to the God of History, who enters into a fateful relationship with the people of Israel." Everett Fox, *The Five Books of Moses*, 361.

2. "Now a new phase of Israel's history is about to commence. God's redemptive acts on Israel's behalf require a reciprocal response on the part of Israel. The liberated multitude of erstwhile slaves must be united not only by a vital sense of shared tragedy and a common experience of emancipation, but even more by bonds of perceived ideals—a vision of a new order of life, namely the establishment of an essentially different kind of society from what had hitherto existed." Nahum Sarna, *Exploring Exodus*, 130.

3. During Moses' prolonged absence receiving the stone tablets of the Ten Commandments from God as well as directions for building the sanctuary, the people beg Aaron for a physical god they can worship, and he makes them a Golden Calf (Exodus 32:1-6). Daniel Hillel suggests that Aaron chose a figure drawn from the people's pastoral tradition, with which they were familiar. See *The Natural History of the Bible*, 133.

4. To clarify: "The sanctuary is referred to by three main terms, each expressing different aspects of it: "*mikdash*" (holy place), "*mishkan*" ("Tabernacle," literally, "abode"), and [elsewhere] "*ohel moed*" ("Tent of Meeting"), referring to it as an oracular site, the place where God would communicate with Moses. "'Sanctuary' refers to the entire compound—the covered structure and the courtyard surrounding it. 'Tabernacle' and 'Tent of Meeting' sometimes refer to the entire compound and at other times only the covered construction." *The Jewish Study Bible*, 165.

5. "Practically all commentators are agreed that the Sanctuary was a symbol; and its purpose, to impress the children of men with spiritual teachings... The Sanctuary reinforced the laws which Moses had been commanded to set before the children of Israel. It kept before them the thought that God was in their midst; and their life, individually and collectively, had to be influenced by that knowledge. As God was holy and as the Sanctuary was holy, so must the Israelites make the sanctification of their lives the aim of all their endeavours. The Sanctuary thus embodies the principle which is the central thought of the whole of the Divine revelation to Moses." J. H. Hertz, *The Pentateuch and Haftorahs*, 325.

6. "The closer to the Ark and the 'Holy of Holies,' the more precious the material." ibid., 164; the source also for probable identity of *tachash*, often mistranslated as "dolphin skins."

7. "In a general way, the intent of the narrator seems to have been close to the intent of the great cathedral builders of the Middle Ages: to reflect divine perfection and order in the perfection and order of a sacred structure." Everett Fox, *The Five Books of Moses*, 395.

8. The Israelites first understood the meaning of the Sabbath as rest from work in the story of collecting manna. Now they rest from the far more significant work of building a sanctuary where He may dwell. In this sense, their work, like their Sabbath rest, is in imitation of God. "The entire section [regarding the sanctuary] is a vehicle of contrast between God's creation and human attempts to reach the divine...Israel, through its religious life as typified by Sabbath and cult, becomes a partner in the process of Creation, either by imitating the divine act or by celebrating it." Fox, 394.

9. Avinoam Danin, *Distribution Atlas of Plants in the Flora Palaestina Area*, 125; *Desert Vegetation of Israel and Sinai*, 117–118.

10. Ibid.

11. Ibid.

12. Yehuda Feliks, *Nature and Man in the Bible*, 21–23. From the Bible's directions, over fifty planks would be needed (Exodus 26:15-25). For a different view of the subject and other possible locations for Migdal Zav'aya, see Nogah Hareuveni, *Tree and Shrub in Our Biblical Heritage*, 118. He shows a photograph of a huge desert acacia which he says would be tall enough to provide for the central bar that ran the entire length of the Tabernacle, or forty-five feet (*The Jewish Study Bible*, 168).

Chapter Seventeen

Mighty Cedar, Lowly Hyssop

Portion-*Terumah* / Contribution (Exodus 25:1-27:19)
  Haftarah **(I Kings 5:26-6:13)**
  He [Solomon] *discoursed about trees, from the cedar that grows in Lebanon to the hyssop that grows out of the wall [in the rock].* (I Kings 5:13)

The *Haftarah* reading from the prophets is linked to the portion *Terumah* by virtue of the building theme: the Israelites make a movable sanctuary where they can worship God and feel His presence in their journey through the harsh desert to the Promised Land. Solomon builds a Temple to God in an urban center, Jerusalem, to fulfill God's promise to his father, David (I Kings 5:19). While both structures contain the Ark of the Covenant and both are faithful to God's plan for housing it, they are very different, not only in scale but in the way each was established: wood for making the desert sanctuary was native acacia, a gift from the people; Solomon used cedar, a costly imported wood. In contrast to the 30,000 unpaid lumberjacks whom Solomon sends to Lebanon

Photograph © Lytton John Musselman

Cedrus libani. Cedar of Lebanon at the Shouf Cedar Reserve, Lebanon.

Photograph © Avinoam Danin

Origanum dayi. Closely related to *Majorana syriaca,* it grows "out of the wall" [of rock] in the Negev Highlands near Sede Boqer.

to help prepare the cedar logs for export, it is the people themselves who undertake the entire construction of the desert sanctuary.

What are Solomon's credentials for such a grand undertaking?

When the *Haftarah* opens, Solomon is described as very wise, a necessary virtue for one so ambitious: "The Lord had given Solomon wisdom, as He had promised him" (I Kings 5:26). We have to backtrack in the text (our justification for working it into the *Haftarah*!) to learn the extent of this wisdom, preserved in a memorable metaphor drawn from the world of plants, and sweeping in its implications: "He discoursed about trees, from the cedar that grows in Lebanon to the hyssop that grows out of the wall" (I Kings 5:13). His encyclopedic knowledge from A to Z is illustrated metaphorically by the pairing of two trees that range in height from the tallest (cedar) to the lowest (hyssop).[1] They are special, too, because they exemplify extremes not only of material worth, but of moral worth: cedar, a costly wood because it does not grow in Israel and has to be imported, is associated with might and wealth; by contrast, hyssop, which grows in many places in Israel, and is freely available to all for its medicinal and culinary use, is symbolic of modesty and humility.

Before he began building the Temple, Solomon had had a dream that God appeared to him and He had said, "Ask, what shall I grant you?" (I Kings 3:5). As a young and newly crowned king, Solomon, eager to know how best to serve Him, asks God to grant him "an understanding mind to judge Your people, to distinguish between good and bad; for who can judge this vast people of Yours?" (I Kings 3:9). God is so impressed with the unselfish nature of Solomon's request that He not only grants him a wise and discerning mind, but riches and glory too. Solomon's virtues, as well as his great wealth and status, are divine gifts. This puts into perspective the later enumeration of details about his unstinting approach to building the Temple.

Just to erect the Temple's basic structure, he "imposed forced labor on all Israel," sending [30,000] men in shifts of 10,000 a month to Lebanon (the source for cedar); also 70,000 porters and 80,000 quarriers were required for the huge blocks of stone to make the Temple's foundation. Solomon's great wealth, which enabled him to carry out this work, came partly from taxes or tribute from the united kingdom over which he ruled (Israel and Judea). To support his growing household of wives with their separate families, as well as the infrastructure that kept it running smoothly, he required *daily* provisions from his subjects consisting of 30 *kors* of semolina [over 180 bushels], and 60 *kors* of flour; ten fattened [grain-fed] oxen, twenty pasture-fed oxen, and 100 sheep and goats, besides deer and gazelles, roebucks and fatted geese. Barley and straw were delivered daily to his 40,000 stalls of horses, kept to run his many chariots (I Kings 5:27; 5:2-8).

These provisions bespeak a high level of agricultural achievement and an economy of plenty, in sharp contrast to shepherd life; in the extreme desert of the Sinai the people had complained bitterly about the lack of water and bread. It is reassuring to know that life in the Promised Land, despite its ups and downs, has turned out so well in the material sense, that many of the shepherds have become successful farmers. But the persistent lure to worship pagan gods has far from disappeared in Israelite life, especially among farmers. Afraid to entrust the bounty of their crops solely to God's blessing, they also turned to the local Canaanite nature gods as a kind of insurance to bring natural forces (rain, heat, wind) to their crops at the right time, depending on where they lived in the Land of Israel. This meant that pagan worship, occurring at various times and places throughout the kingdom, and outside the moral framework embodied in God's covenant, posed a threat to the firm establishment of ethical monotheism. With Solomon's high-profile Temple in Jerusalem, now for the first time in Israelite history there was a centralized sanctuary where all the people from every part of the kingdom were encouraged to come to worship in the *same* way and observe *the three harvest festivals*—Passover (*Pesah*), *Shavuot*, and *Sukkot*—*at the same time* 'in the place that He will choose,' as had been commanded earlier (Deuteronomy 16:16) but never carried out. The grand Temple in Jerusalem, known far and wide, was a major factor in forging religious and national identity.[2] In this sense, the desert sanctuary and the city Temple, although quite different, each served its purpose at a stage in the spiritual development of the Israelites.

In the midst of his building activities, God had spoken to Solomon: "With regard to this House you are building—if you follow My laws and observe My rules and faithfully keep My commandments, I will fulfill for you the promise that I gave your father David: I will abide among the children of Israel, and I will never forsake My people Israel" (I Kings 6:12-13). Peace reigned during Solomon's entire forty-year rule. There was peace on all his borders, and everyone dwelt in safety under his own vine and under his own fig tree (I Kings 5:5). But in the centuries that follow, the monarchy weakens, divisions arise, and pagan worship persists. Eventually the grand Temple will be destroyed.

Is there another message in the pairing of cedar and hyssop?

—∞—

THE CEDAR OF LEBANON, *Cedrus libani* (*erez*), is native to the mountains of the Mediterranean region in Lebanon, west to Syria, and south to central Turkey. It is most abundant at high altitudes where cool temperatures, snow, snow melt, rain, and sunshine provide ideal conditions for the growth of lush forests, as on the mountain ranges of Lebanon as they were in biblical times. In their early growth, trees are pyramidal in form with a dense crown. With age their numerous wide-spreading branches turn slightly upward, well designed to withstand a load of snow for many months of the year, and the top of the tree flattens out. Leaves are needle-like and glaucous green from a coating of wax that helps to protect the needles from drying out in the windy conditions that prevail on the mountain slopes. Flowering, in the form of reddish catkins, occurs in the fall, followed by the development of smooth cones, light green at first, changing to plumy-pink, then brown and upright in maturity. Their scales bear broadly-winged seeds that help to disseminate them in the wind when the cone disintegrates. Despite their slow growth, cedars are said to be easy to grow from seeds as long as they have sufficient moisture and soil nutrients.[3] Trees are slow growing and long-lived. A mature tree can attain a height of eighty to one-hundred-and-twenty feet or more and a crown circumference of more than fifty feet. All parts of the tree are fragrant (woodsy and camphorous, like the refreshing scent of a cedar chest); their resin and distilled oil have antiseptic properties. The ridged bark, even its cones, exudes resin which had many ancient uses, among them to protect wooden structures from deterioration. Its volatile oil, extracted from the wood as well as sawdust, had an ancient history of healing wounds and skin conditions, possibly the 'leprosy' of the Bible, and mummification in Egypt.[4] The wood itself is smooth, fragrant, enduring (resistant to rot and insect damage) and a beautiful honey color.

It is not difficult to imagine why Solomon chose this non-native wood for his building projects over the readily available native sycamore, *Ficus sycomorus*, even though wood from that tree was highly regarded for building in biblical times.[5] The cedar, unlike the sycamore, was associated with strength, glory, wealth and majesty in the Bible, extolled by the prophets as a tree unlike any other "with beautiful branches and shady thickets, of lofty stature" (Ezekiel 31:3), and a sign of God's blessing: "I will be as dew to Israel that he may flower like the lily, take root like the [deep-rooted cedar of] Lebanon" (Hosea 14:6). Cedar had an international reputation throughout the Near East, was widely recognized as the most beautiful and enduring of wood, and no matter how costly, it was used for important buildings as a mark of status.[6] How could Solomon do any less for his Temple?

By using cedar wood ostentatiously throughout his design, he considerably enhanced the Temple's image, and gave it and the entire compound, including the two palaces attached to it, great prestige. His building plans, which took twenty years to carry out, required a great deal of cedar for roofing, paneling, general construction, and in creating the extraordinary House of the Forest of Lebanon (thought to be a kind of reception area to impress visitors), where by clever placement of mirrors, rows of cedar pillars with their branches simulated a forest of cedar trees![7] Within, all the drinking cups and utensils were of gold; Solomon's throne, said to be unlike any other, was made of ivory and overlaid with refined gold (I Kings 10:18-21).

Is there excessive pride and vanity in this enterprise, and has Solomon, singularly blessed by God with wisdom, wealth and glory, gone too far? Like other plants mentioned in the Bible, cedar has both positive and negative connotations. The prophet Jeremiah used the negative symbolism of cedar in railing against Jehoiakim, King of Judah (then a weakened vassal state of Egypt) for his wasteful building: "Shall you rule because you preen yourself with cedars?" He prophesies that Jehoiakim shall be brought low: "For him no mourner... He shall have a donkey's burial, dragged along and flung out beyond the gates of Jerusalem!" (Jeremiah 22:13-19)

The Bible tells us that Solomon heaped up wealth beyond measure: "The king made silver as plentiful in Jerusalem as stones" (I Kings 10:1); he loved foreign pagan women and made them, as well as many others, his wives, as part of his program of diplomatic alliances: "He had seven hundred royal wives and three hundred concubines" (I Kings 11:3); he acquired thousands of horses and chariots and became an exporter to "all the kings of the Hittites and the kings of the Arameans" (10:28-29), in pursuit of his ambitious trading ventures.

Clearly Solomon has violated Torah values. The pairing of cedar with hyssop, to illustrate his wide-ranging knowledge, may also hold a warning for him to control his arrogant pride, or he will be brought low, humbled like the commonplace hyssop. Discussing the ritual of healing lepers (or those afflicted with skin disorders) in the purification ceremony described in Leviticus 14:4, in which cedar wood (symbolic, perhaps, of its healing properties when its oil is extracted) is paired with hyssop as ingredients in the blood mixture sprinkled over the afflicted person, "Said Rabbi Isaac bar Tablai: What is the significance of cedar wood and hyssop ... for the leper? They say to him: You were proud like the cedar and the Holy One, Blessed be He, humbled you like this hyssop that is crushed by everyone" (*Midrash Hagadol, Metzora* 14). Hyssop has a more positive meaning in the saying, 'Israel, God's peculiar treasure, is lowly [modest] like the hyssop."[8] Although hyssop is only one of many plants growing in the Land of Israel, its symbolic use was suggested by the fact that, although very useful in everyday life and accessible to all, it is a plant of low stature and thrives with little encouragement.

Hyssop, also known as Syrian hyssop, *Majorana syriaca* (*ezov*), was discussed in Chapter Fourteen, but this common plant with a fascinating history is worth closer study. It is a low, wide-spreading grayish-green shrub-like herb common in *batha*, (rocky outcrops), rock fissures, wadis, and steppe areas in Israel. It even grows in the Sinai. Hyssop's small, downy oregano-flavored leaves are gathered now as they were in the past, but only for personal use, since due to over-harvesting for commercial purposes, it is now a protected plant. Unlike the mighty cedar that needs cool temperatures, a good supply of moisture, and nutrient-rich soil to thrive, the hyssop 'tree' (regarded by the rabbis as a tree because of its lignified stems), is modest in its needs, finding enough moisture and nourishment even between the cracks of hard rocks, as so graphically described in the phrase "the hyssop that grows in the rock" (I Kings 5:13). Although adaptable, hyssop does *not* "grow out of the wall" the usual translation from the Hebrew (see NJPS, for instance). The inaccurate rendition from the Hebrew text is based on mistranslating "*kir*" as wall, when it can also mean the "wall" of a rock. Over many centuries Bible plant scholars in pursuit of biblical hyssop have produced a vast amount of literature on the subject of "wall plants," unsupported by first-hand knowledge of the land's flora and folklore. Their identifications of hyssop range from moss, lichen, and caper, *Capparis zoharyi* (*Capparis spinosa*), to European hyssop, *Hyssopus officinalis*.

The clue to hyssop's true identity can be found in the ruling from Saadiah Gaon (882–942), born in Egypt and later head of the Yeshiva in Babylon, who identified *ezov* with the Arabic *za'atar*, the name for the plant as well as the spice blend in which the *za'atar* plant is dominant. *Za'atar/ezov* is the hyssop to which the rabbis referred as "crushed by everyone." The traditional blend, still relished by Jews and Arabs in Israel as well as throughout the Middle East for general flavoring—especially to accompany pita bread—is made from hyssop leaves, stripped from their hard stems and dried and crushed or powdered, then combined with the ground, dried, tart-tasting fruits of the sumac tree, *Rhus coriaria*, minus its seeds, roasted or fried sesame seeds, and salt. The unique sharp-sweet flavor of *Majorana syriaca* is the preferred flavoring herb for *za'atar*, but herbs similar in flavor, like thyme, can be substituted where the real thing is not available.[9]

It was not until the twentieth century that the tangled web surrounding the identity of the little plant that grows 'in the rock' rather than 'out of the wall,' was finally cleared away to reveal true hyssop, *Majorana syriaca*. This feat was accomplished by Bible and Talmudic plant authority and botanist Ephraim Hareuveni, who together with his wife Hannah, pioneered a new approach to identifying the plants mentioned in the Bible and Talmud that relies on the veracity of the Talmud (hitherto ignored as opaque), studying native flora on the ground, and exploring local folklore; it was they who recovered the meaning and probable identity of the bitter herbs. This lowly plant, used for everything from kindling to alleviating toothaches, universally associated with the humble fare of everyday foods, required by Jewish law for cleansing and purification rituals, and interpreted to signify Torah values of modesty and humility, was finally given its due.[10]

"Solomon did what was displeasing to the Lord and did not remain loyal to the Lord like his father David" (I Kings 11:6). His building of a shrine to the pagan god Chemosh on a hill near Jerusalem, finally put him over the top, turning his heart away from God who had so generously endowed him. "Because you are guilty of this—you have not kept my covenant and the laws I enjoined upon you—I will tear the kingdom away from you ... But for the sake of your father David, I will not do it in your lifetime" (I Kings 11:6-12).

Solomon, although wise, ultimately chose the path of the lordly cedar, and his descendants would ultimately be brought low, humbled like the hyssop.

ENDNOTES

1. "Because the ezov is a plant with a woody stem and branches, it is listed among the trees of which Solomon spoke." Nogah Hareuveni *Tree and Shrub in Our Biblical Heritage*, 107.
2. The lure of pagan worship is discussed at length in Hareuveni, *Nature in Our Biblical Heritage*, 30-40; 64-68. For the importance of Jerusalem as the site of the Temple and the transformation of religion from spontaneous individual acts to public ritual see Daniel Hillel, *The Natural History of the Bible*, 181.
3. Cedars have been grown in Jerusalem at the Hebrew University on Mount Scopus from seeds collected by the young Nogah Hareuveni in Lebanon, then transplanted to Neot Kedumim (Israel's Biblical Landscape Reserve), where they are thriving.
4. See also Mrs. M. [Maude] Grieve, *A Modern Herbal*, Vol. I, 177 for a description of Libanol, an extraction from the wood or sawdust of the cedar of Lebanon, useful for alleviating bronchitis and various skin eruptions.
5. Hareuveni *Tree and Shrub in Our Biblical Heritage*, 89.
6. Nigel Hepper, *Illustrated Encyclopedia of Bible Plants*, 27. Through overharvesting over millennia, the cedar of Lebanon was reduced to small surviving remnants. It now grows in areas such as the Shouf Cedar Reserve on Mount Lebanon, where it is allowed to naturally regenerate and is protected from browsing goats and other animals.
7. Solomon's design is worked out in convincing detail in Hareuveni, 100–104.
8. Collected in Louis Ginzburg, *Legends of the Jews* (original multi-volume edition), 364.
9. The favored place of *Majorana syriaca*, above all others, in preparing the spice blend, *za'atar*, can be inferred from the qualified names of other *za'atar* plants such as *za'atar romi*, Roman hyssop (*Satureja thymbra*, one of the 'false hyssops'); *za'atar hommar,* donkey or desert hyssop (*Thymbra spicata*); and *za'atar farsi*, Persian hyssop or conehead thyme (*Coridothymus captitatus*). True *za'atar* stands apart from these by its superior flavor, a combination of oregano and sweet marjoram (*Origanum majorana*) with a hint of mint, and the fact that it alone gives its name to the spice blend. Substitutes have a sharper, thyme-like flavor and are often used in other Middle Eastern countries such as Syria, Lebanon, and Jordan. True *za'atar*, like true *ezov* has no qualifying name. See Jo Ann Gardner "Za'atar and Hyssop: Everyday Spice and Ancient Herb," *The Herbarist*, 49–51. Avinoam Danin discusses the various za'atar herbs on the website, "Flora of Israel Online," (see Bibliography for address). Go to "Table of contents, *Plant Stories*, Chapter E, Part 4, 'What shall we eat today?'" The Mishnaic system of nomenclature, he observes, passed with slight changes into the Arabic

language. In both languages there is *ezov* (Hebrew)/*za'atar* (Arabic) without an epithet. Plants related by scent or by morphology (plant form and structure) possess an epithet which aids in differentiating them from (true) *ezov*/*za'atar*.

10. Ephraim Hareuveni presented an overview of the history of identifying hyssop in his 1953 "Research in the Biblical Hyssop, History and Critique," in *Actes du Septième Congrès International d'Histoire des Sciences*, 358–365. Despite the overwhelming evidence, also supported by Immanuel Löw in his widely-acclaimed encyclopedic *Die Flora der Juden* (1924–1938), hyssop continues to be a source of conjecture in popular and scholarly literature.

Chapter Eighteen

HOLY OIL, HOLY AROMAS

❧

Portion-*Ki Tissa* / When you take [a census] (Exodus 30:11-34:35)

Take choice spices: five hundred weight of solidified myrrh, half as much—two hundred and fifty—of fragrant cinnamon, two hundred and fifty of aromatic cane, five hundred—by the sanctuary weight—of cassia, and a hin [gallon] of olive oil. Make of this a sacred anointing oil . . . (Exodus 30:23-25)

Take the herbs stacte, onycha, and galbanum—these herbs together with pure frankincense; let there be an equal part of each. Make them into incense, a compound expertly blended, refined, pure, sacred. (Exodus 30:34-35)

Who has not enjoyed the sweet floating aromas of spring lilacs or the summer's first roses? Perfumes, whatever their source, have an uplifting effect. So it's not surprising that fragrant herbs and spices are featured in the recipes for the Tabernacle's anointing oil and incense. Fragrance is meant to please God as it pleases many of us. A well-equipped ancient household might keep some kind of perfumed oil

Photograph © Lytton John Mussselman

Boswellia papyrifera. A source of frankincense, growing in Ethiopia.

and incense on hand to soothe dry skin in a hot climate, or to burn as a room fumigant. But in its biblical context, it is very important that the oil and incense be set aside solely for sanctifying the Tabernacle.

That anointing with perfumed oil was a common practice can be assumed by the heavy penalty for using the Tabernacle's ingredients for secular purposes: "It [the sacred anointing oil] must not be rubbed on any person's body, and you must not make anything like it in the same proportions . . . Whoever compounds its like, or puts any of it on a layman, shall be cut off from his kin" (Exodus 30:32-33). Later it will be used to anoint kings and prophets as a sign of their dedication to God. The way the ingredients are listed in the text and their amounts[1] suggests their fragrance was imparted to the olive oil by steeping. Olive oil, the means for anointing, carried its own significance as a symbol of light, even of life itself, as we saw in the story of Noah's Ark in Chapter Two, when the dove brought a branch of light-bearing olive leaves as a sign of life to the anxious family awaiting the flood to subside. "The light of the [olive] oil," the rabbis, taught, "is everlasting," (*B'midbar Raba* 9,13). From the earliest Greek and Roman herbals we know it was thought that the order in which the ingredients were added to the oil was significant. Fourth century BCE Greek author Theophrastus, for example, wrote that if one pound of myrrh is added to half a pint of oil, and later only a third of an ounce of cinnamon, the latter scent will dominate[2] (perhaps there is a clue in that to the order of the Tabernacle's ingredients). As the biblical text asserts, the ingredients must be "expertly blended" (Exodus 30:25).

Burning certain ingredients together, usually on hot coals, to produce aromatic smoke (the basic definition of incense, from the Latin to burn, "*incendere*") was a widespread practice throughout the Near East, and although associated with pagan worship,[3] it seems the Israelites took over this custom for their own purposes, as they did various traditions from the surrounding cultures.[4] Aaron, the High Priest, is instructed to burn incense on the altar each morning as he tends the lamps, "and Aaron shall burn it at twilight when he lights the lamps, a regular incense offering before the Lord throughout the ages" (Exodus 30:7-8). Its symbolic significance as a carrier of prayer is evident in David's psalm, "I call You, O Lord, hasten to me; give ear to my cry when I call You. Take my prayer as an offering of incense . . . " (Psalms 141:1-2). Just as God's presence is felt in the pillar of smoke and fire that accompanies the Israelites in their journey to the Promised Land, so too must incense carry a sense of the holy and divine in its smoke and fire. As with the anointing oil, for anyone who violated the taboo against using the same proportions for other purposes, the punishment was severe: "Whoever makes any like it, to smell of it, shall be cut off from his kin" (Exodus 30:37). The incense offering, greatly elaborated, was later associated with hypocrisy and vanity by the prophets, who indicated that God rejected their offerings because they were not carried out with a pure heart (a reference to the Israelites' worship of pagan gods): "Bringing oblations [to God] is futile," Isaiah warns. "Incense is offensive to Me" (Isaiah 1:13).

In Temple times when burning incense was associated with bread offerings, sacrificial burnt offerings honoring the Sabbath, the appearance of the new moon, and festivals (II Chronicles 2:3), the ingredients were mixed together in huge quantities. Approximately five hundred pounds were prepared once a year in the Temple, first pounded in a mortar, each ingredient by itself, then mixed together with a small amount of salt (only the salt of Sodom, "*melah Sedomit*"). On damp days it was piled up; on warm, dry days it was spread out for drying.[5] In Second Temple times, the House of Avtinas, as recorded in the Mishna and Tosefta (*Yoma* 3,11; *Yom Kippurim* 2,7), were skilled perfumers, the only ones who knew the identity of the plant whose name meant "smoke rising." This mystery plant, or an extract from it, was reputed to be responsible for their incense-producing smoke that rose straight up in a column (reminiscent of God's pillar of smoke?), obviously a desired characteristic which none but the Avtinas family could effect.[6]

—⚶—

WHILE THE NAMES of over twenty spice plants and the fragrances extracted from them are mentioned throughout the Bible (especially in the Song of Songs) and in rabbinic literature, translating the Hebrew or Aramaic common name into one in English, then applying a corresponding Latin binomial for the plant source is nearly impossible. Does the word, for instance, refer to a particular plant or only its saps and perfumes, or the compounds mixed from them?

Does the word when it appears elsewhere in the text always have the same meaning? These problems are exacerbated by the secrecy that surrounded the ingredients and their uses, as in the story about the Avtinas family. The appointed perfumer was regarded as an expert, so naturally he (or she?) would want to keep his secrets to himself (like cooks who reluctantly give away their recipes but leave out an important ingredient or crucial step in the process).

Myrrh and frankincense, the most common and sought after and expensive resins in the ancient world (with the exception of the Judean balsam), are widely recognized names, but what do they and the other ingredients in holy anointing oil and incense look like, where do they come from, and why is their perfume so special? Only when we are able to visualize them as real substances does the text come to life, thus giving us a window into the ancient material world in which they were so highly prized.

Myrrh, an ingredient in perfumes, incense, ointments, medicines, and in Egypt used for embalming, corresponds to the Hebrew *mor,* meaning "bitter." It is a solidified oily sap exuded from the fragrant stems and branches of various species of *Commiphora.* It's not clear which one is referred to in the biblical text. All are thorny, unshapely trees that grow on dry, stony soil in semi-arid regions of southern Arabia and northeast Africa, especially in Somalia and Yemen. Despite the legendary reputation of its resin, species such as *Commiphora myrrha* are hardly beautiful: a thorny bush growing up to six feet, its twisty limbs are bare of small three-lobed leaves most of the season, its flowers are white and tiny, the small fruits are beaked. For commercial purposes, now as in the past, the thick stems and trunk are cut to promote the flowing of a fragrant reddish sap or gum,

Photograph Wikimedia Commons

Myrrh, Dhotar region of Oman.

which naturally hardens to a light yellowish-brown resin in crystalized 'tears' of various sizes. Later they are collected in baskets, sorted, and brought to market. This is not as exotic as it sounds. Many trees exude gums, as any woodsman will tell you. Spruce gum, for instance, is a favorite, bitter at first, but then pleasant to chew.

Myrrh has well-known medicinal properties: it is considered a tonic, an antiseptic, and in various forms has been used to treat infected gums, ulcers, throat ailments, and in the manufacture of mouthwashes, gargles, toothpaste, and liniments. Its antibacterial properties, known since ancient times, are acknowledged today in the treatment of cleaning wounds and bedsores in natural medicine.[7] But its main claim to fame is its heavily sweet scent with vanilla and cardamon overtones, mixed with a general woodsy (resinous) aroma. It is not difficult to imagine the proverbial harlot who advertized her scented bed as a means of seducing "a lad without sense" in Proverbs 7:17: "I have sprinkled my bed with myrrh, aloes, and cinnamon."

Like myrrh, frankincense is a resinous, solidified sap, once known as "olibanum," that is extracted from the trunk of *Boswellia* species found growing in the hot, arid conditions of Arabia and East Africa. In biblical times the main producing species were *B. frereana* and *B. carteri* (now included together under *B. sacra*) in Somalia and Arabia; *B. papyrifera* in Ethiopia; and *B. sacra* in Arabia.[8] It is a small bushy tree characterized by peeling, papery bark (probably the source of

Frankincense from Yemen.

the epithet *papyrifera*, meaning roughly "paper-like"). Its compound leaves are small (to conserve moisture) and the flowers are star-like, ranging in color from pink to greenish-white, depending on the species. According to eyewitness accounts, trees seem to grow out from the sides of "nearly polished rock,"[9] (which sounds something like biblical hyssop growing 'in the rock'). Frankincense resins, as they are exuded from the tree after a cut is made, are pearl-like in appearance and have the consistency of condensed milk; after the resin dries it is yellowish in color. The whitish appearance of its sap is preserved in the Hebrew name, *levonah*, and the Arabic name *luban*, meaning "milk." *Levonah* had an elevated role in ritual. Not only was it an ingredient in incense but it was sprinkled on offerings and on the showbread, then a portion was eaten by the priests and scribes as commanded in Leviticus 24:7-9. Frankincense aroma is sharper, more balsamic and woodsy, more penetrating, than myrrh, and not as sweet. "Incense" is virtually synonymous with "frankincense," as preserved in the Latin for frankincense, *francum incensum*, meaning "pure incense."

Resin from Boswellia species has strong antibacterial, antibiotic, antifungal and antiseptic properties, and in the ancient world was used to treat throat and larynx infections, stop bleeding, and as an antidote to poison hemlock, *Conium maculatum*. As a major ingredient in incense, its fragrance was recognized as having a calming effect (it is used today in aromatherapy to create a sense of well-being). Frankincense is used now mainly in perfumes, soaps, and powders and creams, especially for treating skin problems.[10]

Myrrh and frankincense possess fixative properties, which goes a long way toward explaining their prominent role in perfuming oils and incense. Curiously, this important characteristic seems to be ignored in the literature, which focuses almost exclusively on identifying the ingredients and their sources rather than their properties; to a working perfumer this information would be vital. A fixative is like a preservative: it both absorbs the fleeting scents of other ingredients and slowly releases them along with its own scent, as in the prepared roots of certain iris, called "orris root," and sandalwood chips. These, as well as myrrh and frankincense, are still widely used in the production of potpourri, a mix of dried flowers and herbs. A fixative gives the products to which it is added a longer shelf life. Think of those huge piles of a year's worth of incense stored in the Temple.

Who has not heard of cinnamon, an important ingredient with cassia in holy oil? They are often mentioned alone or together in old herbal recipes for making perfumes and ointments. Cassia, (*kez'iah*), also called Bastard Cinnamon because it was (and is) substituted for the more expensive true cinnamon, is the inner bark of the cassia tree, *Cinnamomum cassia*; it is native to East Asia where it may reach thirty feet in height. Its bark is more pungent, less sweet and delicate than true cinnamon bark. Some claim it was oil of cassia that was used in incense rather than its bark, but the process of distilling essential oils from plants was not known until the fourth century BCE. It requires special distilling equipment and huge amounts of raw material to extract any significant amount of pure essential oil: twelve thousand pounds of jasmine flowers, for instance, are needed to produce two pounds of essential jasmine oil. Steeping the plant parts, or in this case, the bark, in olive oil, as already discussed, seems more likely. The true cinnamon tree, *C. verum* (*kinnamon*), is native to Sri Lanka (Ceylon) and the adjacent coast of India. It grows from twenty to thirty feet tall, has large leathery leaves, and its inner bark, like that of cassia when it is peeled off the tree, curls up once dried; in this state it is bundled together in lengths for export. Most cooks and bakers encounter cinnamon as a powder but if you've ever bought stick cinnamon you will notice how the edges of the sticks are tightly curled. Cinnamon has properties beyond simply smelling nice and tasting good in cakes and cookies. It is a digestive, stimulant, antiseptic, and in the Middle East, a key ingredient of a pleasing winter tea.

Exotic spices such as cinnamon and cassia would have had to come to ancient Israel from a great distance. Was that possible? Zohary maintains that they and other drugs and perfumes originating in the East could have reached southeastern Arabia via the Silk Route from the East,[11] and from there, to Israel, Egypt, and other centers by way of the famous camel caravans of the Incense Route that originated in southern Arabia. The Incense Route was undoubtedly the source for myrrh and frankincense. The other well-worn route for moving precious substances not locally available was from Syria to Egypt via Israel (ancient Canaan), and is mentioned in the Book of Genesis when Joseph's brothers, looking up, "saw a caravan of Ishmaelites coming from Gilead, their camels bearing gum, balm, and ladanum to be taken to Egypt" (37:25). Perhaps this route supplied galbanum, *helbenah*, a fragrant resin for incense with a greenish tint, thought to be exuded from the stems and root of a species of *Ferula* native to Persia. The plant looks like an oversize fennel with similar finely cut foliage. Because of its bitter taste (in common with most resinous gums) and its reputed strange aroma (not entirely pleasant) the rabbis drew the moral lesson that "A public fast in which transgressors do not participate is no fast. For though the odor given forth by the galbanum is unpleasant, it is nevertheless one of the essential ingredients of the fragrant spices of the incense offering."[12]

"Stacte," (*nataf*) in the Tabernacle's incense, may be liquid myrrh, that is, a solution of myrrh resin in oil.[13] The incense "*onycha*" (*shehelet*) remains a mystery, although some believe it to be a fragrant part of a shellfish from the Mediterranean coast.[14]

It has been suggested that the *besamim* (perfume) box full of spices at the *Havdalah* ceremony, separating the Sabbath from the rest of the week, is to recall the custom of burning incense in the Temple.[15] A traditional interpretation for the presence and benediction of the spice box is that perceptions and enjoyments through the sense of smell are the most delicate; that they afford not gross, material pleasure, but rather a spiritual one; and that the perfume of spices is, therefore, a comfort to the over-soul of the Sabbath (*neshama yeterah*, the extra soul bestowed to the Sabbath keeper), which grieves when the holy day departs.[16] And that takes us back to the purpose of the Tabernacle's perfumed holy anointing oil and incense—to please God as sweet aromas please us.

Photograph © Ori Fragman

Myrtus communis. Myrtle bloom, fragrant *hadas*, with which the spice box is associated, Lower Mount Hermon.

ENDNOTES

1. Calculations of biblical weights differ. The amount of substances in the anointing oil described in Exodus 30:23-25 can, according to some, range from over six pounds for the fragrant cinnamon and aromatic cane to twice that amount for the myrrh and cassia. See Nigel Hepper, *Illustrated Encyclopedia of Bible Plants*, 140. These would be mixed in a *hin* of olive oil which the *The Jewish Study Bible* in its "Weights and Measures Table" 2105, equates with 1.012 gallons.

2. Lisa Manniche, *An Ancient Egyptian Herbal*, 48.

3. *The Oxford Companion to the Bible*, 301, and many other references.

4. As in the Bible's use of Near Eastern myth themes in the Garden of Eden, the account of Noah and the flood from flood traditions associated with the Epic of Gilgamesh, the themes and practices associated with the three harvest festivals (Passover/*Pesah*, *Shavuot*, and *Sukkot*), that may have originally derived from pagan celebrations. For more on the transformation of ancient festivals see Theodor Gaster, *Festivals of the Jewish Year*, "Old Wine in New Bottles," 21–28.

5. *The Jewish Encyclopedia*, 570; also includes the story of the Avtinas family.

6. Reader and plant expert Elaine Solowey reports that the smoke-making plant, *maaleh ashan*, has been tentatively identified as a species of *Leptadenia*, sometimes called *L. pyrotechnica*. She says that a reference for this is found in Rabbi Zohar Amar's *Ketoret /The Book of Incense*, 143. Elaine has two of these plants and describes them as having "a long bunch of round, skinny branches from a strong central root, with odd little bracts on them instead of leaves, and yes, they do make a column of smoke when a piece of the plant is burned, light grey or white."
7. Shimshon Ben Yehoshua, Bar Ilan University, in his paper on frankincense and myrrh, "Frankincense-Boswellia genus, Fam. Burseraceae," 36.
8. Hepper, 136.
9. Ibid., quoted from a Victorian traveler in 1857.
10. Ben Yehoshua, 9, 10. In his detailed compilation of information about frankincense and myrrh, he focuses on past uses and current research into their medicinal properties and their possibilities for contemporary medicine.
11. Michael Zohary, *Plants of the Bible*, 202.
12. Cited in Louis I. Rabinowitz, *Torah and Flora*, 52–53, in his chapter "Sinner's Spice," as the reason why, prior to the recitation of the *Kol Nidrei* (all vows) on the eve of Yom Kippur during the High Holidays, a public pronouncement is made that "we hereby declare it permitted to pray together with the transgressors."
13. Ben Yehoshua, 31. Mrs. M. Grieve, *A Modern Herbal*, Vol. II, 572, cites Pliny the Elder, a first century CE Roman writer, as the source for identifying stacte as liquid myrrh.
14. *The Jewish Encyclopedia*, 570.
15. Nogah Hareuveni, *Nature in Our Biblical Heritage*, 134. The crushed leaves of *hadas, Myrtus communis*, are also used at the *Havdalah* ceremony, from which the custom arose of calling the spice box *hadas*.
16. *The Jewish Encyclopedia*, 119.

Chapter Nineteen

THE BLOOMING MENORAH

Portion-*Vayyakhel* / Moses convoked (Exodus 35:1-38:20)

He [Bezalel] made the menorah of pure gold. The menorah, its stem and branches were of hammered work; its calyxes, its knobs and its flowers were of one piece with it. There were six branches stemming from its sides: three branches of the menorah stemmed from one side and three branches from the other side. There were also three almond-shaped calyxes with knob and flower on the first branch, three almond-shaped calyxes with knob and flower on the next branch, and similarly for all six branches stemming from the menorah. On the main stem of the menorah there were four almond-shaped calyxes, its knobs and its flowers, a knob under two of its branches, a knob under two of its branches, a knob under two of its branches, knobs under the six branches which stemmed from the menorah. The knobs and the branches were of one piece with it, all a single piece of hammered work of pure gold. (Exodus 37:17-24)[1]

Photograph © Ori Fragman

Salvia palaestina. Land of Israel sage, south Hebron Mountains. See cover illustration for an interpretation of the plant's menorah-like form.

The menorah (often translated "lampstand") is the most dazzling piece of furniture in the Tabernacle and later, the Temple. Hammered out by the chief craftsman, Bezalel, from a solid block of gold (about 150 pounds), and lit with "clear [olive] oil of beaten olives" (Exodus 27:20) it conjures an arresting visual image, one that is considerably enhanced by the idea that it is an oversized plant in bloom. Moses must have been disconcerted, even overwhelmed, when God told him the details for making each item in the Tabernacle, culminating in the difficult directions for the menorah, because he knew he would have to repeat them to the people. God reminds him, as to a bright pupil who must neverthe-less pay strict attention, "Note well, and follow the patterns for them that are being shown you on the mountain" (Exodus 25:40). Bezalel, however, has no problem, as might be expected of one who is con-sidered to be the archetypal master craftsman. He hammers out the menorah without hesitation (we can almost see him in action); his name means "in the shadow of God."[2]

Was the menorah just a rather ornate lamp for lighting the Tabernacle? Its suggested tree-like form—three sets of branches growing opposite one another from the mainstem or shaft—has inspired commentary on the menorah as an idealized Tree of Life, *Etz Haim*, the Jewish symbol associated with the Torah as a source of light that gives form, direction, and meaning to every aspect of the material world.[3] In biblical terms, the seven branches and seven lamps atop each branch, have special meaning, too, the number seven symbolizing completion and perfection, as in God's day of rest, the Sabbath.[4] The only oil permitted for lighting the lamps was "clear oil of beaten olives," for no other gave forth such brilliance. Everything associated with the olive tree, its branches and fruit, as well as its oil, acquired transcendent associations throughout the Bible as, for instance, a source of light for spreading righteousness. The olive tree and its products, as outsiders have observed, "are inseparably bound up with the Hebrew people."[5] Imagine instructions to fill the lamps with the oil of radish or walnut seed!

Why place the menorah facing south, and the golden table with the twelve loaves of showbread (representing the twelve tribes of Israel), facing north (Exodus 26:35)? Does their placement carry a message? According to the Sages, for whom every word of the Bible carried weight, together they represent a silent prayer for the suc-cess of the all-important grains (wheat and barley) and olive harvest:

Photograph © Avinoam Danin

Salvia palaestina. Pressed specimen, Land of Israel sage.

"The northern wind is beneficial to wheat when it has reached a third of its ripening and is damaging to olive trees when they have blossomed. The southern wind is damaging to wheat when it has reached a third of its ripening and is beneficial to olives when they have blossomed. This was symbolized by the table in the north and the menorah in the south" (Tractate *Baba Batra* 147a).[6] The pairing of the showbread and the menorah acknowledged the supremacy of one universal God over all the forces of nature, a meaningful display in a pagan environment. Their placement is a prayer to God to let each wind come at the right time.[7]

Whatever meanings are inherent in the menorah, its design was freely and spontaneously adopted as a symbol without rival of the Jewish people and Jewish nation. Its image is recorded from the Sinai Desert to the Golan Heights, carved into rock walls, worked into mosaic designs on ancient synagogue floors, and used as a motif on countless tombs and monuments. And, with the addition of two more branches to accord with the Talmud's prohibition against copying the Temple menorah,[8] it became the *hanukkiah* of Hanukah, the Festival of Lights. This is the eight-day late autumn/early winter festival that commemorates the rededication of the Second Temple by the victorious Maccabees on Kislev 25, 165 BCE, the third anniversary of its desecration by the Syrian conqueror, Antiochus Epiphanes. The eight-day long festival was first declared by the Maccabees as a belated observance of *Sukkot*, as written in the book of Maccabees (II Maccabees 10:6-8), since in the fall, when *Sukkot* would normally be observed, the Jews were in revolt and the Temple still defiled. After the destruction of the Second Temple, Talmudic legend ascribed the eight day festival to the miracle of the pure oil found in the Temple, which although sufficient for only one day, miraculously burned for eight (*Shabbat* 21b).

In Jewish tradition, the origins of Hanukah have always been rooted in the rededication of the Temple and Torah values, rather than in the idea of bringing light into a darkened world at the winter solstice, as in ancient nature holidays. In the nature cycles of Israel and the Middle East, the season of Hanukah, is a botanical reawakening, similar to a Western spring. In the Land of Israel new growth springs from the dry earth after the fall rains, and then some of the most beautiful bulbs in the world, such as cyclamen, narcissus, sternbergia, and crocus, begin or end their bloom cycle. *Crocus hyemalis*, whose closed white goblet flower resembles a flame, could very well be a floral symbol of the Hanukah season.[9]

— ᛥ —

THE DESCRIPTION OF THE MENORAH is one of the Bible's most fascinating puzzles. The text has such a botanical air about it that it seems reasonable to assume a real plant served as a model. But which one? Even for readers without a background in botany, terms like "stem," "branches," and "flower," are easy to visualize. But what about the repeated "calyxes" (*gevi'im*)? Pick a common field daisy or garden rose and look at the small green leaves that encircle the bud or flower at its base. Separately, these are known as sepals, together they form the flower's calyx. The phrase "almond-shaped calyxes" (*gevi'im meshukadim*) could suggest the way the embryonic fruit of the almond tree (*shaked*) resembles a rounded "knob" with a remnant flower and calyx still attached at its top.[10] The specific phrase "knob and flower" (*kaftor* and *perakh*), together resembling a sort of cup, is repeated so many times in the description of the menorah, that this phenomenon seems to have been drawn from close familiarity with the living almond tree (*shaked* or *luz*).

Botanists believe that the cultivated sweet almond (*Amygdalus communis*) is the result of selection from the wild bitter almond over many generations, going back thousands of years. Jacob sent a consignment of them as gifts to Egypt four thousand years ago, along with other "choice products of the land," such as balm, honey, gum, ladanum, and pistachio nuts (Genesis 43:11) to appease "the man," actually his son Joseph in Egypt, who holds the key to the family's future. In Israel, almond trees are cultivated in groves and they also grow as semi-wild escapes from cultivation near groves and in rocky soil, where roots can reach down deep to find moisture. The first tree in the landscape to break its period of dormancy, its pinkish buds erupt dramatically in massed white-petaled blooms, pink toward their center, opening even before the tree's leaves appear, at or near the end of the rainy season. Its profuse flowering heralds the short spring ahead when the countryside will erupt, too, into a flowering garden, from south to north. The almond tree's Hebrew

Photograph © Avinoam Danin

Amygdalus communis. Bell-shaped calyxes hold buds on a flowering branch of the almond tree in Jerusalem.

name, "*shaked*," is derived from the Hebrew root, *shakod*, meaning to be diligent, reliable, or on watch, virtues that were symbolically associated with the tree itself: "The word of the Lord came to me: What do you see, Jeremiah? I replied: I see a branch of an almond tree. The Lord said to me: You have seen right, for I am watchful to bring My word to pass." (Jeremiah 1:11-12).[11]

Could the "knobs and flowers" of the Tabernacle and Temple menorah be a reference to 'being on watch,' as in the lamp's silent prayer to God to bring the rains at the right time for grain and olives? Ephraim Hareuveni, who with his wife, Hannah, was responsible for setting Biblical and Talmudic botany on a new, more realistic path, investigated the subject of the menorah "knobs" (usually translated as "cups"). The Talmud records that the knobs resembled "a kind of Cretan apple" (*Menahot* 25b). The knobs, as Hareuveni discovered, were actually swellings or galls from an insect sting on *Salvia pomifera*, a species of sage common on the Greek islands, especially on Crete. When the rabbis sought to describe the menorah's "knobs" they looked to a product with which they were familiar, Cretan 'apples.' In ancient times these apples were probably an item of trade between Crete and ancient Israel, as suggested in the Hebrew word for knob, *kaftor*, also thought to be the ancient name for Crete.[12] The galls resemble miniature apples, juicy and sour to taste, and are found on *S. fruticosa* in Israel. I tasted one by the roadside and just as described, the apples swell out from the branch and "were of one piece with it." Even today, dried plant galls are sold in Crete, often preserved with sugar, and are highly regarded as a sweetmeat with healing properties.

What is the link between species of sage (*marvah*, or *moriah*, as named by the Hareuvenis for the hill country where these plants commmonly grow) and the menorah? The Hareuvenis were driven by the belief that the flora of the land were green artifacts that continued to hold the answer to identifying the plants mentioned in the Bible and Talmud long after the Jews were dispersed to many lands and the plants' names and symbolism were forgotten. In their searches throughout the countryside, on hillsides, in valleys, and in the desert, they discovered that not only is Israel rich in salvias (over twenty types), but several of them bear a remarkable resemblance to the basic design of the Bible's menorah. These species have a tall central stem from which grow three side branches directly opposite one another, and as in many Hanukah menorahs, the middle branch is a bit taller than the others. The candle in the socket of this branch is called a *shamas* or helper, and is used to light the others.

The salvias, in varying degree, resemble a menorah not only when dried and pressed (when the calyxes are very prominent), but even when the plants are growing in the ground. Their wide open two-lipped flowers grow around the plant's stem in showy whorls from distinctive calyxes; these remain attractive long after the flowers themselves are spent. Menorah salvias are perennial small shrubs, growing from two and a half to three feet tall, are often heavily musk-scented, and attract bees when in bloom. Leaves, usually rough in texture and tapered, occur mainly at the base of the plant, which allows the branches to show off their *menorah*-like design without distractions.

Salvia fruticosa, three-leafed sage, is the most conspicuous of the menorah-like sages. It is abundant in the Judean Mountains and its foothills, in Samaria, on the slopes of Mount Carmel, and in the Upper Galilee. Its branches bear terminal spikes of pink or mauve florets or flowers from March to May, and its large rough, gray-green leaves are often used as a substitute or adulterant for cooking sage (*S. officinalis*); due to over-harvesting it is a protected plant in Israel. This sage is widely used among Israeli Arabs and Jews from Arab lands for folk remedies to treat, among other ailments, stomachache and earache, and as a diuretic. Herbal doctors in the Middle East use three-leafed sage to regulate menstruation, enhance fertility, strengthen the muscles of the womb before and after childbirth, and to treat problems associated with menopause.[13]

Growing in *batha*, in wadis and from rock fissures in more arid regions, such as the Negev and Samaria, and also in the Upper Galilee and on the Golan, *S. dominica*, pungent sage, is a stunning presence, especially when its strong silhouette, springing from a cliff, is outlined against a blue sky. When backlit on a sunny day the entire plant glows from the presence of many silky hairs on all its parts, a truly brilliant candleabra! Its leaves and calyxes are gray-green and silvery, its April to May flowers are light yellow and white, the total effect, dazzling. Like three-leafed sage, pungent sage (very strongly scented) also bears galls; these have a peach-like taste and are called "little peach" in Arabic.[14] The crushed aromatic leaves are used to make a poultice to relieve external pain.[15] The slender form of *S. hierosolymitana*, Jerusalem sage, and its purple stems and florets combine to create a very ornamental plant, a visual counterpoint to the more vigorous pungent sage. Jerusalem sage grows abundantly in rocky ground in the Judean hills, in Samaria, the Galilee, the Golan, and especially on the slopes of Mount Carmel; it blooms from April to May.[16]

Photograph © Jackie Chambers

Salvia judaica. Violet-purple stem, calyx, and flower of Judean sage in the Jerusalem Botanical Gardens.

Far less prevalent, and growing only in the Arava Valley and Southern Negev, *S. judaica*, Judean sage has a striking resemblance to the biblical menorah. When in bloom in April all parts of the plant turn violet-purple; depending on its conditions, its stems may be crowded with whorls of violet-blue florets. *Salvia palaestina*, the aptly named "Land of Israel sage," is the most menorah-like and has a far wider range. It grows in *bathas*, from the cracks of rocks, and in wadis as far south as Eilat, and in the Negev region, the Dead Sea Valley, the mountains of Judea and Samaria, the Judean Desert, in the Jordan Valley, and north to the Golan. It is more robust than Judean sage, with thicker, hairy stems, rough leaves, and whitish flowers, lightly flushed violet, that bloom in May. Its essential oil has been studied for its anti-microbial activity.[17]

We may never know whether sage plants inspired the design for the ancient menorah, but the fact that they grow in many places in Israel in precisely the same way as described in the Bible, with "*three branches of the menorah stemmed from one side and three branches from the other side . . . its knobs of one piece with it*" is very suggestive. Whatever plant (or plants) the author of the text had in mind, this botanical puzzle reaffirms, in a most graphic way, the close ties between the people of Israel and the plants of their everyday landscape. Some of the sage plants, moreover, like the pungent sage, embody both light and fragrance, characteristics that were associated with all the blessings of the Torah: "As each commandment was spoken by the Holy One, Blessed be He, the world filled with fragrance" (*Shabbat* 88b).[18]

ENDNOTES

1. Translated from the Hebrew by Helen Frenkley in Nogah Hareuveni, *Nature in Our Biblical Heritage*, 126. The usual "lampstand," of the NJPS and other versions, seems stilted and hard to visualize, whereas the image of the *menorah*, the actual Hebrew word in the text, is widely known. See pp. 123–140 for a detailed discussion of the menorah from which I have drawn.
2. In Louis Ginzberg, *Legends of the Bible*, 411.
3. Rabbi Shlomo Riskin, "The Science of Religion," Weekly Portion, *Numbers* 8:2, *The International Jerusalem Post*, 10–16, June, 2005.
4. Riskin, "Menora: a tree of light," Weekly Portion, Exodus 25:31-33, *The International Jerusalem Post*, week ending March 3, 1990.
5. This remark is attributed to the nineteenth century Swiss botanist Alphonse de Candolle, cited in Asaph Goor and Max Nurock, *The Fruits of the Holy Land*, 91.
6. Cited in Hareuveni, 36, in his discussion of the difficult growing conditions of the Seven Varieties.
7. Ibid.
8. See *Rosh Hashana* 24a, *Avoda Zara* 43a, *Menahot* 28b.
9. "This flower [when closed up to protect its pollen during rain] looks like a candle, gleaming in remembrance of the deeds of the Maccabees." Hareuveni, 122.
10. This phenomenon is discussed in Hareuveni, 130–133.
11. Cited in Hareuveni, 133, discussing the almond tree's symbolism.
12. The elder Hareuvenis' research is discussed in Hareuveni, 126–129.
13. D. Palevitch and Zohara Yaniv, *Medicinal Plants of the Holy Land*, 267.
14. Ibid., 268–9.
15. Ibid.
16. I once gave my horticulturist daughter Nell seeds of *S. hierosolymitana* to establish in a Bible garden near Rochester, New York. The following November she brought me a very menorah-like dried specimen just as it had air-dried after having been cut off at ground level.
17. *Journal of Medicinal Plants Research*, vol. 4, pp. 1238–1240, June 18, 2010. *Salvia palaestina* was one of four species represented in a study called "Antimicrobial activities of the essential oils of Four *Salvia* species from Turkey" by botanists from the Faculty of Science at Dicle University in Turkey. They found *S. palaestina* to be very effective.

18. Cited in Hareuveni, 134, in a discussion of how light and fragrance were combined in the Temple through the menorah and incense offering, both of which are now represented in the Sabbath's *Havdalah*, or separation ceremony, in which the menorah's light is symbolized by the special braided candle. See Chapter Eighteen, *Holy Oils, Holy Aromas*, on the spice box, in remembrance of the Temple incense offering.

Introduction

THE BOOK OF LEVITICUS

Vayyikra

The third and shortest book of the Torah, *Leviticus*, picks up where *Exodus* leaves off, at the completion of the sanctuary at Sinai. The book's Greek name means "pertaining to the Levites." The Hebrew name is *Vayyikra*, after the opening words of the text, "And He called [Moses]." Now the Israelites learn what is expected of them in the sanctuary and in daily life. The moral universe encompassed by *Leviticus* includes not only the minute details of priestly duties and animal sacrifice, but the way in which every aspect of human life—diet, marriage, social ethics and the very soil that grows the crops on which life depends—is to be sanctified, made holy.

Photograph © Ori Fragman

Olea europaea. Ripening olive in olive grove, Upper Galilee.

Chapter Twenty

HOLY FRUIT

Portion-*Kedoshim* / Holiness (Leviticus 19:1-20:27)

When you enter the land and plant any tree for food, you shall regard the fruit as forbidden. Three years it shall be forbidden for you, not to be eaten. In the fourth year all its fruit shall be set aside for jubilation before the Lord; and only in the fifth year may you use its fruit—that its yield to you may be increased. I the Lord am your God. (Leviticus 19:23-25)

The essence of Leviticus, its ultimate meaning, is the attainment of holiness, which in biblical terms means always trying to do the right and proper thing.[1] The way to achieve this state, commentators have noted, is through an ideal mirroring of God's perfect ordering of the universe as told in Genesis with His separation of heaven and earth, light from darkness, day from night, water from sky (Genesis 1:1-7). His children strive to imitate Him by creating an order, too, one in which separations and distinctions, such as purity and impurity, are regarded in the light of His own work.[2] In this sense, the seemingly arcane detail of ritual animal sacrifice and the associated priestly duties are very important, for it was believed that through their correct carrying out the priestly or holy character of Israel was to be preserved.[3] Sacrifice, moreover, was not considered to be an end in itself, but rather a means of attaining a state of holiness, a concept preserved in the Hebrew for "sacrifice," *korban*, from the root "to come close." In this sense, *korban* is a way for man to come nearer to God.[4]

The striving to attain holiness extends to every aspect of the material world, including the proper relationship between people and the proper relationship between the people and their land. We see this principle clearly at work in the section of Leviticus known as the Holiness Code (Leviticus 18-26), as in the prohibitions against mixing linen and wool, interbreeding cattle, sowing one's vineyard with a second kind of seed, and against ploughing with an ox and ass together (Leviticus 19:19).[5] These down-to-earth applications of the Holiness Code, drawn from mundane daily life, are interspersed with what almost seem to be casual references to the sublime commandments to love one's neighbor as yourself (Leviticus 19:18) and to "love the stranger as yourself, for you were strangers in the land of Egypt" (Leviticus 19:34). The juxtaposition of seemingly unrelated commands makes the point that every aspect of the Israelite's world should have a holy foundation. This is the way, as Leviticus sees it, to build a holy nation. "Rarely has the drive toward holiness," observed Everett Fox, "found as full expression in a vision of real life society, grounded in the everyday world of people and institutions, as it does in the Holiness Code."[6]

It is within this moral and ethical context that the farmer is commanded to refrain from making use of the food from his newly planted fruit tree until its fourth year when the produce is to be "set aside for jubilation to the Lord." The fruit that the tree bears in its first three years is to be regarded as forbidden (*orla*, uncircumcised or forbidden fruit), either to eat or sell. The tree's fruit in its fourth year, although not sold, may be eaten, but only in the holy precincts of Jerusalem,[7] the spiritual center of the Israelite faith. In this act, the grower acknowledges his debt to God Who is the ultimate owner of the crop and, indeed, of the land ("the earth is the Lord's," Exodus 9:29). In other words, the farmer taxes himself by sacrificing the opportunity to profit from the first significant yield of fruit. If, moreover, the farmer had removed the embryonic fruit (buds) that appears on the young tree during its formative period, a common practice now as it was in biblical times, he was assured of an even *better* crop the fourth and following years because the tree had been encouraged to direct all its energy into producing a strong trunk and branches, vital for prolific fruit production.[8]

Midrash goes to the spiritual heart of the law by bringing out the meaning of planting fruit trees in the first place. To achieve this purpose it links the act of planting, as described in Leviticus, "when you enter the land" (Leviticus 19:23), to a verse in Deuteronomy: "After the Lord your God shall you walk" (Deuteronomy 13:5).[9] How can ordinary humans possibly 'walk like God' (imitate Him), the midrash asks? Spun out in typical homiletic style, it makes the case that although people cannot possibly walk as God walks in the literal sense, it is well within human power to imitate God by copying His horticultural activities. Just as God Himself first planted a fruitful garden in Eden (Genesis 2:8), so the people's first act when entering the Promised Land should be to plant food-bearing trees.[10] Planting trees is, therefore, a holy act, and by following the Leviticus commandment to wait the proscribed time to enjoy its fruit, the fruit itself will have a good and holy flavor.

—᙭—

WHAT FRUIT TREES did the farmers of ancient Israel plant?

Excavations of the oldest strata in Jericho, Megiddo, Beth Yerach on the Sea of Galilee, and elsewhere has revealed olive stones, pomegranate peel, seeds of grapes and dates, all fruits of the Seven Species whose cultivation long preceded the Israelites' appearance in the Promised Land, as did the fig tree.[11] Also found were stones of jujube, *Ziziphus spina-christi*, walnut shells and carob, whose seeds were discovered to be so consistently the same in weight that they were used as weight measures, twenty carob seeds being equal to a shekel.[12] As previously noted, almond and pistachio, reliable producers even under stressful conditions, were among the "choice products" that Jacob sent down to Egypt. In addition, citron (the *etrog* of *Sukkot*), apple, pear, peach, plum, mulberry, and quince fruit trees, known to have been grown since Second Temple times if not before, were available to the Israelite farmer to grow and develop.[13]

The first century CE Jewish historian Josephus described the Land of Israel as "a garden of God," because it was so lush with groves and orchards of "the most precious and most beautiful of trees in amazing variety."[14] From the time of Joshua when the Israelites farmed the hill country, the cultivation of fruit trees, along with grains, was of supreme importance because they were mainstays of the biblical diet. The fruits most favored were those like olives, grapes, figs (true figs and the indigenous sycomore figs), dates and pomegranates that not only thrive in a Mediterranean climate but are amenable to processing for future use. Wine from grapes and pomegranates, oil pressed from olives, honey from dates, and various sun-dried fruits enjoyed a long shelf-life, as it were, when processed in some way, then stored in a cool place (no refrigerators or freezers then!) Fruit and fruit products were also a source of income and trade: oil, wine, raisins, and dates, for instance, could be exchanged for timber, spices, perfumes, cloth, silk, horses, or any number of things farmers did not produce themselves.

From various sources we learn that fruit-tree farming during the biblical period was so successful that ancient Israel became famous for special fruit tree strains: the high quality of olives from the Galilee, grapes and wine from Judea and Samaria, figs from the Plains, and dates grown in the Jordan Valley. Egypt and Persia were among the buyers. The Persian Darius I (522–485 BCE), instructed his officers to procure fruit trees. The Roman Pliny the Elder mentions shipping fruit trees, particularly the fig, plum, pomegranate, and grapevine, from the Land of Israel to Greece and Rome.[15] The Mediterranean climate of cool, rainy winters and dry, hot summers encouraged fruit-tree growth in Israel, but without the Israelite farmer's skill in encouraging that growth by providing the best soil, then pruning, trimming, and irrigating the trees, and carefully selecting the best for breeding or grafting, Josephus' "garden of God" would neither have flourished nor become a center in the region for the development of fruit-bearing trees, as it had during the biblical period.[16]

The cultivation of fruit trees was so highly regarded that the rabbis advised, "If you had a sapling in your hand and were told that the Messiah had come, first plant the sapling, then go out to greet the Messiah" (*Avot D'Rabbi Natan*, 31). Over millennia, the fruits of the land became synonymous with the land itself and with the people who lived from it. The prophet Ezekiel describes Israel as a well-watered vine, (Ezekiel 17:6-8), and conversely, Israel's disobedience to God is portrayed as a ruined vineyard (Isaiah 5:5). Carved, painted, and mosaic images of fruits—heavy clusters of fat grapes and twining vines, stylized olive leaf wreaths, full bowls of figs, stately palms, rosy, round pomegranates—appear on ancient synagogue ceilings and floors and on stone reliefs, on everyday pottery lamps, and on decorated sarcophagi. These beautiful fruit motifs were executed with flair and an eye to detail that time has not diminished. In periods of war, when Israel's nationhood was challenged, ancient Israelite coins proudly displayed the fruits of the land to which the people were attached and with which they identified themselves. A coin from the time of the Second Jewish War against Rome (132–135 CE), for instance, shows an oil pitcher and olive branches with the inscription, "To the Freedom of Jerusalem." [17]

The phenomenal success of Israelite farming, and fruit-producing in particular, must owe a great deal to the discipline imposed upon the farmer by the dictates of a moral and ethical code that always expected him to do the right (proper or holy) thing. The *orla* prohibition, which ensured that only the best fruit would be sold because the farmer had waited until the tree was mature, as well as other laws pertaining to fruit trees—leaving a marginal part of the fruit crop for gleaners (*pe'ah, lekhet*), set forth in Leviticus (19:9, 10) and further elaborated in Deuteronomy (24:20-21)[18]—the offering of the choicest of first fruits (*bikkurrim*) commanded in Exodus 23:19 and Deuteronomy 26:1-11, the seventh year fallowing of the land (*shmitta*) first described in Leviticus 25:3-4—was intended to shape the farmer's character and relationship to the soil. Farming, like every other activity in the Promised Land, was to have a right and proper, or holy, dimension, pleasing to God. The farmer would necessarily closely observe his fruits to meet the requirement of the law. This attention to detail may help to explain the high order of fruit cultivation in the Holy Land during the biblical period. God promises Israel, "If you follow My laws and faithfully observe My commandments, I will grant your rains in their season, so that the earth shall yield its produce and the trees of the field their fruit" (Leviticus 26:3-4). Blessings will then come, moreover, not only to the children of Israel, but to all people: "In the season of plentitude of fruits, there is kindness and peace on earth" (*Midrash Bereshit Raba* 80,4).

How was the voluntary sacrifice of the fourth year fruit actually carried out? Did the farmer load up his donkey and take his entire family with him as well as the crop (which they no doubt helped to produce) on his 'enforced' holiday? Deuteronomy's description of how to carry out the second tithe, *ma'aser sheni*, provides the model: "And you shall eat it [the crop] there before God and rejoice, you and your household" (Deuteronomy 14:26). This

Photograph © Joshua D. Klein.

Ficus carica. Ripening figs, Volcani Center, of Agricultural Research Bet Dagan, near Tel-Aviv.

was a festive occasion in which everyone, the whole household, participated. The farmer could have taken the trip in the autumn when most tree fruits ripen and when pilgrims from all parts of the country would be converging on Jerusalem to celebrate the fall festival of *Sukkot*, the Feast of the Ingathering. It must have been a jubilant occasion as the text suggests, one that helped to deepen the participants' sense of national and religious identity (which is why the fruit was brought to Jerusalem and not to local altars). Did the farmer carry on small talk with other farmers about the weather and whether it had been favorable or not for the season's crop, as farmers invariably do when they meet? Did the farmer share some of his new fruit crop with others? Nowhere do we learn of a prohibition against sharing. An entire fourth year crop would surely be too much for him (and his family) to consume within a single day. How long could he remain away from his farm? These are questions which must intrigue anyone with intimate knowledge of how things actually work on a real farm, whatever its vintage or location. For those with an understanding of farm life, or interested in comprehending it, the Bible's laws relating to agriculture open a window onto a very real world and help to bring us closer to an appreciation of the Leviticus meaning of holiness.

ENDNOTES

1. For James L. Kugel's interpretation of biblical holiness see *How to Read the Bible*, 293–295.
2. See Mary Douglas *Purity and Danger: An Analysis of Concepts of Pollution and Taboo* for her working out of the idea of divisions and divine order as reflected in Leviticus.

3. J. H. Hertz, *The Pentateuch and Haftorahs*, 409.

4. Suggested by the late Rabbi Martin D. Gordon of Knesseth Israel Synagogue, Gloversville, New York.

5. See Chapter Thirteen, *The Seventh Plague*, Endnote 10, with reference to Douglas' concept of divine order, which also applies to Israel's dietary laws, Leviticus 11. Paula Tobenfeld suggests that a traditional way to look at such laws is "to make the point that we cannot ever hope to understand all the ways (including laws and other statutes) of HaShem. In other words, the prohibition against mixing linen and wool (*shaatnez*) and other statutes teach us humility!"

6. Everett Fox, *The Five Books of Moses*, 593.

7. If the distance was too far to transport the crop to Jerusalem, the farmer had the option of converting it into money for the value of the crop (a form of self-taxation) and spending the money in Jerusalem on "anything you want—cattle, sheep, wine, or other intoxicant, or anything you may desire" (Deuteronomy 14:24-26), as for *Ma'aser Sheni*, the second tithe. See commentary to tractate *Orla* in the *ArtScroll Mishna Series*, 37. Also the last chapter of tractate on *Ma'aser Sheni*. Reader Elaine Solowey notes that even today in Israel very few people will eat *orla* fruit (that is, forbidden fruit). To clarify tithes: "Numbers refers to a 'first tithe' [a tenth] of produce given to the Levites, who give a tithe of that to the priests. Deuteronomy 13:21-27 and Leviticus 27:30-31 refers to a 'second tithe,' taken from the remaining ninety percent of produce, which is to be eaten by the owners at sacral feasts in Jerusalem, as is the tithe on cattle (Leviticus 27:32-33). The 'second tithe' on produce is replaced, in the third and sixth years of each sabbatical cycle (see Deuteronomy 15:1), by a 'third tithe' or 'tithe for the poor,' to which Deuteronomy 14:28-29 refers. It is given to the poor and Levites in the farmers' hometowns." Jeffrey Tigay, *The JPS Commentary, Deuteronomy*, 141.

8. Reader Elaine Solowey confirms this practice and adds that buds may also be left on the tree for the birds; Nogah Hareuveni refers to the practice of removing the tree's flowers before they form embryonic fruit in *Tree and Shrub in Our Biblical Heritage*, 46.

9. The NJPS translation of this verse begins "Follow none but the Lord your God . . . " Tigay explains that "walk after," although literally correct, is a biblical idiom against apostasy based on ancient Near Eastern political terminology in which "walking after" a king or a suzerain means giving them one's allegiance. Hence "walking after" another God means defection from the Lord." Tigay, 130. In any case, translations of this phrase differ from one edition to the other.

10. This midrash, Leviticus *Rabba* 25,3, is discussed in Barry W. Holtz ed., *Back to the Sources*, 201.

11. Asaph Goor and Max Nurock, *The Fruits of the Holy Land*, 3.

12. Ibid., 262. Considering that carob was used mainly as animal fodder and only eaten by the poor, it is ironic that "carat," a unit of weight for precious stones, as in carats of gold, is ultimately derived from seeds of this lowly fruit.

13. Goor and Nurock, 3. Individual chapters on these fruits discuss whether they were indigenous (native to the land) or were introduced from elsewhere, and how they were developed. This is a complex subject. The reader is also referred to Michael Zohary, *Plants of the Bible* and Daniel Zohary, Maria Hopf, *Domestication of Plants in the Old World*.

14. Josephus (*The Jewish Wars*, III, 10, 8), cited in Goor and Nurock, 11.

15. References to widespread interest in Israel's fruit trees are cited in Goor and Nurock, 10.

16. Ibid., 1.

17. Illustrated in Goor and Nurock, 99.

18. In the Deuteronomy passage the injunction to be charitable to the poor is vividly linked to the Israelites' redemption from slavery by God: "When you beat down the fruit of your olive-trees, do not go over them again; that shall go to the stranger, the fatherless, and the widow. When you gather the grapes of your vineyard, do not pick it over again; that shall go to the stranger, the fatherless, and the widow." This is followed by the refrain: "Always remember that you were a slave in the land of Egypt; therefore do I enjoin you to observe this commandment."

Chapter Twenty-One

THE FOUR SPECIES OF *SUKKOT*: A SACRED BOUQUET

Portion-*Emor* / Speak (Leviticus 21:1-24:23)

On the fifteenth day of the seventh month, when you have gathered in the yield of your land, you shall observe the festival of the Lord seven days . . . On the first day you shall take the fruit of beautiful trees, branches of palms, and boughs of thick tree-foliage, and willows of the brook; and you shall rejoice before the Lord your God seven days.[1] (Leviticus 23:39-40)

Leviticus moves on to laws regulating what has been called "holiness in time: the sacred calendar."[2] The three Pilgrimage Festivals (Leviticus 23) are each based on the harvest of certain crops: barley on Passover (*Pesah*), wheat on *Shavuot*, and late-ripening tree and vine fruits on *Sukkot*. For Israel, however, celebrations limited to the seasons (as was the pagan practice), were not enough. While each holiday is tied to the rhythms of the agricultural year, so, too, is each connected with the people's remembrance of their history and special covenant with God at Sinai. The linking of physical events, rooted in the land, with a higher vision, was meant to

Photograph Wikimedia Commons

The Four Species/*Arba Minim*: citron/*etrog*; new date palm leaves/*lulav*; myrtle/*hadas*; willow/*arava*.

drive home the ideals of ethical monotheism in a pagan environment. The Bible teaches over and over again, in different ways, that the success of the crops is dependent on the same God Who brought the people out of Egypt, the same "Lord [Who] is our God, the Lord [Who] is One" (Deuteronomy 6:4).[3] It is in acknowledgment of this debt to God that the farmer sacrificed any profit for himself from his newly planted fruit trees until their fifth year, expressed in the law of *orla*, and also the reason that he brought an offering of the finest of his first fruits to Jerusalem to be blessed in the ritual *mikra bikkurrim*. It is in this same spirit that *Shavuot* commemorates both the wheat harvest and God's gift of the Torah at Mount Sinai, and earlier, Passover commemorates both the barley harvest and the Israelites' redemption by God from slavery in Egypt. In this way, the physical and spiritual worlds are bound together and interdependent.

Sukkot, or Feast of Tabernacles, to be observed in the seventh month (later known as *Tishre*, now the first month of the Jewish civic calendar)[4] occurs at the end of the agricultural year just before winter rains inaugurate a new growing season, and is also bound to Israel's history and covenant. The festival's Hebrew name, *Sukkot*, meaning "huts," makes a direct link between the celebration of the harvest and the people of Israel's forty years' wandering in the desert after God had rescued them from slavery in Egypt: "Israel shall dwell in booths [huts], so that your generations will know that I made the Israelites dwell in booths [huts] when I brought them out of the land of Egypt. I am the Lord your God" (Leviticus 23:42-43). A sukka has to be loosely enough made so that the stars are visible through the branches; a sukka that does not fulfill this rule is not kosher. This is a reminder that all human constructions and dwellings are temporary and only the Lord and His works last forever. It is a striking example of superimposing history on agricultural reality, no matter how incongruous, for it is precisely at this time that farmers have left their hut-like shelters in the field.[5] With late crops—olives, grapes, figs, and dates—harvested, processed, and stored, safe from imminent rainfall, there is no longer a need to watch over them. Now, it would seem, is the time to come indoors to celebrate the harvest with a celebratory meal, as at Thanksgiving. Yet this is precisely the time—amidst the plenty of harvest in a settled land—when the people are commanded to camp out in a sukka (singular of the Hebrew *sukkot*) to honor the memory of their humble beginnings and their obligations to God.

—ɯ—

FOUR TREES, together known as The Four Species or *Arba Minim*, play an important role in the rituals of *Sukkot*, as they have from Temple times to our own day. Although the specific plants are not spelled out in the Bible, the rabbis of the Talmud discussed the subject at length and named the ones which they believed fulfill the biblical command. Known collectively as *lulav* after the date palm, the largest of the trees, they are citron/*etrog*—"fruit of beautiful trees" (or more familiarly, "goodly trees")—*lulav*, [new or unfolded] branches of [date] palms—myrtle/ *hadas*—"boughs of thick tree-foliage"—and willow/*arava*—"willows of the brook." When holding the *lulav*, myrtle and willow, bound together, and the citron by itself, a blessing is said every day of *Sukkot*, except the Sabbath (*Shabbat*), before entering the sukka and during the morning service in the synagogue,

Photograph © Joshua D. Klein

Citrus medica. Citron growing on the Coastal Plain. The white foam protects the delicate fruits from rubbing against each other.

at which times the bundles are waved in the four directions of the compass as well as up and down to indicate their all-encompassing blessing. When we examine each of these four tree species, we see how they reflect different aspects of the Land of Israel in the people's history and why they are appropriate choices on *Sukkot*.

Citron, (*etrog*), *Citrus medica*. The Bible's unnamed fruit, *pri etz hadar*, is traditionally regarded as a citron or *etrog*. Considered to be the progenitor of all citrus fruit, it was probably introduced to countries in the Near East from India at a very ancient date.[6] It is a small, graceful, although very thorny, tree, from ten to twenty feet tall, whose evergreen leaves, white flowers, and yellow fruits exude a heady floating aroma. No wonder the rabbis of the Talmud were so taken with it. No other fruit tree came up to the citron's standard of perfection: the pomegranate, for instance, was acknowledged to bear beautiful fruit, but it is not a beautiful tree; carob, on the other hand, is a beautiful tree that bears homely fruit in long pods. "But where fruit and tree alike are beauty," the rabbis concluded, "that is the *etrog* alone" (Jerusalem Talmud, *Sukka* 3,5).

Photograph © Joshua D. Klein

Citrus medica. Citron (*etrogim*), all shapes, sizes, and colors, kosher for use on *Sukkot*. The small, very dark ones are borderline.

Larger than a lemon and oblong-shaped with bumpy, ridged yellow skin, the citron's most arresting feature is the remnant stigma and style, parts of the flower's reproductive organs, which protrude from the opposite end of the stem. Normally, after a flower has been fertilized, it's the stigma and style that wither as the embryonic ovary ripens to form a fruit. This does not happen with a citron. The stigma, resembling a rough knob, remains attached to the fruit by means of its tube-like style. It is this unique characteristic, called in Hebrew a *pitom* or nipple, that suggested citron as a symbol of fertility at *Sukkot*, expressing the hope for a fruitful year ahead. Its association with fertility is also suggested by the fruits' tendency to remain on trees year round, growing larger over time. To be acceptable for ritual use the *etrog* must possess a *pitom*, even though the fruit may be blemished (but only if the area around the *pitom* is clear of blemish), and in different shapes, sizes, and colors.[7] Figuratively speaking, if you've bought an *etrog* without a *pitom*, you've bought a "lemon!" To protect the *pitom* from breaking off, the *etrog* is carried in a special protective container.

In biblical times, both the citron's beautiful wood and its fruit were in demand.[8] Citron also has a history of medicinal use in preparations to alleviate sea sickness as well as pulmonary and intestinal ailments. When its acidic juice was combined with wine it was considered an effective purgative against poison. The essential oil, extracted from the fruit's outer skin, was thought to possess healing and cleansing properties. The fruit, largely rind, was eaten fresh, pickled, or boiled. While modern tastes would probably not find it appealing, it is well to remember that citron was the only citrus fruit then available.[9] Today its use is largely confined to turning the fruit's very thick rind into candied peel, widely used in making fruit cakes. In the post-*Sukkot* season, however, "etrog jam," made at home or available in specialty food markets, is highly prized.

Photograph © Ori Fragman

Phoenix dactylifera. Date palm near Jericho, Lower Jordan Valley.

Date palm (*lulav*), *Phoenix dactylifera*. The tree's Latin name is thought to be associated with the intensive cultivation of date palms in the coastal regions of ancient Phoenicia. The wild progenitors of these date palms could have been selected from wild specimens growing in desert oases as in Israel's Aravah Valley.[10] Its Hebrew name, *tamar*, is derived from "to be upright," and is a popular female name in many cultures. In the ritual of carrying the *lulav* it is the young palm leaf which is used. Derived from *lev*, meaning heart, the *lulav* perfectly describes a young unfolded palm frond, one that grows straight up like a stick from the heart of older leaf clusters, as if reaching for the sky. This characteristic suggested victory, as the upright tree itself was associated with the virtues of a righteous, upright person: "The righteous shall flourish like the palm tree" (Psalms 92:13-14). The tree's form, with its tall, straight trunk and arching branches, added beauty and gracefulness to its symbolic virtues, qualities associated with the biblical character, Tamar, who was driven to seduce her father-in-law in order to perpetuate her dead husband's name; she bore Perez, a predecessor of the royal line. As Judah observed, and tradition affirmed, "She is more righteous than I" (Genesis 38:26).

Date palms have great presence, whether massed in plantations or growing wild in a desert oasis, where they indicate water (fresh to saline).[11] Straight, unbranched trunks growing up to more than eighty feet bear clusters of huge, arching pinnate leaves composed of many leaflets arranged in two rows along a common stalk. As leaves are shed each season they are replaced by new clusters. Male and female flowers grow separately in dense bunches on separate trees. Pollen from the male plant is carried by the wind to female flowers, and after fertilization, the dense bunches of flowers mature into heavy hanging fruit clusters. Even in ancient times date palms were hand-pollinated to ensure more precise fertilization; a single male tree can supply enough pollen to fertilize twenty-five to fifty female trees, so not many are needed. For serious fruit production, propagation was (and still is) by offshoots from desirable female trees, since seedlings would produce inferior fruit and an overpopulation of male trees.[12] Trees live for hundreds of years and even after fire, they send up new shoots, suggesting the date palm as a symbol of life, even of the fabled Tree of Life.[13]

The biblical cultivation of dates was quite sophisticated. We think of plant breeding as a modern endeavor, but named varieties, types selected from among a population for their special qualities, are recounted in ancient literature, including the Mishna, which refers to several of them.[14] Stretching from the Sea of Galilee to the Dead Sea, the warm valley region was extensively cultivated and renowned throughout the Middle East for the quality of its dates. Here, the unchanging warmth was conducive to the production of semi-dry fruit which could be stored for long periods, while fruit grown in cooler, hill country was soft and had to be eaten fresh or it rotted. A 'mountain palm' was a byword for a man of little and profitless wisdom.[15]

The widespread cultivation of dates in biblical times and their importance in everyday life, their fabled medicinal properties,[16] and the date palm's positive symbolic associations, had an impact on Israelite consciousness as reflected in decorative motifs on synagogues, household objects, and coins. The Maccabees used the palm as an emblem of victory on their coins, while the Romans, aware of the date palm's significance, minted a bronze coin, "*Judea Capta,*" after the destruction of the Second Temple, which depicted a woman weeping beneath a date palm. The date palm had become synonymous with both the land and people of Israel.

Growing wild in desert oases, the date palm provides food, fiber, even fodder, for camping shepherds and their flock, now as in ancient times. Nearly every part of the plant has some use. Fibrous strips from the trunk can be braided into rope[17] and its leaves woven into baskets, mats, and household utensils. It is probable that the original *Sukkot* the Israelites dwelt in during their desert wanderings were made from dried-out date palm fronds, just as they are today by Bedouin shepherds.[18] The fruits can be eaten fresh or dried (a plus when traveling). Honey is pressed from the ripe fruit, a juice can be extracted from the tree's trunk, and ground date pits can be fed to camels. Not least of all, the stately date palm provides welcome shade. A date palm grove, even a single tree, is a blessing in the desert, as it must have seemed over three millennia ago to the wandering Israelites.

Both the citron and date palm are associated with water, one of the important themes of *Sukkot*: the cultivated citron must have plentiful water to bear fruit, and the date palm symbolizes the lush plant growth of the dry desert, due to the presence of underground springs. The water theme is carried out in the daily prayer for rain recited beginning on the eighth day of *Sukkot* and continuing until the first day of Passover—the onset of the dry season—when the prayer for dew is substituted (moisture *in any form* was vital for the success of crops on which all life depended). In Temple times elaborate water libation ceremonies were enacted in the Temple, starting at the end of the first day of *Sukkot* and repeated every day except the Sabbath (*Shabbat*). From this distance in time and culture, we

Photograph © Ori Fragman

Myrtus communis. Wild myrtle, lower Mount Hermon.

may not appreciate the depth of anxiety concerning the presence or absence of rain in biblical life when the majority of the population was engaged in dry farming agriculture. After fall ploughing, sown crops were dependent on natural rainfall for successful seed germination and proper growth.

The last two plant species are especially symbolic of the preoccupation with water on *Sukkot.*

Myrtle (*hadas*), *Myrtus communis.* Myrtle is an evergreen glossy-leaved shrub of Israel's riverine thickets and *maquis* that grows not only in damp plains along the banks of the Jordan River and Dan Valley, but also on hillsides, mainly on the Golan and Upper Galilee. The genus name *Myrtus* may be derived from the Greek *myron*, meaning myrrh, a reference to the high oil content and sweet fragrance of myrtle's plentiful, stiff foliage. Five-petalled flowers with prominent fluffy stamens bloom in the dry summer (as do many other maquis shrubs) followed by blackish-blue berries. It was Rabbi Yehuda bar Ilai, one Rabbi Akiva's last students, who proposed that the myrtle be called the "leafy tree." He recommended using branches that had three leaves growing from each node (an occurrence after fire), rather than the usual one.[19] Triple-leaved myrtle, *meshulashim*, are still sought for ritual use by very observant Jews.

Myrtle is an impressive example of a plant adapted to wet winter/dry summer conditions. Its leathery leaves absorb and hold onto enough water during the winter months to protect the plant from drying out during the summer when, although no rain falls, it is not only able to survive but to produce flowers! This ability to manage without rain is indicated when its cut branches remain fresh and upright even when they are not put in water. In the *lulav* ritual this characteristic symbolizes success for the coming agricultural year. The myrtle's associations with success, or good luck, and upright character are preserved throughout the Bible and Talmud: "He who sees a myrtle in his dream, his property will prosper. If he has no property, he will receive an inheritance from somewhere else" (*Brakhot* 57a). Esther's original Hebrew name was *Hadassah* (the female form of *hadas*), because, the rabbis said, she was just, and "those who are just are compared to myrtle" (*Targum*).

The medicinal uses of myrtle are legion, not only in the Holy Land, but throughout the world. These include using the oil of myrtle to relieve earaches and clear the respiratory system, when prepared in tea to reduce fevers and treat colds, and in powders to treat skin conditions (especially on babies). An extract from its flowers was thought to improve blood circulation, and dried leaves have been used to scent skin creams. Scientific research has confirmed oil of myrtle as an effective germicide.[20] Cultivated myrtle is universally admired and is often grown as a hedge.

Willow (*arava*). Willows that grow by water, as described in Leviticus, are acceptable for use as one of the Four Species. Two willows in Israel, *Salix acmophylla* and *S. alba*, as well as poplar or Euphrates poplar, *Populus euphratica*, grow along riverbanks and near streams. The common willow has sharp pointed oblong foliage,

Photograph © Ori Fragman

Salix alba. Common willow by the Hatzbani River, one of the sources of the Jordan River in the north.

while the poplar willow produces two types of foliage: new leaves are oblong—similar in shape to those of *Salix*—while older leaves are rounded. This characteristic suggested the Hebrew name for willows, *arava*, from the root "mix." [21] It is on the branches of the Euphrates poplar, rather than on the familiar weeping willow (*S. babylonica*), an Asian species, upon which the exiles "hung up our lyres [on]," by the rivers of Babylon (Psalms 137:1-2).

In contrast to myrtle, willow boughs bend and wilt as soon as they are out of the soil, so in Temple times fresh branches were brought daily to decorate the altar. In the ritual of *lulav*, willows are a graphic reminder of the people's dependence on water. On the sixth day of *Sukkot, Hoshana Rabbah* (The Great Hoshana), there are seven processions around the synagogue rather than the usual one, known as *Hoshanot* (Save us!). On this occasion, willow boughs are beaten on the ground until all their leaves fall off (perhaps to mimic the sound of running water). It is the last plea for water until the following day when the prayer for rain is instituted.

Whatever their symbolism, The Four Species represent different habitats in the Land of Israel, each with its special water requirements,

Photograph © Ori Fragman

Populus euphratica. Euphrates poplar at Neot Kedumin, Israel's Biblical Landscape Reserve.

and as we have seen, they can be very different, from drought-tolerant myrtle to water-hungry citron.

Maimonides (Rambam), the great twelfth century rabbinic authority, philosopher, physician, and interpreter of Jewish law, understood the meaning of the Four Species as symbols that express the Israelites' rejoicing in having left the desert, a wretched place, "with no grain, or figs, or vines, or pomegranates, or water to drink" (Numbers 20:5) and having arrived in a country full of fruit trees and rivers (*Guide for the Perplexed*). Commentating on Maimonides, Ephraim and Hannah Hareuveni (through the work of their son, Nogah), take this thought further: the Four Species represent the historical move from the desert to the establishment of agriculture in the Promised Land. According to this interpretation, the date palm represents desert life; the willow of the brook stands for the plants that grew along the Jordan River where the tribes entered Israel; the thick-leaved trees or forests that covered the wild hill country are symbolized by myrtle. These plants tell the story of the nation's history while the people rejoice in the fruit of the harvest, epitomized by the fruit of beautiful trees, the cultivated citron. In this way the symbolism of the Four Species teaches the same lesson of humility as the recitation associated with the offering of first fruits, *mikra bikkurim*: it is God, not they themselves, Who has led the people through the desert to the Promised Land and blessed their harvest.[22]

Beyond their agricultural symbolism, the Four Species have generated an extensive literature of stories (*midrashim*) on their moral and ethical associations. In one of the most famous, each plant is considered for its attributes: "The *etrog* is aromatic and tasty like those who combine study of Torah with the practice of good deeds. The *lulav* is tasty, but has no fragrance, like those who study but do not perform good deeds. The myrtle has aroma but no taste, like those who do good deeds but have no learning. The willow has neither aroma nor taste, like those who are both ignorant and do not perform good deeds: What does the Lord do since He does not want Israel to perish? He binds all four species together so that those with taste and aroma—learning and good deeds—redeem the others. Thus, bound together, Israel endures forever (*Vayikra Rabba* 30).

The Four Species, *Lulav* (bound date palm, myrtle, and willow) and *etrog* are available at *Sukkot* in specialty markets. Their ritual use at

Sukkot would never have survived after Temple times if the ritual was tied merely to agriculture or to one place, the Holy Land. When Jews dispersed, they carried the land and its holy associations with them, integrated into festive observance. In this way, the Four Species have retained a presence on *Sukkot* for millennia as a sacred bouquet with deep roots in both the Land of Israel and Judaism.

ENDNOTES

1. I have used the NJPS translation except for the four species, i.e. "fruit of beautiful trees," etc., where Everett Fox's *The Five Books of Moses* is said to come closer to the original Hebrew.
2. Fox, 616.
3. Nogah Hareuveni in *Nature in Our Biblical Heritage* discusses the ongoing battle to inculcate monotheism in a people also influenced by pagan culture. See, for instance, his discussion of the Bible's continuous battle against polytheism, known as 'serving two altars,' (29) and his remarks concerning the "reading for the offering of the first fruits" (*mikra bikkurim*) which emphasize the Oneness of God (50). T. H. Gaster in *Festivals of the Jewish Year* stresses throughout how Israel transformed purely seasonal celebrations to reflect its history and covenant with God.
4. The biblical seventh month is counted from the first of *Nisan,* based on the biblical account of the Exodus from Egypt which marks the great dividing line in the people's history from slavery to freedom ("This month shall mark for you the beginning of the months; it shall be the first of the months of the year for you," Exodus 12:2). In Jewish 'time' there are different New Years, depending on their purposes. In the Mishna, the rabbis cite four different New Years (Rosh Hashana 1,1). Two of them are agricultural: the first one for planting trees and vegetables, the latter for calculating the New Year of the fruit trees. In the modern Jewish or Hebrew calendar the beginning of *Tishrei* corresponds to the Jewish New Year, Rosh Hashana (head of the year).
5. Hareuveni, 69.
6. Asaf Goor and Max Nurock, *The Fruit of the Holy Land,* 152.
7. Reader Michael Solowey adds that this is usually ascertained by circling the end of the fruit with thumb and forefinger, around the *pitom.*
8. "Citron wood," however, may be "thyine wood" from *Tetraclinis articulata,* also known as "citron" or "citrus" for its fragrance.
9. Medicinal and culinary uses of citron are cited in Irene Jacob, *Biblical Plants: A Guide to the Rodef Shalom Biblical Botanical Garden,* 16 and Miriam Feinberg Vamosh, *Food at the Time of the Bible,* 48.
10. Michael Zohary, *Plants of the Bible,* 60.
11. Avinoam Danin, *Desert Vegetation of Israel and Sinai,* 121.

12. Reader Elaine Solowey ran the date orchard at Kibbutz Ketura in the Arava Valley for ten years. She described to me how offshoots grow on date palms and how they are separated from the parent plant: both male and female date palms produce offshoots; these have a woody connection to the parent plant and have to be whacked off with a strong tool (Elaine used a chisel made from a plow blade). Offshoots appear at ground level or above. The ground level ones usually have roots unlike those above ground. The above-ground offshoots are usually rooted in a sack of sawdust or peat moss that is tied around their bottom, with a very small drip line attached to maintain moisture. The resulting plants are complete individual specimens, genetically identical to the parent plant. Readers may be familiar with this phenomenon from cacti or succulent offshoots (also called "offsets").

13. Goor and Nurock, 123.

14. Ibid., 133. Authors cite '*talli*,' which grew in Babylon and Israel, and '*shalfufa*' which is mentioned in the Babylonian Talmud. They go on to note that "Among the better kinds, apparently, is '*ahini*', in name resembling the superior '*hayani*' of today [late 1960s], which is extensively grown in Egypt and Sinai and described as a red date. '*Hayani*,' in Semitic import, belongs to the radical for 'existence,' and that, perhaps links up with the inclusion of the date in the list of competitors for the title of 'Tree of Life'; after all, Eve herself, in Hebrew '*Hava*,' was so named, as the author of Genesis expounds with a startling anticipation of modern philology, because she was the Mother of all the living."

15. Ibid., 131.

16. The now extinct Judean date palm was renowned in ancient times for treating heart disease, chest problems, weakened memory, and possibly symptoms of cancer and depression. Judy Siegel, "Ancient date seed from Masada may yield 'medicinal' bounty," *International Jerusalem Post*, June 20–26, 2008. This was the year the world's media reported the astonishing news of the successful germination of a two-thousand-year-old date seed, one of three discovered in the 1963 excavations at Masada, King Herod's desert palace in Judea overlooking the Dead Sea, where in 73 CE Jewish defenders from Jerusalem took over the palace and made a last stand against the Roman assault. The date seeds, found in a Masada store room and kept in storage, are presumed to have been eaten by the defenders, and Carbon-14 dating confirms that the seeds came from trees that grew when the Romans ruled the land. Elaine Solowey, in her work at the Arava Institute for Environmental Studies, was asked by Dr. Sarah Salon of the Natural Medicine Research Unit of Hadassah Hospital, Ein Kerem, to try to germinate the ancient seeds in order to find out whether the Judean date palm had possible medicinal applications today. In 2005 Elaine planted the pits on *Tu Bishvat*, [a Jewish Arbor Day] for luck, after first soaking them in warm water with

plant hormones and enzymatic fertilizer made from seaweed. By 2007 "Methusalah," as she named the only one to germinate, was a three and a half foot tall flourishing seedling. If it proved to be a female, she observed, "we'll be able to know how dates tasted in Judea in ancient times," as reported in the Israeli newspaper, *Haaretz*, February 15, 2007. Methusalah flowered in 2011 and in answer to my query Elaine reported, "He is a boy, but his pollen may prove interesting." *Update*: Methusalah, now nearly eight feet tall, was planted in the ground on November 24, 2011, at Kibbutz Ketura, accompanied by a tree-planting ceremony. Today, although dates are still widely grown in the Jordan Valley, stock comes mostly from California, so viable authentic Judean date palm would have enormous possibilities.

17. I have a vivid memory of once standing with Avinoam Danin in front of a large date palm by a gas station/restaurant near the Dead Sea area. My friend casually stripped off some fibres from the date palm trunk and expertly twisted them into a strong rope. For instructions, see Avinoam Danin, *Desert Vegetation of Israel & Sinai*, 128–129.

18. Hareuveni, 75.

19. Ibid., 85.

20. D. Palevitch and Zohara Yaniv, *Medicinal Plants of the Holy Land*, 96.

21. The Hebrew name for the poplar willow is *tzaftzafat ha-prat*, but after the destruction of the Temple the names for willow and poplar were confused and switched. To avoid confusion over which willow to use on *Sukkot*, the rabbis differentiated between the poplar willow and the mountain willow (*tzaftzafa*). The former, because it grows by water, was considered a "willow of the brook," and therefore acceptable to use as one of the Four Species, while the latter was not, because it grows in mountainous areas (*Sukka* 34a). For a detailed discussion and illustrations of the Four Species from a rigorously observant viewpoint, see Rabbi Yechiel Michel Stern, *Halachos of the Four Species*, 128–150. For a general discussion of the Four Species see Hareuveni, 76–86.

22. Hareuveni, 76–78. See Chapter Thirty-Four, "First Fruits."

Chapter Twenty-Two

THE HOLY LAND

Portion-*Behar Sinay* / At Mount Sinai (Leviticus 25:1-26:2)

When you enter the land that I assign to you, the land shall observe a sabbath of the Lord. Six years you may sow your field and six years you may prune your vineyard and gather in the yield. But in the seventh year the land shall have a sabbath of complete rest, a sabbath of the Lord. (Leviticus 25:1-4)

Photograph © Avinoam Danin.

Olea europaea. The stone walls of this ancient terraced slope are still maintained in an Ein Kerem olive grove.

There is nothing holy about dirt. But for Jews the very soil in the Land of Israel, and everything that grows from it, becomes holy when God's children live on it and observe His commandments. The seventh day Sabbath or *Shabbat* (meaning "to cease" or "rest') is a unique institution with no parallels in the ancient world,[1] and was considered by God to be so important that He taught the newly-freed slaves to practice it in the desert (Exodus 16) even before they had reached Sinai and formally accepted the covenant. It naturally follows that if the people of Israel rest on the seventh day to honor God's rest on the seventh day after His labors of creation, then the land to which He brought them, and which He blesses through their obedience to Him, must have its rest too. Every seven years the people were to observe a Sabbatical Year.[2] What does this mean? The Sabbath of the land, to be observed in the seventh year, is an extension of the weekly Sabbath, but there are marked differences. In the weekly Sabbath, all work ceases for a single day, from sunset on Friday to an hour after sundown on Saturday, but during the Sabbath of the land, agricultural activity alone is to cease for an entire year. Since the settled Israelites lived mainly as farmers in an agrarian society, observing the Sabbatical Year would have far-reaching consequences.

The biblical laws regarding the seventh year, known as the Sabbatical Year, Year of Release, and *Shmitta* (from "fallow" or "release") are first mentioned in Exodus and express concern both for the land and its poorest people: "Six years you shall sow your land and gather in its yield; but in the seventh you shall let it rest and lie fallow." In addition to the land's Sabbath, "Let the needy among your people eat of it, and what they leave let the wild beasts eat. You shall do the same with your vineyards and your olive groves" (Exodus 23:10-11). In Leviticus the land is personified and explicitly linked to Sabbath rest: "When you enter the land that I assign to you, the land shall observe a sabbath of the Lord" (Leviticus 25:2). Like the weekly Sabbath, the year of release is meant to be more than a cessation of activity, a prohibition with negative import. The command to keep "a sabbath of [to] the Lord" is regarded as a positive one, the soil being devoted to Him as a reminder that the "earth is the Lord's" (Exodus 9:29), as the Sabbath day is a reminder of the earth as God's creation. The law of redemption of land by its original owners is here developed; sales and mortgages of land are conditional and must be redeemable when the original owner "acquires enough [money] to redeem with" (Leviticus 25:23-25).

In addition to fallowing the land and the law of land redemption, in Deuteronomy release in the seventh year is associated also with the remission of debts between Israelites (Deuteronomy 15:2) and the release of Hebrew slaves (Deuteronomy 15:12). Slaves are not only to be freed, they are to be given sheep from the owner's flocks and a supply of grain, and wine, because as God reminds His people: "Bear in mind that you were slaves in the land of Egypt and the Lord your God redeemed you, therefore I enjoin this commandment [to redeem the slaves] upon you today" (Deuteronomy 15:15). A further reference in Deuteronomy mentions a public reading of the Torah at the end of the *Shmitta* year and just before the Feast of *Sukkot* (Deuteronomy 31:10), as a testimony of faith in God though there has been no harvest for which to give thanks.

The Leviticus way of regarding every part of the material world, even dirt, as belonging to the realm of the holy when sanctified by observance of God's commandments, is fundamental to Judaism's moral and ethical vision, and is reflected in the laws of the Sabbatical Year. Four agricultural and horticultural activities are explicitly forbidden: sowing and harvesting grain, pruning grapevines, and harvesting grapes and olives. It is no accident that this group of plants—grains, grapes, and olives—are singled out for special attention in the Bible, for they are the basic crops of the land on which life depends, so observing the prohibitions regarding them would be a true test of the farmer's fidelity to God. The Mishna's tractate *masekhet shvi'it*, in the Jerusalem Talmud's Order of Seeds (*Seder Zerai'im*), expands on what is permissible and what is prohibited during the Year of Release. Discussions and rulings reflect an astonishing familiarity with all the activities that were generally pursued by the Israelite farmer: clearing away stones in fields, hoeing, manuring, making basins (depressions) to catch rain water for irrigation, the many aspects of pruning, thinning branches, shortening canes, shaping vines, and topping them for regeneration, even wrapping vines for defense against sun or cold, dusting, fumigating, and coating them against attack by disease or insects. Anyone who has ever farmed the land or even grown a little backyard garden will recognize these as basic activities necessary for the health of plants.

During the *Shmitta* year, and even during the sixth year, these activities were forbidden, presumably because they could improve the fields (or look like improvements), and thereby improve the seventh year yield of fruit or grain, also forbidden. It is difficult for us to imagine now, when most people live far from the sources of food production, what a challenge the *Shmitta* year was in an agrarian society, where the vast majority of the population was directly involved in farming and horticulture. These were not just enjoyable leisure activities as they are for so many today, they were vital to existence and affected everyone directly.

The utopian social implications are striking. The Year of Release acknowledges that God, not man, is the ultimate owner of the land ("the earth is the Lord's"), so if the land does not truly belong to any one person, then during the seventh year the landowner has no special claim to it or its produce, and anyone—his laborers and indentured servants, his draft animals, even wild beasts—are allowed equal access (Leviticus 25:6,7). By this means, every seven years the wealthy landowner and the landless servant become equals, certainly a humbling experience for the landowner (and liberating for the servant!). Both would prepare only small amounts of olive oil and wine for household use, since harvesting large amounts for sale was prohibited. Rather than employ the usual methods—an animal or human-powered olive or wine press—during the Year of Release the landowner would be reduced to using the same methods as the poor: olive oil would be pressed out by hand in a small container called a *bodeidah*, grapes crushed in a small wooden tub.[3] The scope of *Shmitta* extended to draft animals which, because they would have less to do in the year of release, observed a kind of Sabbath. A concern for the rest of animals was an integral part of the Sabbath of the land for it emphasized that they are a part of the natural and agricultural world which man must cease to dominate during the seventh year.[4] In the Leviticus view, basic to Judaism, there is no separation between the material and moral world. To live a moral life, for instance, one should follow certain dietary rules ("*kashrut*" from "kosher"), and in the Land of Israel, set aside fourth year fruit for sanctification (*orla*), leave the corners of the field unharvested for the poor to glean (*pe'ah*), and in the seventh year dedicate the land to God. In these ways, the material and moral worlds are interdependent, as in the Mishna's saying, "If there is no flour, there is no Torah; if there is no Torah, there is no flour" (*Pirkei Avot* 3,21).

Some have suggested that the Sabbatical Year's laws regarding fallowing the land are the first recorded agricultural policy to provide for replenishment of the soil.[5] Fallowing, that is, leaving a field unsown to restore its fertility after intensive cultivation (as the Israelites pursued), is a form of crop rotation, a very ancient practice. In ancient Israel, a field was planted one year, then left fallow the next. Otherwise, unless some form of fertilizer was added, planting the same field year after year would result in a severe decline in production. In ancient Israel, a fallowed field was not just allowed to rest, but was plowed five to seven times to rid it of noxious weeds.[6] In marked contrast, during the *Shmitta* year, *all* land in Israel was to be fallowed at the same time every seven years, irrespective of necessity, and was not ploughed at all. It is obvious that the health of the soil was not the reason for the Year of Release, although the land may have benefitted. It may also have suffered. Opportunist weeds, the proverbial 'thorns and thistles,' would have invaded untended fields, feeding off their extra nutrients.

Another view is that the *Shmitta* year was not about replenishing the soil, but rather represented a unique and radical attempt to restore the spiritual health of the people by purifying what was felt to be a corrupted agrarian society. This would be accomplished, it was hoped, by returning once every seven years to a semblance of the idyllic period (or perceived to be idyllic) of the people's pre-farming, pastoral desert heritage, when common possession of the land, tribal solidarity, and an altogether less complex society prevailed.[7] In Jewish tradition, shaped by the land, shepherding, in contrast to farming, was regarded nostalgically as the real roots of the people, as the shepherd himself represented purity of spirit and the ideal leader (as in the Patriarchs, and Moses and David, both of whom served apprenticeships as shepherds). This attitude, evident at the very beginning of Genesis in the story of Cain, the farmer, and Abel, the shepherd, whom God preferred, prevailed long after most Israelites were no longer shepherds, as can be seen in the imagery throughout the Bible, drawn from shepherd life. The people themselves are often referred to as God's flock, as God Himself is their shepherd: "Like a shepherd He pastures His flock: He gathers the lambs in His arms and carries them in His bosom" (Isaiah 40:11). There is a very practical reason why farming was regarded as the source of the people's corruption. The difficulties inherent in farming in the Land of Israel (problems associated with the land and climate) tended to lure farmers away from their trust in God to worship pagan idols, as insurance against crop failure.[8] A return to simpler shepherding times, where the complexities involved in tilling the soil and raising crops, where debt release and the redemption of land were not issues, was seen as a social corrective. The Sabbatical or *Shmitta* Year, when considered in this light, was an attempt at social leveling (landowner and servant and slave were all equal in the *Shmitta* year), and a way to bring the people back to God.

Following seven Sabbatical cycles, that is, after forty-nine years, the Bible proclaimed the Jubilee on the fiftieth year. It was to be inaugurated following the Day of Atonement, Yom Kippur, by the blowing of the *shofar*, meaning "ram's horn" or *yovel*, after which the Jubilee Year is known in Hebrew. In addition to the Sabbath of the land, which would result in two consecutive fallow years, all hereditary property that had been sold was to be returned to its original owners or heirs, as the land had been distributed when Israel entered the Holy Land. (Leviticus 25:8-12). The Jubilee Year, as the rabbis deduced from the biblical text (Leviticus 25:10) no longer applied by the time of the Second Temple since all Jews did not then live in the land (*Sifra, Be-Har* 2:3).

Did the Israelite, and later Jewish,[9] farmers and the general populace ever observe the Sabbatical Year? From biblical accounts, the law of land redemption took root in the practical life of the Jewish population.[10] The Year of Release was probably not observed on any scale during the time of the First Temple, for the prophet Nehemiah records that the returning exiles from Babylon, following the destruction of the First Temple, assembled, and collectively agreed to dedicate themselves to rebuild the Temple and return to Torah laws. This renewal of dedication to Torah included a promise to fulfill the laws of the *Shmitta* year, in recognition that the calamities that had befallen them were the result of their transgressions against God (Nehemiah 1:7). For those farmers whose land was left untended, the sight of its current sorry state would have been devastating: unplanted, overgrown, fallowed fields, broken-down stone walls and thorn hedges to keep out grazing animals, unpruned trees and vines. Then the Leviticus warning, that failure to allow the land to rest in the seventh year would result in its desolation, must have seemed prophetic and bitterly ironic. The land, God had warned, will make up for the sabbath rest the erring people had denied it: "Throughout the time that it is desolate, it shall observe the rest that it did not observe in your sabbath years when you were living on it" (Leviticus 26:34).

It is not difficult to imagine the sorrow an agrarian people would feel for the uncared land of which they were once so proud. These are farmers, so close to the land, of whom it was said they could tell the right soil for growing figs, vines, or olives simply by smelling or tasting it![11] It is not so surprising, then, that they should have taken on the challenge of the Sabbath of the land in good heart, however difficult, during the whole of the Second Temple period, if they believed their failure to observe it had resulted in the land's desolation. They would rely on God's promise that He will bring "fruit for three years" in the sixth year (Leviticus 25:21), just as He had blessed His children in the desert with a double portion of manna on the sixth day so they could observe the Sabbath (Exodus 16:29). As recorded in Josephus' *Antiquities*, when Alexander the Great reached Jerusalem during his march through Israel, he acceded to the high priest's request that the Jews be exempted from paying tribute, because it was the Sabbatical Year when they did not work their land (*Antiquities* 11:338). Julius Caesar later reaffirmed the Jews' privilege of tax exemption during the Sabbatical Year since "they neither take fruit from the trees nor do they sow" (*Antiquities* 14:202).[12]

After the destruction of the Second Temple in 70 CE, Jewish farmers found it increasingly difficult to faithfully observe all the *Shmitta* agricultural laws. After the Bar Kokhba Revolt against Roman rule in 132–136 CE, the Roman government withdrew its previous tax exemption for the *Shmitta* year and the people's condition deteriorated. In view of this dire situation, the rabbis relaxed many prohibitions: the buying and selling of vegetables immediately after the close of the Sabbatical Year was now permitted, as was the importing of produce from the Diaspora. Farmers were permitted to till the soil right up to Rosh Hashana when *Shmitta* officially begins (it had been forbidden during the thirty days before the Sabbath Year), and now it was permitted to use the regular olive crushing machine to produce oil, rather than the more time-consuming and less efficient methods of the poor.[13]

The attempt to relieve indebtedness during the *Shmitta* year, to help the poor, was proving to be counterproductive, since lenders, knowing that debts would be cancelled in the year of release, refused to lend money to those who most needed it. Rabbi Hillel the Elder, concerned for the immediate daily needs of his people, issued a *prozbul* (based on a Greek term meaning roughly "in front of the court"), a legal device to encourage loans, whereby the lender, before the onset of the *Shmitta* year, turned over all the debts owed to him to a rabbinic court (*bet din*), which now had responsibility for collecting them. Because the debts were then owed to an institution (the court), rather than to an individual (the lender), they were not subject to the obligation of seventh year debt release which is only between individuals. In effect, the court became the guarantor of the debt which it could then collect for the lender anytime after the seventh year. Thus the lender was now protected against loss of the debt owed him, while the poor could more easily obtain a loan when they needed it.[14] This early rabbinic ruling was justified as *"mip'nei tikkun ha-olam,"* "for the sake of the order of the world" or "for the better organization of society," based on the Mishna's ruling that the presentation of a *get* (divorce document) must be in one's own name rather than an arbitrary name (*Gittin* 34b).[15] Hillel's innovative *prozbul* marked an important turning point in the evolution of rabbinic Judaism, by transforming some of the more impossibly utopian visions of the Mosaic code and the prophetic legacy into workable practice for the good of the people. While this view may seem to be a step down from the lofty ideals of the original Sabbath Year, it reflects as great a passion for achieving the possible in a difficult and complex world. After the destruction of the Temple and the gradual loss of their land, it was rabbinic Judaism's practical regulating system of *halakha* (a way of doing things) that succeeded in holding a defeated and dispersed people together wherever they went, even to the far ends of the earth.

Throughout the vicissitudes of Jewish history, observance of the Sabbatical year was little more than academic, since it is only to be observed by Jews living in the Holy Land. By the late nineteenth century when Jews again farmed the land in significant numbers, the issue of how to observe *Shmitta,* limited now to its central command to fallow the land, was debated. There were those rabbinical authorities who pushed for the restoration of full land release (with all its attendant laws), but the more lenient view took into account the hardships that already existed among Jewish farmers and the possible famine that might result in the struggling *yishuv,* Jewish settlement. Following in Hillel's footsteps, for the good of the people, they instituted *heter mechira,* whereby Jewish-owned land was sold to a gentile for a nominal sum for the duration of the seventh year, then, by agreement, returned to the previous owner. This effectively took the land and its produce out of the realm of holiness and it became ordinary soil for the duration of the *Shmitta* year and could be worked and products sold in the usual way, although there were still some restrictions. In addition, an early sowing of vegetables before the New Year was permitted.[16]

Today *heter mechira* still exists in Israel, although it was originally regarded as a temporary measure. Still, every sixth year before *Shmitta,* issues related to its observance are hotly debated among observant and non-observant. Observance is seen by the non-religious as voluntary acts of piety, and for those who wish to follow its regulations there are several strategies. Jewish farmers may go the route of *heter mechira,* or otherwise pursue ingenious methods to avoid planting in the ground. The most common is to grow vegetables hydroponically, using just water and nutrients rather than soil; another is to raise vegetables in pots filled with a soilless medium (this method is commonly used to grow plants in containers during the summer), and carefully place them in a greenhouse so that the pots never come in contact with seventh year holy soil. Observant consumers can buy refrigerated vegetables and fruits raised in the sixth year, imported food, or food raised by non-Jewish (mostly Arab) farmers.[17]

Some observant farmers, who feel that *heter mechira* is a violation of the principle of the Sabbatical Year, refrain from growing their usual crops, whether chickpeas, watermelons, corn, sunflowers, or wheat, and although they may have a hard time, they are faithful to God's demand to "let the land rest." For them, farming is a way of life, so there is no question of changing occupations to avoid the difficulty of observing *Shmitta*. "You develop sensitivities to the land," a farmer observed, "that the average person does not have. You feel the differences in the soil, the changes in the weather; you know when rain is coming, or when there will be a drought." [18] This sounds very much like farmers in the ancient land, or for that matter, farmers everywhere.

However imperfectly observed, the fact that the millennia-old legislation of *Shmitta* still provokes such lively debate and interest, is a testimony to the powerful and enduring ideal that "every stalk in the field proclaims the truth that God is the master and owner of the soil." [19]

ENDNOTES

1. Jacob Milgrom, *Anchor Bible Series, Leviticus,* Vol. 2, 132-2. Here, he also discusses the number "seven," symbolic of perfection and completion both in the Bible (as in creation's seventh day, seventh year, seven times seven Jubilee year, seven-day festivals, seven weeks between Passover and *Shavuot*), and in ancient Near East literature. It should be noted that although the date of the Bible's major festivals are based on agricultural rhythms, their seven-day observance is ultimately tied to God's time, as in the Torah's account of creation.

2. The origin of the term "sabbatical," as it refers to academic leave every seven years.

3. These processes are discussed in *Neot Kedumim News*, Fall 2000, "The Seventh Year," 4.

4. *Encyclopedia Judaica*, "Sabbatical Year and Jubilee," Vol. 14, 576.

5. *Neot Kedumim News*, "The Seventh Year," 5.

6. *Encyclopedia Judaica*, "Agricultural Methods and Implements in Ancient Eretz Israel," Vol. 2, 375. The special ploughing of fallow fields was referred to as *tiyyuv* (to improve) and *nir* (ploughed field) in Talmudic literature (*Tosefta, Shev.* 3:10; *Men.* 85a), to discourage weeds and keep the soil open (prevent it from becoming compacted).

7. This interpretation is suggested by David Lieber in "Sabbatical Year and Jubilee," *Encyclopedia Judaica* Vol. 14, 578.

8. See Nogah Hareuveni, *Nature in Our Biblical Heritage,* 30–38 and throughout, for detailed discussions of the complexity of farming in ancient Israel, represented by the opposing needs of the Seven Varieties [Species] and the consequent lure of pagan gods as a kind of insurance for successful crops.

9. The word "Jew" is not mentioned in the Hebrew Bible. The Patriarch Jacob's name was changed to "Israel," (meaning "struggle" or "He who fights with God"), following his struggle with the mysterious stranger

near the brook of Jabbok (Genesis 32:29), after which his descendants were called "Israelites," or "children of Israel." Later, descendants of the Tribe of Judah were referred to as *Yehudim*, and eventually became known as Jews.

10. I. Grunfeld, *Shemittah and Yobel*, 4. As examples, the author cites Jeremiah 32:7-8, Ezekiel 7:12; Ruth 4:7.

11. Cited in Asaph Goor and Max Nurock, *The Fruits of the Holy Land*, 58.

12. The history of *Shmitta* observance in Second Temple times is described in the *Encyclopedia Judaica*, 583–584.

13. Ibid., 584.

14. Ibid., 583.

15. *The Jewish Encyclopedia*, 219. There are three different concepts of *tikkun olam* in Jewish sources: The *Aleinu* prayer in the synagogue prayer book, recited at the end of the daily morning, afternoon, and evening services, refers to "perfecting [or repairing] the world under God's sovereignty," with the hope that one day all will recognize God and abandon idolatry. Another is in the Mishna (*Gittin* 4b), and is of a very practical nature (as in Hillel's *prozbul*). It refers to a practice which should be followed, not because it is required by biblical law, but because it helps avoid social chaos, that is, the practice is in the public interest. The third concept of *tikkum olam* from the Lurianic Kabbala, a seventeenth century Jewish mystic movement, is based on incremental spiritual efforts by every Jew to 'perfect the world' through prayer, ritual, and meditation.

16. *Encyclopedia Judaica*, 584.

17. The observance of the approaching *Shmitta* year in Israel was discussed in "'But in the seventh year....'" *The International Jerusalem Post*, 14–17, September 12–20, 2007.

18. Ibid., 17.

19. Grunfeld, 2.

Chapter Twenty-Three

TREE OF DESOLATION, TREE OF HOPE

Portion *Behukkotai* / If you walk in My laws (Leviticus 26:3-27:34)
 Haftarah (Jeremiah 16:19-17:14)

Cursed is he who trusts in man, Who makes mere flesh his strength, And turns his thoughts from the Lord. He shall be like a bush in the desert, Which does not sense the coming of good: It is set in the scorched places of the wilderness, In a [salty] barren land without inhabitant. (Jeremiah 17:5-6)

Blessed is he who trusts in the Lord, Whose trust is the Lord alone. He shall be like a tree planted by waters, Sending forth its roots by a stream: It does not sense the coming of heat, Its leaves are ever fresh; It has no care in a year of drought, It does not cease to yield fruit. (Jeremiah 17:7-8)

The *Haftarah* selection from Jeremiah is linked to this Leviticus Torah portion by the reiteration of the same theme: the people of Israel are free to choose their fate, God's blessing or His curse (Leviticus 26:3-43). In Leviticus "blessing" and "curse" are described in vivid images directly related to the people's lives as farmers in the land. If, for instance, they truly strive to

Photograph © Ori Fragman

Juniperus phoenicea.
Phoenician juniper, southern Jordan near Petra.

become a holy nation by following God's commandments, they will reap the benefits of His blessing in "rains in their season, so that the earth shall yield its produce and the trees of the field their fruit. Your threshing shall overtake the vintage, and your vintage shall overtake the sowing; you shall eat your fill of bread and dwell securely in your land" (Leviticus 26:3-5). If, on the other hand, the people abandon God and behave in ways that violate His moral and ethical code, they will bring down upon themselves a terrible curse: their land, so carefully cultivated, will become desolate. The "skies will be like iron and your earth like copper . . . Your land shall not yield its produce, nor shall the trees of the land yield their fruit" (Leviticus 26:19-20).

Jeremiah speaks to this same issue, but in a strikingly different way. For him, images of blessing and curse are drawn not from the farmer's life, but from the experiences of a seasoned shepherd. God's blessing on His people is exemplified by the fruitful tree "planted by waters," near a desert spring, while His curse is symbolized by the forlorn juniper tree, just managing to survive in the bare, waterless desert.

Who was the prophet Jeremiah? And why is his prophetic voice so distinctive?

Jeremiah (meaning "God elevates") was from the village of Anatot (Jeremiah 1:1), a few miles northeast of Jerusalem, between the hill country of the Tribe of Benjamin to the west, and the desert descending to the Dead Sea to the east, an area devoted to shepherding rather than farming. Descended from Hilkiah, one of Anatot's priests, Jeremiah was a shepherd, and so was intimately familiar with all the details of a shepherd's life: the importance of protecting his flocks from predators, and the need to lead the animals under his care to good grazing land and water. He was also intimately familiar with the way shepherds and farmers, Cain and Abel notwithstanding, co-exist harmoniously on the same land, each using it according to its features: in fertile hill country and valleys that were easy to cultivate, fruit trees and vineyards were established and grains were sown, while difficult steep areas and desert were left for grazing.[1] This arrangement, as far back as biblical times, is an early example of sensible land management.

Like Moses, Jeremiah was a reluctant prophet, arguing, when he was called upon by God, that he was young and inexperienced and didn't know how to speak (Jeremiah 1:6), but God knew Jeremiah's powers better than he did. He knew, for instance, that Jeremiah's experiences as a shepherd had strengthened his character to meet the challenges ahead, as shepherding had done for Moses. God needed Jeremiah's leadership qualities, honed as a shepherd, to try to turn His erring children away from the paths that were taking them away from Him, unraveling the special covenant forged at Sinai. Jeremiah knew the importance of choosing the best paths from his experience of leading flocks over difficult terrain, and the dire consequences that would result when a dangerous way was taken. God had chosen well.

Jeremiah's prophetic service began in the thirteenth year of the reign of King Josiah (627 BCE) and lasted until the fall of Jerusalem to the Babylonians in 587/586 BCE. Although he remained active in Judea and Egypt after the destruction of the Temple and the city of Jerusalem, Jeremiah's major prophetic role is associated with the last forty years of Judea as an independent state. He comes through the text as a real, feeling person, one who suffers for the defects of his people and yearns for the restoration of their covenant with God (Jeremiah 11:1-13; 33:1-26). That God chooses him to deliver the hard message of His punishment if they do not reform is agonizing to him (Jeremiah 11:18-23). With his contemporary, Ezekiel, he felt it was politic to submit to the rising Babylonian power (Jeremiah 25:1-29:32), was imprisoned for his view, then later thrown into a mud-pit (Jeremiah 32:1; 37:14-16; 38:6). Offered sanctuary in Babylon after the fall of Judea (Jeremiah 40:4-5), he refused, ending his days in exile in Egypt (Jeremiah 43:6-7).

Jeremiah's prophetic voice was infused with imagery directly drawn from his life as a shepherd. He began his prophetic service by reminding the people how they had followed God with devotion through "the wilderness, In a land not sown" (Jeremiah 2:2), "Who brought us up from the land of Egypt, Who led us through the wilderness, A land of deserts and pits, A land of drought and darkness" (Jeremiah 2:6), as the best shepherd would do for his flock, yet His people had abandoned Him. Jeremiah points to a failure of leadership in Judea: "My people were lost sheep: their shepherds misled them, the hills led them astray; they roamed from mount to hill [to worship false gods on high places] they forgot their own resting place" (Jeremiah 50:6). As Jeremiah sees it, the source of the people's temptation toward pagan worship is farming. Because of the complexities involved in successfully raising grains and fruits in a land with uncertain rains and drying, searing winds, the people turned to idol worship, afraid that reliance on God alone would be insufficient for the success of their crops.[2] For Jeremiah, shepherding, without the complexities of cultivating the land, offers a return to a state of purity and the renewal of worshiping God. He holds up the faithfulness of the Rechab family as an ideal. They neither built houses and sowed fields, nor planted vineyards; they eschewed drinking wine (as a symbol of cultivation) and preferred to live in tents (Jeremiah 35:1-10, 13-14), although they were not shepherds. This may be the first recorded theme of 'returning to the simple life,' a state of being where one is thought to be more 'in touch with nature,' where one is free to pursue life uncontaminated by the compromises and struggles inherent in day to day living in an ordinary environment with its many temptations. Jeremiah had to have known in his soul that a call for a return to the past, exemplified by the Rechab family's behavior, was purely utopian, for whatever calamities are to come (the burning of Jerusalem and the downfall of Judah are described in detail in Jeremiah 52), he holds out hope for rebuilding Zion in stirring terms; these encompass the full possibilities of viable Israelite life, combining farming with shepherding, as he had experienced this arrangement in his youth.

"Judah and all its towns alike shall be inhabited by the farmers and such as move about with the flocks" (Jeremiah 31:24). "I will build you firmly again, O Maiden Israel! Again you shall take up your timbrels And go forth to the rhythm of the dancers. Again you shall plant vineyards on the hills of Samaria; Men shall plant and live to enjoy them" (Jeremiah 31:4-5). "He Who scattered Israel will gather them, And will guard them as a shepherd his flock" (Jeremiah 31:10).

The biblical narrative often seems to go in different directions, and Jeremiah is, perhaps, juxtaposing two entirely different ideas for the future of his people, one based solely on shepherding, the other on the restoration of mixed farming and shepherding, thinking aloud about which one would be best for his people. The Leviticus legislation for *Shmitta*, as we have seen,[3] anticipates this conflict and resolves it by a symbolic return to the past in the context of a farming life.

JEREMIAH VENTS HIS WRATH against those who turn from God by comparing them to the most desolate tree specimen he can think of, *arar*, which some believe to be Phoenician juniper, *Juniperus phoenicea.*[4] Dramatically opposite in looks and habitat to the "juniper" (*brosh*)—a tall coniferous tree, or group of trees, with scale-like leaves that grows in forests[5]—the Phoenician juniper grows in Israel in desert conditions to only fifteen feet tall from a thick trunk. Its young branches bear needle-like leaves that change to scale-like leathery leaflets in maturity, light green to bluish-green, pressed tightly against twiggy growth. Its cones are berry-like, round in shape, fleshy, and reddish in color. The Phoenician juniper now grows mainly among rocky outcrops at high elevations in northern Sinai and Petra, in Jordan, but from fossil records it is believed that the remaining stands of *J. phoenicea* were once bridged by scattered growth all across the Negev. Jeremiah may have been referring to individual, desolate specimens that had survived during biblical times but are now extinct.[6] In any case, it appears to be a Mediterranean, rather than desert, species, so its appearance in the context of Jeremiah's metaphor for those who turn away from God, makes its point. Here is a tree that doesn't belong where it grows, is an anomaly, a lonely specimen occurring in scorched places and saline or salty soil, far away from human habitation with nothing to recommend it. It is not a pleasant thing to be compared to a Phoenician juniper!

Photograph © Ori Fragman

Juniperus phoenicea.
Phoenician juniper fruits,
southern Jordan near Petra.

Juniper trees in general are characterized by a resinous aroma in all their parts: wood, branches, and berries. Among the berries' most well-known uses is to flavor gin, but they have many medicinal applications, too: as an antiseptic, diuretic, stimulant, and to staunch bleeding.[7] The Bedouins of the Sinai and Israel use the resinous berries of Phoenician juniper to prepare incense for religious purposes.[8]

There is an entirely different way to regard Jeremiah's cursed "bush." According to painstaking research by his parents, Nogah

Hareuveni presents their case for the apple of Sodom, *Calotropis procera*, as the *arar* in Jeremiah's metaphor for those who turn from God, as well as for the lowly man (*arar*), whose prayers God does not spurn (Psalms 102:18).[9] The elder Hareuvenis based their identification partly on Jericho Bedouins' traditional association of the "cursed lemon," with the apple of Sodom, known in Arabic as *osher*. Although the fruit is large, yellow, and attractive, like an oversize lemon, it is actually fleshless, containing only flat seeds attached to tufts of fluff (similar to milkweed), which float away in the air as soon as the fruit is opened; its juice is poisonous. According to Bedouin shepherd folkways, whose traditions have been passed on for many generations, the fruit was once as juicy and tasty as it looked, but became cursed when it was associated with the sinners of Sodom and Gommorah. "When mankind repents of its evil ways," the Bedouin are taught, then "the fruit of the cursed lemon will be cleansed and its juice will be as delicious and satisfying as it was before the destruction of Sodom and Gommorah."[10]

The apple of Sodom is a peculiar-looking small tree from nine to fifteen feet tall loaded with fruit on corky stems. Its bark is peeling and its branches are full of milky latex, irritating to the skin. The tree grows in hot oases in the Dead Sea and Lower Jordan Valley. For a cursed tree it has a surprising number of good uses, including material for making ropes and fishnets from its stems, and filling for pillows and mattresses with its fleece-like inner seeds.[11]

It is not difficult to envision the fig tree, *Ficus carica*, as Jeremiah's symbol of the man who is blessed by his faith in God.[12] The symbolism of the 'cursed' as opposed to 'blessed' tree comes to life when we consider the special landscape of desert oases. For here, beside desert springs, fig trees flourish, impervious to extremes of heat and cold. These are conditions that in hill country, where they commonly grow, would adversely affect their growth and fruit production. Fig trees in other parts of the

Photograph © Joshua D. Klein

Ficus carica. Fruit bearing fig tree at the Volcani Center of Agricultural Research, Bet Dagan, near Tel-Aviv.

country, for instance, normally shed their leaves in the cooler winter temperatures, and bear fruit only from summer to fall; when they are steadily watered by desert springs, they seem to miraculously retain their foliage most of the year, and bear fruit almost continuously.[13] As the experienced shepherd Jeremiah knew from observation, the fruit-bearing fig tree "does not sense the coming of heat, Its leaves are ever fresh; It has no care in a year of drought, It does not cease to yield fruit (Jeremiah 17:8)." In the prophet's vision, God's blessing to Israel is vividly embodied in "a tree planted by waters," an ideal state which we can attain by trusting in Him.

ENDNOTES

1. Nogah Hareuveni explores the phenomenon of mixed farmholds in *Desert and Shepherd in Our Biblical Heritage*, 19.
2. Ibid., 21.
3. See Chapter Twenty-Two, "The Holy Land" for the suggestion that the reason for the *shmitta* legislation concerning the land was "a radical attempt to restore the spiritual health of the people by purifying what was felt to be a corrupted agrarian society," by returning to the perceived idyllic state of the people's pre-farming, pastoral desert heritage.
4. Michael Zohary, *Plants of the Bible*, 117.
5. The precise identity of "*brosh*," which occurs more than thirty times in the Hebrew Bible, is uncertain. Michael Zohary, in *Plants of the Bible*, 106–107, considers it a collective term for similar evergreen forest trees with tightly packed scale-like leaves. He includes under "*brosh*" the evergreen cypress, *Cupressus sempervirens*, rare in the Galilee, once common in the Judean Mountains; Cilician fir, *Abies cilicia*, which grows with cedar in Lebanon; and the cedar-like eastern savin, *Juniperus excelsa*, another coniferous species which grows in Lebanon in the same conditions as true cedar, *Cedrus libani*, as well as on Mount Hermon in Israel. See Chapter Fourteen, "Teaching Torah in the Field," for reference to "juniper" as a substitute for cedar in the ceremony of the leper.
6. Zohary 117. Avinoam Danin charts the distribution and fossil remains in *Desert Vegetation in Israel and Sinai*, 104.
7. Lise Manniche, *An Ancient Egyptian Herbal*, 110.
8. Danin, 105.
9. Hareuveni, 70-71.
10. Ibid.
11. Zohary, 122. The apple of Sodom is also discussed in Chapter Thirty-Six, *The Vine of Sodom*.
12. Hareuveni, 68.
13. Ibid., 68.

Introduction

THE BOOK OF NUMBERS

B'midbar

The name of the fourth book of the Torah, Numbers, is derived from the Greek *arithmoi*, and refers to the census-taking that occurs at the beginning of the Book. The Hebrew name, the fourth word in the opening sentence, *b'midbar* means "in the wilderness," and sets the scene for the Israelites' long, eventful, and protracted journey from Sinai to the Promised Land. In the desert they are faced with many challenges. They rebel against Moses and God, and are punished. Only their free-born children (and Caleb, who argued, along with Joshua, in favor of the conquest of Canaan), further instructed in laws and ordinances, and with a new leader (Joshua), will be permitted to enter the land. They gather on the plains of Moab, another census is taken, future borders are outlined, and they prepare for the conquest.

Photograph © Nell Gardner

Citrullus lanatus. Watermelons for sale at Wegman's Supermarket, Rochester, New York.

Chapter Twenty-Four

FOOD LUST

Portion *Behaalotkha* / When you set up (Numbers 8-12)

We remember the fish we ate in Egypt for nothing, the cucumbers, the melons, the leeks, the onions, and the garlics; but now our gullets are shriveled. There is nothing at all! Nothing but this manna to look to!" (Numbers 11:5-6)

During the desert trek toward the Promised Land the people's growing dissatisfactions and complaints culminate in a series of rebellions against Moses' leadership (ultimately, God's).[1] What is especially disturbing is not so much the insurrections themselves, but the fury of God's response to them: offenders are put to death in terrible ways (by plague or fire, for instance). In Moses' case, he and his brother Aaron are denied the honor of leading the people to their final destination "because you did not trust Me enough to affirm My sanctity in the sight of the Israelite people" (Numbers 20:12), a reference to Moses' striking the rock to produce water rather than trusting in God's instructions simply to order the rock to produce water (Numbers 20:8), so that the people may see this miracle before their eyes and attribute it to God's power.[2]

What lies behind these recurring challenges, and why is God's reaction so unforgiving, so brutally final, so swift? After all, God has, until now, shown the greatest compassion toward His recalcitrant children, parting the sea for them in their flight from slavery so they can escape their Egyptian pursuers (Exodus 14:21), turning bitter water to sweet to satisfy their thirst (Exodus 15:23-25), and raining down manna from heaven to allay their hunger (Exodus 16:4), all the while enduring the former slaves' ingratitude, as in the idea that "it is better for us to serve the Egyptians than to die [or suffer] in the wilderness" (Exodus 14:12).

The unique features of the virtually barren and dry desert landscape, so starkly different in character from the Nile region of Egypt, where lush crops were grown in well-watered soil, sets the scene for the first rebellion, after the Israelites have completed the Tabernacle and resumed their journey in the Sinai wilderness in the second year after their departure from Egypt (Numbers 10:11). It is not difficult to imagine how numbers of people, described negatively as a mixed multitude (Numbers 11:4)—or as we might say, "riff-raff"—could become obsessed with a lack of succulent vegetables and fruit during their desert journey, once their spiritual fervor has cooled and the privations of desert living no longer seem worth enduring for the sake of freedom. Whatever their route, the land would present a daunting aspect. In the south, site of the tall massive rock heights, where, according to tradition, all the people heard God from the top of the mountain and with one voice accepted the Ten Commandments (Exodus 19:8), vegetation occurs only in wadis, dry riverbeds fed by occasional rains, and oases, watered by underground springs, both of which occur throughout the Sinai Desert. Elsewhere, the land would be flatter and undulating, the soil rocky or gravelly, encrusted and salty, or covered by sand dunes shaped by the wind.[3] For the uninitiated, the endless stretches of this odd terrain would appear to be entirely devoid of life, yet since time immemorial, small tribes of nomads and their animals have managed to live off what little the desert has to offer.[4] It isn't a rich living by any means, but it is life-sustaining. For the food complainers, however, who are new to such life and would rather be elsewhere, the desert is a great burden, made even heavier by their highly colored remembrance of the abundant foods they left behind in Egypt.

The people's earlier complaints, which began as soon as the exodus from Egypt was underway, were pressed during a time when they had actually experienced fear, thirst, and hunger, but there is no indication they are now starving since God is still supplying manna to supplement their diet (Numbers 11:6). But not content with enough to eat, they want variety, pining for the sweet, pungent, juicy vegetables and fruit, and readily available fish they enjoyed in Egypt, none of which the desert can supply. Worse is their craving for flesh that cannot be satisfied: "Who," they ask, "will feed us meat to eat?" (Numbers 11:4, Judaica Press) Their demands drive Moses to distraction. This former Egyptian prince turned shepherd, who gave up everything to accept God's mission to free the Israelites from slavery and lead them safely through the hazardous wilderness to the Promised Land, has reached the limit of his endurance as their leader.

In an astonishing scene, Moses unburdens himself to God in language deeply colored by bitter irony. He, who neither gave birth to this people, nor promised them a land of their own, has been charged by God "to carry them in his bosom as a nurse carries an infant" (Numbers 11:12). It has been a thankless task and now the burden seems overwhelming. Where, he demands from God, could he ever find enough meat to feed all these people? (The modest number of sacrificial animals among the tribal gifts, listed in Numbers 7:13-82, indicates they were not everyday fare.) He winds up his own list of complaints by begging God to kill him, "and let me see no more of my wretchedness!" (Numbers 11:11-15). Then we understand that Moses' anger is directed not toward God, but to himself, for his inability to carry on with his mission.

God removes some of His prophet's burden of responsibility by having Moses appoint a council of seventy elders (Numbers 11:16-17), who will help him in his tasks. As for meat, the people will have plenty in the form of quails which God blows in from the sea (Numbers 11:31).[5] Unlike the manna, with which God blessed Israel and through which He taught the people to observe the Sabbath (Exodus 16:30), the quails He sends will be a punishment for their rebellion, for He understands that it is neither about hunger nor about the special foods of Egypt, but represents rejection of Him and all He stands for: a moral and ethical standard which they seem incapable of ever achieving. They have conveniently forgotten the bitterness of slavery in Egypt and do not look forward to the goal of living as free people in their own land. Their souls, in other words, are still imbued with a slave mentality, "preferring the garlic of Egypt to the bread of freedom."[6] God sees into the depth of their being and knows they are beyond reforming, and His punishment, graphically described, is in its way, appropriate. God sends them the flesh they wanted—a symbol par excellence of the material world—but

He sees to it that they will eat it until it comes out of their nostrils and they loathe it (Numbers 11:19-20). Even as they gather the quail in great numbers, God strikes them with a plague and the riff-raff complainers die. They are buried at *Kivrot Ha-Taava*/Burial Places of the Craving (Numbers 11:34).

The relatively trivial complaint about diet was a stark sign to Moses that all was not well with his charges. Always more in God's orbit than in touch with the common people, Moses fails to recognize that the complainers' lust for food reflects a deep spiritual emptiness rather than physical hunger. It is apparent that he will stumble again, unable to prevent more serious rebellions in the future, not to speak of his own momentary loss of faith in God, with tragic consequences for his own future.

WE ARE FAMILIAR with the foods on the complainers' list: cucumbers, melons, leeks, onions, and garlic. Whether heaped up in colorful displays in open air Middle Eastern food stalls or in the local supermarket, they are always desirable for their mouth-watering succulence and pungency. It is no wonder that, having become discouraged with the entire enterprise to serve as a holy nation, the grumblers should pine for fruits and vegetables with a refreshingly high water content, as they travel through the daunting landscape of the parched desert. In ancient Egypt the former slaves' favorite fresh foods were cultivated in the steadily moist, nutrient-rich soil left behind by the annual flooding of the Nile. Crops were abundant and formed the mainstay of the everyday diet, even for slaves, according to the text (Numbers 11:5).

These foods are classified botanically into two groups. Cucumbers, melons, and squash belong to the cucumber family (Cucurbitaceae), and are characterized by their sweet flavor and juiciness. Lily family (Liliaceae) members, which include onions, leeks, and garlic from the genus *Allium*, are known for their pungency. All were developed from wild plants very early in mankind's history, were plentiful and cheap, and helped to expand the limited ancient diet of grains, pulses, fruits, and when available, meat. Not only were the favorite foods good to eat, most had an important place in the ancient world's pharmacopeia.

The "cucumbers" (*kishuim*) of the text were not the well-known cucumbers of today, *Cucumis sativus*, since these were developed in India and were not widely cultivated in the Middle East until the early centuries of the common era. The "cucumbers" the grumblers had in mind could have been muskmelon, *Cucumis melo* or a variant known as snake cucumber, *C. melo* var. *flexuosus*. Originating in Africa and Southwest Asia, they and their wild ancestors grow all over Egypt,[7] where they have been cultivated for millennia.[8] All variants of muskmelons grow on sprawling stems with lobed leaves and yellow, bell-shaped flowers that produce fruits from four to sixteen inches in diameter, varying in shape from oval to round, with a smooth or sutured, netted or unnetted outer surface and juicy, aromatic flesh ranging in color from white, yellow and light green to orange; the latter are called "cantaloupes" in North America,

Photograph © Shirley P. Sidell

Cucumis melo. Muskmelon grown in California.

although true cantaloupes are more common in Europe. The snake cucumber is common in Middle Eastern markets and in countries like Sudan it may be the only 'cucumber' available.[9] Sometimes called "Armenian cucumbers," snake cucumbers resemble ordinary cucumbers in their sweet taste, but their skin is ridged and light green (rather than stippled and dark green as in the cucumber we are familiar with), their flesh is firmer than a cucumber's, and their shape, as the common name suggests, is narrow and curved, rather than cylindrical. Mature coiled specimens can grow as long as three feet, but are usually harvested much earlier in their growth cycle and can be eaten just as they are, without peeling. Short, young snake cucumbers are often pickled. In the ancient Egyptian pharmacopeia, melons were used in mixtures to treat bladder ailments and diseases of the stomach or anus and in soothing inflammations.[10]

Watermelons, *Citrullus lanatus*, translated as "melons" in the text from the Hebrew *avatihim*, were grown in pharonic times and are believed to be the one the grumblers had in mind.[11] What could be more refreshing, even vital, on a hot summer's day, or in

Photograph © Shirley P. Sidell

Allium porrum. Small leeks similar to salad leeks (*Allium kurrat*), purchased at an Asian food market in Washington State.

Photograph © Nell Gardner

Allium cepa. Onions for sale at Wegman's Supermarket, Rochester, New York.

the dry desert, than a thick slice of this sweet pinkish-red fruit, nearly ninety percent of which is water! Watermelons, like cucumbers, grow from sprawling vines. Modern fruits can be as large as ten inches in diameter and are full of large black seeds which are roasted as a snack in Egypt, Sudan, and surrounding countries,[12] including Israel, as they must have been in ancient times. Their oil content satisfies a hunger for edible oil that is prevalent in people who live in arid zones.[13] Oil, expressed from watermelon seeds has been used for soap and lighting, and is considered to be useful as an antiseptic, laxative, and vermicide.[14]

The Hebrew *hatzir* of the text is traditionally translated "leeks," *Allium porrum*, but most likely refers to "salad leeks," *Allium kurrat*, the kind grown in Egypt's Nile Delta;[15] *kurrat* is Arabic for leeks. Both leeks and salad leeks are derived from the wild *A. ampeloprasum*, wild leek, native to Israel and the Mediterranean region. Although they are closely related, leeks and salad leeks are quite different in their growth and use. Anyone familiar with leeks recognizes them from the long, thick white stems that grow straight up from a slightly swollen base. The sweetly pungent stems are the highly desirable part of the plant, prized in the French soup, *vichyssoise*. In contrast, salad leeks are smaller and slender, and are grown for a successive harvest of leaves, which regrow after being cut. They are eaten in salads, hence the common name, and also used to flavor the traditional Egyptian fried cake dish, *tameeah*, made with broad beans. Bundled leaves are common in the markets of Alexandria in the spring.[16]

Onions, *Allium cepa* (*betzalim*), like leeks, originated in Central Asia, but were known in ancient Egypt from about 3200 BCE.[17] Onions were extensively cultivated in the light soils of ancient Philistia along the Mediterranean coast of Israel, as preserved in the place name, "Ashkelon," based on the Latin for "scallion." These are especially delicious immature onions with little bulbous growth and long green leaves. There's no mistaking a mature onion, which forms a solitary round bulb of fleshy, extremely pungent, overlapping layers. Just the smell of a pungent onion, released by chopping, produces tears. The English word "onion" is derived from the Latin *unio*, which means "large pearl" and graphically describes the beauty of a well-grown large white onion (onions can also be yellow-fleshed or purplish). Ancient accounts by the fifth century BCE Greek writer Herodotus, and others, suggest that Egypt was renowned for the high quality of its sweet onions, a favorite staple food[18] as they remain today throughout the Middle East. Onions are represented in Egyptian tomb paintings, have been found inside mummies. In the Egyptian pharmacopeia, the juice was used to treat snake bites and to staunch bleeding.[19]

If the wish list of foods is arranged according to type, with the first two belonging to the cucumber family, and the last three to the alliums (lily family), they seem to be further organized according to taste, since so much emphasis is placed on flavor. The grumblers consider manna, the food they were forced to eat in the desert, the most boring food imaginable: "Now our gullets are shriveled," they whine, from this terrible experience. Thinking about the great foods they once ate, the first two are rated from sweet and juicy (snake cucumber) to sweetest and juiciest (watermelon). Next come the alliums, whose flavor

Photograph © Shirley P. Sidell

Allium sativum. Garlic grown in California.

ranges from sweetly pungent (leeks), to the more pungent, but still sweet, onion, and finally hits the jackpot with garlic, *Allium sativum* (plural in the Bible, *shumim*), the mother of all pungent foods, the one that brings other food to life with its ultra-pungency.

Garlic is of Eastern Mediterranean origin and is believed to have been known throughout the ancient Middle East for millennia, which helps to explain why it is so prevalent in the Middle Eastern cuisine, used to flavor everything from fava bean, chick pea, and lentil dishes, to soups, salads, and cheeses. Unlike onions, which produce seeds, garlic is sterile and must be grown from the individual cloves that make up a whole bulb, the kind you see in the supermarket when you are looking for fresh garlic. Strap-like leaves grow from a solid stem, and when the leaves turn yellow or fall over, it's time to dig up the bulbs.

Herodotus reported that great quantities of onion, garlic, and radishes were eaten by the slaves who built the pyramids at Giza, based upon inscriptions on them.[20] Whether true or not, these were undisputed foods of all the people, from slave to royalty. Garlic has been found in Egyptian tombs, including the tomb of Tutankhamun.[21] The medicinal uses of garlic are legion. It has long been recognized as an antiseptic, used in various preparations to soothe asthma, coughs, and disorders of the lungs, and in cooked dishes it is said to aid digestion; today it is being examined as a possible anti-oxidant. In the Egyptian pharmacopeia it was used in preparations to soothe skin diseases and to stimulate milk production in women. The Egyptian complete 'garlic cure,' which has survived in one form or another in many cultures, is based on eating fresh garlic every day.[22]

With the aid of drip irrigation, modern Israel produces tons of sweet, succulent fruits and vegetables—Israeli-bred melons are especially famous—more than enough to have satisfied the ancient grumblers.

ENDNOTES
1. The rebellions, after the one about food, appear in Numbers 12:1 (Miriam and Aaron speak against Moses); 14:2 (the people against Moses and Aaron); 16:1-3 (Korah and his followers against Moses and Aaron); 17:6 (the people against Moses and Aaron); 20 (the sin of Moses and Aaron against God); 25:1-2 (apostasy: idol worship).

2. Many commentators through the ages have sought to account for God's harsh punishment of Moses and Aaron at the Waters of *Meribah* ("strife"), among them that their offense was attributing the pouring forth of water from the rock to their own powers, rather than to God's. See Numbers 20:10.

3. For a non-scientific, accessible description of the different areas of the Sinai, see Daniel Hillel, *The Natural History of the Bible*, 123–126.

4. For a description of useful desert plants ranging from those which indicate a water source to those that can be used for food, seasoning, and, among other things, making rope, see Avinoam Danin, *Desert Vegetation of Israel and Sinai*, 121–129.

5. See Hillel, 129 for an explanation of quail migration and a possible natural basis for quail being borne inland from the sea.

6. J. H. Hertz, *The Pentateuch and Haftorahs*, 614.

7. Reader Elaine Solowey.

8. Maude Grieve, *A Modern Herbal*, Vol. II, 528. *In An Ancient Egyptian Herbal*, 95, Lise Manniche includes drawings based on a depiction of a basket of snake cucumbers or melons found on a wall painting in a Theban tomb dating from the 18th Dynasty, the period which included Tutankhamun (1567–1320 BCE), 95, 96.

9. Lytton John Musselman, *Figs, Dates, Laurel, and Myrrh*, 106.

10. Manniche, 95.

11. F. Nigel Hepper, *Illustrated Encyclopedia of Bible Plants*, 126.

12. Musselman, 286.

13. Elaine Solowey adds that she has seen Bedouin children buy a bag of chips or a shwarma and then lick the oil off the paper wrappings.

14. Irene Jacob, *Biblical Plants: A Guide to the Rodef Shalom Biblical Botanical Garden*, 48.

15. Musselman, 173.

16. Ibid., 174.

17. Michael Zohary, *Plants of the Bible*, 80.

18. Louis I. Rabinowitz, *Torah and Flora*, 102 and elsewhere.

19. Manniche, 69.

20. Hepper, 127.

21. Ibid.

22. Manniche, 71.

Chapter Twenty-Five

BEAUTIFUL POMEGRANATES

Portion-*Shelach Lecha* / Send for yourself (Numbers 13:1-15:41)
They reached the wadi Eshkol, and there they cut down a branch with a single cluster of grapes—it had to be borne on a carrying frame by two of them—and some pomegranates and figs. (Numbers 13:23)

Photograph © Joshua D. Klein.

Punica granatum. Pomegranate flowers and fruit in the Moshav Gimzo orchard on the Coastal Plain.

The desert wilderness journey in Sinai to the Promised Land has become very difficult. The physical challenges—lack of water and food—are not as hard to overcome as the people's lack of faith in their leader, and ultimately, in God. No sooner is the food rebellion quelled than complaints come from an unexpected quarter: Aaron and Miriam, Moses' own brother and sister, first express dissatisfaction with Moses because "He married a Cushite woman," (perhaps because she is not one of their own?),[1] then they go to the heart of their grievance. They challenge Moses' role as God's principal prophet, the one through whom His word is spoken to the people. "Has He not spoken through us as well?" the disgruntled siblings demand to know (Numbers 12:1-2). God answers them decisively, telling them in tones that must have sobered them (but too late), that Moses was called by Him not in a dream, as prophets are usually called, but directly, "mouth to mouth, plainly and not in riddles, and he beholds the likeness of the Lord" (Numbers 12:8). God may have helped Moses when the burden of his mission seemed to overwhelm him, but there can be no doubt that he, and he alone, stands closest to God. For her part in this challenge Miriam is punished, and later so are Aaron and Moses himself. None will ever reach the Promised Land.

The spirit of rebellion deepens. From the encampment at Kadesh in the Wilderness of Paran, Moses sends twelve scouts or spies, drawn from each of the tribes, to the land of Canaan on a secretive forty-day fact-finding mission. The Promised Land, after all, is wholly unknown to him and there are certain things of a practical nature he wants to know: What is the land like? Where are people already settled and what are they like? Is the land fat (fertile) or lean (unproductive)? Are there trees? These are the natural concerns of a people who will settle the land as farmers and shepherds. Farmers need nutrient-rich soil to grow crops, shepherds need lush grazing areas. Almost as an afterthought, Moses charges the scouts to "take pains to bring back some of

Dr. Avishai Teicher Pikiwiki Israel.

Israelites carrying grapes of Canaan. Mosaic in Or Torah Synagogue, Israel.

the fruit of the land" (Numbers 13:17-20). Perhaps he hopes a good showing of tasty fruit will avoid a repeat of the food rebellion.

Forty days later when they return, the scouts confirm before Moses and the whole community that, as God has promised, the land does, indeed, "flow with milk and honey, and this is its fruit" (Numbers 13:27). The image of two scouts struggling to bear a single enormous cluster of grapes on a stout pole has become indelibly associated with the abundance of the Holy Land.[2] Shouldn't these fruits inspire joy in the hearts of the scouts and the people to whom they show them? What better support could there be for the land's favorable conditions for growing food than seeing actual cultivated specimens from the land, for the fruits they bring are not wild. The grapes, for instance, were cultivated by people already settled in the fertile Valley of *Eshkol* (meaning "cluster"). The land that "flows with milk and honey," on the other hand, is the untamed, unsettled hill country, where the scouts noted that the characteristic thick undergrowth of forest land supported wild goats, the source of milk, and a profusion of wild flowers from which wild bees produce honey.[3] Such land would provide superior grazing ground for the people's sheep and goats, but according to the scouts there are major problems: the wild areas shelter beasts that "devour its settlers," the cities are well fortified and the men are so big they are like giants, while "we looked like grasshoppers to ourselves" (Numbers 13:32-33). There can be no doubt that despite proof of the land's potential abundance, the scouts have brought back a very discouraging report, one that exaggerates all obstacles and discounts entirely God's plans for Israel. "We cannot attack that people," they declare to the assembled Israelites, "for it is stronger than we are" (Numbers 13:31). Two of the scouts, the stalwart Caleb and Joshua, disagree and try to undo the damage of the negative report. They exhort the people to remember that God is with them, the land is good, and it will be theirs if they do not rebel against Him. But the people are now so stirred up, so hysterical with fear, that they are ready to turn around and return to Egypt at once (!)—"Let us head back for Egypt"—and threaten to stone Caleb and Joshua for even suggesting that they carry on towards the Promised Land (Numbers 14:2-10).

This rebellion, deep and widespread among the Israelites, one that was inspired, moreover, by hand-picked leaders from each of the twelve tribes, strikes a new low, one for which the whole people, not just the agitators will be punished by a wrathful God. Moses intervenes on their behalf and God pardons them but promises that none of the slave generation will live to see the Promised Land. They and their children will wander and suffer in the desert for forty years, one year for each of the days of the scouts' mission. The scouts themselves, with the exception of the faithful Caleb and Joshua, will die of plague (Numbers 14:11-38).

The slave generation has proved, beyond doubt, that they are incapable of throwing off the chains of slavery and living as a free people. Only their children, who were never slaves, who were born into the "free air of the wilderness, can be readied for the orderly transition into conquest and life on their own soil."[4]

—⟅ᴡ⟆—

POMEGRANATES, *Punica granatum* (*rimmon*), like figs, are overshadowed by the grape cluster that two scouts find so heavy to carry between them. Why are these other fruits so obscured? Aren't they also desirable products of the land? The clue to their diminished stature may be the time of year in the land to which Moses sent the scouts: "Now it happened to be the season of the first ripe grapes" (Numbers 13:20). In ancient Canaan, as now in modern Israel, this season occurs in certain areas in June or July, while the heavier crop ripens in August and September. The text rightly places pomegranates in a secondary position on the carrying pole because in common with other fruits of the famous Seven Species with which the Holy Land is blessed (Deuteronomy 8:8), pomegranates blossom between Passover and *Shavuot* (March–April and May–June) and mostly ripen in August and September; in the south of the country they ripen in June and July. Figs, on the other hand, can produce fresh fruit for as long as five months of the year on old and new wood, beginning before *Shavuot* and extending beyond *Sukkot* (mid to late October). Since fruit does not ripen all at once and, therefore, has to be picked daily, perhaps the Scouts were forced to pick figs which were not at their peak of ripeness. Yet even if the pomegranates and figs had not achieved the full, mouth-watering state of the early grapes, they would at least give an idea of the land's bounty. Olives and dates, the other fruits of the Seven Species, would still be in the embryonic stage and not worth bringing to show to Moses and the people.

Rank and thorny wild or semi-wild ancestors of the cultivated pomegranate, originally from the south Caspian sea area, have been found in Israel on Mount Carmel, in Gilead, and northern Syria.[5] Through gradual selection over thousands of years, growers tamed pomegranates into a neater, rounded or vase-shaped shrub or small tree that grows from twelve to sixteen feet tall or more. Stiff branches bear narrow, glossy and leathery leaves—a sign of the plant's heat and drought tolerance—and gleaming buds that open to waxy, red bell-shaped blossoms of crinkled petals surrounding numerous, showy stamens. Each bloom is encompassed by a fleshy red calyx, the floral envelope that first covers the bud, gives way to the flower, and then remains as a ruff around the flower's base. Fruit, the size and shape of an orange or apple, hangs down from the branches, turning from yellow to glowing shades of pink or deep red, tinged with yellow beneath. The calyx, which should have dropped with the petals as it does in other flowers, persists at the tip of the fruit as a tufted crown, giving the whole ripe fruit its characteristic beauty of form. When the hard rind of the fruit is opened, it reveals its treasure: delicious seeds from medium-hard to softer, contained in a mass of juicy reddish sacs, groups of which are separated into sections by membranous walls and white, spongy, bitter tissue. It is the juicy seeds, and the juice from them (like the flavor of sweet strawberries and tart cranberries combined) that make the fruit desirable.

After the Israelites finally entered Canaan under Joshua and settled down as farmers, they spread the cultivation of pomegranates throughout the land, improving the fruit and introducing new varieties. We tend to think of plant improvement and breeding as a modern phenomenon, but people have been tinkering with plants from the beginning of recorded history. By taking cuttings and rooting them from trees which showed promise of bearing larger or sweeter fruit, or that did not split before harvesting, or were earlier bearing, the pomegranates of ancient Israel became famous for their quality. Pomegranates were introduced to Egypt from Syria and Israel, and better varieties were imported from the Holy Land.[6] Preserved rinds, parts of the fruit, and hardened whole fruits, thousands of years old, have been discovered in Gaza and near Ein Gedi on the western shore of the Dead Sea, attesting to the pomegranate's ancient cultivation, as does a plethora of biblical place names, such as Rimmon-perez (Numbers 33:19), Rimmon (Joshua 15:32; 19:7), and Ein Rimmon-Spring of the Pomegranate (Nehemiah 11:29).

A fruit of such distinction would become, over time, closely associated with the land in which it thrived, a source of artistic inspiration. Its image was used to adorn buildings, garments, and objects of daily use such as lamps. On the hems of the priestly robes pomegranate fruits were fashioned from twisted blue, purple, and crimson yarns, and the alternating pomegranate flowers into "bells of pure gold" (Exodus 39:24-26). Solomon's kingly crown was said to be fashioned after the plant's persistent crown-like calyx. Pomegranate images were cast in bronze by the artisan, Hiram, on the Temple's columns (I Kings 7:18), and on ancient coins they were represented by a stylized cluster of three pomegranate flowers signifying sanctity (the Temple), fertility, and abundance. A silver half shekel, minted during the first Jewish revolt against Rome in CE 66–70, uses the same image,[7] obviously one that was intended to inspire faith in a return to Jewish sovereignty by invoking a recognized symbol of nationhood. This motif was used again in modern times on Israeli coins.

Although not a staple of the diet, the fruit had many uses: as edible seeds, a refreshingly tart juice (especially welcome in the heat of late summer when pomegranates ripen), wine, and when the seeds were dried, as popular *pered*: "The *pered* and raisins and carobs were heaped up (Mishna, *Maasarot*, 1,6)." The tough rind, used to make nara-water, or ink, and with the flower's stamen roots, to color fabrics and tan leather, were subject to the laws of *Shevi'it* on the Sabbatical Year because they had commercial value.[8] The fruit itself was a convenient yardstick of size to which household utensils were compared (Mishna, *Kelim*, 17,1), and, more poetically, to compare the beauty of the beloved in Solomon's Song of Songs: "As a piece of pomegranate are thy temples [cheeks]" (Song of Songs 6:7, KJV). The pomegranate branch itself was used as a moisture retentive skewer for roasting the paschal offering (Mishna, *Pesahim* 7,1).

Among the pomegranate's other virtues, recognized throughout the biblical region, were those associated with healing, perhaps due to the fruit's astringency. The flesh and rind were used in preparations to soothe respiratory ailments and dispel intestinal worms, an infusion of flowers steeped in wine was taken to relieve the symptoms of dyspepsia, and pomegranate juice was recommended as a gargle for laryngitis.[9] Powdered pomegranate seeds were (and still are) used to cure dysentery and alleviate food poisoning.[10] Today there is a renewed interest in pomegranate seeds, whose red colored juice indicates a high level of anti-oxidants (such as those found in red wine) for reputedly fighting cell aging. The fruit is also being investigated for its potential to help in treating certain kinds of cancers, to treat drug-resistant infections, protect the heart, and prevent or treat diabetes. As a rich source of plant estrogens, it also holds the promise of preventing Alzheimer's disease.[11] Perhaps the recalcitrant slave generation would not have been so hasty to return to Egypt had they known of the near-miraculous powers of the beautiful pomegranate.

Photograph © Shirley P. Sidell

Punica granatum.
Pomegranates grown in California.

The rabbis of the biblical and post-biblical times had an uncanny ability to invest all growing things with a moral purpose. This is not surprising since they were dedicated to teaching the Bible's instructions on being a holy nation devoted to God. They saw in the pomegranate not only its outward beauty, but deep into its heart, where its multitude of seeds (six-hundred and thirteen, they said, the number of Torah commandments) suggested the hope that "even the worthless members of the Jewish people are as full of good deeds as is the pomegranate of seeds" (*Eruv* 82).[12] Because of this association and since they ripen in late summer, pomegranates are often eaten at Rosh Hashana, the New Year, when they are used for the blessing of new fruit on the second day. In the synagogue, you may notice the silver bell-like *rimmonim* (plural, "pomegranates,") atop the rollers of the Torah scrolls, inspired by the bells (pomegranate flowers) that once adorned the hem of the High Priest's gown. Despite having been overshadowed by the scouts' ripe cluster of grapes, pomegranates have maintained an important place in Jewish ritual, lore, legend, and among those who look forward to drinking its refreshing, health-giving juice.

ENDNOTES

1. The issue of Aaron and Miriam's grievance against Moses' Cushite wife has been the source of much commentary, both ancient and modern.
2. It is now the symbol of Israel's Ministry of Tourism.
3. In *Nature in Our Biblical Heritage*, 11–22, Nogah Hareuveni discusses his interpretation of the phrase "land of milk and honey." It would have to be wild honey, Hareuveni reasons, since apiculture (beekeeping) did not develop until centuries later. See Hareuveni, 12.
4. Everett Fox, *The Five Books of Moses*, 649. And as reader Michael Solowey observes, "Rebelliousness was not the only reason why most never saw the Promised Land. The slave generation was not used to taking care of itself, they had to be fed. Nor were they used to defending themselves. Only a new generation born into freedom could appreciate the opportunities and stand against the dangers."
5. Asaf Goor and Max Nurock, *The Fruits of the Holy Land*, 70.
6. Ibid., 70, 71.
7. See cluster of fruits on the coin in the photo p. 213.
8. Goor and Nurock, 79.
9. Ibid., 74.
10. Reader Elaine Solowey.
11. In "Israeli pomegranates worth their weight in gold," Judy Siegel reported on work in developing new pomegranate varieties at the University of the Negev and of their health benefits in fighting aging and certain cancers, in the *International Jerusalem Post*, Oct. 3–8, 2008. New varieties are also being tested at the agricultural research station, Neve Yaar, in Israel, where the focus is on developing fruit with soft, easily digested seeds. In *The Herb Companion*, Nov. 2008 "Pomegranate: Fruit of Life," 12, herb expert Steven Foster reported on the latest information about the health benefits of pomegranates.
12. In Louis I. Rabinowitz' *Torah and Flora*, 62, the author recounts having spent time actually counting pomegranate seeds to "gauge the accuracy of that rabbinical simile." His report: "I had hoped to find that the sum total was 613 or a near approximation to that number: the pips in my 'test pomegranates' varied in number from a low of 404 to a high of 550. On consideration, however, I realized that I had expected too much. The optimistic view of the transgressor may make him as full of *mitzvot* as the pomegranate is of seeds, but it was not to be expected that he would be a paragon of all the *mitzvot*! And in any case, it has been pointed out that 613 represents the totality of the commandments which can be fulfilled only by all Jews collectively. Some are confined to the king, others to priests, etc., while others can be performed only while the Temple stands. This being so, my pomegranates were fuller of seeds than the number of commandments which the most observant Jew can perform. So perhaps my experiment was not entirely in vain."

Chapter Twenty-Six

THE BLOOMING ROD

Portion-*Korah* / Korah (Numbers 16:1-18:32)

The next day Moses entered the Tent of the Pact, and there the staff [rod] of Aaron of the house of Levi had sprouted: it had brought forth sprouts, produced blossoms, and borne almonds. (Numbers 17:23)

The spirit of rebellion deepens. Endless vistas of barren rock mountains in the vast dry desert wilderness of Sinai seem to have unsettled the people, who look backward to the lushness of Egypt where they were enslaved, instead of forward to life as a free people in their own land. From malcontents at the fringes of the community to Moses' own family, voices are raised against his leadership, and through him, against God Himself.

The Great Rebellion follows a section of legal instructions (Numbers 15), giving the reader a sense of the tensions that exist between the ideal of the laws and the reality of the less-than ideal behavior of the ex-slaves, a situation which inevitably results in disaster: the complainers, who wished they'd never left Egypt and pined for the food they left behind, were struck with a severe plague, even as the meat they were granted "was still between their

Photograph © Ori Fragman

Amygdalus communis. Blooming almond tree branch at the Jerusalem Botanical Gardens.

220

teeth" (Numbers 11:33), the ten scouts who brought back slanderous reports about the Promised Land also died from plague (Numbers 14:37), while the entire ex-slave community who listened to them and believed them were destined to "roam the wilderness for forty years suffering for your faithlessness, until the last of your carcasses is down in the wilderness" (Numbers 14:33). The rebellions are decimating the Israelites, yet there is no doubt that even though they have violated their covenant again and again, God has not given up on them. He prefaces a set of instructions concerning gifts to the Lord with "When you [your children] enter the land to which I am taking you" (Numbers 15:17-21), a comforting thought in light of the people's penchant for backsliding.

Who is Korah, the leader of the Great Rebellion, how does he fit into the pattern of mutiny we have already seen, and what does this have to do with a rod that sprouts blossoms and bears almonds although it is separated from the soil?

The Korah-inspired revolt is the most serious challenge yet, one that seeks to undermine the order of sanctity as ordained by God. Korah is a Kohethite Levite[1] who demands a share in the Aaronite priesthood, not content with the Levite's auxiliary role in sanctuary procedures. What begins as a personal grudge gathers momentum as Korah combines forces with the Reubenites, descendants of the first-born Reuben, who also feel slighted. Moses and Aaron face a serious mutiny as two-hundred and fifty "chieftains of the community, chosen in the assembly, men of repute" (Numbers 16:2) enter the fray. All charge Moses and Aaron with unjustly raising themselves above everyone else: "You have gone too far! For all of the community are holy, all of them, and the Lord is in their midst. Why then do you raise yourselves above the Lord's congregation?" (Numbers 16:3)

Moses is devastated but he (inspired by God, we assume) has a plan to resolve this latest rebellion. He instructs all the mutineers (directing himself especially to their ringleader, Korah) to appear at the entrance to the Tabernacle on the following day, and to take with them fire pans with a smoldering incense offering, strictly a priestly duty. There, Moses tells them, God will decide who is holy, and in what appears to be an unscripted moment, undirected by God, he heatedly attacks the Korah-led mutineers: "[It is] You [who] have gone too far, sons of Levi!" (Numbers 16:7). This angry outburst is reminiscent of his flare-up of temper against the stubborn Pharaoh who refused to let the Israelites go (Exodus 10:25-29). This, we feel, is the authentic man speaking with real passion, selfless in his mission to bring the Israelites through their difficult journey towards fulfillment, not for his own personal gain (unlike Korah), but for the good of the people themselves. In his impassioned speech to the Levites ("Hear me, sons of Levi."), which does not appear to move them, he reminds those present that the God of Israel has singled them out, set them apart from the community so they may serve it and assist in the carrying out of priestly duties that occur within the holy space of the Lord's Tabernacle. Shouldn't this be enough of an honor? Their mutiny, he warns, is not about seeking the priesthood, but is a challenge to God's authority over them (Numbers 16:8-11), and that is the great danger of the revolt.

The following day Korah—whose persuasive oratory is suggested—has roused the entire community to stand with his side at the entrance to the Tent of Meeting, thus presenting a united front against Moses and Aaron (Numbers 16:19). The moment of truth comes with God's warning to Moses and Aaron to stand back from the mutineers, for he intends to annihilate them all "in an instant" (Korah, his followers, and everyone else standing with them). Moses intervenes to save the very people who oppose him (the community at large), and they are saved for now, but the sinners themselves are swallowed up, "all Korah's people and all their possessions. They went down alive into *Sheol* with all that belonged to them; the earth closed over them and they vanished from the midst of the congregation."[2] Then a fire "went forth from the Lord" and consumed the two-hundred and fifty men who had offered incense (Numbers 16:33-35).[3]

For commentators on the Bible, the rebellions in general and their horrific consequences were conceived as warnings for future generations: this—suffering, disaster, death—is what happens to those who take it upon themselves to challenge God's authority, whose lust for material gain, whose fearfulness, divisiveness, and moral failure lead to national disaster.[4] The Korah-led Rebellion, which was especially imprinted in the minds and hearts of later generations, was regarded as "typical of all controversies that had their origin in personal motives—'not in the Name of Heaven' and that could not therefore lead to any beneficent results."[5] The very name "Korah" became synonymous with demagoguery and failed leadership.

Two memorable devices were employed in the Bible to drive home its efforts against backsliding, the text's most persistent theme: the firepans, by God's instructions, have been removed from the fire and hammered into a cover for the altar to serve as a warning to the Israelites against instigating future calamities (Numbers 17:3).[6] The other device draws us back to the Israelites' shepherd roots, to the shepherd's indispensable staff for guiding his flock, now consecrated as "the rod of God" (first endowed with divine power to help Moses in his mission to Egypt to free his enslaved people in the story of the burning bush).[7] The rods (staves or scepters) from the chief of each Israelite tribe, symbol of his authority, shall be inscribed with his name, as Aaron's will be inscribed on his, and the rods shall be placed in the Tent of Meeting. The one whose rod sprouts blossoms is the person whom God has chosen as his priest and priestly line. The next day when Moses enters the Tent, Aaron's rod of the house of Levi is not only blossoming, but putting forth its fruit! It is kept on display as a final lesson to the rebels about God's authority, "so that their mutterings against Me may cease, lest they die" (Numbers 17:25). Thus this very disturbing rebellion is finally brought to an end.

—⁂—

WHY WAS THE BRANCH of the almond tree, *Amygdalus communis*, endowed with such miraculous powers? The text tells us that overnight, Aaron's rod (fashioned from wood) had "brought forth sprouts, produced blossoms, and borne almonds" all at the same time. The answer is suggested by the Hebrew name of the almond tree, *shaked* (*luz* in Aramaic and other Semitic languages), which is derived from *shoked*, a root word indicating to be diligent, persevering, reliable, watchful, vigorously wakeful, early rising, and to hasten events, meanings corroborated by the almond tree's chief characteristics. Able to grow and thrive in dry, stony soil, its roots penetrate deep into the ground to find water. Unlike the Seven Species which are vulnerable to drought and wind during their growth cycle, the almond tree takes these in stride, unfailingly producing its crop. Jacob, remember, was able to include almonds among the "choice

Photograph © Jackie Chambers

Amygdalus communis. Almond tree in bloom, Jerusalem hills.

products" he sent down to Egypt during a time of drought in Canaan (Genesis 43:11). And while all other trees in the landscape are still in their winter dormancy (biologically asleep, as it were), the almond tree 'watches' carefully in late winter for conditions which signal its moment to awake, to burst vigorously into bloom. God is watchful, too, to bring His words to pass (Jeremiah 1:11-12).

Anyone who has witnessed the enormous cloud of whitish bloom produced by a single tree, or better, a grove of almond trees, will never forget its impact, especially because it has the landscape all to itself, most other flowering plants still awaiting rain and warmer conditions to bloom. Coming at the end of winter, around late January or early February, it is a reliable sign that winter is nearly at an end and the warmer season lies just ahead, when "The blossoms have appeared in the land/ The time of pruning [or singing] has come/ The song of the turtledove is heard in our land (Song of Songs 2:12).

While the almond tree itself is of modest stature, from about thirteen to twenty feet, its bloom is unforgettable. Every inch of its bare branches is covered with white or light pink flower clusters, each bloom loosely petalled like a wild rose (to which family the almond tree belongs) and held by a bell-shaped calyx as described in the design of the Tabernacle's golden menorah in Exodus 37:17-24. When massed, their sweet, heady aroma floats on the air. Such dense bloom must seem miraculous, since one day the flowers are in bud and the very next they burst open, their impact even greater since the tree's branches are still bare of leaves. In this sense, it is not difficult to imagine the almond as a divine sign on Aaron's rod. |

Although we think of it as a nut, the almond is classified as a fruit tree. In pre-historic times wild and semi-wild bitter almonds grew in the Middle East and western Asia. In Israel three bitter wild species, similar in habit to the cultivated version (which arose from a genetic mutation) persist, suggesting that Israel (ancient Canaan) was one of the original countries in which the sweet almond tree was domesticated.[8] Place names in the Bible (Genesis 28:19, Judges 1:26), based on the Aramaic "*luz*," reflect the almond tree's prominence in ancient life. The almond tree is closely related to other stone fruits such as apricots, peaches, and cherries, but unlike these, in which the inedible stones are discarded and the flesh eaten, in the almond tree, the fleshy outer covering becomes leathery, dries up and splits open to reveal a brittle shell or husk, within which lies the edible kernel, the delicious almond! In biblical times, almonds were eaten raw, roasted, ground into a paste, and made into a relish, similar to the ways they are still used; even bitter almonds, containing prussic acid, could be rendered edible by boiling them.[9] In Sephardic cooking, based on long-established traditions, not only from Spain, but southern Europe, North Africa, and the Middle East—places where almond trees thrive—almonds in different forms are featured in everything from chicken dishes to omelets and sweets.[10] In the Ashkenazi cuisine, almonds also have an important place, especially in baking (*mandlebrodt*, "almond bread," a biscotti-like classic sweet). Oil for cooking, always a valuable product, was expressed from the kernels, which contain fifty percent fat.[11] It is likely that almond-oil was also used medicinally, as it was throughout the classical world. The first century CE Greek writer Dioscorides records it to treat respiratory and intestinal problems and also skin blemishes. Honey and almond hand cream is still highly regarded. Bitter and sweet almonds were discussed in the Talmud with regard to their distinctions—soft-shelled, hard-shelled, modes of grafting, the tree's longevity, its various uses, and how they are to be tithed or taxed.[12]

Of special interest is a section of the Talmud (*Bekhorot* 8a) where the parturition times of various animals are compared with the time of fruit ripening: the dog goes with young for fifty days, corresponding to the fig which produces its fruit in fifty days; the fifty-two days of the cat corresponds to the fifty-two days of the mulberry; and the hen, which lays its eggs after twenty-one days corresponds to the twenty-one days from the blossoming of the almond tree to the ripening of its fruit. This is not overnight, as was the case with Aaron's rod, but it does suggest hastening, with which the almond tree is symbolically associated. In fact, embryonic fruits develop just after the flower petals drop, but they do not fully ripen until seventy days after fruiting, in late summer, not twenty-one days according to the Talmud. A Jewish proverb, moreover, warns, "Be not in a hurry like the almond, first to bloom and last to ripen; be rather like the mulberry, last to blossom and first to ripen."[13] This discrepancy can be explained by the almond's two ripenings: the first, after twenty-one days, yields the unripe green, furry fruits, a popular Middle Eastern snack food, tasty but sour and usually sold with a packet of salt; the second ripening yields the more familiar sweet-tasting beige-white almond, the kernel within the mature fruit. In Talmudic times, as today, the unripe green almonds were considered a treat and regarded as ripe enough to eat.

The rabbis, always keen to linger over the text and enhance upon it to further their teachings, did not forget Aaron's rod. Its blossoms were, accordingly, the flowers of the priesthood, while the almonds represented the eagerness with which the priests carried out their duties. Their rich commentaries passed into Jewish legend, where the rod itself, the story goes, never lost its blossoms or almonds, was used by the Judean kings until the time of the destruction of the Temple, then disappeared; but, in miraculous fashion, Elijah will in the future fetch it forth and hand it over to the King Messiah.[14] "The Lord shall send the rod of thy strength out of Zion: rule thou in the midst of thine enemies" (Numbers *Rabba* 18 end).

ENDNOTES

1. A Kohethite Levite is descended from Kohath, one of the three sons of Levi whose descendants made up the three clans of the Levites. "Their duties [the Kohathites] comprised the ark, the table, the lampstand, the altars, and the sacred utensils that were used with them, and the screen—all the service connected with these" (Numbers 3:31).

2. "*Sheol*" is where the dead, both righteous and sinners, dwell: I Kings 2:6. When ethical viewpoints are involved, however, as in the punishment of the Korah rebellion, *Sheol* is said to be a place of punishment. See *The Oxford Companion to the Bible*, 277–278 for a detailed discussion of the concept of *Sheol* in the Bible. "Hell," from a Germanic root meaning "to cover" is the English translation of the Hebrew *Sheol*, which is mentioned sixty-five times in the Hebrew Bible. In Jewish legends "*Sheol*" is translated as "hell" and there is no doubt it is a place of perpetual torment. In one colorful description, the sinners of the

rebellion sink slowly and painfully into the earth, acknowledging finally that "Moses is truth, and his Torah is truth." Not only were the sinners swallowed up alive by the earth, but their possessions disappeared with them, "even their linen that was at the launderer's." Louis Ginzburg, *Legends of the Bible*, 444. In their telling and re-telling, these folk tales, woven around biblical narrative, became richly embroidered with homely details drawn from ordinary everyday life, thereby strengthening their effect. Anyone listening to the story of how the sinners of the Korah rebellion were punished would know that it was total, for even their laundry was punished!

3. The two strands of rebellion stories, Korah's and the Reubenites', can be confusing for the reader. What actually happened to Korah? Was he swallowed up with the Reubenites or consumed by fire? In post-biblical Hebrew tradition Korah is sometimes represented as having been buried alive and sometimes as having been incinerated. Robert Alter, *The Five Books of Moses*, 767.

4. Alter, 677.

5. J. H. Hertz *The Pentateuch and Haftorahs*, 638.

6. The fire pans and their ultimate use as a covering for the altar has been a subject of much commentary through the ages. According to one interpretation, the fire pans are a metaphor for any seductions that turn us away from the God-inspired moral life. See "The Lesson of the Fire-pans" on *parasha* Korah by Rabbi Ephraim Buchwald online at the National Jewish Outreach Program. See Bibliography for Internet address.

7. See Exodus 4:2-5 for the first instance of the staff-magic rod as a symbol of divine authority.

8. Michael Zohary, *Plants of the Bible*, 67.

9. Asaph Goor and Max Nurock, *The Fruits of the Holy Land*, 245.

10. There are a wealth of Sephardic recipes from these lands in Gilda Angel's *Sephardic Holiday Cooking: Recipes and Traditions*. This book is available now from the publisher, Decalogue Books, via its distributor's website: www.adinfinitumbooks.com.

11. Zohary, 67.

12. Goor and Nurock, 245.

13. *Jewish Proverbs*, 44. A pocket-size book charmingly illustrated by Brenda Rae Eno.

14. Ginzburg, 447.

Chapter Twenty-Seven

THE SHELTERING BROOM BUSH

Portion *Phinehas* / Phinehas (Numbers 25:10-30:1)
   ***Haftarah* (I Kings 18:46-19:21)**
   He [Elijah] *came to a broom bush and sat down under it, and prayed that he might die.* (I Kings 19:4)

Photograph © Jackie Chambers

Retama raetam. White broom bush, Ramon Crater/Makhtesh Ramon in the Ramon Nature Reserve, Negev.

A reading from the prophets is linked to the Numbers portion, *Phinehas*, by the zeal with which Phinehas (also Pinhas, Pinchas) and the prophet Elijah defend the God of Israel. Before they reached the Promised Land, during the Israelites' encampment at Shittim, many of the men formed sexual relationships with the local Midianite women who invited them to partake of their pagan sacrifices and worship the local god, Baal-peor, a manifestation of the fertility storm-god Baal.[1] Thus did these Israelites shamefully desecrate the entire moral underpinnings of the new moral and ethical order they had sworn allegiance to at Sinai. God orders the slaying of the ringleaders of this serious apostasy so that His wrath may turn away from Israel (Numbers 25:5) and save it from death by plague. Phineas steps forward to execute both the Israelite Zimri, son of a chieftan, and his Midianite woman, who had brazenly entered the encampment together (Numbers 25:6-8), thus saving the community. Much later, Elijah fiercely attacks worship of the pagan god Baal in the Northern Kingdom, headed by the weak-minded King Ahab and his fearsome queen, Jezebel, a Phoenician. Despite the centuries that separate the events described in the Book of Numbers and those in the Elijah stories, the text confirms that instilling the heretofore unimaginable idea of an invisible God Who alone created the heavens and earth and all they contain, Who transcends nature yet brings the "early rain and late rain" so essential to life, and Who demands adherence to a moral code wholly outside the realm of the pagan gods, is an ongoing struggle. Elijah's bold campaign against the royally sanctioned prophets of Baal, who urge the people to worship the pagan god Baal alongside of (or instead of) the "Lord," is part of an emerging movement in the eighth or ninth century BCE toward establishing Him as the sole God of the Israelites.[2]

Given Elijah's passion for God's cause (his name means "Yahweh is my God") and the fiery Jezebel's full embrace of idolatry (Ahab is a follower), the high drama which ensues is not surprising. To set the scene for Elijah's challenge to the reigning authority of Ahab and Jezebel, the narrative details how low the Northern Kingdom had already sunk, when past rulers, including the father of the present king, Ahab, had been involved in civil war, treason, intrigue, assassination, drunkenness, and idolatry—"what was displeasing to the Lord" (I Kings 16:13-25). Could things get worse? It seems so, since

Ahab "did more to vex the Lord, the God of Israel, than all the kings of Israel who preceded him." He not only worshiped Baal, but built a temple for Baal in the kingdom's capital, Samaria, an altar to him, and a sacred post (or grove), a symbol of Baal's consort, the goddess Asherah, thus conferring national status on pagan gods (I Kings 16:32-33). We can assume that under his kingship Baal worship deeply pervaded Israelite life,[3] corrupting the underlying moral and ethical foundation of monotheism.

Who was Elijah, challenger not only to the current regime, but to the two that followed (873–843 BCE)?

Before we know anything about him, except that he is "the Tishbite, an inhabitant of Gilead [in Transjordan]," Elijah appears before Ahab, and bluntly declares, "As the Lord lives, the God of Israel whom I serve, there will be no dew or rain except at my bidding" (I Kings 17:1). This is a broadside against Baal, since *he* is supposed to be the storm god, the "cloud rider," whose arrival is announced by thunder and lightning, who is thought to bring the life-giving rain associated with the seasonal renewal of vegetation.[4] In an agriculture-based economy that relies mainly on moisture from rain and dew (rather than on irrigation), it's not difficult to imagine how Baal worship, whether as primary or supplemental deity, would seem like a good idea to farmers whose lives were tied to natural phenomena, but Elijah's warning should give Ahab pause to reconsider his allegiances. In a prolonged drought, crops, especially the vital grains, will fail, and famine will ensue, as indeed it does, as predicted (I Kings 18:2).

God instructs Elijah to withdraw into the countryside and go into hiding by Nahal Kerit,[5] east of the Jordan. Here He promises Elijah that ravens will feed him and supply him with water from the wadi (I Kings 17:4). When the wadi dries up from the drought, God instructs Elijah to go north to Zaepath, south of Sidon, where He has designated a widow to feed him. The widow, however, explains that she is very poor and has only a handful of (barley) flour left and a little (olive) oil to feed herself and her son, after which they will starve. Elijah assures her not to be afraid, and then performs the first of two miracles. In the first one, the near-empty jar of barley flour and jug of olive oil are filled up "until the day that the Lord sends rain upon the ground" (I Kings 17:14). She must have been impressed, but when he then performs a second miracle, reviving her son after he has drawn his last breath, she knows that "the word of the Lord is truly in your mouth" (I Kings 17:24). It seems that God wants us to know that not only is His prophet zealous in pursuing His enemies, but His prophet is a force for life and good: just as God feeds Elijah in time of need, so Elijah will feed others in want.

In the third year of the terrible drought, Elijah commands Ahab to summon all the population to Mount Carmel, as well as all the prophets of the Canaanite gods, in order to settle the issue that has brought on such dreadful conditions. In characteristically forthright style Elijah asks, "How long will you keep hopping between two opinions?" (I Kings 18:21). In Elijah's view the choice is simple. "If the Lord is God, follow; and if Baal, follow him!" He devises a test: two young bulls are to be offered on altars but the fires beneath them are not lit. First the prophets of Baal are to invoke the name of Baal to send fire, but no matter how hard they try (Elijah eggs them on with caustic comments such as 'Shout louder! Maybe he is asleep.'), nothing happens. Then Elijah calls to God and "fire from the Lord descended and consumed the burnt offering" even though the altar has been soaked with water (I Kings 18:38). The people cry out that (for the moment) "The Lord alone is God," then Elijah, with the people's aid, slaughters the four-hundred and fifty prophets of Baal, and finally, rain is signaled by rumbling, "the sky grew black with clouds; there was wind, and a heavy downpour fell" (I Kings 18:45). With the end of the drought, Baal, the "cloud rider" has been defeated by God at his own game, but the drama is not yet played out.

When Elijah learns that Jezebel is still in control and threatens retaliation, he is devastated and flees southward into the desert wilderness. There he finds comfort beneath a broom bush, and just as he has fed the impoverished widow, God's angel now provides him with food and water to sustain him on his walk to Mount Horeb/Sinai, where he opens his heart to God. He cries out that he has failed in his mission, the people have already forsaken God's covenant, torn down His altars, and killed His prophets. In a most remarkable scene, God calls to Elijah to stand on the mountain before the Lord, "And Lo, the Lord passed by. There was a great and mighty wind, splitting mountains and shattering rocks by the power of the Lord; but the Lord was not in the wind. After the wind an earthquake; but the Lord was not in the earthquake. After the earthquake fire; but the Lord was not in the fire. And after the fire "a still small voice" (I Kings 19:12), a sound of the thinnest silence.[6] Only recently on Mount Carmel, Elijah had called on God to prove His might against the Cannanite god, Baal, by sending down fire to consume the sacrificial bull, but here, in the vastness of the desert at Horeb, God is reduced to virtual silence, yet His power is overwhelming. Like Moses who hid himself from direct contact with the presence of God in the burning bush, Elijah, too, wrapped his face in his cloak and was overcome. Was there a lesson here for him, one that could help him understand his failures? Perhaps God means Elijah to know that the good he had tried, but failed, to accomplish by vanquishing Baal worship, was not defeated. Even though evil appears mighty, loud, and triumphant, it can be overcome, not by the sign of God's might that Elijah had invoked, but by indomitable faith in God's purpose and persistent, patient work in His cause.[7] Elijah's foe, the powerful Jezebel, who strove to superimpose her alien values over those of Israel, only temporarily triumphed. She is later punished for instigating the death of Nevot, whose vineyard she coveted. Although her overthrow is long in coming (she outlives her husband), it represents a stirring of the true spirit of the kingdom.[8]

However much Elijah felt he had failed his mission on earth, his later spectacular ascent to heaven in a chariot of fire (II Kings 2:1-12) transformed him into a spiritual force invested with great powers. According to Jewish legend, his removal from earth marked the beginning of a new life as a tireless helper in time of need, a teacher, a guide, and a vigilant protector of the innocent.[9] His heavenly ascent became the source of messianic expectations that he would return to earth and turn the hearts of the parents to the children and the hearts of the children to the parents before the coming of the great and awesome day of the Lord (Malachi 3:23-24), when Israel will be created anew.[10]

—ɷ—

AS ELIJAH FLED deeper into the desert after leaving his servant in Beer Sheva, the vegetation thinned out, occurring now mainly in dry riverbeds (wadis) and rocky outcrops. When the prophet had walked an entire day and could go no further, he took shelter beneath a quintessential desert shrub: the white broom bush, *Retama raetam*, the *rotem* of the Bible. Wide at the top, narrow at the bottom, six feet or taller, it is the sort of growth one is thankful to shelter in, especially when a breeze freely circulates through white broom's numerous narrow branches. According to tradition, Hagar, when sent by Abraham from Beer Sheva into the desert, "thrust the child [Ishmael] under one of the [white broom] bushes" (Genesis 21:14-15).

The text does not explicitly say what time of year Elijah fled into the desert, so we do not know what he saw. White broom changes in appearance as it adapts to changes in available moisture, which varies from year to year during the winter months and is notoriously unreliable. In early winter white broom sprouts soft new green stems covered with silvery hairs and tiny leaves, then by late winter and early spring, it produces a multitude of showy white bean-like flowers ringed brownish-purple at their base and held by a distinctive purple calyx. Their honey-scented flowers attract bees so pollination is assured. This is very important for white broom's survival in the brutal conditions of excessive heat and irregular desert rainfall,

Photograph © Jackie Chambers

Retama raetam. White broom bush flowers, Ramon Crater/ Makhtesh Ramon in the Ramon Nature Reserve, Negev.

for once the flowers are pollinated, they will form many egg-shaped pods, each containing one to three seeds, some of which are bound to germinate to grow more plants. Pods are dispersed by flood water washing through wadis, by wind rolling them over the sands, and by animals eating them and excreting the seeds. In lean years, the seed pods of white broom provide nearly the only food for foraging goats in southern Sinai.[11]

As the dry season approaches, white broom sheds its tiny leaves, and most of its silvery hairs, to conserve the moisture so vital to its survival. The remaining stems harden but remain green. Photosynthesis, the process by which green plants absorb the sun's energy and turn it into food for growth, usually carried out via minute openings (stomata) on the backs of green leaves, occurs within the green stems of the white broom.[12] The openings, sunken in furrows in the stem to lessen water loss during the process, allow for the exchange of the necessary gases: carbon dioxide, absorbed from the atmosphere, combines with hydrogen to produce glucose, from which the waste product, oxygen, is released into the atmosphere. In addition to these adaptations for survival, white broom's underground roots, thirty to forty feet long, penetrate deep into the desert soil to find water, and during prolonged drought, the bush sheds excessive stems. Despite these features, white broom does not always endure successive dry winters, but generous seed dispersal ensures its survival.

White broom's stems are a source of slow-burning, high-heat fuel whose coals are well known as a source for cooking. The miraculous cake, that appeared along with water, when Elijah awoke from his sleep beneath the broom bush, was said to have been "baked on hot stones [embers]," a reference to rotem's amazingly long-lasting coals. In rabbinic literature these remarkable properties were likened to the long-lasting damage of an evil or slanderous tongue (*lashon hara*): "All other coals, when they are extinguished on the outside are extinguished inside; whereas these coals, even though they are extinguished on the outside are not extinguished inside. The story is told of a person who left coals burning on *Sukkot* and found them still burning on Pesach" (Jerusalem Talmud *Pe'ah* 1:1).[13] The production of charcoal from white broom's roots, trunk, and stems was common among Negev Bedouin until recent times when white broom became a protected plant in Israel to prevent its extinction from over-harvesting.

Elijah chose well when he sat beneath the white broom. It offered him not only shade and perhaps a mattress of fallen branches,[14] but food cooked on its slow-burning embers, food that sustained him all the way to Sinai, a trip of "forty days and forty nights" (I Kings 19:8), at the end of which God spoke to him in a "still small voice" and transformed his mission as a messenger for a reborn Israel.

ENDNOTES
1. *The Jewish Study Bible*, 334.
2. James L. Kugel, *How to Read the Bible*, 431.
3. *The Oxford Companion to the Bible*, 70.
4. Ibid.

5. This is the original Hebrew. In the NJPS translation and other versions, "*nahal*" is translated into the Arabic "*wadi*," [as in "Wadi Cherith"], although these words are not synonymous. A wadi is a dry creekbed, with seasonal water in it; the rest of the time it does not flow. A nahal is a flowing river or creek, or a very large wadi with a flat bottom that can turn into a flowing river. As reader Elaine Solowey in the southern Negev describes these terms: "In our area, Nahal Zin is called Wadi Zin because all but its end by the Dead Sea is canyon-like rather than river-like." From the context, Nahal Kerit could be a place where one usually finds water but it is dried up due to God's punishment of drought (not just a lack of seasonal rain as would be the case with a wadi).

6. I have substituted the familiar "still small voice" of the JPS 1917 edition rather than the latest translation's (1985) "a soft murmuring sound," which seems far less impressive. The original Hebrew, "*kol demama daka*," literally, "a voice [or sound] of thin silence," or "the sound of silence" conveys the awe that Elijah must have felt. The prophet hears God's call in the sound of silence. As reader Paul Tobenfeld pointed out, the same idea has been preserved in the well-known Rosh Hashana *Unetaneh tokef* prayer when Jews are invited to hear God in the sound of the shofar [ram's horn]: "The great shofar is sounded, the still small voice is heard." (*U'vshofar gadol yitaka, b'kol demama daka yishama*).

7. The lesson to Elijah is suggested in J. H. Hertz, *The Pentateuch and Haftorahs*, 700.

8. See Adin Steinsaltz, *Biblical Images: Men and Women of the Book*, for his interesting analysis of Jezebel according to her own perspective, 177–184.

9. Louis Ginzburg, *Legends of the Bible*, "After His [Elijah's] Translation," 589–594.

10. Among the Jewish traditions associated with Elijah's return to earth are those at the Passover Seder when, at a point in the service, a participant, often a child, is appointed to open the door for him so that he may announce the advent of the Messiah (*Moshiach*), and wine is poured into a special cup for him, known as "Elijah's cup" (*kos shel Eliyahu*). One of my most lingering childhood memories of Passover is opening the door on a dark, cool spring night to let in the prophet, who has not yet arrived.

11. Avinoam Danin, *Desert Vegetation of Israel and Sinai*, 94.

12. Plants that carry the main burden of photosynthesis on their stems throughout the year are called "stem assimilants" as defined in Danin, 135. *Retama raetam* is a leading example of plants that have diminished or no leaf area as a consequence of xeric (dry) conditions.

13. According to this interpretation, Elijah's "*ugat retzafim*" (coal-baked cake) is linked to his sin of slandering Israel when the prophet says, "They have forsaken Your covenant" (I Kings 19:10). The rabbis

comment on Psalms 120:3-4, "What will the slanderous tongue gain you [which is itself] a warrior's sharp arrows and *rotem* embers?" The midrash explains that since rotem's embers burn inside even when they are extinguished on the outside, "So it is with someone who is the butt of slander, even though you have appeased him and he has (seemingly) been appeased, he still seethes on the inside" (*Bereshit Raba* 95, 19). This midrash is discussed in Hareuveni, *Tree and Shrub in Our Biblical Heritage*, 31.

14. Hareuveni, 32, describes in detail how to construct a warm bed from fallen white broom branches: "These branches burn readily when gathered into a pile for kindling. Amazingly, this fire does not go out as quickly as expected. On the contrary, it grows quietly, producing great heat, dying down very gradually, leaving a pile of gray, charcoal-covered branches. A gentle puff into the pile proves that there is still a fire smoldering inside. The hiker who knows how to utilize this characteristic of the white broom branches will prepare a layer of broom embers on the ground to suit his size, cover them over with a layer of sand or fine soil to a depth of five to ten centimeters [two to four inches], and then enjoy a warm mattress in the cold desert night."

Chapter Twenty-Eight

WARNING OF THE THORNS

Portion-*Masei* / Journeys (Numbers 33:1-36:13)

If you do not dispossess the inhabitants of the land, those whom you allow to remain shall be stings in your eyes and thorns in your sides. (Numbers 33:55)

In the fortieth year of their wanderings in the desert, as the Israelites are poised to enter the Promised Land, God warns that unless they dispossess its inhabitants, the Canaanites shall be like thorns in the Israelites' sides, leading them astray to follow pagan practices wholly antithetical to the moral and ethical basis of monotheism.[1] This warning follows another, one that is implicit in Moses' report of the entire journey from Egypt to the plains of Moab (Numbers 33:1-49). Although the text does not tell us why the itinerary is recalled, such a document would inevitably remind the people of the places where an earlier generation had suffered for their lack of faith in God, and this would serve as a warning for those present not to repeat the sins of the wilderness.[2] In this sense, both warnings reflect the Bible's persistent campaign against faithlessness. The recollection of the places where they had

Photograph © Avinoam Danin

Sarcopterium spinosum. Thorny burnet with thorns and fruit near Beer Sheva.

been would also remind the present generation of how God had protected and encouraged them, and even wrought miracles for them.

The journey had begun with the Israelites' hasty departure from Egypt on the day following the first Passover. God, as promised, had struck down every first-born among all the Egyptians, high and low, even their animals, and Pharaoh, at last, had ordered Moses and Aaron to take all the Israelite slaves and leave Egypt at once: 'Up, depart, begone, go!' (Exodus 12:31). And they went, six hundred thousand men on foot, in addition to the women and children, including "a mixed multitude,"[3] along with many flocks of sheep and herds of goats, a large, jostling crowd. The women hurriedly baked their unleavened cakes of dough on the way, since they had been driven out of Egypt and could not delay (Exodus 12:37-39). What a tumultuous, exhilarating time as they rushed from slavery to freedom, committed to follow a momentous course they did not yet understand. God had delivered them and now they must move on into the unknown.

There was no turning back on this journey, only forward, up to the Land, despite whatever difficulties the people encountered. To test them, God had deliberately chosen the long, arduous trek around by the Sea of Reeds and thence out to the desert wilderness, rather than the straight way from Egypt to Canaan "by way of the land of the Philistines" (Exodus 13:17-18).[4] We are so used to the phrase "desert wanderings," suggesting a long, arduous trek in a challenging terrain, that we cannot imagine the unfolding drama taking place anywhere else. Try recasting the Exodus journey from Egypt to Canaan, along the Mediterranean Coast (the Philistine Way), a journey then of about eleven days. It doesn't work because the more difficult journey in the desert wilderness, an endless vista of rock-strewn ground and rising, jagged stone mountains, and encounters with hostile nations (the Edomites, Amorites, Bashanites, Moabites and Midianites),[5] provides the right dramatic setting where God would have time to teach His newly-liberated people the rudiments of a new spiritual order so that they would be fit, in every sense, to enter the Promised Land. A landscape that challenges at every turn—in striking contrast to the relatively smooth course along the Mediterranean Coast—and that forces one to draw on inner strength to survive, would inevitably toughen and mature the former slaves. It is impossible to separate their journey from slavery to freedom from the desert landscape, which comes across, not as incidental background, but as a character in itself, a powerful force in the Israelites' physical and spiritual journey.

Every stop in the beginning of their travels exposes the former slaves' inadequacies. The conditions of their new life in the desert, entirely outside their experience in the lush land of Egypt, were difficult, but the people's lack of will, their undeveloped spiritual state, was even worse. Mentally and emotionally they were still slaves, showing extreme anxiety at every turn of events. Their refrain, when faced with hardships, was not to try to overcome them, but to complain, always hitting the same theme: "Let us be, and we will serve the Egyptians, for it is better for us to serve the Egyptians than to die in the wilderness" (Exodus 14:12).

At *Marah* ("bitter"), only three days into the desert wilderness, they had complained about finding bitter water. God responded with compassion and instructed Moses to sweeten it with a stick, but in return He expected something from them (their first lesson).[6] His straightforward 'fixed rule' was to do what is upright in His sight, give ear to His commandments, obey His Laws and He will protect you (Exodus 15:26). Since they have been instructed, so far, only to remember the Passover, God is not yet demanding very much from them (although this first lesson will be hard to learn). He knows they are still unformed, still children, as it were, far from adulthood, and in need of His protection. From the very beginning He protected them in their journey by displaying His presence in a marvelous pillar of cloud by day and pillar of fire by night (Exodus 13:21), and at the very next encampment after Marah, Elim, He showed them what paradise could look like, even in the desert: an oasis of twelve springs and seventy (date) palm trees (Exodus 15:27),[7] more than enough food and water for their needs.

In the Wilderness of Sin, a month after the Exodus, when they complained bitterly of hunger, the people had learned another very important lesson: to gather God's heavenly provision of manna for six days, trusting that God would provide them with a double portion then, so they could rest on the seventh day (Exodus 16). They were not told why, but simply to follow instructions. Initially, they lacked faith in God to provide them with sustenance, and so continued to gather manna on the seventh day, but through trial and error they passed the test. Only later, in the framework of the covenant, would they understand the importance of the Sabbath as a unique rest period based on divine time rather than on the cycles of nature as in the celebration of Passover at the time of the barley harvest. By then the seventh day rest had become a natural part of their lives (Exodus 31:15-17; 35:1-3).

This was great progress, but at Rephidim lack of water again became an issue when the people quarreled with Moses about their predicament and uttered their usual complaints, questioning the point of their liberation and even the presence of God, despite all He had already done for them (Exodus 17:1-7). Although God did deliver water (Moses was instructed to strike a rock and water poured forth),[8] future generations regarded the place where this event occurred, *Massah* ("trial") and *Meribah* ("strife"), as a warning: "Do not be stubborn as at *Meribah*, as on the day of *Massah*, in the wilderness, when your fathers put Me to the test, tried Me, though they had seen My deeds [for them]" (Psalms 95:8-9).

Three months later, the Israelites arrived at Sinai, encamped at the foot of the great rock mountain, and through a series of miraculous events, actually heard the voice of God speaking to Moses. The entire people—men and women together—gathered at the foot of the mountain, felt the power of God directly, and were transformed (Exodus 19-24). All their complaints were forgotten in the grandeur of the experience, in the awe-inspiring surroundings at the mountain of God, and no matter how future events were to unfold—the shame of worshiping the Golden Calf, their rebellions, their years of desert wandering without ever reaching the Promised Land—this moment imprinted itself on the minds of all the future generations, so they felt as if they, too, had stood with their ancestors at Sinai and heard the divine voice.[9] And for God, too, in the words of His prophet Jeremiah, the desert sojourn would be remembered as the time of "the devotion of your youth, your love as a bride—when you followed Me in the wilderness, in a land not sown" (Jeremiah 2:2).[10] Now another generation is about to enter the land, God's Promised Land, where gradually, shepherds would become farmers, sowing and reaping their crops. In this new setting, there would be new hazards, new temptations, to overcome. Thus, the warning of the thorns.

—⟋⟍—

THE GARDEN PATH is not always smooth, especially in Israel and the surrounding semi-arid and arid regions where, in order to survive drought conditions, many plants have evolved to fend off grazing animals (especially sheep and goats) by producing sharp points on their stems, leaves, flowers, buds or fruits (they cannot afford to lose them!).[11] Animals that dare browse such plants may come away with a mouthful of wounds, a damaged digestive system, or otherwise incur harm in some way to their bodies. Thorny and prickly plants can actually infect large herbivores with bacteria and fungi as a form of biological warfare. If you have ever grasped stinging nettle by mistake, you will never forget the burning sensation which comes from an injection of acetic acid into your system (fortunately, it is short-lived) from the barbed leaves. So when we read that the Canaanites will be "stings in your eyes and thorns in your sides," if the Israelites fail to take action against them, we know that the warning is drawn from experience with the thorny plants with which the land abounds.[12] The Bible's metaphorical use of these plants, as warnings of impending doom or punishment for Israel's disobedience to God, was a sure way to get its message across.

But to which plants does the text refer? The Hebrew words and their context do not always offer clues to a prickly plant's botanical identity, particularly to those unfamiliar with the land. "No other group of plant names in the Bible," observed Michael Zohary, "is so frequently misidentified and arbitrarily translated."[13]

Over twenty different Hebrew words in the Bible relate to some kind of prickly growth, but since the Hebrew words are very difficult to attach to specific plants, such words are usually translated into English simply as "briar," "nettle," "thorn," and "thistle." The phrase *shamir va-shayit* (in variant forms), for example, is mentioned eight times in the Bible in the Book of Isaiah,[14] and is usually translated "thorns and thistles," but what does it mean? The Hebrew phrase may be a collective term for thorny plants in general (just as we use the term, "thorns and thistles," familiar from Bible translations, to mean prickly, weedy plants in general), or Isaiah may have tacked on the second name as a figure of speech to emphasize the thorniness of a particular plant.[15] For biblical narrators, the identity of the thorny plants was not important. Everyone, after all, lived among them, would probably know which ones were meant, and would have understood their symbolic use. When, for instance, Isaiah predicts that the farmer's carefully cultivated and guarded grapevines will be destroyed when God breaks down the protective wall and hedge surrounding it, and the ground will become overgrown with *shamir va-shayit* (Isaiah 5:5-6), we can be sure that an audience of farmers were able to envision this terrifying fate, because they were all too familiar with the thorny plants that invade cultivated ground.

When specific thorny plants fit the Hebrew text by virtue of their linguistic parallels or ecological setting, images of thorniness are brought to life. Zohary, for instance, proposes on linguistic grounds that *tzinim* or *tzininim* (plural) translated as "thorns" in the Numbers passage (33:55) is cognate with *sinim* in Talmudic and Mishnaic literature, and "possibly identical with the bramble, *Rubus sanguineus*" [16] (the rabbis' metaphorical 'burning bush'). This is a true bramble, a prickly shrub of the genus *Rubus*, similar to the blackberry bush. Those who have ever picked wild blackberries will appreciate how their tall stems and branches, fiercely armed with hooked prickles, can inflict 'thorns in your sides' as you reach into a tangled thicket to get that nice large berry. As the proverb tells us, "Thorns and snares are in the path of the crooked; He who values his life will keep far from them" (Proverbs 22:5). In Israel wild brambles grow up to six feet or more, along river banks and by swamps in the central and northern areas of the country.

Golden thistle, *Scolymus maculatus*, *hoah* (plural, *hohim*), mentioned several times in the Bible, grows in abandoned and fallow fields and at the edges of uncultivated fields, in heavy, deep soils. As an annual that grows up and completes its growth cycle in a single season, its seeds sprout during the rainy season to form a nearly spineless rosette of leaves, but gradually, to conserve water in the approaching drought, the entire plant changes as its soft leaves turn leathery and very spiny all along a rigid stem from two to three feet tall; the stem itself is whitish and fearsomely armed with sharp-tipped spiny wings. The plant's appearance, first in bud, then in full bloom from April to July when topped by tufted, bright yellow flowers caged within sharp spiny bracts, is formidable, but the flowers are

Narcissus tazetta and Scolymus maculatus.
Narcissus flowering at the foot of the skeletal
form of golden thistle in a wet field, Golan.

Narcissus tazetta. Golan.

pretty in bloom. Well-rooted in the ground, the thistle's gray skeletal
form remains behind after it has completed its growth cycle, and thus
serves as a dramatic foil for the emerging native daffodil, *Narcissus
tazetta* (*narkiss*), which grows in a similar habitat. Blooming in the
winter months from December to February, its dainty form, relatively small stature (twelve to eighteen inches tall), and its bouquet-
like clusters of fragrant flowers—white-petaled with a prominent
deep yellow central crown (Latin, *tazetta*)—are in marked contrast
to the tall, dead, angular thistle, and in this way we see how a natural
pairing of strikingly dissimilar plants in the ground suggested the
graphic imagery in Solomon's Song of Songs when the lover declares,
"Like a lily among the thorns, *shoshanat ha'amakim*, so is my beloved
among the maidens" (Song of Songs 2:2).[17]

Elsewhere, the *hoah* is an invader, taking over wheat fields. Job cries
out, "If I have eaten its yield without payment . . . let thorns [*hohim*]
grow instead of wheat, and foul weeds instead of barley" (Job 31:39-
40, RSV), from which the rabbis concluded that the presence of *hohim*
indicated rich soil for growing wheat.

Weeds like *hoah* remind us of God's curse upon the land, our fate
since Adam and Eve were expelled from the first garden (*gan eden*)

for their disobedience in eating the forbidden fruit. In Eden, the well-watered garden was filled with wonderful fruit trees, "pleasing to the sight and good for food" (Genesis 2:9), and free of weeds. Conditions for the growth of food plants were ideal, but in the post-Eden universe God decreed, "All the days of your life thorns and thistles [*kotz ve-dardar*] shall it [the ground] sprout for you" (Genesis 3:17-18); some identify this "*dardar*" with star thistle, *Centaurea iberica*, its common name in Hebrew, although it does not grow in fields. Even though many people live far from the sources of their food, and so are unaware of the daily struggle to maintain productive land (whatever the technology), even a backyard gardener is familiar with the travails of trying to keep a vegetable garden free of weeds (among them thistles and other troublesome, unwanted plants). And so we must work to live. Jeremiah drew from this condition a moral lesson: If the land is kept 'open' (well cultivated), the peoples' hearts, by analogy, would open toward God. "Break up the untilled ground," he advised, "And do not sow among thorns. Open your hearts to the Lord" (Jeremiah 4:3-4).

None excelled the prophet Isaiah in invoking thorns and thistles to give heft to his visions. Just as thriving crops were associated with blessings, the desolation of the land was considered a consequence of wickedness, as embodied in the *sirim* of the Bible, always plural (singular, *sira*), usually translated as "thorns." It is identified as a dwarf, thorny shrub, *Sarcopoterium spinosum* or thorny burnet, one of several easily burned low shrubs that help to spread a whirlwind of fire, as in the one that will consume the wicked (Psalms 58:10).[18] Isaiah predicts that "*Sirim*" will grow up in its [Edom's] palaces, and nettles and briers/thorns (*kimosh* and *hoah*)[19] in its strongholds (Isaiah 34:13), a shorthand way of bringing home in a vivid image the total destruction of Edom's civilization; God's wrath is turned, at times, not only on His faithless people, but on their enemies. We can appreciate the depth of His curse when we envision the various ruderal plants (those found in ruins and garbage heaps) that move in where the soil is unattended but rich in nutrients. Since the prophet leaves out what must occur before the *sirim* take hold (his audience would not need this spelled out), we must imagine what might happen: The first weeds to appear after the destruction of the palaces would probably be carpets of sharp-leaved nettles and the little pink-flowered mallow, *Urtica pilulifera* and *Malva parviflora*, and when the fertile soil had undergone a lengthy period of leaching by rain water, the yellow-flowered crown daisy and white mustard, *Chrysanthemum coronarium* and *Sinapis alba*, would thrive in their place. Many years later, after additional leaching, the very spiny artichoke cotton-thistle, *Onopordum cynarocephalum*, would spring up. Then, years after the establishment of *Onopordum*, when the polluting influence of the palace ruins had disappeared, *sirim* would take over. Unable to compete with weedy plants, this thorny shrub would now have all the ground to itself. In just a few well-chosen words, Isaiah conveys the utter destruction of Edom, where weeds, rather than nourishing cultivated plants, will always grow up in its soil, its civilization irrevocably destroyed.[20]

Sirim are typical of the low shrubby growth that grows over abandoned, deforested, once-cultivated land, turning it into a wasteland or *batha*, a Hebrew term adopted from Isaiah's prediction of Israel's coming "desolation" in the parable of the vineyard (Isaiah 5:5-6). *Sirim* are compact shrubs, rounded in form, and springy that cover vast areas, especially in the once-forested hill country. Only twelve to eighteen inches tall and prickly all over, they hug the ground to survive winds. When the rains begin in the fall, young shoots appear below the dried, spiny branches of the previous season. The new shoots branch out to produce more pointed thorns. Until the dry summer season, the thorns remain green or reddish, but with increased heat and drought, these turn hard and become very sharp, then turn grayish-white and die after producing flowers and fruits. Flowers are small, occurring in tight clusters

Photograph © Ori Fragman

Sarcopterium spinosum.
Mounds of colonizing thorny burnet with anemones at the Pura Nature Reserve on the highway to Beer Sheva.

at the tips of short spikes. The light spongy fruits, changing from reddish to brown and dispersed by the wind, resemble pots, hence the former Latin name, *Poterium*, based on the Greek for a drinking cup, *poterion*. The modern Hebrew name for thorny burnet is *sir kotzanit* (literally, sharp little pot). The little 'pots' of *sirim* resemble the laughter of the fool because they crackle when the branches of the shrub are used as cooking fuel: "For as the crackling of the *sirim* under the pot, so is the laughter of the fool" (Ecclesiastes 7:5-6).[21]

Sirim, still widely used for cooking fuel, to pen livestock and to top off stone walls against grazing animals, is considered to be the thorny barrier in Isaiah's warning that God will "remove the thorn cover that it may be eaten [by goats]." Removal of this thorny protection against grazing sheep and goats would open the way to the utter destruction of the once fruitful grapevine [Israel].

Prophets do not confine themselves to dooming their people. On the contrary, they always hold out hope, even in the midst of impending disaster. In Isaiah's vision, both Assyria and Israel will fall, their wickedness embodied in a fire that "burns and consumes its *shayit va-shamir* [thorns and thistles] in a single day," leaving behind so few trees that "a boy may record them." But a saving remnant of Israel will survive, truly repentant (Isaiah 10:17-20). This is signified by a shoot that will grow from the stump of Jesse, a mere twig that shall sprout from his stock and in it "the spirit of the Lord shall alight upon him" (Isaiah 11:1-2). From thorns and thistles to regeneration from the stump of a tree, the Bible brings the natural world to the fore, charging nature with warnings as well as hopes for Israel's future.

ENDNOTES

1. For the Bible's concerns about pagan practices see Deuteronomy 12:31; 18:9-12. Traditional and modern scholarly sources consider that the policy of unconditional destruction of the peoples inhabiting the land (as in Numbers 33:55; Deuteronomy 7:1-2; 20:15-18) was purely theoretical and was never in effect. See Jeffrey Tigay, the *JPS Commentary, Deuteronomy*, 470–471; also *The JPS Study Bible*, 382.

2. Another, more fleshed out, review of the wilderness itinerary follows in Deuteronomy 1:6-3:29, emphasizing that mistrust and disobedience to God lead to disaster, while trust in and obedience to Him lead to success. These reviews are to ensure that Israel is fully prepared to enter the land, "with a new generation, new leadership in the wings, a full set

of societal rules, an operative cult, and, above all, a collective memory of experiences that serve to instruct and warn future generations." Everett Fox, *The Five Books of Moses*, 649.

3. *Erev rav*, undefined but thought to refer to non-Israelites from the underclass of Egyptian society who took the opportunity of the Exodus to flee the country. Fox and others link *erev rav* to the *asafsuf* of Numbers 11:4 who instigated the food rebellion; see Fox, 713. See also Chapter 24, *Food Lust*. It is assumed that over the forty years of wandering in the desert wilderness, the *erev rav* eventually blended with the people of Israel.

4. The presumed route of the Philistine Way (called "The Ways of Horus" by the Egyptians) from Egypt to southern Canaan ran parallel to the Mediterranean coast, was the shortest route to Canaan, and would take an army nine or ten days to reach Gaza. *The JPS Study Bible*, 133.

5. Numbers 20:14; 21:21, 33; 22:2-24:25.

6. On the need to teach and discipline His still unformed children, J. H. Hertz cites the following midrash in *The Pentateuch and Haftorahs*, 265: "It is like that king who wished to give his son his inheritance. He thought to himself, My son is young; he hardly knows how to read and write. If I give him all my possessions now, will he be able to keep them? I will wait until he has grown in strength and wisdom. In the same way God thought, the children of Israel are still children; first let Me teach them to understand and practice My precepts and commandments, then will I give them the Promised Land."

7. "Twelve" as in the twelve tribes; "seventy," considered a number of perfection, being a multiple of "seven," the number of days of the Creation.

8. Some thirty years later the scene almost repeats itself except that this time God orders Moses and Aaron to *speak* to the rock [my emphasis], rather than strike it. They disobey God and are severely punished; they will not be allowed to lead their people into the Promised Land (Numbers 20).

9. "In classical Jewish thought [based on the writings of Judah Halevi and Maimonides], the fact that the entire nation witnessed God speaking to Moses is the definitive evidence that the Torah is from God." *The Jewish Study Bible*, 146. In the magazine *Azure: Ideas for the Jewish Nation*, the author analyzes the origins of equality in the Bible, a concept that was unknown in the surrounding pagan culture. "Although the account of the revelation at Sinai is usually conceived in religious terms, its political implications are no less dramatic and constitute the bedrock of the Bible's egalitarian theology. Elsewhere the gods allegedly communicated only to the kings and had no interest in the masses. At Sinai, God spoke to the entire people, without delineating any role whatsoever for kings and their entourage . . . and transformed the entire people of Israel into a collective of king-like individuals." Joshua Berman, "The Biblical Origins of Equality," *Azure*, Summer 5769/2009, p. 80. Popular understanding of this event is that all Jews, through time, heard God's words together.

10. The wilderness [*hamidbar*] in a land "not sown" (Jeremiah 2:2) may be arable land that only needs water to make it suitable for growing. Jeremiah was familiar with the phenomenon of pockets of green land in a desert environment that, because of their topographical location and soil composition, could absorb available moisture and become fertile, but in this passage he is recalling the people's courage in leaving the lushness of Egypt for the unsown, barren land of Sinai. Suggested in Nogah Hareuveni, *Desert and Shepherd in Our Biblical Heritage*, 24.

11. See description of *Scolymus maculatus*, 242.

12. It is difficult to be exact when counting the number of thorny plants in Israel. Sources differ, but as a knowledgeable friend observed, in one way or another, as many as 2,300 [out of 2,875 plant species] may leave a spiny tip in one's finger.

13. Michael Zohary, *Plants of the Bible*, 153.

14. Isaiah 5:6; 7:23, 24, 25; 9:17; 10:17; 27:4; 32:13;. An entirely different phrase in Hosea 10:8, "*kotz v'dardar*," is also translated "thorns and thistles."

15. Occurring pairs are known as "*hendiadys*," from a Greek phrase which means "one thing by means of two."In this instance *shamir va-shayit* could have been used to strengthen the concept of thorniness, as suggested by Zohary, 153.

16. Zohary, 157. See Chapter Twelve, "At the Burning Bush," for another discussion of this plant.

17. *Narcissus tazetta* as the probable candidate for the "lily among thorns" is based on the teachings of Nogah Hareuveni. At Neot Kedumim, Israel's Biblical Landscape Reserve, which he established, visitors can see the "lily" and "thorn" growing together in their ecological setting as they do in nature.

18. The *sira* or *sirim* of the Bible and post-biblical literature was first identified as *Sarcopoterium spinosum* or thorny burnet by G. E. Post (1896) and I. Loew (1924), then, after thorough field research in Israel, by Ephraim Hareuveni (1933). See Nogah Hareuveni, *Tree and Shrub in Our Biblical Heritage*, 66-67, for his father's methods.

19. For Ephraim Hareuveni's identification of *kimosh* as *Ammi visnaga*, a weed that quickly spreads in abandoned wheat fields, see Hareuveni, 70. The *hoah*, as already discussed, is an invader weed, especially in water-saturated fields during the rainy, winter months. Same source.

20. This ecologically-based sequence of plant succession is based on "Thoughts about the replacement of ruderal plants in human-induced habitats in relation to the scriptures," by Avinoam Danin in Table of contents, *Plant Stories*, Chapter D, part 6 from "Flora of Israel Online." See Bibliography for Internet address.

21. Nogah Hareuveni discusses *sirim* (*seerim*) in detail, in Biblical passages as well as its many uses in biblical times and today. See Hareuveni, 66–78.

Chapter Twenty-Nine

Tzelafkhad's Daughters
and the Persevering Caper

Portion-*Masei* / Journeys (Numbers 33:1-36:13)

*The daughters of Tzelafkhad did as the Lord had commanded Moses:
Mahlah, Tirzah, Hoglah, Milcah, and Noah, Tzelafkhad's daughters,
were married to sons of their uncles, marrying into clans of descendants
of Manasseh son of Joseph; and so their share remained in the tribe of
their father's clan.* (Numbers 36:10-12)

A second census has been taken so that the land which the Israelites are about to enter will be properly divided among the tribes. At this point something unheard of occurs: The five daughters of someone named Tzelafkhad[1] have stepped up, not only to Moses, but to all officials of the tribe and cult, in fact, to the entire assembly at the entrance to the Tent of Meeting, and made a sound case for inheriting their father's land: their father had died "in the wilderness" (he was not, they assured everyone, associated with the rebellious Korah faction) and there were no male heirs. "Let not our father's name be lost to his clan just because he had no son! Give us," they plead, "a holding among our father's kinsmen!"

Photograph © Avinoam Danin

Capparis zoharyi. Bees making a beeline at dusk to collect pollen grains from open caper flowers, Jerusalem.

249

(Numbers 27:1-4). Moses, having no precedent for such an intervention in established law, consults God, Who sees the justice of their cause and rules in their favor, further clarifying the procedure with regard to inheritance (Numbers 27:6-11).

All legal and ritual matters and land appropriations are then settled. But are they? Later, the males of the same tribe as the daughters see a loophole in the law and they step up, too (perhaps the consequences of female inheritance were not immediately apparent to them). This is a very serious matter for which the male family heads, descendants of Manasseh of the Josephite clan, appealed, not to the entire assembly as had Tzelafkhad's daughters, but directly to Moses and the other tribal chieftains. Their complaint is that if the daughters marry out of their tribe, as they would be allowed to do in the adjusted law, the tribe would lose part of its ancestral portion forever (Numbers 36:3-4). Moses, at God's suggestion, sees the justice of this view, and so the daughters are still allowed to inherit their father's land, but they must marry within the tribe, which, as dutiful daughters, they do.

The first thing that strikes the reader is the daughters' bravery (or effrontery) in bringing their case forward in what is so apparently a patriarchal setting. The second is that the Bible not only respects their right to do so, but takes care to give us their names each time they are mentioned: "Mahlah, Noah, Hoglah, Milcah, and Tirzah" are repeated three times: when they bring their case to Moses (Numbers 27:1-2); when they marry within the clan (Numbers 36:10-12); and when they receive their inheritance (Joshua 17:3-6).[2] Evidently the text means us to know them intimately, not only as Tzelafkhad's daughters, but as individual women in their own right, troubled by an injustice that directly affects them. The resolution of their case is an example of the case-law approach, similar to common law, within the Torah itself,[3] and is embodied in Jewish Responsa literature, *she'elot u'teshuvot*, "questions and answers." This is a body of work, from post-Talmudic times to the present day, that covers every aspect of Jewish life, and shows in detail the elasticity of the Torah when confronted with specific cases that cannot be dealt with within the confines of existing law.[4] The laws of female inheritance were not written into the original Torah law, but circumstances called for a new ruling (twice!). A judicial decision, therefore, founded a rule of law. The case of Tzelafkhad's daughters passed into legal history.[5]

Post-biblical literature continues to find something fresh to say about the legal case as well as the character of the daughters.[6] The Talmud, for instance, has nothing but praise for them. One midrash teaches the lesson that the women of the wilderness generation repaired the breaches made by the men. In contrast to the scouts who slandered the land in their report to Moses, thus frightening the people away from the Promised Land (Numbers 13:31-33), the daughters of Tzelafkhad, braving disapproval, made a passionate appeal not to be denied their portion (Num. *Rabbah* 21:10).[7]

Rabbi Akiva (50–135 CE), considered to be the greatest of all Mishnaic Sages opened up a creative line of thinking about the daughters' father when he proposed that the name of the man who gathered kindling wood on the Sabbath was Tzelafkhad, who "died in the wilderness . . . for his own sin" (*Shabbat* 96b), as the daughters had reported (Numbers 27:3). With hindsight, it seems like a perfect fit, for his name can be broken down to mean sharp caper (*tzalaf*-caper; *khad*-sharp); the caper bush's plentiful dry stems make good kindling, especially in winter when most shrubs sprout new growth, while the caper bush remains leafless and its thin, dead stems, quite dry. As a shepherd, Rabbi Akiva would know all the uses of desert plants; perhaps he had this in mind when he linked the Sabbath-breaker to Tzelafkhad.

The caper is an endless source for homiletic expression in the Talmud. In a story about a righteous man who refrains from mending his broken fence on the Sabbath, the hole is mended by the miracle of a sprouting caper bush that effectively covers the break. "He and his family lived off [the income] from that caper for the rest of their lives" (*Shabbat* 150b). In Kabbalistic tradition many centuries later, the strands of thought inspired by Rabbi Akiva, are woven together in the story that the soul of the Sabbath-breaker, Tzelafkhad, whose name was said to suggest the caper tree, finally found rest when it transmigrated to the soul of the righteous man who had refrained from mending his fence on the Sabbath (*D'vash L'pi*, Hida).[8]

—⁕—

WHAT IS THE CAPER BUSH and why was it so popular a subject in rabbinic literature?

Photograph © Avinoam Danin

Capparis zoharyi. June-blooming caper bushes on the Western Wall, Jerusalem.

There are six caper bush species in Israel. The most widely distributed is *Capparis zoharyi,* formerly *Capparis spinosa* (*tzalaf kotsani*), literally, thorny caper, a deep-rooted, low mounding shrub (a tree, according to Talmudic nomenclature), two to three feet tall, with arching reddish stems that may trail to seven feet. Native to the Mediterranean region, it characteristically grows in the crevices of rocks or stone walls, over ruins, or wherever other plants could not survive. When standing at the Western Wall, look up, and you will see its spreading, lax form hanging down against the ancient stones. The caper's association with the walls of Jerusalem is preserved in the name, Tzalaf, whose sixth son is named as one of the helpers in the reconstruction of the city's walls (Nehemiah 3:30). Another species, the ever-blooming *C. aegyptia,* grows out of solid rock in the Negev and persists between boulder cracks at the top of King Herod's fortress, Masada, in the Dead Sea desert, truly a miracle of growth.[9]

The rabbis, familiar with the caper's ability to flourish in difficult places by means of its penetrating roots, would see in its strength an analogy to Jewish endurance: "Three are persevering [strong]: Israel among the nations . . . the goat among cattle, and . . . the caper among the trees" (*Beitza* 25b). The KJV mistranslation, followed by others, about Solomon, who knew everything "from the cedar in Lebanon to the hyssop that grows out of the wall," rather than "in the rock," led Bible plant scholars to misidentify the hyssop as the caper bush, which travelers noted growing from ancient walls. True biblical hyssop, *Majorana syriaca*, is a strong-scented herb that grows between the 'walls' or sides of rocks on the ground.[10]

After caper seeds sprout, they send down their roots to find life-giving moisture. As plants grow, their arching stems sprout drought-resistant waxy, round green leaves, accompanied by hooked spines or thorns at the base of their stalks, effectively protecting the plant from predators; the previous Latin epithet *spinosa* means spiny or thorny. Rounded, reddish buds open to unfurl a delicate white, four-petaled flower, two to three inches wide. When fully open, a profusion of purplish-pink stamens extend beyond the white, cupped petals, adding to the flower's beauty and airy grace, similar to cleome, *Cleome hassleriana*, a closely related popular garden flower in the West. The caper flower's ovary, positioned on an elongated stalk, thrusts up in the midst of the stamens. When the petals fall, the fruit, called caper berry, is revealed. When ripe its oval shape, two to three inches long, hangs down from the stem. Caper berries contain as many as three-hundred seeds and when these are eaten by birds and widely dispersed, their high number ensures that at least some of them will find a favorable spot to germinate. The caper is well-designed to survive difficulties.

Caper plants produce hundreds of buds during their long flowering period from May to August, so although each flower lasts only twenty-four hours, fresh ones are continually opening, blooming, and quickly forming fruit. The show begins in late afternoon when the white tips of the petals can just be seen in the caper bush's round, fat buds; by evening the fragrant flowers open, attracting bees as well as the hovering hawk moth (similar in the sound of its whirring wings to a hummingbird). Fluttering near the flower in search of nectar deep within the bloom, it picks up pollen from the tips of the stamens (the anthers) on its long beak and in the course of its hovering, deposits it on the ovary, thereby accomplishing fertilization: the following morning, as the heat of the day increases, the petals wilt, then fall, revealing the embryonic fruit.[11] The phenomenon of a plant producing both flowers and fruit within a twenty-four hour period did not escape the rabbis, who were aware of the natural world to a remarkable degree and effectively brought it into their teachings.

Over two thousand years ago, Rabban Gamaliel of Yavne (80–110 CE)[12] taught his students that the prophet Ezekiel's vision of trees that would bear fruit every day in the world to come (Ezekiel 17:23) was already true. When questioned about this improbability by a skeptical student who pointed to Ecclesiastes 1:9 ("There is nothing new under the sun"), Rabban Gamaliel replied: "'Come and I will show you an example in this world.' He went out and showed them a caper" (*Shabbat* 30b). If, as seems likely, he drew his students' attention to a single branch, they would see, all along its length, buds, opened flowers, spent flowers, and fruit in various stages of ripening, a graphic demonstration of Ezekiel's prophetic vision.

The caper's major economic value has always been its pungent-flavored pickled buds called "capers," which are marketed around the world as a condiment for appetizers, salads, sauces, meat dishes, and as a garnish. About the size of peas or smaller (the smaller ones are more desirable and expensive), they are sold packed in a salt-vinegar brine. The Talmud's discussions on tithing included the caper: "The caper shall be tithed on its [edible] *timorot* [young leaves at the tip of the branches], its [edible] *avionot* [young fruit], and its *cafrisin* [young flower buds], a decision Rabbi Akiva did not agree with because, he argued, "only the *avionot* shall be tithed because only they are fruit" (*Ma'asrot* 4,6). From this debate and other discussions in rabbinic literature, it is clear that the caper bush was an economic crop in ancient Israel and was subject to the rule of *orla*, the prohibition against making use of the fruit from a newly planted tree until its fourth year.[13] The taste of the caper bud, young leaf tips, and partially ripe fruit, all of which are still prepared in brine and sold, is like a peppery mustard with bitter overtones from the presence of the bitter properties also found in species of rue (*Ruta*). To get the most value from a caper bush, it is essential to pick the buds, leaf tips, and young fruits every day at their height of perfection before they turn bitter and are of no use. This added to the caper's reputation as a tree that produces new fruit every day.[14]

For a common plant of economic importance with a distinctive growth habit (sprouting from walls) and virtually indestructible, it seems odd that the caper bush, as a plant, rather than embodied in a name (in Tzalaf, father of the wall builder), did not suggest itself as a subject for metaphorical or symbolic use in the Bible. Or did it? The single possible reference to the caper bush, in Ecclesiastes 12:5, is to "*avinoah*," the name generally used in Talmudic literature for the caper's bud or fruit. But although translations differ, they manage to vividly convey the speaker's view of man's debilitation and mortality. One approach is to assume "*avinoah*" is a symbol of man's failed sexual desire because of the caper's known association as an aphrodisiac. "The almond tree blossoms, the grasshopper drags itself along and desire [*avinoah*] fails [to work]."[15] Another interpretation, assumes that "*avinoah*" is synonymous with the caper bush itself (*tzalaf*) and in this view, it is symbolic of regenerating plant life: "For the almond tree may blossom, The grasshopper be burdened, And the caper bush may bud again."[16] In other words, while nature carries on its seasonal cycle—living and seeming to die (an apt description of the caper bush), but ever-renewing itself—man ages, becomes infirm, and finally "sets out for his eternal abode" (Ecclesiastes 12:5). Just as "there is hope for a tree; if it is cut down, it will renew itself . . . but mortals languish and die" (Job 14:7-10).

The entire caper plant is a virtual pharmacopeia. Every part has been recorded for medicinal use. Fruits and roots, and the skin of the roots, have been used to soothe toothache and spleen complaints, reduce fevers, treat joint infections; and the sap of the plant, to kill worms. The prepared leaves are also used to relieve toothache and cough, and when applied in a poultice, for relieving back and joint aches. The caper leaves, with those of tamarisk (*Tamarix*), are reputed to be a remedy for sterility in women, and for men as well in a tea from the roots. The flower buds have been used to disinfect kidneys, as a mild laxative, and in a dressing to treat eye afflictions, and the flowers themselves when rubbed on the penis, are believed to strengthen erection. Roots, leaves, and fruits are also used to treat lung diseases, diabetes, infections, and nervousness. Modern research has found various compounds in the plant that affect blood clotting and, in common with rue, irritate the skin (rutin, the bitter property the caper shares with rue, is an anti-oxidant); flower buds contain antihistamine properties. Extracts from the caper are used in the cosmetics industry and to treat wrinkled skin.[17]

The strength the daughters show in their appeal to Moses over inheriting their share of the land was linked to the caper, a plant of uncommon strength, by virtue of their father, Tzelafkhad, whose name means "sharp caper." What happened to the daughters after they married? We know their property remained in the family tribe, but where and how did they live? Archeological data has revealed three place names in the northern regions of Samaria that match three of the daughters' names: Noah, Hoglah, and Tirzah.[18] It's a good thing the biblical narrative has preserved these names, for now we can envision the daughters living in a hilly area of poor soil, where few but the caper 'tree' could not only survive, but thrive, putting forth its new flowers and fruits every day. Like the righteous man who refrained from mending his fence on the Sabbath and thereby gained his living from the caper, we like to think that the brave and dutiful daughters, too, lived a full life, enriched by the same plant, thereby redeeming the sin of their father in the wilderness.

ENDNOTES

1. Transliterations of the name vary considerably: Tzlafchad, Tselafchad, Tzlafchad, Zelafchad, Zlafchad, Tzelafchad, Tzelofhad, Zelophehad, and the transliteration of the Hebrew letter *chet* as kh, as in Zelafkhad, rather than as ch; *chet* is pronounced like Ba*ch*, a sound that is difficult for non-Hebrew speakers. Rabbi Lawrence Kushner describes it as "It is the top of your throat and the bottom of your throat fighting against one another." *The Book of Letters*, 39. I have used the spelling I think most closely reflects the name's original Hebrew and plant origin: *tzalaf*=caper; *khad*=sharp [thorn].

2. The discrepancy in the order of the daughters' names in Numbers 36:10-12 compared with the other references signifies their equal merit (*Baba Batra* 120a).

3. For other examples see Leviticus 24:10-23 (the blasphemer); Numbers 9:1-14 (the second Passover); 15:32-36 (the Sabbath wood gatherer). The special circumstances of each case required a new binding law.

4. "Each of the recent centuries has produced scholars ready to deal with new problems. Thus, as new a technique as artificial insemination in

human beings is already the subject of numerous responsa." *The New Standard Jewish Encyclopedia*, 1619.

5. In its discussion of ancient law, The *Albany Law Journal* of 1873, Vol. VI, offers an extract from *The Law Magazine and Review*, p. 203, on the development of Jewish law: "The case, however, of the daughters of Zelophehad, reported in the Pentateuch as for the first time introducing inheritance by females into Hebrew law, with its attendant restriction, that the heiress should marry within her tribe, is a valid instance of a judicial decision, founding a rule of law. Here the statute was silent, and circumstances called for a decision which, when once pronounced, introduced a rule which obtained a force as obligatory as that which attached to the written code of Moses."

6. There is a growing body of work, for instance, on Jewish feminist and traditional perspectives on women in the Bible, including the daughters of Tzelafkhad. For a detailed analysis of how the daughters were regarded in Midrash and Aggadah, see Tamar Kadari, "Daughters of Zelophehad: Midrash and Aggadah," *Jewish Women: A Comprehensive Historical Encyclopedia*, available online at "Jewish Women's Archive." See Bibliography for Internet address.

7. Reader Paula Tobenfeld has written, "According to tradition, the daughters did not participate in the making of the Golden Calf, but are noted for their generosity to the tabernacle to which they contributed their most valued possessions, including their private mirrors, earrings, and precious dyed clothing, as valuable as gold, for the sake of the new sanctuary."

8. In *Tree and Shrub in Our Biblical Heritage*, 42–53, Nogah Hareuveni devotes a chapter to the caper bush, tracing its link to the Sabbath-breaker of Numbers 15:32-36 through Talmudic commentary and beyond. I have drawn on his insights in my own discussion of the subject. From outside sources, we learn that his father, Ephraim Hareuveni, "was apparently the first to suggest that the name Zelafhhad actually means 'sharp caper,' and in this he has largely been followed by later Israeli botanists." See Louis I. Rabinowitz, *Torah and Flora*, 122.

9. On an excursion to the top of Masada when I was in Israel in 1998, I observed *Capparis aegyptia* with one open blossom. It appeared to be trailing from a crack in the stone. Seven years later I saw this species in the same area, with a spent blossom.

10. See Chapter 17, "Mighty Cedar, Lowly Hyssop."

11. Avinoam Danin described the life cycle and fertilization of the caper flower in "The Resourceful Caper" in *Israel-Land and Nature*, p.139, Summer, 1980.

12. He was of the second generation of *tannaim*, those Sages mentioned in the Mishna or of the Mishnaic period: about 20 CE to the final redaction of the Oral Law (the Mishna) circa 200 CE. The title rabbi or

rabban was given to all the *tannaim*. Rabban Gamaliel was the accepted national-political leader of his day, recognized by the Roman government as spokesman for the Jews.

13. This rule ensured that the fruit tree would not be exploited before it had reached maturity. For more about *orla*, see Chapter Twenty, *Holy Fruit*.

14. Hareuveni, 48.

15. Cf. KJV and Judaica Press. The latter is the source for the complete online *Tanakh* (Jewish Bible) at the Chabad website. See Bibliography for Internet address.

16. NJPS.

17. D. Palevitch and Zohara Yaniv report the specific medicinal uses of the caper in Israel by Arabs and Jews from Arab lands, as well as modern research findings on its properties, in *Medicinal Plants of the Holy Land*, 67–69.

18. Hareuveni, 53.

Introduction

The Book Of Deuteronomy

Devarim

The Greek name for the fifth and last book of the Torah means "Second Law," apparently based on an erroneous translation of an older Hebrew name, *Mishne Torah*, "copy of the Torah."

The Hebrew name, "*Devarim*," is derived from the opening words of the first verse: "These are the words that Moses addressed to all Israel on the other side of the Jordan." This all-important speech or teaching, in the spirit of true Torah, crystallizes the relationship between God and Israel, and Israel and God. It is intended to strengthen the Israelites for life in their land, to deepen their commitment to God so they will not be lured away to serve unworthy pagan gods. Moses reviews their history, God's care of them through the desert, and exhorts them to follow His ways, the ways of life over death. He goes over the laws in detail, reaffirms the covenant, and blesses the tribes, before passing from the scene, mourned by his people. Under the leadership of Joshua they are now prepared to enter the land that God had promised their ancestor Abraham.

Photograph © Jackie Chambers

Ceratonia siliqua. Carob tree near Luzit caves in the Jewish National Fund Britannia Park west of Jerusalem near Beit Shemesh.

Chapter Thirty

THE EVERLASTING CAROB

Portion *Devarim* / **Words (Deuteronomy 1:1-3:22)**
Haftarah **(Isaiah 1:1-27)**
But if you refuse and rebel [against God], *You will be devoured* [by]
the sword. (Isaiah 1:20)

This selection from the Prophet Isaiah is always read on the Sabbath
before *Tisha b'Av*, a fast day commemorating the destruction of
the First and Second Temples, and is chosen for its theme of affliction. In the portion from Deuteronomy that precedes this reading,
Moses reviews the failures of the older generation in the wilderness
and the disastrous consequences of their behavior, to warn the new
generation not to make similar mistakes. Now, it seems, his warnings were ignored, for generations later the prophet Isaiah warns
of imminent catastrophe to a people who have lost their way and
"rebelled against Me!" (Isaiah 1:2)

Who was Isaiah, one of the most widely-known (and quoted)
of Israel's prophets? As we learn from the text, Isaiah (*Yeshayah*),
whose name means "help [or deliverance] of God," was the son of
Amoz. He lived in Jerusalem, Judah (Judea), the Southern Kingdom,
during the last half of the eighth century BCE and received his prophetic mission in the last year of the reign of King Uzziah. Isaiah
was active in Judah for forty years, from 740–701 BCE, throughout
the reigns of Jotham, Ahaz, and Hezekiah, and was a contemporary of the Prophets Micah and Amos. His wife, to whom he refers
as "the prophetess" (evidently an honorary title) bore him a son,
whose symbolic name, "*Maher-shalal-hash-baz*," meaning "swift to

plunder and quick to carry away," pointed to the speedy downfall of both the Northern Kingdom (Israel), and Syria (Isaiah 8:3-4), which occurred in 721 BCE. Another son was called "*Shear-jashub*" (Isaiah 7:3), meaning "a remnant shall return." [1]

Isaiah was on the scene, then, during the time of the Assyrian empire's domination of the region and the destruction of the Northern Kingdom, when most of its inhabitants were exiled. This was a terrible blow, leaving Judah as the lone representative of a struggling monotheism in a pagan world. It is against this background that Isaiah's voice rings out as a call to the people to mend their ways and repent, for if they do not, God's punishment will be severe. Isaiah, who sees punishment for Judah's sins coming not from worldly forces (the Assyrians), but directly from God, prophesies disaster ahead: "Your land is a waste, Your cities burnt down; Before your eyes, the yield of your soil is consumed by strangers—a wasteland as overthrown by strangers!" (Isaiah 1:7). In 701 BCE the Assyrians overran Judah and besieged Jerusalem, but the capital was miraculously saved. [2]

For a man of the city, of what we would now call an urban environment, it is surprising how often Isaiah frames his arguments, his words of chastisement, of condemnation and comfort, in the imagery of the everyday working world of agriculture, even from the household skills of dyeing wool. Because Judah is corrupted it will be punished. Jerusalem, he predicts, will be stranded like the fragile, temporary structures of "a booth in a vineyard" or "a hut in a cucumber field" (Isaiah 1:8)—erected to oversee the crop—a graphic metaphor for the capital surrounded by desolation. We see the color of Judah's sins in the prophet's imagery of wool dyed a brilliant scarlet, and its unblemished faithfulness in the wool "as white as snow" of those who repent (Isaiah 1:18). [3] His incomparable parable of the vineyard (Isaiah 5:1-6), an indictment against various moral lapses, is so true to the agricultural methods of his time that it could be used as a farming guide for viticulture. Isaiah's ability to see beyond his immediate place inspires his visions, infusing them with a power that spoke to the audience of his time and still thrills us today, although we may not wholly understand the specific references to land and flora.

The prophet's most serious charge against the people of Judah was the sin of idolatry, the worship of Canaan's nature gods. This was beyond any other offense; it represented a broken covenant, the violation of the first of God's Ten Commandments. Here was a people worshiping the very trees that God Himself had caused to grow. In his indictment, Isaiah goes right to the source, the trees themselves: "For they shall be ashamed of the terebinths [*Pistacia* spp.] which you have desired, and you shall be confounded for the gardens [pagan sacred groves] that you have coveted" (Isaiah 1:29). In Isaiah's clever metaphorical use of these emblems of nature worship, based on what appears to be an intimate knowledge of the tree's growth cycle, the worshipers themselves become the object of their devotion, as "a terebinth leaf that fades [dies in the autumn and is shed] and a garden that has no water." This is a telling description of a corrupted people with no future unless they return to the path of righteousness. His audience would have no difficulty associating decay with bare-limbed trees and an unwatered garden, but they could take some comfort in the prophet's imagery of possible redemption in the idea of a surviving remnant, the "the holy seed," (Isaiah 6:13) that would make a holy life true to God.[4]

A casual reading of the opening chapter of Isaiah, and the entire book, has led to the misconception of him as a prophet of social justice who characterized ritual as empty of meaning. Judah had become corrupted by wealth and Isaiah *did* severely castigate the current elite for its failure to deal justly with the poor, the oppressed, the orphans, and widows, but his chastisements and warnings were given within the context of Torah, in which there is no separation between ritual or law and morality; they are one.[5] His remedy for restoring "the faithful city" (Jerusalem), characterized as a harlot for the faithlessness of its people, was not to do away with rituals and laws, but to fulfill them (Isaiah 1:17). It was not that the people offended God with their sacrificial gifts and the rituals associated with the festivals, new moons, and sabbaths (Isaiah 1:13-14), but that these had become hollow gestures without the fulfillment, also, of laws concerning social justice. For Isaiah (and all the prophets), true holiness, the state that most pleases God, is achieved by carrying out His laws. To truly love God, one must carry out and obey His commands "with all your heart, and with all your soul, and with all your might" (Deuteronomy 6:5). Isaiah's was an abiding, never wavering, faith in God ... "Holy, holy, holy! The Lord of hosts! His presence fills all the earth!" (Isaiah 6:3). In the same vein, while he envisioned a time of universal peace when nations "shall beat their swords into ploughshares," this will happen only when "many peoples" come up to Zion [Jerusalem], where "He will teach us of His ways, and we shall walk in His paths" (Isaiah 2:3).

"Swords," in rabbinical interpretation can have another meaning. If the people reform, Isaiah promises that they will "eat the good things of the earth," but if they disobey and do not return to God, they will be "devoured by the sword" (Isaiah 1:19-20). There could be a worse fate in store for them. Taking note of a lack of a preposition in the original text,[6] combined with a play on the similarity between *herev* ("sword") and *haruv* ("carob"), the rabbis came up with a homiletic rendering of the text: "'You shall devour sword': that should read 'ye shall devour carobs,' and thus be as paupers and folk of feebleness" (*Vayikra Raba* 13,4). Some authorities believe that, in fact, *haruv* is derived from *herev*, based on the sword-like shape of the carob pod.[7] Just one word, "*haruv*," brings Isaiah's scene of desolation to vivid life for those familiar with the carob's associations. The citizens of Judah, whose productive land will be destroyed because of their iniquity, are reduced to eating carobs, the despised food of the poor, that grows, by inference, in waste ground, eaten only as a last resort in times of famine. No other food, apparently, was considered to be so far from "the good things of the earth."

—⚬—

WHAT IS THE CAROB and why was it so despised?

The evergreen carob, *Ceratonia siliqua*, indigenous to Israel, has been cultivated for millennia in the entire region, where the climate of cool winters and hot, dry summers is favorable to its growth. In Israel it grows in scrub or *maquis* forests with the mastic pistacia bush, *Pistacia lentiscus*, and is common in the Coastal Plain, adjacent foothills, and on the eastern slopes of Galilee and Samaria. A medium-sized tree of the pea or bean family, carob grows up to forty feet tall, a fine shade tree with a many-branched wide crown of leathery foliage that nearly obscures its trunk. Odd, petal-less flowers, male or female, usually appear on separate male or female trees in short, crowded spikes that sprout from thick old wood on the tree's branches, limbs, and even trunk. In the female flower, a long, projecting ovary grows out from reddish perianth scales (the envelope that encloses the flower bud); in the male, short white stamen filaments are topped by reddish anthers, giving male trees a reddish cast. Pollen from the male flowers is distributed to the female flowers (which bear the fruits or pods) by wind and bees; one male tree can fertilize about thirty female trees. Although flowers bloom in autumn, fruits are not ripe until the following year, when old, dry fruit and young fruits can be seen together on the same tree. Carob trees grow slowly, their yield increasing year by year, averaging two-hundred pounds of fruit at thirty years. Ancient Mediterranean specimens with gnarled and twisted trunks are reported to have borne three thousand pounds in a season.[8]

The carob's sweet, edible pods are its claim to fame (or infamy?). Four to twelve inches long, straight or curved, they hang down from the tree's branches, green at first, then turning dark brown and leathery in maturity. When the dry pods are opened, a sugary syrup, something like honey, drips from them. The seeds, about eight to a pod, are brown and shiny, and rattle when dry. Unlike various peas and beans in the same family, which split their pods when ripe, the carob's drop, whole, to the ground. The easiest way to make use of them is simply to chew the tough pod and spit out the seeds. The pod's pulp contains a high degree of sugar from the soft, semi-translucent pale brown pulp inside its walls, and is also a source of protein. Traditionally, carobs were considered animal fodder since they are not very digestible in their raw form (opinions vary on their taste). Unlike more demanding and desirable fruits that are subject to the vagaries of nature, carob trees consistently yield a good crop and so were stockpiled for famine emergencies and as cheap food for the poor and indigent. In this regard, carob resembled barley, another fodder crop more reliable than wheat that could be ground to make a cheap, coarse bread.[9]

The Hebrew name *haruv* influenced the Arabic, *khatub*, and is preserved in the common names in the countries to which it was introduced, as in the French, *caroube*, and the English, carob. The Greek, *keration*, little horn, from the shape of the carob pod, is preserved in the Latin genus name *Ceratonia* and the epithet *siliqua*, meaning pod-like. In Yiddish the carob is *boxser*, a corruption of the German *bockshorn* (ram's horn), indicating carob's widespread use in eastern Europe among Jews. Based on passages from the Christian Bible,

Photograph © Avinoam Danin

Ceratonia siliqua. Ripe carob pod with seeds, Jerusalem.

carob is also called St. John's bread and locust bean.[10] It is widely believed that in Mishnaic times, carob seeds, because of their near uniformity of weight (200 milligrams), were used as a standard measure for small weights known as *gera* in the Bible.[11] The term "carat," derived from *keration,* is a unit of weight against which to determine the value of precious gems, and was once also based on the weight of the carob.

Carob is not mentioned directly in the Hebrew Bible but some commentators believe it to be the source of honey that Jacob sent down to Egypt as one of the "choice products of the land" (Genesis 43:11).[12] Carobs are inferred in a description of the siege of Samaria by the Assyrians when sources of food were so hard to come by that "[even] a donkey's head sold for eighty shekels of silver, and a quarter *qav* [about two cups] of 'dove's dung' [carob][13] for five shekels" (2 Kings 6:25). These were inflated prices for lowly foods, with carobs being the lowliest.

In rabbinic literature carob comes into its own, and it is through the rabbis' eyes that we better understand its varied role in agriculture, in daily life, and as a traditional symbol of humility.

Not only was the carob widely cultivated, but farmers took care to improve their stock by grafting good variants onto seed-grown trees,[14] strongly suggesting the importance of producing good crops for whatever purpose. As an economic crop, tithes were levied against it beginning when the fruit blackened. Although recognizing the close relationship between the carob and other members of the bean family such as chickpeas and lentils, the rabbis ruled that it was ritually acceptable to plant carob side by side with Egyptian beans;[15] it is unclear why this should ever occur since these beans were raised as a field crop for animal feed and would need to be planted far away from the carob, with its ramifying roots. The

Jerusalem Talmud acknowledges this potential hazard by enjoining the farmer to keep both the carob and sycomore fig tree (*Ficus sycomorus*), another food for the poor, at least fifty cubits (about seventy-five feet) away from habitation or well (*Berahot* 9, 3).[16] The carob's value can be appreciated relative to other common commodities: a *qav* of carobs (about two quarts) was worth one quart of fig-cakes or a *log* (about half a quart) of wine or a quarter of the value of olive oil.[17]

However lowly, processed carob had many uses in daily life, a tradition that continues in the Middle East and Mediterranean countries where it is an abundant, cheap alternative to other sweeteners and thickeners. Today carob products enjoy a reputation as a health food (a healthy alternative to chocolate, for instance). Ripened pods were (and still are) cooked to yield a molasses-like general sweetener, milled into flour for baking breads and other products, and fermented into carob-wine and carob-brandy. Ground carobs, cooked like porridge, were considered digestible food for the elderly, thus their reputation as food for feebleness; modern investigation supports the carob's soothing, digestive properties. Leaves, high in tannin, were used in preparing leather, and when dried, served as a kind of stationery, and green pods yielded a golden dye.[18] Ripe seeds (locust bean) could be ground into a powder with thickening and glue properties, for which there are untold applications today.[19] The tree's close-grained reddish wood, in high demand in the ancient world for construction and to make utensils, was, according to Egyptian records, used to carve idols.[20] Those who worshiped the work of their own hands also, it appears, prayed to the trees themselves, not only to the terebinth, as Isaiah recognized, but also to the carob and sycomore.[21] The punishment to eat carobs can be seen in another light, as the fruit of the peoples' sin against God in the pagan worship of nature gods.

Legends in rabbinic literature abound about carob as a miraculous source of nourishment. In a well-known example, Rabbi Simon bar Yohai, a famous second century CE teacher, mystic, and outspoken critic of Roman occupation, fled Jerusalem with his son to find refuge in a cave where he hid for thirteen years, surviving solely on the fruits of a carob tree and a spring of water, both of which miraculously appeared at the mouth of his cave (*Shabbat* 33,2). The lowly status of the carob lent it an aura of holiness in the minds of the rabbis, who saw in its unfailing growth and bountiful crops, even in adversity, virtues of humility and perseverance, exemplified in teachings inspired by the lowly hyssop in which 'Israel, God's peculiar treasure, is lowly and modest, too.'[22] One could do no better than to plant this humble tree for the next generation when it will feed the poor and all who seek nourishment.

The Babylonian Talmud recounts this story: "While walking along a road a sage saw a man planting a carob tree. He asked him: 'How long will it take for this tree to bear fruit?' 'Seventy years,' replied the man. The sage then asked: 'Are you so healthy a man that you expect to live that length of time and eat its fruit?' The man answered: 'It was in carobs that I found the world, and just as my forefathers planted them for me, so shall I plant them for my sons that follow.'" (*Ta'anit* 23a).[23]

ENDNOTES

1. "to the true worship of God," according to Abarbanel, note to verse 3 in *The Soncino Books of the Bible*, Hebrew text, translation, and commentary of *Isaiah*. Rabbi 'Don' Yitzhak Abarbanel was a classical Jewish Bible commentator and thinker who left Spain during the expulsion of 1492.

2. Assyrian records indicate that Assyrian troops vanquished forty-six Judean cites, but not Jerusalem. *Jewish Study Bible*, 853.

3. Further along in this verse, "though they [your sins] be red like crimson, They shall be as wool," suggests two different states of sinfulness: if you have sinned by yourselves and you repent, your sins [scarlet] will be forgiven completely, signified by wool as "white as snow," but if "your sins be red like crimson, They shall be as wool." In other words, if you caused others to sin, your sins will not be wholly forgiven, "wool" in its natural state being slightly off-white. This interpretation is based on Rashi's commentary of this text (Isaiah 1:18) as discussed in the *Soncino* edition, 6.

4. See Chapter Three, *Abraham's Trees*, for a discussion of *Pistacia atlantica* and *P. palaestina* and the symbolism associated with these trees. The terebinth to which the prophet refers is most likely *P. palaestina*.

5. See Chapter Twenty, *Holy Fruit*, for a discussion of the unifying principle connecting practical and moral concerns in the Holiness Code.

6. The NJPS *Tanakh* offers two translations: "You will be devoured [by] the sword," or alternatively, "You will be fed the sword."

7. Nogah Hareuveni in Part 2, *Fruit in the Land of the Bible*, 19, educational material published by Neot Kedumim. He discusses other possibilities

that scholars have considered for the derivation of *haruv*: from *horev*, a synonym for dryness because the carob is a dry fruit in maturity; from the root word, *hurban*, meaning "destruction," because the carob tree grows in desolate areas.

8. Julia F. Morton, *Fruits of Warm Climates*, "Carob," 65–69.

9. Hareuveni explains a midrash (*Sifri, Parahat Beha'alotkha* 89) in which a man is asked why he is eating bread made out of barley? "'Because I don't have bread made out of wheat.' 'Why are you eating carobs?' 'Because I don't have any dried figs.'"

10. Many people are familiar with carob as "St. John's bread" or "locust bean" from the story in the Christian Bible of John the Baptist who was nourished on a diet of "locusts and wild honey" (Mark 1:6; Matthew 3:4). Some authorities believe "locusts" were thought to mean carob: Harold N. and Alma L. Moldenke, *Plants of the Bible*, 73. Carobs, a popular animal feed, were probably the "husks" of Jesus' parable of the prodigal son (Luke 15:16).

11. See Exodus 30:13, Ezekiel 45:12.

12. In Louis Rabinowitz, *Torah and Flora*, 127, the author refers to Bible commentators such as Saadiah Gaon and Ibn Janah who identified carob with the delicacies Jacob sent down to Egypt.

13. "Apparently a popular name for carob." *Jewish Study Bible*, 738.

14. Asaph Goor and Max Nurock, *Fruits of the Holy Land*, 259–260.

15. Discussed in Goor and Nurock, 259. "Egyptian beans" are cowpeas (*Vigna unguiculata*), a very ancient legume that is high in protein and drought tolerant.

16. Ibid.

17. Ibid.

18. Ibid., 263.

19. Among its uses, seed gum (locust gum) is used in producing cosmetics, detergents, paints, ink, shoe polish, photographic paper, and in tanning; the gum is a high quality thickener in food products such as ice cream, desserts, and soups.

20. Goor and Nurock, 257.

21. Ibid., 261.

22. Collected in Louis Ginzburg *Legends of the Jews* (original multi-volume edition), 364. See Chapter Seventeen, *Mighty Cedar, Lowly Hyssop*.

23. Reader Michael Solowey points to another version of the midrash in which the questioner is a Roman legate, Titus Rufus, and the old man is Honi Ha Maagel (Honi the Circle Maker), a mystic of Talmudic times and a sort of Jewish Johnny Appleseed. When the Roman legate asks Honi why he plants a tree that he will not live to eat the fruit of, Honi says, "The world was not empty when I came into it. There were carobs enough for me because those before me planted them."

Chapter Thirty-One

FLOWERS OF THE FIELD

Portion *Va-ethchanan* / I besought [the Lord] (Deuteronomy 3:23-7:11)
Haftarah **(Isaiah 40:1-26)**
All flesh is grass,
All its goodness [beauty] like the flowers of the field:
Grass withers, flowers fade
When the breath of the Lord blows on them.
Indeed, man is but grass:
Grass withers, flowers fade—
But the word of Our God is always fulfilled![1] *(Isaiah 40:6-8)*

Photograph © Avinoam Danin

Anemone coronaria. Anemones carpet in the Shefela (foothills of the Judean Mountains), Lahav near Beer Sheva.

This *Haftarah* is the first of the "Seven of Consolation," all drawn from the Book of Isaiah, which are read on successive Sabbaths following *Tisha b'Av* (the Ninth of *Av* according to the Hebrew calendar).[2] While there is no formal thematic link between the portion from Deuteronomy and this *Haftarah* selection, Moses, too, offers consolation to his charges as they are about to enter the Promised Land under Joshua's leadership.[3] Even if you stray from God, Moses tells them, if you "seek Him with all your heart and soul" you will find Him. Although the people may, at times, forget the covenant at Sinai, God remembers and will not fail to redeem them. Because He loved their fathers, He had chosen their heirs after them (Deuteronomy 4:29-31), and although the relationship will always be fraught with difficulties, it is eternal.

Many generations later, when the Southern Kingdom has been destroyed, the Temple in ruins, and the people are captive in Babylon,[4] God sends a message through his prophets to speak tenderly to "Jerusalem" (the Jews or people of Judah), to tell them that their "term of service" (punishment) is over, that they have paid double for their iniquities (Isaiah 40:2), and they soon will be returning home (as they eventually do, under a new ruler).[5] Just as He had once led them from captivity in Egypt across the desert to the Promised Land, so He will now be with them on their return journey from captivity in Babylon. In the glorious (and familiar) imagery of the prophet, "Every valley shall be lifted up, / And every mountain and hill shall be made low; / And the rugged shall be made level, / And the rough places a plain."(Isaiah 40:4).[6] What stands out in this description (whatever the translation), is that God's highway—the one to be prepared for the Lord Who will lead His people back—is nothing like the endurance trip from Egypt through the difficult desert of jagged mountains and rock-strewn ground. God is no longer testing His people, He is comforting them, so the road ahead is made smooth. Like a good shepherd that carefully pastures his flock, God, the ultimate Shepherd, is bringing His people home, gathering them like lambs carried in His bosom, while gently, He drives the mother sheep ahead (Isaiah 40:11). This evocative imagery, drawn from real shepherd life and so familiar to all (either from life experience or preserved in the nation's memory as an ideal) would surely have cheered the fallen people, as the entire reading has consoled generations of Jews in their exile and times of travail.

The prophet strives to impress upon the exiles that their current troubles will pass, because their God, Who created the seas by measuring "the waters with the hollow of His hand (Isaiah 40:12)," is omnipotent and their enemies are weak. He convincingly proves his point by employing a memorable metaphor drawn from a natural phenomenon, as true in Babylon as in the Promised Land. Surely the captives would recall how the winter rains on the parched earth, after summer's drought, had brought forth a mass of wild grasses and brilliant flowers that spread across the land, covering valleys, hills, and plains, extending even into the desert, and they would remember, too, how the hot, dry winds (the breath of God, as the prophet describes it) had caused the withering of this once vigorous growth, leaving no trace behind, as if it had never existed. This, Isaiah proclaims, is what will happen to your enemies for "man is but grass [mortal],[7] but the word of our God is always fulfilled!" (Isaiah 40:7-8).

The poets of the Bible saw in this natural occurrence of rapid growth, followed by a quick shriveling up of life, different ways to exalt God. His loving-kindness, for instance, is everlasting, unlike man's, "whose days are as grass; he blooms as a flower of the field"[8] (Psalms 103:15). Wickedness, it follows, is transient. David, the psalmist, advises against being vexed or incensed by evil doers since "they soon wither like grass" and fade as the green herb. Trust in the Lord and do good, abide in the land and remain loyal, for those who look to the Lord, "they shall inherit the land" (Psalms 37:1-2, 9). These are wise words for the returning exiles from Babylon.

—〰—

THE PROPHET SPEAKS to the exiles in imagery that vividly recalls the landscape that produced the "flowers of the field," imagery that depends for its greatest impact on knowledge of the two distinct seasons of the year in the Middle East, winter and summer. Summers are hot and dry, dew the only source of moisture until around October when the early rain, *yoreh*, falls from heaven. This event, the first rain, is greeted with rejoicing, now as in biblical times, even with sophisticated water technology. It is difficult for those in a temperate climate to appreciate the joy that the sound of the first drops of rain can bring to those who live in a semi-arid climate, or the sight of puddles where once there was cracked earth. Temperatures cool down, grasses and weeds spring up (like the early growth of the *merorim* of Passover),[9] and by late January to early February when the rainy season is at its height, the almond tree, *Amygdalus communis*, the first tree to break its winter dormancy, bursts into bloom, signaling the beginning of the main flowering season (crocus and other bulbs have already bloomed).[10] This is the time when hundreds of flowers rush to bloom and set seed before the late rain (*malkosh*), usually around the end of March or early April, after which "the grass withers, the flowers fade," in response to the *sharav* heat wave (Arabic, *hamsin*). To understand its effect, 60 degree F temperatures in the north may, overnight, rise to 90 degrees F, while 80 degrees F in the south may soar to 110 degrees F, accompanied by a hot, dry east wind causing a dusty haze in the air.[11] While the phenomenon of brief flowering is characteristic of the region, it is especially dramatic in the Land of Israel. "The flowers of Palestine," wrote a late nineteenth century observer, "come and go so swiftly that it dazzles and bewilders one who for the first time observes this peculiarity of

Photograph © Jackie Chambers

Adonis aestivalis and *Anthemis sp.* Adonis and chamomile, detail of the annual carpet just outside Nazareth.

the Syrian landscape. This floral procession, so brilliant and yet so rapid in its many-hued changes, is found in its highest perfection in the Holy Land." [12]

The Babylonian exiles would remember when "The winter is past/ The rains over and gone/and the flowers [*nitzanim*] have appeared on the earth" (Song of Songs 2:11-12), the general period when the rain-soaked ground encourages hundreds of annual flowers to spring up and bloom in such a bewildering and intricate range of colors and design that they bring to mind an oriental carpet: rosy flax, pink ricotia (of the mustard family), the blues and purples of low centaurea (like a dwarf cornflower), lupine, bugloss, veronica, orange calendula, creamy scabiosa, all sorts of daisies, some yellow and large, others small and white-petaled like Peter Rabbit chamomile. In the desert, colors appear on hillsides, changing almost daily, to form waves of mauve, yellows, and pinks. Various species of perennial wild iris bear beautiful garden-like flowers from the palest yellow to the deepest purple, almost black. But the most conspicuous flowers are the vibrant reds, a group of four different

Photograph © Jackie Chambers

Iris atropurpurea. Dark-purple iris near Ashdod.

species which appear in succession over several months, beginning as early as December and continuing until May. These glistening flowers, progenitors of some of the most beautiful and desirable plants of the garden world, are often produced in great drifts or carpets, from north to south, and may have been the ones the prophet had in mind.

The connection between the four different red flowers, known collectively as *nitzanim* in *Song of Songs*, and 'tzitz,' Isaiah's 'flower of the field' (*tzitz ha-sadeh*)[13] is suggested in the meaning of their root word origins: *tzitz* derived from *tzutz*, means "to twinkle" or glisten; *nitzan* (singular of *nitzanim*) also conveys the idea of a flower that glows, from the root word *notzez*, "to sparkle"; *notzez* can also mean "fresh" or "fragile," characteristics that could apply to spring flowering plants. The red flower group, known collectively as *nissan* in Iraq

(biblical Babylonia), all bear glistening or sparkling blooms of varying intensity. This name corresponds to the Hebrew month *Nisan* (of
Babylonian origin),[14] when in March through April, as the rains are
ending, all four of the reds are in bloom, suggesting that the month's
name may be linked to this phenomenon.[15]

The flowering reds are an impressive sight, no less now than in
the prophet's time.[16] The first red to bloom is the crown anemone,
Anemone coronaria, a popular flower of the crowfoot or buttercup
family (Ranunculaceae) known in Hebrew as *kalanit* (*klonita* in the
Talmud), from *kala* or "bride," a reference to the flower's beauty.
After the early winter rains, a rosette of finely cut foliage (likened
to a crow's foot) sprouts from a small brown tuber close to the soil's
surface. Flowers, on stems under two feet tall, are cup-shaped like a
poppy (poppy anemone is another common name) with five to six
rounded, overlapping tepals—undifferentiated outer sepals and
petals. Nutrient-poor soil, as in steppe and desert areas, produce
spreading red populations, except where ants leave behind a richer
soil to support other species.[17] In the more favorable soil conditions
elsewhere the anemone's color range extends to flowers in varying
shades of purple, pink, violet, and light blue to white. Blooming in
January and lasting into April, flowers open in the morning and
close at night, and although they don't contain nectar, insects come
to feed on pollen at the tips of the numerous blue-black stamens
in the center of the bloom. Seeds, which quickly develop after the
flowers fade, are dispersed by the wind.

Next to bloom, beginning in March and continuing to May, is
Persian crowfoot or red buttercup, *Ranunculus asiaticus* (*nurit*),
closely related to the familiar yellow buttercup, *R. acris*, of European
or Asian origin, naturalized in North American wet meadows. The
Middle Eastern version has a larger, showier red flower on stems
to eighteen inches tall, and grows up from a tuberous, rather than
fibrous, root. Geophyte or bulbous flowering plants are plentiful
in the Middle East, well adapted to survive long periods of drought
because they store nutrients in their underground tubers and bulbs.
Foliage, similar to that of the anemone, is finely cut, and the five petals are noticeably shiny, as if painted with lacquer (buttercup petals
are similar). It has been observed that the *nitzanim* of the *Song of
Songs* may refer, not to the entire groups of reds, but to this particular

Photograph © Jackie Chambers

Ranunculus asiaticus. Persian crowfoot blooming in cracked ground near Beer Sheva in semi-desert conditions.

flower, the most sparkling of the four, which Jews of Kurdistan (in northern Iraq) know as *nissana*.[18]

Who is not familiar with red tulips, the floral symbol of spring in the West? Red tulips are native to the eastern Mediterranean region in forests and scrub land along the Coastal Plain from Syria to Israel and Cyprus. The progenitor of garden tulips (after intensive breeding), it was probably introduced to Europe in the 16th century. The sharon or sun's eye tulip, *Tulipa agenensis*, is a classic red: emerging from an underground bulb, stout stems, with strap-shaped leaves, grow up to fifteen inches tall or less, bearing a flame-red flower of narrow petals (tepals)—the outer ones noticeably longer and more pointed than the inner ones—with a large yellow-rimmed black splotch at their base. Plants flourish in *batha, maquis,* and open scrub land on the Coastal Plain, especially in the north, on Mt. Carmel, and on the hills of Judea, Samaria, and the Galilee, where they bloom from March to April. A smaller, daintier version, *Tulipa agenenis* subsp. *sharonensis*, is restricted to sandy soils and hills along the Coastal Plain. The red tulips are regarded by many as the "rose of sharon," *havatzelet hasharon,* of Song of Songs (2:1), one of the two flowers to which the young maiden compares herself: "I am the rose of Sharon, the lily of the valleys [*Narcissus tazetta*]."[19] (In North America, the "rose of sharon" refers to quite a different plant, the late summer blooming *Hibiscus syriacus*). A desert species, *Tulipa systola*, creates red carpets of bloom during February and March in a rainy year, transforming, at least for a short time, a barren landscape.

The last of the reds to bloom is the more heat-tolerant common field poppy *Papaver* sp. (*parag*), an annual flower of which there are several species in Israel, each having evolved to grow in specific habitats. Red carpets, as far as the eye can see, spread out in different areas of the land, from the Dead Sea in the south to the Golan in the north, over a long period from March to May (and in cooler places into June), blooming in mountainous regions and deserts, in waste ground and cultivated, aerated soil. The most common is *P. umbonatum (subpiriforme)*, which to the untrained eye looks virtually the same as the familiar European corn poppy, *P. rhoeas*, also known as the Flanders Field poppy. Strong wiry stems to about eighteen inches tall grow up from a rosette of hairy, divided gray-green leaves. When the flower is ready to open, the nodding bud lifts its head, and throws off the green sepals that tightly wrapped its four crimson, silky petals. Unfurled and smoothed out they form a two-inch wide delicate, nearly translucent flower, usually blotched black at its base, its center filled with numerous stamens and an oblong pistil. Petals fall two to three days after the flower has opened, then the narrow pod, with its hundreds of small seeds, quickly ripens and its seeds are dispersed. Unlike the other reds, which all leave behind underground tubers or bulbs, the annual field poppy, like other annuals, completes its growth cycle in one season, from germination to fruiting, then dries up, leaving no trace of its former glory. Could this fragile, short-lived flower be the symbol of mortality the prophet had in mind?

Photograph © Jackie Chambers

Tulipa aegenensis. Wild Sharon tulips growing among rocks in the Martyrs Forest on the outskirts of Jerusalem.

Photograph © Jackie Chambers

Papaver umbanotum. Field poppy outside Nazareth.

Like the desert wilderness that shaped the narrative of the Israelites' arduous journey to the Promised Land, the flowers of the field in the prophet's wonderful imagery become a force for driving home his message of the everlasting power of God. The Bible's ever-present land is a rich source for teaching Torah in the field for those who are familiar with its features and its wealth of flora.

ENDNOTES

1. NJPS version. In more traditional translations, as in the Hertz and the King James: "But the word of our God stands forever." In the Christian Bible, the metaphor is used again in nearly identical wording: "For all flesh is as grass,/ and all the glory of man as the flower of grass./The grass withereth,/and the flower thereof falleth away:/ but the word of the Lord endureth for ever." (I Peter 1:24-25). This is to be expected since the imagery was drawn from the same land.

2. A day of fast and mourning that commemorates the destruction of the First and Second Temples and other catastrophes in Jewish history.

3. God has told Moses that because of his lack of faith at *Meribah* (Numbers 20:12), he will not lead the people into the Promised Land. Despite Moses' final pleading, the verdict stands and Joshua is appointed successor (the case is reviewed in Deuteronomy 3:23-28). Therefore, Moses imparts, directly to his charges, his last teachings.

4. In 586 BCE Babylonia, succeeding Assyria as the ruling regional power, destroyed Judea and ransacked the Temple. See II Kings 25:1-17 for a graphic description of these events which included the starvation of the Jerusalemites, the breaching of the wall of the city, the slaughter of the Judean king Zedekiah's sons before his eyes, then the putting out of the king's eyes, his exile to Babylon in chains, the burning of the House of the Lord (the Temple) and the king's palace and the house "of every notable person," the carrying off of the Temple's treasures (bronze and gold objects used in ritual service), great bronze columns decorated with pomegranates, and finally, the exile of the remnant population (those that had not already gone over to Nebuchadnezzar), leaving behind the poorest of the land, "to be vinedressers and field hands."

5. That "all flesh is grass," is exemplified dramatically by historical events. In 539 BCE Persia (Iran) conquered Babylon, and the new ruler, Cyrus, issued a proclamation in 538 BCE allowing the Judeans to return home and rebuild their Temple. See II Chronicles 36:22-23 and Ezra 1:1-3. The period of exile proved fruitful. The Jews were able to maintain themselves as a distinct community and develop and shape Judaism. Lacking the Temple and its associated sacrificial rites, there was more emphasis on the spiritual and ethical aspects of the religion, on dietary

laws, and on observing the Sabbath. Communal worship took place in a new setting: the synagogue. The exilic experience also provided the impetus for collecting and adding to the old scrolls (canonized after the return to Jerusalem), and later, the recording of the Oral Law in the Babylonian Talmud (*Talmud Bavli*) around 200 CE. See Daniel Hillel, *The Natural History of the Bible*, 193–205 for an insightful discussion of the impact of the Babylonian Exile.

6. This is the traditional Soncino version (similar to the King James Version in its poetic effect), with the interesting note that "the rugged" for the Hebrew *akob* should probably be translated as "crooked road" (referring to the comments of Kimchi, a famous family of 12th and 13th century Hebrew Bible commentators and grammarians). "Its equivalent in Arabic denotes 'a steep mountain path.'" The NJPS translation may be more authentic, but seems prosaic (at least to our unaccustomed ears): "Let every valley be raised, / Every hill and mount made low. / Let the rugged ground become level / And the ridges become a plain."

7. Reader Elaine Solowey points out that "grass" is often a code word for quick growing things with no roots. In Psalms, for instance, grass-like things are wicked and are destroyed, or wicked people are like grass on rooftops which bear no fruit, have no real roots (Psalms 129:6).

8. The symbolism of "grass" carries over in the Christian Bible (James 1:10; Matthew 6:30).

9. See Chapter Fourteen, *Teaching Torah in the Field*, for an explanation and discussion of *merorim*.

10. The almond tree's flowering as a signal of new growth is associated with the Jewish holiday, the New Year of the Trees or *Tu b'Shvat* (Fifteenth of *Shvat*, which occurs in different years from late January to mid-February) when thousands of saplings are planted in Israel as a sort of arbor day. All sorts of dried fruits are eaten then, including carob. The holiday's date is based loosely on the Talmud's reckoning of a "new year of the trees," (discussed in Tractate *Rosh Hashana* in the Mishna) for the purposes of tithing. *Tu b'Shvat* was recognized as the average date when fruit trees awaken from dormancy, begin to draw water from the ground, and form leaf buds. The best time to plant fruit trees is, however, not *after* they break their dormancy, but before, when they are leafless. As Nogah Hareuveni points out in his far-ranging discussion of *Tu b'Shvat*, the holiday grew out of a general enthusiasm for the Land of Israel among people unfamiliar with its growth cycles (initially 17th century Kabbalists in Safed). See Nogah Hareuveni, *Nature in Our Biblical Heritage*, 103–118.

11. Azaria Alon, *The Natural History of the Land of the Bible*, 60.

12. George Sandison in *Wild Flowers of Palestine* (1895), typical of the charming books of Protestant origin of the period. The pressed wild flowers mounted in this book were collected in Palestine by Rev.

Harvey B. Greene, and remarkably, some of them, like the anemone, still retain some of their original colors. In an introductory essay, "A Divine Bouquet," the author points out that "this may be the first time you have ever held a part of Palestine in your hand. These are not pictures of flowers . . . but were wrought and spun and colored by the hand of God."

13. Singular in the text but often translated in the plural, perhaps to indicate a mass of bloom.

14. When the Jews returned to Zion after the Babylonian Exile they brought back Babylonian names for the months of the year, gradually displacing the numerical system ("the first month" became *Nisan*, "the twelfth month," *Adar*, and so on).

15. Michael Zohary, *Plants of the Bible*, 169.

16. Nogah Hareuveni discusses the possible role of this succession of red flowers amid white and later light colored flowers in the drinking of red and white wine at a seder-like meal developed by the Kabbalists for *Tu b'Shvat*. Neot Kedumim was one of the earliest institutions to develop a *Tu b'Shvat* seder for the holiday.

17. At "Flora of Israel Online," edited by Avinoam Danin, go to Table of Contents, *Plant Stories*, Chapter H, part 8, "Plants and ants" to read about this phenomenon. See Bibliography for Internet address.

18. Hareuveni makes the case for why he thinks the *nitzanim* in *Song of Songs* refers specifically to *nurit* (from *nur*, "fire") in educational material from Neot Kedumim, "*Flowers in the Land of the Bible*," Guide to Filmstrip NKF-14, p.14.

19. See Chapter Twenty-Eight, *Warning of the Thorns* for a discussion of *Narcissus tazetta* as the 'lily among thorns.'

Chapter Thirty-Two

THE SEVEN SPECIES: SPECIAL CROPS OF THE LAND

Portion *Ekev* / If you obey [these rules] (Deuteronomy 7:12-11:25)
For the Lord your God is bringing you into a good land, a land with streams and springs and fountains issuing from plain and hill, a land of wheat and barley, of vines, figs, and pomegranates, a land of olive trees and honey. (Deuteronomy 8:7-8)

Photograph © Ori Fragman

Olea europaea. Olive grove in the Upper Galilee with *Silene aegyptiaca* (Egyptian campion), a common sight in spring.

Moses, in his last teaching, appeals to all the people—"Hear, O Israel"—urging them to remain faithful to the covenant, to grasp its laws as one would grasp a heel (*ekev*, literally "on the heels of"),[1] an act that will enable them to move forward in the right direction toward God.[2] Moses wants to be sure the people understand that their future actions in the Promised Land will have consequences. If they 'walk' in God's ways and always revere Him, then they will be blessed. He spells out how: Before you, he tells his audience, lies the Promised Land, a land of diverse features, of plains and hills, and streams, springs, and fountains, a land where the people will be farmers and shepherds, "where He will bless the issue of your womb and the produce of your soil, your new grain and wine and oil, the calving of your herd and the lambing of your flock " (Deuteronomy 7:13). But if the people take the wrong direction, if they are lured away (or turn away of their own will) to other gods, all will be lost, God's anger will "shut up the skies," their crops will fail and they will perish (Deuteronomy 11:17).

Moses appeals to the nation's highest ideals, the aspirations that set them apart from their neighbors, that had transformed them from a rough shepherd people into a holy nation with laws and regulations based upon moral and ethical values. His audience did not directly experience this transformation from its beginnings, did not directly participate in their forebears' early history, but Moses, the great teacher (who once described himself as "slow of speech and slow of tongue"),[3] makes it live for them, so that it is as if they, too, had all been present during the great exodus from Egypt, had all heard the covenant directly from God when they stood at the foot of Sinai, and had all suffered through the entire arduous wilderness journey. Not only would they (and all subsequent generations) now always remember these events and the lessons to be learned from them, but they would instruct their children about these matters.[4]

Yes, the wilderness journey was difficult, he tells them, a long, roundabout way to get to the Promised Land, but, as Moses points out, God had to test you (the slave generation), to find out what was in your hearts, and whether you would keep His commandments. You complained that you were hungry and He fed you with the miraculous grain from heaven, a substance the people called *manna*,[5] for it was an unknown substance. God taught you, from this experience, that "man does not live on bread alone, but may live on anything that the Lord decrees" (Deuteronomy 8:2-3). That is, to truly thrive, man must feed his spiritual needs, his soul, as well as his body.

There is the danger, Moses warns, that when you prosper in the Promised Land, when you have made your own bread from seed you have planted with your own hands, and "eaten your fill, and have built fine houses to live in, and your herds [of goats] and flocks [of sheep] have multiplied," (Deuteronomy 8:12-13) then you will turn away from God, thinking that you accomplished all this by your efforts alone, forgetting that it was the Lord your God Who freed you from Egypt and allowed you to live in freedom, Who tested you by hardships which built your character, so that, in the end, you would benefit from your experiences. Therefore, Moses urges, when you have eaten, "give thanks to your God for the good land which He has given you," (Deuteronomy 8:10)[6] and walk in His path, upholding, as He does, the cause of the fatherless and the widow, and befriending the stranger, "for you were strangers in the land of Egypt" (Deuteronomy 10:19).

We can feel, in some measure, how impressed Moses' audience must have been by his eloquence. Their ancestors, he declares, had gone down to Egypt seventy persons in all; "and now the Lord your God has made you as numerous as the stars of heaven" (Deuteronomy 10:22). We can imagine how thrilled they must have been (and by extension all generations that follow) by the retelling of their past when God had "wrought for you [your ancestors] those marvelous awesome deeds that you saw with your own eyes," such as rolling back the waters of the Sea of Reeds upon your pursuers when you fled slavery in Egypt,[7] bringing forth water from a flinty rock to slake your thirst;[8] feeding and clothing you when you had nothing.[9] Moses reminds them of their destiny: "Keep, therefore, all the Instruction that I enjoin upon you today, so that you may have the strength to enter and take possession of the land that you are about to cross into and possess, and that you may long endure upon the soil that the Lord swore to your fathers to assign to them and to their heirs, a land flowing with milk and honey" (Deuteronomy 11:8-9).

—⚭—

WHAT IS THIS PROMISED LAND, the goal of the long journey through the wilderness, and what's so special about the Seven Species (*Shivat Haminim*)?

In their exploration of Canaan, the scouts had explored both cultivated and wild areas so they would be able to give Moses an assessment. "See what kind of land it is," he had ordered them (Numbers 13:18). It is a land naturally divided into distinct belts running its entire length from north to south, dissected laterally by deep valleys and mountains, the same physical characteristics that exist now as then. The Coastal Plain is an undulating strip of varying width and soils that runs alongside the Mediterranean from Mount Carmel to the Negev desert, with sandy plains on the coast, red loam in the Sharon Valley at its center, and to the east, the rich, dark earth of the traditional wheat growing area. The Hill Country rises east from the Coastal Plain. To the north lie the mountains and hills of Upper Galilee and Lower Galilee, farther to the south, the Samarian hills with small, fertile valleys, and to the south of Jerusalem, the Judean hills. Several valleys cut across the highlands from east to west, the largest of which is the Jezreel Valley (also known as the Plain of Esdraelon), stretching from Haifa southeast to the valley of the Jordan River. Its legendary fertility is preserved in its Hebrew name, *Yizr'a-El* ("sown by God"). To the east, the Rift Valley runs the entire length of the country from the north southwards through the Jordan Valley and the *Arava* (derived from the Hebrew root "to mix," a reference to the area's intermingling of arid and green regions). The rift has been called not merely a valley, but a chink ploughed deep in the bowels of the earth.[10] In its northernmost section, the Dan Valley is traversed by three important brooks, the Dan, Baniyas, and Hasbani, which merge to form the Jordan River, the land's largest river, which descends southward, flowing into Lake Kinneret or Sea of Galilee, then meanders down and down, emptying in the Dead or Salt Sea, 1,312 feet below sea level, the lowest point on the surface of the earth.

The land you are about to enter, Moses advises, is unlike Egypt, where crops were irrigated by channeling the seasonal overflow of the Nile. In the Promised Land "its hills and valleys soak up water from the rains of heaven," where not you but God "will grant the rain for your land in season, the early rain and the late" (Deuteronomy 11:10-14).[11] The Israelites will be entirely dependent on seasonal rainfall to grow their crops. When we consider that the Promised Land lies in the climatically unstable zone between moisture in the north and aridity in the south, we begin to appreciate the problems inherent in the establishment of agriculture. The early rain and the late rain vary from season to season, can take the form of heavy downpours causing erosion and flooding, and are unevenly distributed; rainfall in the north averages over forty inches, down to less than three inches annually in the south. The condition of the soil, furthermore, determines how (or if) moisture is absorbed into the soil. In the uplands of the hill country, soils, while fertile, are relatively shallow and therefore unable to hold moisture on their slopes.[12] Rain was anxiously awaited (and still is), but what form it would take determined the fate of entire crops. Worst of all was a prolonged dry spell, which would mean total crop failure and the spectre of famine.[13]

These conditions help to explain why Baal, pagan god of the sky and rain, was central to Canaanite worship, and that the Seven Species, a group that encompasses both staples and luxuries— the basic grains, wheat and barley, grapes for wine, olive trees for producing lighting oil, as well as figs, pomegranates, and honey, assumed to be from dates[14]—are singled out in Moses' description of the bounty that awaits them in the land. Unlike the more weather-tolerant trees represented in the "choice products" such as pistachio and almond,[15] all of the Seven Species are extremely sensitive to the heat wave winds (*sharav/hamsin*)[16] and the cold, northern winds, accompanied by thunder, lightning and driving rain typical of the unsettled conditions that prevail during the fifty days between Passover and *Shavuot*. The hot winds may be beneficial if they come at the right time when the olive, grapevine, pomegranate and date are budded, and the fig is in its embryonic stages. Successive days of dry heat encourage the buds to open, allowing the pollen to reach the pistils for pollination. If pollination is not achieved before a blast of cold northern winds accompanied by driving rain, the blossoms of these fruits may be blown away, lost forever. Neither the almond nor pistachio tree, which blossom earlier, are affected by these conditions. Date palms, moreover, need a very long dry period to flower and mature. If it rains at the wrong time the bunches can become moldy or the flowers can rot. Figs and grapes, on the other hand, are very sensitive to lack of water. Thus, a dry spring can blight them and ruin or affect the size of the crop.

The same hot winds, moreover, that are beneficial to the fruits if they come at the right time, are detrimental to the grains (wheat and barley) if they come before the kernels have filled with starch, at about a third of their ripening. Then the grain is scorched and the crop lost, as in Pharaoh's dream (Genesis 41:6). When the wheat is ready to harvest, around *Shavuot*, a driving rain will flatten and may ruin the crop.[17]

The Israelite farmers, anxious for the success of these weather-sensitive crops, might have been tempted to copy their neighbors by worshiping the various pagan gods thought to rule the 'warring' or opposing elements, rather than depending on God alone. In this context, the Seven Species are a botanical emblem of the challenges the Israelites will face in the new land, and a reminder (warning) to be faithful to Him so as to bring about the 'rain in its season,' so that "you may gather in your new grain and wine and oil" (Deuteronomy 11:14). Their task was made more difficult because the Israelites established themselves, not in the fertile valleys and plains, but in the rugged central hill country, the most desirable areas having already been settled by the Canaanites.[18] The new arrivals were faced with limited sources of water, shallow, stony, erosion-prone soil, and a lack of flat land.[19] "Go up to the forest country and clear an area for yourselves," Joshua had advised (Joshua 17:14-18). This sounds like the same land the scouts had described in glowing terms, as if it was "flowing [literally, "oozing"][20] with milk and honey" (Numbers 13:27), and so it would seem to shepherds who had lived for so long under harsh, desert conditions. By contrast, the hill country was covered with virgin forests of oak, pine, terebinth, storax, wild olive, arbutus, carob, and various shrubs, which supported a thick undergrowth of wild grasses for foraging, and masses of wild nectar-rich flowers in their season.[21] Here, as the shepherds may have envisioned, their goats and sheep would keep them supplied with milk, and honey could be gathered from the activities of wild bees.[22] But it was hardly farmland. The huge cluster of grapes (so large it had to be suspended on a pole carried by two men), and the figs and pomegranates the scouts had brought back as samples from their expedition into Canaan, were picked from fruit cultivated by the Canaanites under the favorable conditions in the rich soil of the Valley of Eshkol near Hebron (Numbers 13:23).

Photograph © Ori Fragman

Vitis vinifera. Large clusters of green grapes, Cyprus.

In the centuries-long transformation from shepherds to mainly farmers, the Israelites developed techniques to grow their crops on the cleared slopes so that precious soil would not be lost during heavy downpours; these rock-enclosed, terraced beds are still evident today and some of them are maintained and used.[23] The steepest hillsides were left for pasture, and cisterns, hewed out of rock, collected and stored rainwater.[24] Only much later did they move out to the plains and valleys.[25] Perhaps first settling on forested land helped to build up the people's character (just as their wilderness journey had toughened them), for

Photograph © Avinoam Danin

Olea europaea. Olive trees growing on well-maintained ancient terraces, Ein Kerem.

the shepherds turned out to be industrious farmers. Although they did not, themselves, leave us a written record of their achievement, it is clear from all available sources, and what can be extracted from Greek and Roman manuscripts—from Theophrastus, Pliny and Varro, from Cato and Columella, from Virgil and Dioscorides, as well as from the Oral Tradition preserved in the Mishna (the closest link to biblical times)—that the Jewish historian Josephus was not exaggerating when he called the Land of Israel, "a garden of God," [26] where in the Galilee, a once wild land was cultivated, and so successful were the farmers in raising diverse fruits and preserving them, especially in the long-growing season around the Sea of Galilee, that they supplied for ten months, without interruption, those kings of fruits, the grape and the fig.

ENDNOTES

1. *Ekev* can be translated "as a consequence of" or more commonly as "if."
2. This interpretation was inspired by "From Heel to Soul," a commentary on Portion *Ekev* by Rabbi Steve Chester, Temple Sinai, Oakland, CA online at Union of American Hebrew Congregations website. See Bibliography for Internet address.
3. Exodus 4:10.
4. "Apart from the liturgy, Deuteronomy is the source of the idea that religious life should be based on a sacred book, and hence of the obligations of all Jews, not only an elite class, to learn the Torah and teach it to their children (5:1; 6:7). Deuteronomy 6:4 and 33:4 are the first verses to be taught to a child as soon as the child is able to speak... Other fundamental [Jewish] practices rooted in Deuteronomy are affixing *mezuzot* to doorposts and the wearing of *tefillin* (6:8-9; 11:18, 20) and fringes (*tsitsit*) (22:12)." Jeffrey H. Tigay, *The JPS Torah Commentary, Deuteronomy*, Introduction xxviii.
5. Exodus 16. See Chapter Fifteen, *Heavenly Grain*.
6. The source for Grace after Meals, *Birkat Ha-Mazon*.
7. Deuteronomy 11:4; see Exodus 14:28.
8. Deuteronomy 8:15; see Exodus 17:6 and Numbers 20:7-11.
9. Deuteronomy 8:3, 4. See Exodus 16. "Another indication of Israel's dependence on God and His control of nature: Israel's clothing and feet were immune to the effects of nature during the years in the wilderness." Tigay, 93.
10. H. B. Tristram, *The Natural History of the Bible*, 5. Tristram was a 19th century English clergyman and traveler whose work is a classic of the genre.

11. See Chapter Thirty-One, *Flowers of the Field*, for a description of the seasons of the year in Israel. Jeffrey Tigay, 112, notes that the rabbis discussed whether the dependence of the land on God for irrigation (Deuteronomy 11:10-12) is meant to praise the land or denigrate it. "In the end, they decided that the passage is one of praise but, as Rashbam [Rabbi Samuel ben Meir, 1080–1174] observed, 'This land is better than Egypt and all other lands to those who observe God's commands, but worse than all other lands to those who do not observe them.'" He goes on to quote 19th century Bible scholar August Dillmann: "The very land is suited to educating a pious, Godfearing people," because, in Tigay's words, "it makes their dependence on God obvious." In a similar vein, from a naturalist's point of view, "In reality, Canaan was very possibly the least convenient location for a small nation to try to establish itself. Not only did it lie between the two competing regional centers of power, Mesopotamia and Egypt—the hammer and the anvil, as it were—but it lay at the climatically unstable transition zone between the arid and humid zones." Daniel Hillel, *The Natural History of the Bible*, 149.

12. Hillel, 146 discusses the effect of rainfall on the soil the Israelites worked. These soils are terra rossa, a loam or clay-loam formed on hard limestone, and rendzina, a darkish or grayish loam formed on soft limestone and on chalk or marly bedrock. While both are receptive to rain, they are shallow, seldom exceeding two feet in depth and less on steep hillsides.

13. Famine from delayed rain is often a feature of the biblical narrative, as when Abraham left Canaan to sojourn in Egypt (Genesis 12:10); as did Jacob and his sons in the Joseph story (Genesis 42:2; 43:1); there was famine in both Egypt and Canaan during the time of Joseph (Genesis 47:13); in the time of Elijah (I Kings 17:1); and in the Books of Ruth and Second Samuel.

14. Dates, like the other plants on the list, not only reflect the agricultural bounty of the land but share the perils of successful pollination at a season of unsettled and possibly unfavorable weather conditions, unlike carob, another tree source of honey.

15. See Chapter Twenty-Six, *The Blooming Rod*, for a discussion of almonds that Jacob sent down to Egypt.

16. The *sharav/hamsin* phenomenon is discussed in Chapter Fourteen, *Teaching Torah in the* Field, as an explanation of one of the plagues, and in Chapter Thirty-One, Flowers of the Field, as the cause of their withering.

17. I have drawn on Nogah Hareuveni's interpretation of the effect of weather on the Seven Species in *Nature in Our Biblical Heritage*, 30–37, and comments from reader Elaine Solowey.

18. Hillel, 150. He cites Judges 1:34 on the scarcity of available land: "The Amorites pressed the Danites into the hill country, they would not let

them come down to the plain." See n.12, 300. Hareuveni, 16, also discusses settlement of the hill country citing Joshua 17:14-18 and archeological research, from which he concludes that settling the hill country was "clearly the situation during the time of Israelite settlement in the middle of the 13th century BCE: the fertile valleys were inhabited by the Canaanites, while much of the hilly region was uninhabited and retained the natural cover of forest and thicket. This is almost identical to the environment described by the scouts Moses had sent to survey the land."

19. Hillel, 150. The central hill country, as Hillel observes, presented further difficulties since the east-facing slopes, which drop steeply towards the Jordan Valley, are in the rain shadow, and are virtually desert. See 141.

20. Jeffrey Tigay's more graphic "oozing" for "flowing" is based on the meaning of the Hebrew verb *zavat*, "which refers to bodily organs leaking fluids and, in poetry, to water gushing (see Leviticus 15 and Psalms 78:20)." Tigay, 75. It is a favorite phrase, repeated in Deuteronomy 6:3; 11:9; 26:9, 15; 27:3; 31:20, and elsewhere. As Nogah Hareuveni has pointed out it is a shorthand for the bounty of wild, uncultivated land, with its good connotations, as well as a "frightening description associated with the destruction of productive farmland." See Hareuveni, 11–22, for an analysis of the phrase, also discussed in Chapter Twenty-Five, *Beautiful Pomegranates*.

21. Zohary, 28–33, discusses the probable forested landscape of biblical times based on surviving remnants.

22. Prior to the discovery of clay cylinders identified as beehive remains at an archeological dig in northern Israel at Tel Rehov from 2005–2007, the earliest actual evidence of beekeeping dated from the Hellenistic period. The period to which the Tel Rehov beehives relate is the second half of the tenth century BCE and beginning of the ninth century, corresponding to the biblical era of Solomon and the divided Kingdoms. In their report, the Tel Rehov archeologists note that "Though the Bible does not mention apiaries, the example from Tel Rehov shows that they were known at that time and functioned very much like those from Egypt that are dated much earlier, as well as like the much later beehives known from the ethnographic record." Amihai Mazar, Dvory Namdar, Nava Panitz-Cohen, Ronny Neumann & Steve Weiner, "Iron Age beehives at Tel Rehov in the Jordan valley," *Antiquity* 82 (2008): 629–639.

23. "Over the centuries the terraces have not altered greatly. They continue to be cultivated without major reorganization and are merely maintained and repaired when necessary." Gershon Edelstein and Mordechai Kislev, "Mevasseret Yerushalayim: The Ancient Settlement and its Agricultural Terraces," *Biblical Archeologist*, Winter, 1981, Vol.

44, pgs. 53–56. They date the earliest layer of terraced land use to the period of the Kingdom of Judah (8–7th centuries BCE) and discuss the discovery of a water cistern cut into bedrock, as well as basins and channels characteristic of the oil and wine industries. As the authors note, much work remains to be done to better understand the phenomenon of terraced agriculture in ancient life.

24. Hillel, n.5, 299, discusses various sources of water, other than rainfall, that are mentioned in the Bible. Gershon and Edlestein refer to an extensive study of ancient terraces by geographer Zvi Ron in 1966 in which he discussed the irrigation of terrace beds by natural springs.

25. There are various theories regarding how/when the Israelites settled in the Promised Land. In Hillel's view, "The takeover of Canaan, as best can be discerned from available evidence, was not a single victorious march from east to west and from south to north until 'all the land' was conquered. Instead it seems to have taken place gradually over several centuries. Israelite tribes apparently infiltrated into Canaan and settled wherever they could find room between the existing city-states. Eventually, they absorbed those city-states, either by peaceful assimilation or by violent action, or by both means." Hillel, 147.

26. *The Jewish Wars*, III, 10,8. See Chapter Twenty, *Holy Fruit*, for a discussion of the achievements of fruit farming in the Land of Israel.

Chapter Thirty-Three

GIFTS OF THE GRAIN HARVEST

Portion *Ki Tetse* / When you go out [to war] (Deuteronomy 21:10-25:19)

When you reap the harvest in your field and overlook a sheaf in the field, do not turn back to get it; it shall go to the stranger, the orphan, and the widow—in order that the Lord your God may bless you in all your undertakings. (Deuteronomy 24:19)

Photograph © Joshua D. Klein
Triticum aestivum. Winter wheat growing in a field in Rehovot.

Thus far, Moses has appealed to the people's common bond, to their sense of connection to all they and their forbears had endured for the sake of reaching the Promised Land. Failure in the future to obey what God requires of them, they have been told in many different ways, will result in catastrophe. Moses, unexcelled as a teacher, knows that the time has come for the people to hear a detailed review of the laws and regulations of the covenant by which they are expected to live when they are settled in the land (in this portion, alone, seventy-two are reviewed), and on the whole, they are more expansive than previous accounts in Exodus (20:3-23:19; 34:17-26) or throughout Leviticus. In Deuteronomy there is more emphasis on moral and ethical issues, especially on charity laws protecting the classic triad, the stranger, the orphan, and the widow. While the Torah affirms that holiness can be achieved in the simplest act, as in the farmer not going back to retrieve the forgotten sheaf of grain in his field but leaving it for those in need, the fact that the charitable act is mandated, rather than left to the inclinations of the individual farmer, acknowledges the central role of the covenant in shaping Israel's character.

Concern for others, even for strangers, is evident in the biblical narrative from the earliest days of the Patriarchs, when, for instance, Abraham "ran [not walked] from the entrance of the tent" to offer approaching strangers unstinting hospitality (Genesis 18:2), and when Rebecca cheerfully hauled up all those buckets of water to slake the thirst of Eliezer and his ten camels (Genesis 24:17-20). These acts could serve as a model for the Leviticus commandment to "love the stranger [and your neighbor][1] as yourself, for you were strangers in the land of Egypt" (Leviticus 19:34). Extending food and drink to strangers and their animals in the setting of the harsh desert environment, however, while an integral part of shepherd culture, would be an insufficient guide for the more developed society of farming life, and so we see how the law develops to extend legal protection, not only to the stranger, but to the orphan and the widow, in other words, to the poor and most vulnerable; in an agricultural-based society this would mean those without land.

Laws concerning the seventh year release of the land, or *shmitta*, in Exodus 23:10 and Leviticus 25:2-7, when most agricultural activities were to be suspended, required that the poor be allowed to eat whatever grew of itself or had been left in the field, on the vine, and in groves: "Let the needy among your people eat of it" (Exodus 23:11). Some believe that the driving force behind *shmitta* (which also included redemption of the land by its original owner),[2] was to restore the ideal, at least for a time, of social equality exemplified by shepherd life, or an idealized memory of it. In contrast, land owner-ship and agricultural activities opened the way to a widening gulf between the rich and poor, the land owner and the landless. During the *shmitta* year, the owner, the landless servant, and the poor would, as it were, drink from the same cup (all were allowed to harvest just enough for sustenance).[3]

The law of the seventh year of remission in Deuteronomy, while not specifying fallowing the land, stresses one's duty to lend to the poor and requires the freeing of the indentured servant. The owner is told not to let him go away empty-handed, but to be generous, to give him sheep from his own flock, as well as a supply of basic foods such as grain and wine from the "threshing floor and [wine] vat" (Deuteronomy 15:14). The social welfare system, expanded in the Poor-tithe, *ma'aser oni*, (Deuteronomy 14:28-9), is an expansion of previously stated tithing which had been restricted to giving produce to the priests and Levites (Leviticus 22:10; 27:21; 30-33; Numbers 18:21-32). Now in every third and sixth year of the seven-year tith-ing cycle, the farmer was to bring forth "the full tithe of your yield" (a tenth) and leave the produce in his own village or town where the landless Levite and "the stranger, the orphan, and the widow in your settlements shall come and eat their fill" (Deuteronomy 14:28-29).[4] Presumably the food was distributed by a town official and at least some of it had to be in a form that could be stored for future use until the next Poor-tithe three years later.[5]

Such charity, dependent on an intermediary and subject, there-fore, to the vagaries of interpretation (or corruption), was strength-ened by other agricultural legislation, first in the Holiness Code (Leviticus 19:9-10; 23:22), which dealt with leaving a corner of the grain field uncut (*pe'ah*), leaving the gleanings *lekhet*—stalks that fall to the ground behind the reaper and not picked up in the sheaf (*omer*)—and unpicked grape clusters as well as fallen grapes for "the stranger, the orphan, the widow" to take for themselves. This legis-lation was expanded in Deuteronomy to include the forgotten grain sheaf (*shikhehah*), along with olives remaining on the trees after the main crop had been beaten off with a stick (Deuteronomy 24:19-21). In this way, the poor could, by their own initiative, provide for themselves without having to beg, since what they took was considered by law to be rightly theirs. Deuteronomy (and subsequent Talmudic interpretation) regarded such charity as just and righteous acts, qualities subsumed in the Hebrew word *tzedakah* (justice). "Justice, justice you shall pursue" (*Tzedek, tzedek tirdof*) is considered the supreme duty of Israel and its people, which "you shall pursue, that you may thrive and occupy the land that the Lord your God is giving you (Deuteronomy 16:20)." If the law protected the destitute, it also blessed the provider, instilling in the Israelite psyche the link between giving and blessing.

—〰—

HOW DID SUCH LAWS, based on mostly unenforceable moral obligations, affect daily life?

We are offered a unique insight into this question in *Megillat Rut* (*Scroll of Ruth*),[6] a tight and brilliantly crafted story suggestive of a lively drama in four acts, which takes place in the town of Bethlehem ("house of bread") in Judah. The laws of charity are never spelled out, but a biblical audience, listening to the story, would know when various well-known duties and obligations were neglected, violated, or re-interpreted. The events that occur in *Ruth* begin at the time of the barley harvest around March–April at Passover and extend to the wheat harvest, which begins in May–June at *Shavuot*.

To better understand the story we must go directly to the field, then the threshing floor, where important scenes take place. If it was a large field belonging to a wealthy landowner, crews of men were employed to cut the standing grain. With one hand, the worker would clasp as much as his hand could hold, and with the other hand, he cut the stalks with a sickle. The resulting small heaps were gathered together into larger bundles and either left lying on the ground or tied together in sheaves, work that was often done by groups of young women. The weather at harvest time was increasingly hot and could bring on sunstroke (II Kings 4:18-20). However you look at it, working in the field, whether as a reaper, binder, or gleaner, was hard work. After the sheaves were dry, they were piled in large stacks, then they were transported to the nearby threshing floor (*goren*), where the ears, or heads, were separated from the stalks by beating them to release the individual kernels from the husks. In the evening when there was a cool breeze, they were winnowed of chaff that floated away in the wind.[7]

What exactly was due the destitute in the grain field? Ruth, the heroine of the story, was both a stranger and widow and so would be entitled to *leket*, (gleaning), *pe'ah* (uncut corner), and *shikhehah* (forgotten sheaf), referred to collectively as *matanot aniyim* ("gifts for the poor"). At the time the events occurred there probably was an informal system, later spelled out in the Mishna's tractate, *Pe'ah*, in the section *Zeraim* ("Seeds"), where it is clear that this form of charity had always been considered as a way for the poor to earn their daily bread, nothing more: two fallen stalks from the hand of the reaper, as he went along, could be picked up by the gleaner, but not three, which were regarded as belonging to the field's owner.[8] On the other hand, there was no upper size limit to the area of his field that the farmer could leave uncut, only a minimum (one sixtieth), thus giving him latitude for generosity, but he was admonished not to show favoritism. The gleaners of uncut corners, limited to using their hands, since it was forbidden to bring cutting tools, might be able to pick up enough stalks for only slightly more than a single meal, considering the work involved. The forgotten sheaf was most difficult for the farmer to observe, since if he remembered to forget it, he would be violating the law's intent (inadvertent generosity).[9]

Into this complex world of obligations and duties and informal arrangements known to all, enter Naomi, a widowed and destitute Israelite returning from Moab with her daughter-in-law, Ruth, often referred to as "the Moabitess" as a sign of her outsider status. According to law, on no account were Israelites ever to have anything to do with Moabites, Israel's sworn enemy "because [among other charges] they did not meet you with food and water on your journey when you left Egypt" (Deuteronomy 23:4-5); in other words, they had violated the shepherd code of hospitality. Ruth, however, has married into an Israelite family and has sworn allegiance, not only to Naomi, personally, but to Naomi's people, in her famous declaration: "Wherever you go, I will go; your people shall be my people, and your God my God. Where you die, I will die, and there I will be buried" (Ruth 1:16-17). Essentially, Ruth has converted to the Jewish faith.[10] In any case, it seems that in the ordinary course of life the law was not always strictly upheld. As soon as Naomi realized that Ruth would not be deterred from following her from Moab back to Bethlehem, she did not hesitate to bring her Moabite daughter-in-law home with her.[11]

Naomi's former neighbors and friends, however, do not rush up to offer even minimal hospitality, or even a kind remark of welcome, but, rather, are aghast at Naomi's appearance (in traditional interpretation, she is barefoot, in rags, and thin).[12] They are only able to utter, "Can this be Naomi?" the once well-off wife of the respected Elimelech. Bethlehem buzzed with this news (Ruth 1:19). Not only had she returned in disgrace from her sojourn in Moab—her husband had taken the family there during a famine at home (Ruth 1:1-2)—but she had brought with her her Moabite daughter-in-law! The contrast between the conduct that was expected of an Israelite toward the needy stranger or widow—not to mention former neighbor—and what actually occurred in Bethlehem, is striking, as a biblical audience would appreciate.

In the second 'act,' Ruth, who has stayed in the background until now, takes stock of their desperate situation and asks Naomi's permission to "go to the fields and glean among the ears of grain, behind someone who may show me kindness" (Ruth 2:2). The text does not indicate that anyone has stepped forward to offer them any help, despite the fact that Naomi "has a kinsman on her husband's side, a man of substance of the family of Elimelech, whose name was Boaz" (Ruth 2:1). Apparently Naomi cannot bring herself to remind him of his family obligations (although he must be aware of them since he knows of Naomi and Ruth's presence and their condition—how could it be otherwise in a small town?). It is unthinkable to Ruth that her beloved Naomi, whom all the town knows, should stoop to the level of gleaning, an activity associated with paupers. Ruth, having no qualms herself, but based on her negative experience thus far, is anxious to find a place where she will be allowed in the field. Her singular purpose, before which all obstacles will fall, is to bring relief to her mother-in-law. Hers is a spontaneous act of *hesed*, of lovingkindness, a central Jewish value which she naturally possesses in abundance.

How impressed an audience of ordinary people must have been as they came to know Ruth's sterling character!

Ruth goes to the fields of Boaz (unaware they are his), where she "gleaned in a field, behind the reapers" (Ruth 2:3). Surely something is out of place here, as a biblical audience would know at once because it was against all the prevailing mores of modesty that a young, unattended woman would place herself among the company of groups of men in this way. It is this discordance that prompts Boaz to ask about her as soon as he arrives from Bethlehem and observes the scene: a lone woman moving around in the rough society of his young male workers, perhaps jostled here and there for being out of place, perhaps subjected to unwanted physical contact, as seems likely in the light of Boaz's subsequent orders to his men. Ruth appears to be wholly unfamiliar with the etiquette of gleaning, perhaps picking up whatever fell from the reapers' hands, which would help to explain why she was being harassed. Thoughtless of her own peril, she has been singularly intent on her purpose to feed her hungry mother-in-law and nothing would deter her, neither law nor custom.[13] "Whose girl is that?" Boaz asks his overseer (Ruth 2:5), who tells him her origin ("a Moabite girl") and of her association with Naomi, about which he must already have known. He learns that "She has been on her feet ever since she came this morning. She has rested but little in the hut" (Ruth 2:7).

How does this prosperous landowner act toward the destitute gleaner who has caused a commotion in his fields because she has acted improperly? Not only does he not chastise her for her unusual activities in the field, which he has seen himself, but takes steps to protect her. "Listen to me, daughter. Don't go to glean in another field. Don't go elsewhere, but stay here close to my girls [female workers]. Keep your eyes on the field they [the men] are reaping and follow them [the girls who are tying the sheaves]. I have ordered the men not to molest you." As a further sign of his concern, he tells her that "when you are thirsty, go to the jars and drink some of [the water] that the men have drawn" (Ruth 2:8-9).

Ruth prostrates herself on the ground, overcome by his kindness (especially in light of what she and Naomi have experienced since they arrived in Bethlehem), and asks, "Why are you so kind as to single me out, when I am a foreigner?" (Ruth 2:10).

Boaz's reply puts him in a new light, as one capable of *hesed* himself. What unlocks his reserve is that he sees directly into Ruth's heart and he is overwhelmed. To him, the fact that she violated customs of modesty in the field and perhaps even violated law by gleaning more than was her due, is of no account. What matters are her good deeds. He tells her that he knows her entire history (but not that they are related and so he would have family obligations to her and Naomi), how she left her parents and the land of her birth to accompany her mother-in-law and live among "a people you had not known before. May the Lord reward your deeds. May you have a full recompense from the Lord, the God of Israel, under whose wings you have sought refuge!" (Ruth 2:11-12).

Later, he invites Ruth to lunch with his staff—bread dipped in a cooling wine vinegar and *kali*, roasted or parched grain—then, when she goes out again to glean, Boaz is careful to instruct his work-

ers to violate the law, as described in Leviticus 23:22, by ordering them to let her glean even among the sheaves; they were also instructed to pull out some stalks from them for her to glean, and on no account to scold her (Ruth 2:15-16). His is a two-fold violation, since justice would demand that owners not show favoritism among the gleaners, equality before the law being a staple of Deuteronomy.[14] He is well on his way to earning a *hesed* title for himself, inspired by Ruth's actions! His over-the-top generosity is revealed when, after she has threshed what she has gleaned, we are told it came to about an *ephah* of barley (Ruth 2:17), reckoned to be enough for a ten-day supply for one, or five-day supply for two,[15] in addition to which she brings home some of the roasted grain Boaz had given her for lunch. This must have been a very liberal amount since

Photograph © Joshua D. Klein

Hordeum vulgare. Barley growing at the Volcani Center of Agricultural Research, Bet Dagan, near Tel-Aviv.

"she ate her fill and had some left over" (Ruth 2:14). Altogether, it was an unprecedented haul for a gleaner.

Although generous to a fault, Boaz has confined his generosity to going beyond what is required of him as a landowner, but he has not yet fulfilled his family obligations. Urged on by Naomi, who, selflessly concerned about her daughter-in-law's future, hopes to force the issue with Boaz, Ruth is told to make herself attractive and when Boaz is asleep (after helping his men winnow the grain), to uncover his feet and sleep there. When he is startled by her presence and demands to know who she is, she goes beyond Naomi's advice and boldly, against all custom, proposes to him, explaining that "you are a redeeming kinsman" (Ruth 3:9), which means that he is obligated to buy Naomi's inheritance (land owned by Elimelech) and take Ruth with it as his wife, so they can produce a child who will carry on her late husband's name, a version of levirate marriage (*yibbum*) mandated in Deuteronomy 25:5-10.[16] Boaz, suddenly awakened (literally) to his duties, assures her he is more than agreeable—in fact, he is stunned by her loyalty to the family and is ready to do "whatever you ask" (Ruth 4:10-11)—but first he has to give a chance to a closer kin, who declines; he wants the land but not the Moabite widow.

And so it is a pauper Moabitess who ensures that the good citizen Boaz of Bethlehem will fulfill the law, and by doing so bring fulfillment to Naomi, who went away "full" (wealthy, with a family), returned "empty" (widowed, poor, and childless) (Ruth 1:21), and who is now truly fulfilled, with a grandson (more like a son) to carry on the family line that eventually produces David, founder of Israel's Royal House (Ruth 4:16-17).

What was the purpose of *Ruth*? Beyond tracing the lineage of David (which we don't find out about until the very end), the storyteller presents Ruth, a stranger from a rejected nation, as an example to the ordinary citizens of Bethlehem who, like people everywhere, often fail to come up to the mark. He shows how, unfamiliar with the etiquette of the gleaner, she violates custom, but Boaz, so impressed with her selflessness in the cause of supporting her mother-in-law, is moved to violate the letter of the law in the service of its spirit (he, it is assumed, knows the law, she does not, so his violation is greater). Is this to be condemned or condoned by the storyteller? Nothing in the text hints at disapproval. On the contrary, it is due to Ruth's *hesed*, and its impact on Boaz, moving him to *hesed* on her account, that convinces Naomi he has an interest in Ruth and therefore will act as the redeemer, thereby providing for her future. It is his duty, to be sure, but Naomi, sensitive to being a burden to her kinsman, is reassured by how generous Boaz has been to Ruth in the field. In this way, the story shows us how real people confront their obligations. It is not always a straightforward matter, given the complexities of human feelings. It is Ruth, who, standing above all the rest with her pure motives, moves those around her to fulfill their duties, and in this way the law is fulfilled. The rabbis have nothing but praise for Ruth, and see in her actions the fulfillment of Torah.

"The Torah is composed entirely of kindness, as it is said, 'And the Torah of lovingkindness is on her tongue.'"[17]

ENDNOTES

1. "Love your fellow as yourself," Leviticus 19:18.
2. Leviticus 25:23-25.
3. See Chapter Twenty-Two, *The Holy Land*, explaining the *shmitta* year.
4. In the intervening years (except for the seventh year), he is to sanctify his crop by consuming a tenth of it with his household in the holy precincts of Jerusalem, or converting its value into money and spending it there on food (Deuteronomy 14:22-26), as in the tithe on fourth year fruit trees. See Chapter Twenty, *Holy Fruit*.
5. Suggested in Jeffrey Tigay, *The JPS Torah Commentary, Deuteronomy*, 144.
6. The second of the Five Scrolls (*Hamesh Megillot*) (after Song of Songs, Ruth is followed by Lamentations, Ecclesiastes, Esther), and placed in the third section of the Hebrew Bible, *Ketuvim* (The Writings); in the Christian Bible, Ruth appears after the Book of Judges. Both the authorship of the book, and its date of composition are difficult to establish, although there are many opinions. Dates range from 950–700 BCE, between the time of David and the Assyrian conquest of the Northern Kingdom of Israel; during the period of the Babylonian Exile or in the early period of the return, that is, between 586 and 500 BCE. Jewish tradition holds that Ruth was composed by the prophet Samuel to legitimize David's dynasty about which there was question since he traced his ancestry to Ruth, the Moabitess and Deuteronomy 23:4 states that no descendant of a Moabite "shall [ever] be admitted into the congregation of the Lord." Oral law (Mishna) interprets this verse to mean only a male Moabite is prohibited from marrying an Israelite, referred to in the phrase, "Moabite, not Moabitess" (*Yevamot*

76b). *Ruth* is read in synagogues on *Shavuot* (Feast of Weeks, Pentecost) because, among other reasons, it is associated with the wheat harvest which occurs on *Shavuot*, and because Ruth's acceptance of the Torah parallels Israel's acceptance of it, the historical theme of the holiday. "This element of the feast is related to the prevalent rabbinic theme of Ruth as the ideal convert to Judaism who takes the Torah upon herself just as the Israelites did at Mount Sinai" (*The Jewish Study Bible*, 1579). For a traditional view of Ruth, see *ArtScroll Tannach Series—The Book of Ruth* and *The Soncino Books of the Bible—The Five Megilloth*; for a scholarly, and very readable, approach, see *Ruth*, in the Anchor Bible series, by Edward Campbell. All of these, as well as *The Jewish Study Bible*, include translations and commentaries. Only the *Soncinco* and *ArtScroll*, however, include the Hebrew text.

7. Harvesting, threshing, and winnowing in ancient Israel is discussed at length in the *Encylopedia Judaica*, 378.

8. *Mishna Pe'ah* 6:5. This and other Mishnaic laws in the tractate called *Zeraim* can be found in the ArtScroll Series *The Mishna*, Seder Zeraim Vol. IIa which contains the Hebrew text with translation and commentary from Talmudic, Midrashic, and Rabbinic sources.

9. There is a well known story about the pious Rabbi Zadok who "grieved over the fact that he had never carried out this *mitzvah*. When at last he forgot some sheaves in his fields, he rejoiced, and made a festival for himself and his household." J. H. Hertz, *The Pentateuch and Haftorahs*, 853.

10. There are many rabbinic interpretations concerning Ruth's conversion, mostly centering around the question of whether or not Ruth and Orpah converted when they married Elimelech's sons or when Ruth pledged her loyalty to Naomi. For a review of traditional responses see the *Soncino*, "Midrashic Approach to Ruth," 94–95.

11. Archeologist John Gray points out that there must have been many from the mountains of Palestine who, like Elimelech and Naomi from Bethlehem, sought relief in the plains of Moab, (probably located just north-east of the Dead Sea and well-watered by perennial wadis), when the seasonal rains failed. See *Archeology and The Old Testament World*, 13–14.

12. For interpretations along this line see *ArtScroll-Ruth*, 83.

13. This interpretation was suggested by Rabbi Moshe Shulman's inspiring classes on *Ruth* at Shaarei Shomayim Synagogue in Toronto, 2003.

14. As in Leviticus 19:15: "You shall not render an unfair decision: do not favor the poor or show deference to the rich; judge your kinsman fairly."

15. This reckoning is explained in *ArtScroll*, 101: An *ephah* equals ten *omers*. Since an *omer* is considered a day's food for one person, Ruth's yield from her first day of gleaning was sufficient to feed Naomi and herself for five days.

16. There it is restricted to a brother of the deceased brother (as the term, from the Latin *levir*, meaning husband's brother, implies), but in the story it is extended to include closest kin. See Genesis 38 for this treatment of levirate obligations in the story of Judah and his widowed daughter-in-law, Tamar. See also Genesis 19:30-38 for another story of carrying on the family name (this one features the seduction of Lot by his daughters); the offspring of these unions were Moab and Ammon, patriarchs of their respective nations. And so we see another layer of meaning in the story of Ruth, where past dubious, but necessary, actions are reconciled by the present.

17. Recounted from *Lekach Tov* (literally, "Good Lesson"), a compilation of *midrashim* by Rabbi Toviah ben Eliezer HaGodol (1036–1108), in the *Soncino* edition, *Ruth*, 93.

Chapter Thirty-Four

FIRST FRUITS

**Portion-*Ki Tavo* / When you enter [the land] (Deuteronomy
26:1-29:8)**

*When you enter the land that the Lord your God is giving you as a
heritage, and you possess it and settle in it, you shall take some of every
first fruit of the soil which you harvest from the land that the Lord your
God is giving you. (Deuteronomy 26:1-2)*

Photograph © Ori Fragman

Phoenix dactylifera. Clusters of
ripening dates, Tel-Aviv.

Moses' teaching (*Torah*) continues.
He instructs his charges regarding the offering of first fruits (*bikkurim*), the very best of the farmer's
earliest ripened fruit from his trees
and vines. We have already encountered this law in Exodus: "The choice
first fruits of your soil you shall bring
to the house of the Lord your God"
(Exodus 23:19; 34:26). The principle
of the "first fruits of everything" in the
land belonging to God, from "all the
best of the new oil, wine, and grain,"
to the first-born among animals and
man (who is to be redeemed)[1] is not
new, having been stated in different
ways elsewhere in the Bible.[2] It is clear
that the law has been fleshed out with
an elaborate ceremony that includes

a declaration to accompany the offering of first fruits (*mikra bikkurim*). From Moses' description we can envision, in a general way, what takes place: the farmer selects the best of his earliest fruits, puts them in a basket that he takes up to the Temple in Jerusalem where he verifies before God what he has done. Moses' audience of rough shepherds, soon to be transformed into farmers, must have wondered about their new role. Not only were they expected to bring an offering of fine fruit (which they must learn to grow), but they will be required to make a speech! Fortunately, every word to be uttered is supplied.[3]

The declaration begins by reviewing the Israelites' history from its very beginning with Abraham ("My father was a fugitive Aramean"),[4] then moves on to a description of how he had gone down to Egypt with few in number, had become a populous nation, and was later enslaved and sorely oppressed. The farmer clearly identifies with this experience, as if he, himself, were there: "We cried to the Lord, the God of our fathers, and the Lord heard our plea, and saw our plight, our misery, and our oppression. The Lord freed us from Egypt... and brought us to this place and gave us this land, a land flowing with milk and honey."[5] It is only then that the farmer makes the connection between what God has done for him, personally, and the fruits he has brought. He is bringing his offering in acknowledgment of the land which, like the fruit, is a gift from God: "I now bring the first fruits of the soil which You, O Lord, have given me" (Deuteronomy 26:2-10).

This is so very different from what we imagine might occur in a ceremony of thanksgiving for the fertility of the land (Why a review of the people's history?) that Moses needs once more to explain, as he has been doing from the beginning of his teaching, that the people are embarked on a much different course from any they had known about before, one that defines and sets them apart forever from the surrounding pagan culture. Lest the farmer believe that he alone produced his fruit, he is led to think beyond his immediate material world, represented by the basket of fruit, to a more transcendent vision: the role of God in shaping and fulfilling Israel's destiny, and its consequences: dependence on God and the obligation to follow His laws.[6] Linking agricultural events to the people's history, as embodied in the *mikra bikkurim* ceremony, is typical of the Bible's ongoing effort to forge a distinctive religious and national identity. Many temptations lie ahead for the people, especially in light of the difficulties inherent in cultivating a semi-arid land with uncertain rainfall. The Israelites' adherence to God's laws needs to be fortified and strengthened at every opportunity. A shepherd people needs to understand, for instance, that the opposing forces of nature they will encounter in the land they are about to enter, forces that will greatly influence the success or failure of their crops, are ruled not by a pantheon of nature deities as their neighbors believe, but by the same God Who brought them out of slavery and gave them the means to become a holy nation, the same God Who created the universe and everything in it, including the *hamsin* winds, periods of drought, blessed rain, and thriving crops.[7]

A great deal will be expected of an Israelite farmer within the moral and ethical framework of the covenant, but commitment has practical advantages. It seems probable that the very discipline imposed by law—to sacrifice the fourth year fruit from a young tree (*orla*), to leave a corner of his field uncut (*pe'ah*), to set aside a tenth of his crop for the poor (*ma'aser oni*), for instance—became the very means whereby the Israelite farmer was motivated to raise the level of his farming activity. If he was conscientious in fulfilling the law he would have to keep a sharp eye on his crops and thus would be bound to observe flaws in plant growth due to disease, insect infestation, competing weeds, poor siting, or lack of water, conditions that might otherwise not be noticed so soon, and he could make the necessary improvements.[8] He might also become more aware of variant growth (earlier ripening fruit or grain, for instance) and select for improved varieties. Any good farmer would watch carefully over his fields and groves, but the law may have added another dimension to the Israelite farmer's work. This may help to explain his better-than-average skill, famous throughout the region, in raising and developing various fruits, a considerable achievement in itself, but even more so when taking into consideration the difficulties inherent in farming in the Promised Land.

Moses' teaching now draws to a close, having ended with a description of the farmer's declaration that he has fulfilled the third year Poor-tithe (Deuteronomy 26:13-15), and although Moses states that the two-way covenant first made at Sinai (Exodus

19:5-6) has been now reaffirmed, one feels a growing tension, a sense of unfinished business. Moses is near his end, aware that soon he will die and Joshua will be left to lead the people on to their new life. Are his charges truly prepared for this great venture? Will they adhere to the demands God requires of them to live as a holy people? What follows are measures to be enacted when the people reach the other side of the Jordan. These are designed to impress the laws into the people's memory (Deuteronomy 27:2-8), and to drive home the consequences of failure to obey them. The proclamation of blessings, a short, compact list (Deuteronomy 28:1-14), is followed by a much longer series of curses (Deuteronomy 28:15-68), so terrible that they are traditionally uttered in a low voice in the synagogue liturgy.[9]

—

LIKE THE *ORLA* SACRIFICE of fourth-year fruit, *bikkurim* is a sacrifice, too, a gift to God in return for the gift of the land and its produce.[10] As with the grain offerings in their season (at Passover and *Shavuot*), only after he has brought the first fruit of the season to Jerusalem and made his declaration (*mikkra bikkurim*) and presented his offering, is the farmer allowed to eat any of the season's new crop. The question is, which fruits qualify as *bikkurim*? Which fruits should the farmer load into his baskets and take up to Jerusalem? The text seems to say that *bikkurim* can come from any of the fruit he raises on his own land, "some of every first fruit of the soil." The Israelite farmer cultivated a variety of fruits, among them citron, apple, peach, apricot, plum, pear, walnut, almond, carob, and mulberries.[11] None of these, however, were ever considered appropriate for fulfilling the commandment of first fruits. According to the Mishna, only the five fruits from the Seven Species, *Shivat Haminim* (grapes, figs, pomegranates, olives, and dates that produce honey) are acceptable as *bikkurim*,[12] the reasoning being that these are the fruits in God's own description of the "good land" (Deuteronomy 8:7-9). But given their susceptibility to damage from unsettled conditions at that time of year—fluctuating rain, drought, wind, cool and hot temperatures—that prevail during the fifty days between Passover and *Shavuot* when these fruits blossom, are pollinated, and form their fruit, these fruits themselves represent a temptation to the Israelite farmer to forsake God in favor of (or in addition to) the local nature gods, by propitiating them to bring the right weather conditions for his crops. By contrast, the "choice products" sent down to Egypt, are not a source of anxiety to the farmer, because they are more tolerant of adverse weather conditions and would bear their fruit even during times of drought and famine, as was the case when Jacob sent his gifts. The Seven Species are, in effect, emblematic of the Israelites' trust in and commitment to God alone.[13] By bringing fruit only from this group of plants, the farmer acknowledges that it is He who has blessed the harvest, rather than the Canaanite gods.

The rabbis stipulated that because certain of the Seven Species grow better in one part of the land than another, only *bikkurim* growing in the most favorable conditions are acceptable. Dates, for instance, must come from the warm valley areas, rather than the cooler mountainsides, because dates grown in warm valleys produce more date honey. Other fruit trees, however, grow better in the cooler areas, so their fruits are favored as *bikkurim*. Olives must be the best of those grown for producing olive oil (oil-olives), rather than from inferior types which would be grown for pickling.[14] The Mishna gives us a glimpse into the complex agricultural world of biblical times, about which the rabbis appeared to be intimately familiar.

Photograph © Avinoam Danin

Phoenix dactylifera. Date palms growing spontaneously on wet saline ground, Beit Shean Valley.

The rabbis ask and answer all the practical questions that come to mind concerning *bikkurim*. How does the farmer set aside his first fruits? It is very simple. "A person [farmer] goes down into his field and sees a fig that has emerged [budded], a cluster [of early grapes] that has emerged [budded],

[or] a pomegranate that has emerged [budded], he ties it with a reed, and says: 'These are *bikkurim.*'" [15] He then leaves them in the field until they are ripe and ready to be transported to Jerusalem. Rabbi Mordechai Ziemba, a great twentieth century Polish Torah scholar, commented that figs, early ripening grapes, and pomegranates are precisely the fruits the scouts brought back from their mission to report about the land to Moses (Numbers 13:23), and as had been observed earlier, by the sixteenth century Rabbi Isaac Luria ("The Lion"), bringing these fruits as a sacrifice in gratitude for the land serves to rectify the sin of the scouts who disparaged the land.[16]

Photograph © Ori Fragman

Punica granatum. Pomegranate fruit, Israel.

When does the farmer bring his first fruits to Jerusalem? Only during the time of year when people rejoice over their harvest: "And you shall enjoy, together with the Levite and the stranger in your midst, all the bounty that the Lord your God has bestowed on you and your household" (Deuteronomy 26:11); that is, between *Shavuot* and *Sukkot*, the period when the people rejoice over the crops they harvest from early to late summer before the winter rains inaugurate a new growing season. *Shavuot*, therefore, was the time for bringing the earliest ripening fruits from among the Seven Species to Jerusalem.

Shavuot (from "weeks"), one of the three Pilgrimage Festivals (*shalosh regalim*), goes by several names: Feast of Weeks or *Hag ha-Shavuot* (Deuteronomy 16:9-10); Feast of the Harvest or *Hag ha-katzir* (Exodus 23:16); and Day of the First Fruits or *Yom ha-Bikkurim* (Numbers 28:26). In post-biblical literature (the Mishna and Talmud) it is referred to as *Atzeret* ("closing"), because it brings to an end the seven-week period between the barley and grain harvests; on the fiftieth day, the wheat harvest begins, from which the festival is also known by its Greek name, Pentecost ("fiftieth day").

The seven-week period is known as the Counting of the Omer (*Sefirat Ha'omer*), and is an oral counting of days that began on the eve of the second day of Passover after the first ripe *omer* (sheaf) of barley was brought to the Temple as a sacrifice. The counting of days was accompanied by much anxiety over the fate of the wheat crop, which, like the fruits of the Seven Species, is also subject to the damaging effects of unsettled weather during this period. *Hamsin* winds, for instance, can scorch and ruin standing wheat; by contrast, barley, considered animal fodder, a last resort in famine, or for the very poor, was a surer crop, able to grow well even in less than ideal conditions, and ripening before *hamsin* weather. There must have been a collective sigh of relief on the fiftieth day when the wheat harvest was officially launched, when "they have rejoiced before You, As they rejoice at reaping time" (Isaiah 9:2). We cannot imagine today how dependent people were on the success of the wheat crop, the staple, above all others, of daily sustenance.[17]

Bringing the very first fruits of the Seven Species to Jerusalem at *Shavuot* was a colorfully festive national affair, as we know from accounts in the Mishna, *midrashim*, and from outside sources.[18] Families gathered in the early morning in the open squares of towns, then traveled, by whatever means, in processional style to Jerusalem, the column headed by someone leading a sacrificial ox whose horns were gilded in gold and silver, his head garlanded with an olive-leaf wreath, the procession accompanied along the way by musicians playing flutes.[19]

It must have been a source of pride to the farmer and his family to present an attractive basket of fruit. Great effort would have gone into selecting and watching over the earliest and best fruits, then, after picking them, displaying them in a basket, with the very best on top. If the farmer lived too far from Jerusalem to bring in fresh fruit, dried figs and raisins were allowed. The edges of the basket were adorned with fruit, too, perhaps with a handsome cluster of grapes, and even live pigeons. The rich brought their fruit in baskets of gold and silver (which were returned), the poor wove theirs from willow branches; these hand-made baskets were considered an integral part of the fruit offering and were not returned.[20]

With the destruction of the Second Temple, the pilgrimages came to an end, but not the observance of *Shavuot*. It was the genius of the rabbis who saved this purely agricultural festival, based on the wheat harvest and first fruit offering, from extinction. They calculated that

Shavuot commemorated the day of the giving of the Torah on Mount Sinai, from the suggestion that this occurred in the third month, *Nisan*, after the Exodus from Egypt, when the Israelites entered the wilderness and camped "in front of the mountain" (Exodus 19:2); this is the same month of the year, *Sivan*, when wheat ripens in the Land of Israel. Thus *Shavuot*, like the other Pilgrimage Festivals, Passover and *Sukkot*, became a portable holiday that could be practiced wherever Jews lived in a widely scattered diaspora, and the prayers, rituals, and traditions that developed from this interpretation could be observed in the synagogue and by the family at home. Also known as the Giving of the Torah (*Matan Torah*), it brings the Exodus saga to its logical conclusion, when the freed slaves stood at the foot of the mountain and declared, "All the Lord has spoken we will do!" (Exodus 19:8). By this linkage, even a scattered and landless nation continued to renew its commitment to God through new interpretations of its festivals and observances. The land was not forgotten, though, for it is inextricably bound to the people's history from its beginnings. Passover still commemorates the Jews' freedom from slavery in the season of *aviv* when stalks of barley in the Land of Israel become hard and their heads swell with ripened kernels of grain, as *Shavuot* commemorates the Jewish acceptance of God's laws in the season of ripened wheat and first fruits in the Land of Israel.[21]

ENDNOTES

1. This takes place in a ceremony called *Pidyon HaBen*, literally "Redemption of the First Born Son," on the thirty-first day following his birth, when his father takes the infant before a descendant of a *kohen* (priest), blessings are made, and a symbolic ransom of five silver coins is paid, symbolizing the five shekels prescribed in the Torah as the redemption amount [Numbers 18:16]." See Rabbi Hayim Halevy Donin *To Be A Jew*, 276–279.

2. Exodus 23:19; 34:22, 26; Numbers 15:17-21; 18:12-13; Deuteronomy 26:1-11.

3. The declaration was to be recited in the original Hebrew from a Torah scroll. At the beginning of the Second Temple period, when Jews returning from Babylon were not fluent in Hebrew, the text would be dictated to them and they would repeat it. Realizing that by being singled out, they would be embarrassed and this would discourage them to come to Jerusalem to make the declaration, the rabbis made an enactment that the declaration of *bikkurim* should be recited to everyone. See Yad

Avraham commentary to *Bikkurim* 3.7 in *ArtsScroll Mishnah Series, Bikkurim*, 125–126.

4. This very ancient alliterative phrase, *Arami oved avi*, conducive to memorization, was adopted for inclusion in the Haggadah at the Passover Seder where it is interpreted to mean "Laban the Aramean sought to destroy my father," perhaps "due to a disbelief that the Bible would describe one of Israel's ancestors as an Aramean [aggressors toward Israel in the ninth century BCE]." Jeffrey Tigay, *The JPS Commentary, Deuteronomy*, 240.

5. A wild, uncultivated land. See Chapter Twenty-five, *Beautiful Pomegranates*.

6. Tigay, 238, discusses the theme of fertility as having a secondary role in the first fruits ceremony, "as the farmer is led from his immediate situation to a recognition of the land's fertility as merely one aspect of a larger picture, namely God's guidance of Israel's history from its humble beginnings, freeing it from oppression and giving it the land."

7. Linking historical events to seasonal harvest celebrations drives home the central concept of monotheism: of One God, the same God Who redeemed the Israelites in Egypt, Who brings forth the crops of the land. This concept is worked out in detail throughout Nogah Hareuveni's *Nature in Our Biblical Heritage*.

8. For instance, the *omer* offering, an armful or sheaf of the first ripened barley (as much as a hand-held sickle can cut) *had* to be brought to the Temple on the second day of Passover every year.

9. "The list of curses and its companion in Leviticus [26:14-38] were considered so frightening that in later times the custom developed of chanting them in an undertone during the Torah reading service in the synagogue, and many people were reluctant to be called to the Torah when they were read." Tigay, 261.

10. After the ceremonial offering the fruit was given to the priests as part of their livelihood. See Numbers 18:12-13; Deuteronomy 18:3-5.

11. Asaph Goor and Max Nurock discuss these in *The Fruits of the Holy Land*.

12. *Bikkurim* 1.3.

13. See Hareuveni, 30–42 and Chapter Thirty-Two for the significance of the Seven Species.

14. *Bikkurim* 1.3; 1.10.

15. Ibid. 3.1.

16. These interpretations are cited in a note in the *ArtScroll*, 5. Rabbi Ziemba (1883–1943) was murdered in the Warsaw Ghetto Uprising shortly after the beginning of Passover, 1943. His body was buried by his comrades, exhumed after the war, and reburied in Israel where his funeral was attended by thousands. His story is told in the *ArtScroll/ Mesorah Publications Judaiscope Series*. Rabbi Isaac Luria (1534–1572), also known as "The Ari," who lived in Safed in the Galilee of Ottoman Palestine, is considered the father of contemporary Kabbala.

17. Biblical scholar E. P. Saunders estimates that grain constituted over half of the average person's total caloric intake, followed by legumes (such as lentils), olive oil, and fruit, especially dried figs. Most people ate red meat only a few times a year during the Pilgrimage Festivals when they sacrificed an animal, and fowl or fish at the Sabbath or on festival days they did not spend in Jerusalem. *Judaism: Practice and Belief, 63 BCE–66 CE*, 129.

18. As in Philo's *De specialibus legibus*, a work which expounds on special Jewish Laws. He was a first century CE Alexandrian Jew who devoted much of his efforts toward trying to impress gentiles as well as Hellenized Jews with the greatness of Scripture and the Law.

19. *Bikkurim* 3.2, 3.

20. Ibid. 3.3, 5, 8.

21. In modern Israel, kibbutzim hold *bikkurim* celebrations on *Shavuot* with colorful parades displaying agricultural produce grown on the kibbutz.

Chapter Thirty-Five

POISON PLANTS AND WORMWOOD

Portion *Nitzavim* / You are standing [today] (Deuteronomy 29:9-30:20)

Perchance there is among you a stock sprouting poison weed and wormwood. (Deuteronomy 29:17)

Photograph © Ori Fragman

Conium maculatum. Poison hemlock in Zipori, Lower Galilee.

Moses introduces his last exhortation by referring back to all that God has done for his charges: led them out of Egypt through the wilderness for forty years,[1] and when it was evident they were incapable of surviving without His help, He had provided for all their material needs, from the clothes on their backs and the sandals on their feet to the 'food' (manna from heaven) that sustained them, "that you might know that I the Lord am your God (Deuteronomy 29:5). And having arrived at "this place"[2] before crossing the Jordan River, did not God defeat their enemies?[3] To Moses, the evidence is indisputable. Having witnessed God's power over all things, there should be no question about the people's commitment to the covenant, yet there is doubt, or why should Moses expend so much passion in exhorting them to be faithful? Perhaps because he knows all too well where even momentary doubt can lead. For failure to obey God at the waters of Meribah, Moses is fated to die shortly thereafter.[4] He will look down on the Promised Land, but Joshua, not he, will lead his people there. All the more reason for the faithful shepherd to put his flock on the right path.

Moses summons everyone to listen carefully to his words. "Everyone" includes every single person within the camp, from officials to entire families, from "the woodchopper to waterdrawer," and beyond them, to all future generations, even though they "are not with us here this day" (Deuteronomy 29:9-14). Each one is invited to participate in the affirmation of Moses' teaching, which establishes for all time the special relationship between God and His people. We can imagine this standing assembly as real people—from the exalted to the most humble—all aware of the seriousness of the occasion as they listen intently to Moses, who warns them yet again of the consequences of disobedience.

Wouldn't this become tiresome? After all, the consequences of disobedience have been spelled out in graphic detail. Surely the point has been made: obedience brings the blessings of abundance; and contrary behavior brings grief in every conceivable form, from barrenness to the loss of one's land, a terrible fate in a farming-based existence.

Moses' genius as a teacher is to frame the subject repeatedly in different ways in order to press home his message most effectively. Now, for instance, he anticipates that even as they are listening to him, some among his audience (man or woman) are turning away from God, thinking that the sanctions don't apply personally to them. He assures his listeners that this "stock sprouting poison weed and wormwood," these doubters, will bring disaster and death, like a spreading poison, to the utter ruin of "moist and dry alike" (Deuteronomy 29:18, 22), to both the righteous and sinner.[5] The very land will be destroyed by "sulfur and salt," so that it is beyond sowing and producing grass, similar to the destruction of Sodom and Gomorrah, the cities of wickedness (Genesis 19:24).

Moses skillfully contrasts this scene of devastation with one of "abounding prosperity in all your undertakings, in the issue of your womb, the offspring of your cattle, and the produce of your soil (Deuteronomy 30:9)," blessings that mean everything to a society of farmers. But this will only come about when, having been sent into exile by God for their disobedience (turning to other gods), the people have a change of heart and return to Him. Moses describes in moving terms how God will "take you back in love," from wherever you are scattered. From wherever you are, God will "fetch you," and "bring you to the land that your fathers possessed, and you shall possess it; and He will make you more prosperous and more numerous than your fathers" (Deuteronomy 30:3-5). And not only will the people return to God, but He will return to them.[6]

When he observes that his teachings are not beyond the reach of the most humble among his flock, Moses makes a telling point. The commandments are not some esoteric code that only the initiated can understand. Just as all the people stood together at the foot of Sinai and heard the Law, now they have heard it again from Moses. God's commandments, Moses concludes, are readily accessible to all, "they are in your mouth and in your heart" (Deuteronomy 30:14).[7]

Once again, he goes over his argument for being true to the covenant. He reminds them that his purpose has been to set before them two clear paths and their consequences: simply put, one path leads to life, the other to death. The path of life is to walk in God's ways and thereby gain life and prosperity; the other is to turn away from God, to be lured to the worship and service of false gods, and thus bring about death and adversity. "I have put before you life and death, blessing and curse. Choose life." Moses urges, "If you and your offspring would live—by loving the Lord your God, heeding His commands, and holding fast to Him. For thereby you shall have life . . ." (Deuteronomy 30:19-20). "Life" (*hayim*), then, goes beyond mere physical survival. It means living according to the covenant the Israelites have made with God, just as living outside the covenant is regarded as death in a spiritual sense, even if the body survives.[8] In a final effort, Moses lays out the choices his people will face once they are settled in the Promised Land. There they will be exposed to the temptations of pagan culture, to which they have already shown their susceptibility in the incident of the Golden Calf.[9] He has to get across the idea that it is not enough to *affirm* the covenant (to pay lip service), it must be *obeyed*, and the choice is theirs.[10]

WHICH ARE THE POISONOUS and bitter plants, *rosh ve-la'anah*, that symbolize the bitter poison of doubt that could spread throughout an entire nation and bring about its destruction?

The phrase is variously translated as "poison plant and wormwood" (NJPS); "hemlock and wormwood" (Alter); and "gall and wormwood" (Hertz, KJV). The traditional rendering, "gall and wormwood," has passed into the English language as an expression for something very disagreeable, a deep bitterness of the spirit, based on the idea that gall and wormwood have very bitter, as well as poisonous, properties. Gall, or bile, is the bitter greenish fluid contained in a sac on the liver of most vertebrates, which helps digestion. If even a little bit of the dark green fluid spills onto the carcass in the process of butchering, it taints the meat, as most people in the past would know from experience. Trappers and American Indians are said to have spiced up their food with a little bile,[11] but if consumed in sufficient quantity it could be toxic. Wormwood is the common name of *Artemisia absinthium*, so described because it is especially strong in the bitter property *absinthin* and most famous for flavoring the drink, absinthe. What could more vividly convey God's punishment for those who turn away from Him than a metaphorical combination of "gall and wormwood?" But "gall" doesn't get us very far in identifying *rosh*, a term in the Bible usually associated with a poisonous plant, as in "a stock sprouting *rosh*" and "Justice degenerates into *rosh*, breaking out on the furrows of the fields" (Hosea 10:4). The translation of *la'anah* as "wormwood" is problematic, too, because *A. absinthium*, one of the most bitter of artemisias, is a European plant.

In virtually every reference to *rosh* meaning "poison," it is spelled the same as *rosh* meaning "head" as in Rosh Hashana, "head of the year": *resh-aleph-shin*; the exception is "Their grapes are the grapes of *rosh*," (Deuteronomy 32:32, Judaica Press), where *rosh* is spelled *rosh-vav-shin*, specifically meaning "poison." Commentators have taken this as a clue to the identity of a particular poisonous plant or a group of them with head-like flowers or seed heads. Several candidates for *rosh* have been advanced, among them poison hemlock, *Conium maculatum*. Known in Hebrew as *rosh akod*, or simply *rosh*, the Latin genus name is from the Greek *konas*, "to whirl about," from the vertigo and death that follow eating any part of the plant. Poison hemlock is native to Europe and to many other parts of the world, including Asia and the Mediterranean region, and is naturalized in many other areas. In Israel it grows along roadsides, on refuse dumps, and at neglected sites in most parts of the country except desert areas. It is a member of the Umbelliferae family whose flowers form a characteristic umbrella-like head (the origin of the Latin genus name), as in parsley, fennel, parsnip, and carrot. Poison hemlock reaches three to six feet in height, has a fetid odor, and often densely covers large patches of ground wherever conditions are favorable. Leaves are large, finely cut, and feathery, tapering as they grow up the plant. Small, clustered white flowers in rounded umbels or heads are held on radiating branches on purple-spotted, hollow stems that grow from a long, white taproot. All parts, especially its seeds and roots, contain the powerful alkaloid coniine, a minute quantity of which can cause death through paralysis of the respiratory system. Widely known throughout the ancient world, it was administered to criminals; according to Greek tradition it was hemlock extract that Socrates chose as his death potion in 399 BCE.

What better poison to administer to the erring people of Israel than a draft of poison hemlock, whose stock sprouts a poisonous head?

Despite its ancient reputation as a killer, poison hemlock, in common with other poisonous plants such as foxglove (source of the heart medicine, digitalis) has curative powers too. Greek and Arab physicians used it to treat tumors, swellings, and pains in the joints. In medieval times hemlock was used with a mixture of herbs to create an anesthetic preparation, and later as an antidote to strychnine poisoning. Because of its sedative properties, it was used in the past for treating nervous spasms, cramps, epilepsy, and whooping cough,[12] and in North Africa a preparation is used against hardening of the arteries, convulsions, and to alleviate insect stings as well as the pains of cancer.[13]

Henbane, *Hyoscyamus*, has been linked to *rosh* through its Aramaic name *shikhrona* (intoxicating plant) and its hood-like flowers. Golden henbane, *H. aureus* (*shikaron zahav*), is preserved in the Bible as the place name Shikrona or Shikkeron (Joshua 15:11) in

Photograph © Avinoam Danin

Hyoscyamus aureus. Golden henbane perched on rock in Acco Plain, Acco.

Judea, where this plant is abundant. The most common of the five species of henbane that grow in Israel, it has the habit of tumbling indiscriminately out of cracks in ancient walls and ruins, whether on the Western Wall in Jerusalem, mosque walls in the Galilee, or on Crusader fortress walls in Acco. Hiking in the Negev, the eye is led upward, where golden henbane clings to a high rocky ledge, its flowers the only bright color as far as the eye can see. Plants grow from twelve to twenty inches in height, their branched stems bearing large lobed leaves, sticky and covered with glandular hairs. Flowers are showy with flared back yellow petals, dark purplish in the center, with prominent stamens extending beyond the funnel-shaped bloom. Josephus compared the shape of the flower to the head-like 'cups of gold' that decorated the High Priest's crown.[14]

Pliny the Elder stated that eating just four leaves of henbane had the power to drive a person crazy.[15] The active ingredients, to a greater or lesser degree in all henbane species, are the powerful alkaloids atropine, scopolamine, and hyoscyamine, which have antispasmodic, hypnotic, and narcotic properties, the last preserved in the Hebrew word for "drunk," *shikor.* In small doses henbane preparations have a beneficial effect as a tranquilizer and have been used to treat acute mania and delirium tremens. Externally, it has been used to relieve rheumatism, and treat arthritis, earache, toothache, eye problems, and asthmatic conditions, but it must be used cautiously and in small quantities. *H. muticus*, which grows in the Sinai and is sometimes referred to as Egyptian henbane, is cultivated in Egypt as a source of chemicals which act on the nervous system.[16]

Wild gourd, *Citrullus colocynthis*, according to some scholars, could be biblical *rosh*.[17] Its fruits—round, very bitter, and poisonous—were gathered by the prophet Elisha's servant to make a stew for the hungry disciples of the prophet. Searching the land in a time of famine, he must have been glad to see a potential source of food in the sprawling desert vine, for he picked a lot of the wild gourds, stuffing them in his clothing, but after he had sliced them up and cooked them and the men began to eat the stew, they were suddenly struck, and called out, "O man of God, there is death in the pot!" Elisha quickly threw flour into the stew, thereby neutralizing the effect of the poisonous fruit (II Kings 4:38-41). Also called bitter apple and bitter cucumber, this member of the cucumber family (Cucurbitaceae) is the biblical *pakuot-sadeh*. The plant looks

Photograph © Avinoam Danin

Citrullus colycynthis. Wild gourd, Nahal Nekarot near Hatzeva, Arava Valley.

something like a small cucumber vine with similar yellow flowers. Its thick roots enable it to store water and survive in harsh desert conditions. The fruit (a gourd), about the size of an apple is four to five inches across, striped green in early growth, then later turns brownish yellow as it ripens. The pulp is spongy, and the seeds, which are surprisingly edible, are white or brown.

It would be a terrible mistake to try to eat a wild gourd, as Elisha's disciples discovered. Its properties include the glucoside colocyntin which could cause hemorrhaging of the bowels. But in common with other *rosh* candidates, it is also a healing plant and its many uses have been known for millennia. Since the time of the Pharaohs, the dried pulp of the fruit has been used as a moth preventative, and preparations have been widely used for treating urinary tract and liver diseases, jaundice, to relieve muscle pains, rheumatism, and menstrual discomfort. In the beginning of the twentieth century, significant quantities of the fruit were exported from Gaza to Europe for use as a laxative drug. According to the Mishna, it was permissible to use the oil, extracted from the seeds, for lighting ceremonial candles.[18]

The annual opium poppy, *Papaver somniferum*, is the candidate favored by some commentators for its known poisonous properties and its conspicuously rounded seed head after its petals have fallen. A steeped solution of poppy heads has been thought by some to be the 'water of gall' of Jeremiah 8:14, KJV.[19] It is native to the eastern Mediterranean (but not Israel), Asia Minor, and Central Asia. It has been extensively cultivated in Europe, China, and India, and in North America for its seeds and oil, and highly regarded garden forms. Closely related to the red field poppy[20] it is taller, growing up to five feet when intensively cultivated for opium, seed, or oil production; it is much shorter when found as an escape from cultivation (growing on its own after it has been abandoned). Plants grow up on hollow stems from a spindle-shaped tap root, the stems clasped by large, grayish, jagged leaves, and topped by a large wavy-edged, silky flower, white to lilac to pinkish-purple, sometimes with a darker blotch at its base. As the petals fall, the immature seed head (the source of opium) is revealed. The Latin epithet *somniferum*, derived from the Greek meaning "sleep-bearing," indicates the poppy's narcotic properties.

Raw opium, a white milky juice, is extracted from the fast-ripening seed head, and when hardened contains a number of important alkaloids, the most important of which are morphine and codeine. It is likely that readers have benefited from preparations that contained these properties and other opium alkaloids to treat coughs, diarrhea, or pain. The healing properties of opium have been known since earliest times. In ancient Egypt, for instance, it was used as a sedative, and only much later was it consumed as a drug for its narcotic properties.[21] Although the plant's products are potentially deadly if not administered with care, its seeds have no narcotic properties. On *Shabbat* we may enjoy delicious *hallah* loaves thickly sprinkled with poppy seeds. The Talmud refers to this poppy-seed bearing poppy, *parag*, and declares that it is subject to tithing for its seeds (*Halah* 1, 4); the seeds of the native red poppy are not harvested for use. Thus we understand that *Papaver somniferum*, although not native to Israel, was an important crop, cultivated for its seeds and for the oil expressed from them since poppy seed oil is known to be a cheap substitute for olive oil.[22] Because poppy seeds were sprinkled over the hallah dough but were not part of it, they, like sesame seeds, were tithed separately. A small population of opium poppy flowers survive in Israel as escapes in several parts of the country.

And wormwood, *la'anah*? Commentators seem to be unanimous that the *la'anah*, of the phrase *rosh ve-la'anah*, is "wormwood," a plant synonymous with bitterness. But which one? Some support *Artemisia absinthium*, a European plant, while others point to the local white wormwood, *A. siberi*.

The common name "wormwood" is a corruption of "vermouth," and is applied to *A. absinthium*, one of the herbs used to flavor the drink. It is widely distributed in Siberia, Eurasia, North and South America and New Zealand. The genus is named after the Greek goddess Artemis; the Latin epithet, *absinthium*, means "without sweetness." Once you have tasted just a few drops of an infusion you will know that the epithet is surely an understatement, for its taste is beyond bitter, the bitter of bitters. It is a shrubby plant, from three to four feet tall, growing up from a woody base. Its stems are covered with aromatic, deeply divided leaves, silver-gray in color, soft and velvety in texture. Insignificant yellow flowers occur in small clusters, nearly hidden by the long leaves.

Photograph © Avinoam Danin

Artemisia sieberi and *Helianthemum vesicarium*. White wormwood and sun-rose growing wild in the Negev, as if planted in a garden.

Bitter properties, present to some degree in all artemisias, are due to the chemical thujone, which gives them their bracing aroma and medicinal value. This chemical is so powerful that preparations made with it, including the drink absinthe, can be fatal. Based on my own experience growing this herb, brushing the fresh leaves or being near the drying leaves can produce a severe headache. In small quantities wormwood has a history of being beneficial as a vermifuge (to kill or expel intestinal worms), to relieve indigestion, heartburn, regularize menstrual periods, relieve fevers, assuage rheumatism, as a tonic for the liver and gallbladder, and when infused in brandy it is purported to be a remedy for gout.[23]

Artemisia sieberi (*A. herba-alba*), white wormwood, is the most common of several wormwood species native to Israel. It is a dwarf shrub about sixteen inches tall, heavily branched from its base, covered with hairy gray, finely cut leaves that are shed at the end of the winter and replaced by very small, scale-like summer leaves. White wormwood covers vast areas of dry, rocky land in the Negev desert.

In a good rainy year, sun-rose, *Helianthemum vesicarium*, a dwarf silvery shrub that grows among white wormwood, produces masses of flowers as far as the eye can see, ranging in color from shades of dark and light pink to white, as if planted in a garden rather than growing spontaneously in barren, rocky desert ground.

But does white wormwood fit the context of an extremely bitter, poisonous plant? Its uses in local folk medicine do not support this interpretation. White wormwood's fresh winter leaves and stems are boiled in water with sugar to produce a drink. All commentators agree that the flavor of the tea, regarded as a digestive, is pleasant, even "tasty."[24] White wormwood tea is also used to alleviate nervousness and as a vermifuge.[25]

A better candidate for wormwood is the less common but very bitter *Artemisia judaica*, Judean wormwood. Short and shrubby, the plant is densely covered in light-reflecting hairs that gives it a silvery-gray appearance and protection from drying out in dry, hot desert conditions. In Israel it grows in the southern Negev, Arava Valley, and Eilat, and is also found in extreme deserts in the Sinai, Arabia, Jordan, Egypt, and Libya where it has a long history of medicinal use. In Bedouin desert folk medicine it is used in similar ways to those of *A. absinthium*: to relieve stomachache, constipation, intestinal worms, and to strengthen appetite,[26] and in common with the European wormwood, it is very bitter and an overdose could be fatal.

In summary, commentators do not agree on the identity of the plants referred to in the phrase "*rosh v-la'anah*." It may be a collective term for a number of plants that yield bitter and or poisonous extracts, just as the phrase "*shamir va-shayit*," ("thorns and thistles"), may be a collective term for armed or thorny plants.[27] The prophets often drew inspiration from the plants of the everyday landscape, seeing in them the embodiment of terrifying punishments for those who strayed from God's path. Moses' audience, presumably acquainted with various poisonous plants that were prominent in the ancient world from their experiences in Egypt, would know how they worked, and so would understand Moses' metaphorical reference to doubters as a "stock sprouting poison weed." They knew that some among them, even they themselves, had doubted before and could doubt again, and they felt the power of Moses' unequivocal warning to stay on course and "Choose life" rather than a spiritual death.

ENDNOTES

1. In biblical terms a generation, or a period of time the exact duration of which is unknown (Genesis 7:4;12;17). *Jewish Encyclopedia* (1901–1906), 349.

2. "Place" is used loosely for the territory of Transjordan." Jeffrey Tigay, *The JPS Torah Commentary: Deuteronomy*, 276.

3. " ... King Sihon of Heshbon and King Og of Bashan came out to engage us in battle, but we defeated them. We took their land and gave it to the Reubenites, the Gadites, and the half-tribe of Manasseh as their heritage" (Deuteronomy 29:6-7).

4. Numbers 20:2-13. God's punishment of Moses and Aaron, for a moment's indiscretion, is very harsh, and as I have suggested elsewhere, has been the source of endless discussions among Bible scholars for generations. It is beyond the scope of this work to detail them, but one of the leading points of view is that God's appointed leaders disobeyed His instructions so publicly.

5. Tigay's linkage of "the ruin of moist and dry alike" (Deuteronomy 29:18) with "the righteous and sinner alike" is based on "Jeremiah's comparison of the righteous with a tree planted by water and the sinner with a bush in the desert [Jeremiah 17:6-8]." See Tigay, 280 and Chapter Twenty-Three, *Tree of Desolation, Tree of Hope*, which discusses this reference in detail.

6. This paragraph (Deuteronomy 30:1-5) with the theme of return is read in the synagogue on the Sabbath preceding the ten days of repentance (*teshuva*, literally "return") that extend from Rosh Hashana to Yom Kippur.

7. "This manner of speaking reflects a predominately oral culture in which learning and review are accomplished primarily by oral recitation." Tigay, 286.

8. *The Jewish Study Bible*, 436.

9. Exodus 32:1-35.

10. Joshua reiterates this idea, making a very reasoned argument for free choice. See Joshua 24:14-15.

11. Mentioned in *Across the Wide Missouri*, Bernard Devoto.

12. Among other references, *The Random House Book of Herbs*, Roger Phillips and Nicky Foy, 126.

13. Palevich and Yaniv, *Medicinal Plants of the Holy Land*, Vol. II, 213–214.

14. Josephus' *Antiquities*, Book 11, 7:6.

15. Palevich and Yaniv, Vol. I, 145.

16. Ibid.

17. The various opinions concerning the wild gourd as *rosh* are considered in Harold N. Moldenke and Alma L. Moldenke, *Plants of the Bible*, 78-80.

18. Palevich and Yaniv discuss the various uses of the wild gourd Vol. I, 49–50.

19. Moldenke and Moldenke, Vol. I, 80.
20. See Chapter Thirty-One, *Flowers of the Field*, for a detailed discussion of Israel's red field poppies.
21. The long history of opium poppy use is discussed in detail in Mrs. M. Grieve, *A Modern Herbal*, Vol. II, 652 and Phillips & Foy, 119.
22. Phillips and Foy, 119.
23. Ibid., 80.
24. Avinoam Danin, *Desert Vegetation of Israel & Sinai*, 77. When I was on a hiking trip in the Negev in which kibbutzniks from all parts of Israel gathered the winter leaves of white wormwood, I discovered that they were picking them to make a highly regarded digestive tea. I can vouch for its pleasant taste, which is nothing like an infusion of *Artemisia absinthium*, with which I am also familiar.
25. Palevich and Yaniv, Vol. II, 324, 310.
26. Reader Elaine Solowey, who grows Judean wormwood as a crop at Kibbutz Ketura in the Southern Negev, reports that it is used at Hadassah Hospital as an anti-parasitic by the Natural Medicines' Research Center and is being researched for use against infectious diseases. She says that in alternative medicine, Judean wormwood is used to treat arthritis, rheumatism, and leishmaniasis, a disease transmitted by the sand fly, common in desert areas.
27. See Chapter Twenty-Eight, *Warning of the Thorns*.

Chapter Thirty-Six

THE VINE OF SODOM

Portion *Haazinu*/Listen (Deuteronomy 32:1-52)
Ah! The vine for them is from Sodom, from the vineyards of Gomorrah; the grapes for them are poison, a bitter growth their clusters. (Deuteronomy 32:32)

Photograph © Joshua D. Klein

Vitis vinifera. Normal, still unripe grapes in May–June at Moshav Mevo Horon in the foothills of Jerusalem.

Photograph © Joshua D. Klein

Vitis vinifera. Shriveled grapes during the same period, May–June, at Moshav Mevo Horon. They will fall off in 2–3 weeks.

One imagines Moses standing above the people as he calls on heaven and earth to witness his last teaching, which takes the form of a great poem or song. In imagery drawn from the Promised Land, he likens his final words to the rain and dew, without which the people will not be able to live. "May my discourse come down as the rain," he tells them, "My speech distilled as the dew" (Deuteronomy 32:2). Moses' audience must be aware, from the scouts' report, of the nature of the climate in the hill country in which they will first settle. This will be nothing like the lush, flood-irrigated land of Egypt with which their ancestors were familiar. In the new land, without timely rain and dew in their season, the people will be lost. How, then, must they have hung on Moses' carefully chosen words.

Although his theme is familiar—urging Israel to obey God or disaster will befall them—Moses frames his argument in such new and compelling ways that each word seems fresh and telling. He exhorts his audience to remember their history, and if they cannot recall it, to ask their fathers or elders to tell them how God found their ancestors in the desert, in a howling waste fraught with danger,[1] how he took them for His own special portion among all the other nations, and how through His efforts they not only survived their treacherous journey to the land He had promised them, but, through His patient efforts, they were encouraged to rise above their lowly circumstances. Moses likens God's protection and teaching of the untried Israelites to an eagle which tenderly teaches its young to fly (Deuteronomy 32:11). We have only to recall the ways in which God not only supplied the ex-slaves' physical needs—food, water, clothes—but taught them the rudiments of spiritual discipline in the gathering of manna for six days, while resting on the seventh, Sabbath, day,[2] and how He brought them to the foot of Sinai where they all stood together, heard God from the top of the mountain, and with one voice accepted the Ten Commandments and the way of life it signified. What an achievement for these former slaves who had probably never been encouraged to think much beyond the cruel demands of their taskmasters! During their days of wandering in the desert toward the Promised Land, they had begun to comprehend that their freedom entailed obligations to the God Who had redeemed them.

Moses, the prophet, sees beyond their past history to his people's life in their new land as shepherds and farmers. With God's blessing, they will prosper, despite difficult circumstances. In vivid terms drawn from pastoral and agricultural life, Moses describes how God fed the shepherds so well they were even able to find honey in rocks, how the farmers grew olive trees on flinty ground, produced oil, the very best of wheat and wine, and all the good things of life (Deuteronomy 32:13-14). But influenced by their neighbors who pray to idols, they turn away from their God to worship the pagan "no-gods" who never did anything for the people Israel but who demand abominable practices from them. As predicted, God punishes Israel with catastrophes which include devastating wars, famine, and plague (Deuteronomy 32:23-24). God, however, never forsakes His backsliding people. On the contrary, he punishes those who persecute them: "O nations acclaim His people! For He'll avenge the blood of His servants, Wreak vengeance on His foes, And wipe away His people's tears: (Deuteronomy 32:43).[3] Israel's enemies will know the vine of Sodom and bitter grapes from the vineyards of Gomorrah, which produce poison wine.

Moses' words, which follow his formal recitation, go straight to the heart of everything he has taught: remember my teaching and pass it down to your children, that they may faithfully observe all its terms. This is not a trifling thing, he points out, "it is your life" (Deuteronomy 32:47), just as he had told them earlier, choose life, the life that springs from loving the Lord your God and being faithful to the covenant (Deuteronomy 30:16-19). Moses then blesses each tribe, and passes from the scene with his death on Mount Nebo.

—ποι—

WHAT IS THE VINE OF SODOM, *gefen s'dom*? What would be the characteristics of a plant named after the incorrigible city of depravity that God utterly destroyed (Genesis 19:25), a plant whose features suggest the terrible fate that will befall Israel's enemies: "Ah! The vine for them is from Sodom." Is it actually a vine? Does it grow in the area of the biblical Sodom, that is, along the southern shore of the Dead Sea?

These questions have vexed Bible scholars, who over centuries have offered several plants ranging from vines to shrubs, some of which are found near the Dead Sea, others which grow throughout the Land of Israel. All bear fruits which are bitter, poisonous, or markedly peculiar, and although none are regarded definitively as the "vine of Sodom" referred to in the text, they, like the candidates for Biblical *rosh* or poison,[4] give us a wider view of the varied flora that grow in the Land of Israel.

Two of the candidates are vines.

Wild gourd, *Citrullus colocynthis* (*avatiah ha 'paku'a'*), is a candidate for *rosh* as well as the vine of Sodom. It grows in hot deserts and sandy soils in various parts of the Land of Israel and it is the vine whose very bitter fruit the prophet Elisha's servant was sorry he gathered and fed to the hungry disciples of the prophet (II Kings 4:39-40). An appealing round, striped fruit, about the size of an apple, its looks are deceiving. The nineteenth century naturalist, Canon Tristram, was thoroughly convinced that "the simile of the Vine of Sodom is taken from the fruit of the colocynth, which has long straggling tendrils or runners like the vine, with a fruit fair to look at but nauseous beyond description to the taste, and when fully ripe, [is] merely a quantity of dusty powder with the seeds inside its beautiful orange rind."[5]

Others have identified the vine of Sodom with the squirting cucumber, *Ecballium elaterium* (*yeroket ha'hamor*), referred to in the Mishna as "the spitting donkey."[6] A trailing, bristly plant that grows along roadsides, garbage dumps, and wastelands in most parts of the Land of Israel, it bears juicy berries—shaped like small cucumbers—which, when ripe and just touched, spray their seeds and bitter juice a considerable distance. Like the wild gourd, it has a history of use as an emetic and laxative all over the Middle East and North Africa.[7] It has also been used to treat headaches, aching joints, malaria and rabies, and in small doses, to avoid nausea, vomiting, and dehydration. In local folk medicine it has many applications: to relieve severe constipation,

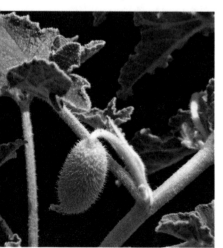

Photograph © Avinoam Danin

Echballium elaterium.
Squirting cucumber ready to
'shoot,' Sharon Plain.

eat the sliced fruits; for hemorrhoids, apply a dressing soaked in the juice from the fruits; for jaundice, drip the sap into the nose.[8] Obviously, one has to harvest squirting cucumbers with care!

Another candidate, gray nightshade, *Solanum incanum* (*hahedek*) belongs to the deadly nightshade family (Solanaceae). Growing in hot deserts, wadis and oases in the Jordan Valley and Dead Sea region, it is a tropical, thorny shrub with large grayish leaves. Its flowers are attractive: wide open and lilac-colored, followed by an appealing, but poisonous, large yellow fruit. The deadly property solanine is present in all members of this family (even in potatoes when their skin is inadvertently exposed to sunlight). But like many poisonous plants, gray nightshade possesses healing virtues, too, in preparations to relieve toothache, chest pains, and sore throat.[9]

The apple of Sodom, *Calotropis procera* (*ptilat hamidbar*) is considered a candidate because, although not a vine, it is associated with the city of Sodom and grows in the right place: in oases and deserts in the Jordan Valley and Dead Sea area. It is a strange looking shrub or small tree from nine to fifteen feet tall, various parts of which are filled with a poisonous milky sap. Its branches and trunk are white, the latter covered with a thick layer of cork, while its leaves are large, fleshy, and grayish-green; flowers range in color from almost white to purple-pink, sometimes in combinations, and wax-like. The fruits, shaped like apples or oranges, grow in clusters of three or four and look good to eat, but when touched they explode with a puff, leaving behind only their fluffy, poisonous seeds. Josephus, the authoritative Jewish historian in the Roman period, noted that in his day the remains of the destruction of Sodom were still apparent in the ashes from the Sodom apple, which if plucked dissolves into smoke and ashes.[10] What better symbol of the depravity of the city of Sodom? According to Arabic folklore, the apples were once fine fruits, but when God cursed Sodom, the curse fell on the fruits of the tree and emptied them.[11]

Does the apple of Sodom have any redeeming features? Folk medicine in subtropical countries where Sodom apple grows, records many uses for its leaves to reduce fevers, treat malaria, typhus, and syphilis. The dried leaves are smoked as a cure for asthma and coughs, and to clear the respiratory system. Powder made by grinding the leaves is used in an ointment to treat sores, skin ulcers, abscesses and infections. In India, the outer skin from the dried root is used to make

Photograph © Ori Fragman

Calotropis procera. Apple of Sodom, fruits and flowers, North Dead Sea area near Kumran.

mudar, sold commercially to prepare an ointment for treating skin complaints such as eczema and leprosy.[12] The unfriendly Sodom apple, the mere touch of which can cause severe skin irritation, is, like many poisonous plants, also a source of healing.[13]

There is another view: in the Bible, the vine of Sodom is inseparable from Gomorrah; one cannot mention either without the other as symbols of what is utterly corrupt. The prophet Isaiah, for instance, refers to the morally compromised leaders of Judea and its people in the same breath as "chieftans of Sodom, folk of Gomorrah" (Isaiah 1:10). If Sodom is bound to Gomorrah, then the vine of Sodom is the same as the grapevine that grows in Gomorrah, where the grapes are, for Israel's enemies, a poison and the wine from them is like the venom of asps (Deuteronomy 32:32-33). When regarded in this light, the blighted grapevine of Sodom and Gomorrah is a more telling metaphor for the punishment Israel's enemies will suffer than any of the plants that have been identified by countless commentators as the 'vine of Sodom.' Grapevines that 'go bad,' for instance, turn up in Isaiah's parable of the grapevine (Isaiah 5) where the vines that God had planted on a fruitful hill and had hoped would grow choice grapes produced 'bad' or stunted grapes (*beushim*). Here, the imagery of bad grapes is a powerful metaphor for wayward Israelites whose stunted belief encouraged them to stray from the path of God.[14]

To the very end of his life, Moses draws on imagery inspired by the land. Moses' final blessing, before he ascends Mount Nebo to die, includes the assurance that the people he has led through the desert, will dwell in safety, "in a land of grain and wine, under heavens dripping dew" (Deuteronomy 33:28). This is a vision of bounty that leaves the reader with hope for the future of the Israelite people.

ENDNOTES

1. This is not the way it happened according to the biblical account, but Moses makes his point.
2. See Chapter Fifteen, *Heavenly Grain*.
3. NJPS alternate rendering of uncertain Hebrew passage (Deuteronomy 32:43: "And cleanse the land of His people."
4. See Chapter Thirty-Five, *Poison Plants and Wormwood*.
5. H.B. Tristram, *The Natural History of the Bible*, 184.
6. Cited in Louis Rabinowitz, *Torah and Flora*, 155.
7. Palevitch and Zohara Yaniv, *Medicinal Plants of the Holy Land*, Vol. II, 255.
8. Ibid.
9. Ibid., Vol. I, 54.
10. Many commentators refer to the observations of Josephus, in his *Jewish Wars*, Book IV, 8:4.
11. Palevitch and Yaniv, 37. See also Chapter Twenty-three, *Tree of Desolation, Tree of Hope*, for other folk references.
12. Ibid., 37.
13. For more uses, see Chapter Twenty-three.
14. NJPS translates the grapes that 'go bad' as "wild grapes" (*beushim*) in the parable ((Isaiah 5:4), but as Nogah Harueveni shows in his discussion of the subject, *beushim* refers to a disease that stunts the grapes, preventing them from ripening properly. A biblical audience of farmers would be well aware of this condition, known in modern Hebrew as *zoteret*, and would understand the implications of comparing the people to stunted grapes: the Israelites did not perceive the full meaning of belief in One God and so were easily led astray. See *Tree and Shrub in Our Biblical Heritage*, 72–73.

EPILOGUE

WHEN WE THINK BACK to the Bible's stories, poems, and laws, beginning with Genesis, we see that they all comprise a "teaching"— the very meaning of the word "Torah." In this sense, every blade of grass, every flower, every weed, every tree, the land itself, has meaning beyond its physical existence. Flowers are likened to what is transient, unlike the word of God which endures forever; the common hyssop that grows from a rock embodies the Torah virtues of humility and modesty; the bitter herbs remind the participant of a shared history of bitterness in Egypt; and the almond tree that watches and hastens to blossom before all other trees is compared to God, Who also watches and hastens to perform His word. The land becomes a force for teaching the values of ethical monotheism, as in the injunction to observe the seventh-year sabbath of the land. In Moses' final discourse, his very words, likened to rain, distilled as dew, imitate God's blessing on the land and everything that grows from it.

We have traveled very far from the beginning, when Abram, the Aramean, left all he had known in his previous existence to answer God's call to found a new people who will live by a different code from the surrounding cultures. Abram, the shepherd, became Abraham, father of a multitude. Beginning as a rough shepherd people, whose roots were deep in the soil of semi-arid lands, they were transformed into a holy nation, destined by God's commandments to walk by the light of His presence.

WHERE TO SEE PLANTS OF THE BIBLE

There is a great deal of enthusiasm for creating Bible Gardens, not only across the United States but internationally. The following is a partial listing, subject to change. Consult recommended websites at the end of this entry to find others.

UNITED STATES

California

B'nai Shalom Synagogue
74 Eckley Lane
Walnut Creek, CA 94596
925-934-9446
office@bshalom.org
http://www.bshalom.org
    Designed by Shirley Pinchev Sidell who was inspired by a trip to Israel, and dedicated in 2002, the planting is spread out over the synagogue's 7.5 acre hilltop site. Identification tags include botanical and biblical references. The fig and olive trees, grapevine, salvias, and many other plants thrive in a climate similar to Israel's. Open to the public, no charge.

St. Gregory's Episcopal Church
6201 Willow Street
Long Beach, CA 90815
562-420-1311
stgregs1@aol.com
http://www.stgregoryschurch.com
    Started by Betty Clement in the 1980s, the garden is in the Church courtyard. Laid out to take advantage of the most favorable temperatures, there are plants in pots as well as in the ground. Just as in Israel, the almond tree's bloom heralds a new growing season. Among the stars of the garden are Judean sage (a possible model for the menora) and acacia (*shittim* wood

for the Ark), grown from seed, as well as carob, fig, olive, pomegranate, citron (*etrog*), and cinnamon trees in tubs. Devoted volunteers carry on the legacy of the garden's founder. Open to the public, no charge.

Church of the Wayfarer
Lincoln Street at Seventh Avenue
P.O. Box 2205
Carmel-by-the-Sea, CA 93921
831-624-3550
http://www.churchofthewayfarer.com/church/

The Master's Garden, formerly the Biblical Garden, is an integral part of the picturesque church and grounds, tucked into the 'downtown' area. Plants mentioned in the Bible are featured along brick pathways. Wooden arbors and a fountain add to the beauty and peacefulness of the surroundings. Open to the public, no charge.

CONNECTICUT

Naugatuck Valley Community College
750 Chase Parkway
Waterbury, CT 06708
Michael Schwartz, Grounds Maintainer
203-596-2135
mschwartz@nvcc.commnet.edu

The layout of this garden of about 1700 square feet, is unusual: four triangular beds surrounding a square courtyard with a central circular bed. The beds are oriented to the points of the compass with each of the twelve sides corresponding to one of the tribes of Israel; there are plaques on each with a tribe name and appropriate passage from the Hebrew Bible. There is a similar treatment of Christian Bible quotes, with the names of the four evangelists on them, outside the perimeter of the central circle. Plants include barley, emmer wheat, lentils, and wildflowers (anemone, poppy, tulip). Open to the public, no charge.

FLORIDA

Temple Beth Shalom
355 43rd Avenue
Vero Beach, FL 32968
772-569-4700
rabbi@tbsvero.org
http://www.tbsvero.org

The idea behind the planting is to create and care for a Garden of Eden. Inspired by the flora and agriculture of the land of Israel and the Hebrew Bible, the garden helps congregants connect with the experiences of their ancestors and the stories and values of the Torah. Six of the Seven Species mentioned in Deuteronomy are grown alongside a series of plantings: exploring spirituality through the five senses; plants that host and attract pollinators; and a vegetable garden to nourish the body. The congregation participates in pressing olives from the garden's olive tree, and makes hallah and matzah from the wheat planting.

INDIANA

Warsaw Biblical Gardens
Warsaw, IN 46580
574-267-6419
http://www.warsawbiblicalgardens.org
Extensive gardens of more than 100 plants on 3/4 acre, hardy enough to survive the Mid-western climate; tender plants are wintered over in a greenhouse. Bulb display April 1–May 1; May 15–July 4, best color; September–early October, grasses. Guided tours May 15–September 15. Plants include Syrian hyssop, mandrake, *Salvia judaica* (a menorah plant), and the caper bush. Open to the public, no charge.

NEW YORK

Cathedral of St. John the Divine Biblical Garden
1047 Amsterdam Avenue
New York, NY 10025
212-316-7540, ext. 7490
http://www.stjohndivine.org
The Biblical Garden was founded by Sarah Larkin Loening in 1973, restored in 1988, and further developed in 2001 by the Cathedral Guild with the assistance of designer Keith Corlett. Designed to complement the grandeur of the adjacent Cathedral, the effect is stunning. Trees, shrubs, vines, perennials, and bulbs referred to in the Bible are planted in formal design around a main axis cross with numerous stone and wooden seats throughout. Narrow-shaped conifers and vertical vines (including climbing rose) further link the Garden to the soaring Cathedral. Look for the resident peacocks. Open to the public, no charge.

OHIO

Herb Garden at Inniswood
Inniswood Metro Gardens
940 South Hempstead Road
Westerville, OH 43081
614-895-6216
http://www.inniswood.org
The Central Ohio Unit of the Herb Society of America maintains an Herb Garden within the Inniswood Metro Gardens, and a Bible Garden within the Herb Garden which features many plants of the Bible. Among

these are fig, carob, and myrtle, as well as a hand-hewn watering trough from the 1880s planted to miniature thymes and conifers. Tender plants are wintered over in a green house. Open to the public, no charge.

Rodef Shalom Biblical Garden
4905 5th Avenue
Pittsburgh, PA 15213
412-621-6566
http://www.biblicalgardenpittsburgh.org

An ambitious 3-acre garden in the Shadyside area near Carnegie-Mellon, established in 1987 on the grounds of the synagogue. There are more than 100 plants presented in recreated habitats: waterfall, desert, and a representation of the Jordan River from the Sea of Galilee to the Dead Sea. Ongoing in-depth programs and educational materials on aspects of biblical life. Open to the public, no charge, handicapped access. Group tours (8 or more) available.

Shir Ami Synagogue
101 Richboro Road
Newton, PA 18940
215-968-3400
http://www.shiraminow.org

The Stan Averbach Biblical Garden on about a half acre was dedicated on October 29, 2010. The main garden features a winding path and a producing grape arbor. Among the plants there (69) are date palm, citron, myrtle, papyrus, and wheat. The Children's Garden is established in an area by the school entrance and features a cement walk bordered on each side by handprint cement pavers created by the children, with their names, dates of birth and a hand or footprint. Assorted vegetables and herbs (32) are planted here. The synagogue library includes works useful for research on biblical gardens. Open to the public, no charge. Call to arrange for a garden guide or to use the library for research.

Temple Beth-El Biblical Garden
70 Orchard Avenue
Providence, RI 02906-5425
401-331-6070
http://www.temple-beth-el.org

The planting features wheat, barley, grapes, figs, pomegranate, olives (of the seven species), as well as poppy, oak, cedar tree, and anemones. Open to the public, no charge.

Biblical Garden at Magnolia Plantation
3550 Ashely River Road
Charleston, SC 29414
800-367-3517
http://www.magnoliaplantation.com/gardens.html
Historic house and gardens of one of the oldest plantations in the U.S., dating from 1676, on 70 acres. Biblical garden features plants from the Hebrew Bible in the shape of a Star of David to commemorate the 12 tribes of Israel; the cross planting, representing the Christian Bible, commemorates the 12 disciples. Admission charge to the Plantation.

TEXAS

Kavanaugh Biblical Garden
United Methodist Church
2516 Park Street
Greenville, TX 75401
903-455-2869
http://www.kavumc.com/bible-gard.htm
Extensive plantings based on the Hebrew Bible and Christian Bible, attractively presented, include pomegranate, fig, acacia, papyrus, wheat, barley, flax and thistle. Open to the public, no charge.

VERMONT

Fair Haven Biblical Garden
First Congregational Church
19 West Street
Fair Haven, VT 05743
Rev. Marsh Hudson-Knapp (hkfamily@sover.net)
802-265-8605
http://www.fairhavenucc.org
Marsh and his wife, Cindy, established the Garden in 1983 to include flowers, herbs, and shrubs, in the hope of making the stories of the Bible become real and alive for people. Gardens wrap around the south and east sides of the church and contain many biblical plants including some like dwarf pomegranate and dwarf papyrus that are wintered over indoors. A children's garden, which includes cucumbers and gourds supported on a trellis, has been added, as well as a water garden. A very active group and a very informative website with information about other biblical gardens and related matters. Open to the public, no charge.

Edward E. Kahn Memorial Biblical Garden

Temple Sinai
11620 Warwick Boulevard
Newport News, VA 23601
757-596-8352

Inspired by a 1970's trip to Israel, Edward E. and Anna Lee Kahn began a biblical garden on an acre of land at Temple Sinai in Newport News. The garden now has more than 100 types of plants, each marked with a metal plaque listing the Hebrew plant name, common name, botanical name, and a Bible verse that mentions it. Plants include Tulip (rose of Sharon), wormwood (*Artemsia judaica*), olive tree, pomegranate, and persian buttercup (*Ranunculus asiaticus*). Open to the public weekdays during daylight hours; stop by the Temple office for a brochure. Large groups should call in advance.

ISRAEL
JERUSALEM

Neot Kedumim, Israel's Biblical Landscape Reserve

In memory of Nogah Hareuveni
Route 443 between Jerusalem and Tel-Aviv
10 minutes from Ben Gurion Airport
972-8-977-0777
info@neot-kedumim.org.il
http://www.neot-kedumim.org.il

The Biblical Landscape Reserve in Israel
In memory of Nogah Hareuveni

One of the world's foremost biblical gardens and a model of restoration ecology, Neot Kedumim is a 620+ acre landscape of recreated biblical

Courtesy Neot Kedumim, Israel's Biblical Landscape Reserve

Fall color at the Willow Pond in Neot Kedumim.

habitats that include the Four Species Ascent, Solomon's Pool, and Menorah Hill (several salvias) with the Syrian hyssop (*Majorana syriaca*) and all the 'false' hyssops (aromatic herbs) mentioned in the Talmud planted nearby. Developed over decades, Neot Kedumim is the culmination of the Hareuvenis' vision (Nogah and his parents, Ephraim and Hannah) of teaching the connections between the Bible (Hebrew Scriptures and Christian Bible) and Talmud to the nature and landscapes of the Land of Israel. Top soil, added to eroded hillsides, has produced hundreds of wild flowers in season, so in addition to organized plantings, visitors can see, among many wild flowers, cyclamen, anemone, and an annual carpet of creamy scabiosa, rosy flax, and purple bugloss in season. Self-guided and guided tours, many activities and programs. Closed Sabbath and Jewish holidays. Handicapped accessible. Admission charge.

Photograph © Jackie Chambers

Amygdalus communis and *Lupinus pilosus*. Almond blossoms and wild lupin in spring at the Jerusalem Botanical Gardens.

Bible Path
Jerusalem Botanical Gardens
Hebrew University,
Givat Ram Campus
Jerusalem 91904
972-2-679-4012
jbotanic@botanic.co.il
http://www.botanic.co.il

An outstanding botanical garden where more than 10,000 species of flowers, trees, and other vegetation from southern Africa, Europe, North America, southwest Asia and the Mediterranean are grown in separate plantings. The Bible Path seeks to bring biblical and botanical stories alive through some 25 plants, among them the almond, pistachio, and fig tree, holy bramble, hyssop, mandrake, myrtle, broom, and rockrose. There are signs in three languages (English, Hebrew, Arabic) as well as an audioguide which provides additional information about the plants. Paths are handicapped accessible. Admission charge to the Gardens. The website offers a link to a new interactive, accessible online course that looks at more than 100 plants in the context of the Land of Israel and the Bible. The course has 10 lectures and ends with an optional one-week tour of Flora of the Holy Land. A charge for course and tour.

Yad Hashmona Biblical Village

972-2-5942000
info@yadha8.co.il
http://www.yad8.com

About 40 minutes from Tel-Aviv and 10 minutes from Jerusalem. At the center of the Village, opened in 2000, is a reconstructed Galilean synagogue. Fig, pomegranate, almond, date-palm, olive, and other trees, as well as grape-vines, are planted all around the compound. A reconstructed marketplace shows ancient crafts such as clay manufacturing, the minting of coins, pottery, copper, glass, wood and stone work. There is a guest house and restaurant. The name "Yad Hashmona" is a memorial given by the original Finnish Christian settlers to eight Austrian Jewish refugees surrendered by the Finnish Government to the Gestapo in 1942.

WEBSITES OF INTEREST

http://www.biblicalgardens.com

Founded by Shirley Pinchev Sidell to bring together people from around the world who have an interest in the research and growing of Bible gardens. It offers a wealth of information on Bible plants, where to find them and how to grow them, with help from experts. Lots of wonderful photos.

http://www.bbgsusa.com/contact-us.php

Founded by Dr. Ed Bez, it is a vast source of information about plants of the Bible in depth; presentations; articles; bibliography.

http://www.fairhavenucc.org

Where to find international Bible gardens, what's going on in the world of Bible gardens, experts, books and reviews.

http://www.mechon-mamre.org

Described as Bible and Mishneh Torah (Oral Law) for all Jews and Gentiles, this site offers five editions of the Hebrew Bible in Hebrew and English, Maimonides' Restatement of the Oral Law, an encyclopedia of Torah basics, and more.

http://www.torahflora.org

Devoted to the study of Biblical and Talmudic ethnobotany (plants and nature in Torah and Jewish tradition), this site offers Dr. Jon Greenberg's in-depth essays, announcements of events, and a wealth of resources.

A GLOSSARY OF JEWISH TEXTS
AND RELATED TERMS

Haftarah (addendum)

The supplemental reading in synagogues from the Prophets, following the Torah reading during the Sabbath morning service, and on festivals and fast days. The *Haftarah* reading is usually related to events described in the Torah reading. Both the *Haftarah* and Torah selections are read, preceded by the removal of scrolls from the Ark and the recitation of appropriate blessings and rituals.

Midrash (plural, *midrashim*; from Hebrew root meaning "to seek" or "to search")

A technique for interpreting Torah developed by the rabbis or Sages (recognized learned authorities). One form focused on interpreting the law (*halakha*, "the way to walk"), while the second type (*aggadah*, "narration" or "story") was concerned with inspiring and strengthening faithfulness to Torah, using homiletics, ethics, history, and legend, often in very striking and imaginative ways. Collections of *midrashim* were later committed to writing.

Mishna ("oral instruction," or "teaching," from the Hebrew root, *shanah,* meaning "to learn by rote")

When the exiles returned from Babylon and rededicated themselves to Torah (as recorded in Ezra 7:6), the need arose for a practical, detailed guide for everyday life. So Oral Law traditions were transmitted over generations from teacher to disciple as a way of clarifying and fulfilling written law, the Torah (according to tradition, they were both given to Moses by God). The laws, and the questions and comments about them, culminated in a written version, the Mishna, around 200 CE. Rabbi Judah Ha-Nasi is credited with compiling and arranging the material into six orders, each order divided into two tractates, each tractate into chapters, and each chapter into paragraphs. The orders are *Zeraim* (Seeds), having to do with agriculture; *Moed* (Appointed Times), the laws of festivals and feasts; *Nashim* (Women), on marriage, divorce, and vows; *Nezikin* (Damages), civil and criminal law; *Kodashim* (Holy Things), pertaining primarily to Temple service; and *Tohorot* (Purity), laws of ritual purity and impurity. As soon as the Oral Law was written down, it became the focus for further study and commentary, and was the basis of the Talmud.

Portion/Portions *(parasha/parshiot)*

Designated verses from the Torah, read in the synagogue from a scroll at every Sabbath morning service, with accompanying blessings and rituals. There are fifty-four designated readings, the extras calculated for a leap year. In years with fewer Sabbaths, readings are combined. The Five Books of Moses are the sum total of all the *parshiot*.

Rabbi/Sage (teacher of Torah)

A term in general use by 100 CE that came to mean a person qualified to give decisions regarding Jewish law, also recognized teachers of the tradition. The rabbinic movement had begun to take shape during the Babylonian Exile, continued through the Second Temple Period, and beyond the destruction of the Temple. Its first literature was the Mishna, culminating in the Talmud. Its crowning achievement was "rabbinic Judaism," the form of Judaism that has existed from post-Temple times to the present.

Rabbinic literature

Used in this book, the phrase refers to rabbinic works of the Talmudic era (ca. 200 CE to 560 CE) compiled by generations of rabbis, as distinct from rabbinic literature produced since medieval times to the present. The ancient writings include the Mishna, *Tosefta* ("appendix" or "supplement," commentary on the Mishna, ca. 220–230 CE or later), Jerusalem Talmud (ca. 400 CE), collections of *midrashim* (ca. 400–500 CE), and the Babylonian Talmud (ca. 500 CE).

Talmud ("study")

There are two talmuds, vast compilations of rabbinic laws, legends, and interpretations of Torah extending over eight centuries by rabbis in the academies that existed in the Land of Israel and in Babylonia: the Jerusalem Talmud (*Talmud Yerushalmi*)—also called the Palestinian Talmud—and the Babylonian Talmud (*Talmud Bavli*). At their center is the Mishna, but their texts differ in size and the content of their *gemara* ("completing of the learning") the final commentary on the Mishna in the Talmud. A page of the Talmud would be indecipherable to the uninitiated even when translated into English (there are different editions with commentaries) and one would need a teacher or guide just to understand the layout of each page, then the condensed nature of the text itself. The Jerusalem Talmud discusses thirty-nine tractates of the Mishna belonging mainly to the first four orders; the text, considered rather obscure, contains 750,000 words. By contrast, the Babylonian Talmud, while commenting on thirty-six tractates, is nearly four times longer than the Jerusalem Talmud, with 2,500,000 words, one third of which is aggadic material. The rabbis made no distinction between halakhic and aggadic methods for interpreting Torah, both of which they considered equally important. The more complete Babylonian Talmud has long been considered the more authoritative and accessible, especially after it was first printed in the 1520s with extensive commentary by Rashi (Rabbi Shlomo ben Isaac, 1040-1105), the great medieval French scholar and rabbi renowned for his clear and concise interpretations. For anyone interested in biblical agriculture and flora, however, the Jerusalem Talmud is invaluable. Since its final editing, the study of the Babylonian Talmud has been the basis of Jewish religious life, ever renewing itself as the source for fresh studies, discussions, debates, legal rulings, and commentaries on many issues.

Torah ("teaching," "instruction")

In its special sense, "the Torah" refers to the Five Books of Moses, the Pentateuch, of the Hebrew Bible. But traditionally, it is understood to mean the study of the entire Hebrew Bible and/or the study of Jewish tradition in its entirety.

A GLOSSARY OF BOTANICAL
AND RELATED TERMS

Alkaloid A powerful substance in plants, often very poisonous, as in poison hemlock.

Annual A plant that completes its growth cycle in a single season from seed germination to seeding, then dying, as in the red poppy.

Anther Pollen bearing structure at the tip of a stamen.

Anti-oxidant An enzyme or other organic substance capable of counteracting the damaging effects of oxidation on human cells. Certain plants such as pomegranates are said to contain high levels of anti-oxidants.

Astringent A chemical compound in plants that helps blood clotting and reduces secretions or discharges.

Bract A modified leaf beneath a flower, often small.

Bulb Underground fleshy storage organ of certain perennial plants like narcissus.

Calyx The outer circle (whorl) of floral leaves (sepals) on a flower.

Capsule Dried fruit containing seeds, as in the red poppy.

Catkin Spike of stalkless flowers often without petals, almost always either male or female, as in the common oak.

Compound A leaf divided into two or more leaflets borne on the same leafstalk.

Cone Conifer fruit arranged in stiff, leaf-like modified leaves.

Conifer A cone-bearing tree like the cedar of Lebanon.

Crown Top portion, as in the upper area of a tree with much branching and foliage.

Cutting A portion of a leaf, stem, or root separated from the plant and treated in a special way so that it produces roots that will develop into a duplicate or clone of the original plant.

Deciduous   Describes trees and shrubs that lose their leaves in autumn.

Decoction   Herbal preparation made by boiling a plant part in water.

Ear   The grain or seed-bearing spike of a cereal plant such as wheat.

Escape   A plant once cultivated, now growing on its own in the wild.

Essential oil   A concentrated liquid obtained from a plant by a process of distillation and bearing the plant's characteristic fragrance.

Evergreen   Describes trees and shrubs that retain their leaves all year.

Female flower   Bearing pistil only; lacking stamens.

Fertilization   When pollen, the male part of the flower, has been successfully transferred to the pistil, the female part of the flower, and seed is produced.

Fixative   A plant substance capable of preserving the scents of other plants, as in frankincense and myrrh.

Frond   A large divided leaf as in the date palm.

Fruit   The seed-bearing structure of a plant, as in a dry capsule, nut, or grape.

Gall   An abnormal outgrowth of plant tissue caused by an insect irritation as in some salvias.

Genus   In plant classification, indicates a group of closely related plants, as in plants belonging to the genus *Quercus* (oak); ranked between "family" and "specie."

Glaucous   A thin, light-colored waxy or powdery bloom on a plant, most noticeable on leaves, that gives it a blue-green color; a plant adaptation to certain conditions thought to give protection from extremes of heat, cold, drought, wind, salt spray, and unrelieved sun.

Habitat   The natural home of a plant, or the type of environment in which it usually grows.

Head   A dense cluster of flowers.

Life cycle/Growth cycle   The period during which a plant grows up, flowers and fruits (produces seeds).

Male flower   Contains only pollen-bearing stamens.

Nectar   The sweet secretion from glands in flowers such as those of the caper, and sought by bees and other insects.

Needle   The stiff linear leaf of a conifer.

Netted   Net-veined marking as on the outside of a melon.

Nitrogen-fixing   The conversion by certain plants, of atmospheric nitrogen into nitrates, essential for vigorous growth.

Oasis   A productive place in an otherwise dry, barren area where plants flourish due to the presence of heat and water.

Ovary   The basal part of the pistil that ripens into a fruit when fertilized.

Perennial   A plant that persists for two years or more.

Pistil   The seed-bearing female organ of a flower consisting of stigma, style, and ovary.

Plant community   A group of plants adapted to the same habitat.

Pollen   Spores of a plant borne on the tip of the anther.

Pollination   The transfer of pollen from the (male) stamen, to the (female) stigma in a flower, by the wind, insects (bees and butterflies, for instance), or birds.

Progenitor   Wild ancestor of a cultivated plant.

Rhizome   Thick horizontal underground stem of a plant producing roots and shoots from its nodes.

Rosette   A circular cluster of basal leaves around a plant's stem.

Scales   A greatly reduced leaf or other outgrowth on a plant surface to conserve moisture as in the small tightly compressed leaves of many juniper trees and the minute hairs on the leaves of some plants such as the olive tree.

Sepal   Outermost part of a flower which collectively forms the calyx.

Shrub   A woody multi-stemmed plant smaller than a tree, producing growth from its base as in white broom.

Sp.   The abbreviation for "species" when the particular plant of a genus is unspecified or not known; or "spp." to represent more than one unspecified or unknown plant in the genus.

Species   A single, distinct kind of plant; in botanical nomenclature a descriptive word or epithet used to describe a plant belonging to a certain genus, as in the Latin binomial *Cistus incanus*; the species name or epithet, "*incanus*," refers to the plant's gray, hairy foliage.

Spike   A flower cluster formed of many flower heads attached directly to a long stem.

Spine   Sharp-pointed projection on a plant; slender, thorn or needle-like growth.

Stamen   The male organ of a flower composed of a filament, or thin stem, and pollen-bearing anther.

Stigma   The part of a pistil, or female organ of a flower, which becomes receptive to pollen.

Style   A stem or channel between the stigma and ovary down which pollen grains must grow to achieve fertilization with the ovary.

Subspecies   The first sub-division of a "species" abbreviated as "subsp.," indicating that the plant has characteristics significantly distinct from other populations of the species, as in *Tulipa agenensis* subsp. *sharonensis*.

Tendrils   Thread-like modified leaves capable of attaching themselves to a support, as in the grapevine.

Thorn   A short, sharp woody outgrowth of the stem or branch of a plant.

Tincture   The preparation of an herb steeped in a mixture of alcohol and water.

Tree   A woody plant with a distinct main stem or trunk carrying a head or crown of branches.

Tuber   A modified plant structure enlarged to store nutrients underground as in the anemone.

Umbel   An umbrella-shaped flower cluster spreading from a central point as in poison hemlock.

Variety   The second sub-division of a species, abbreviated as "var." as in *Cupressus sempervirens* var. *horizontalis*, indicating a lesser variant of the species than a subspecies.

Whorl   Three or more leaves radiating around a stem and originating from a single point.

BIBLIOGRAPHY

Alon, Azaria. *The Natural History of The Land of The Bible*. New York: Doubleday & Company, Inc., 1978.

Three-Hundred Wild Flowers of Israel. Israel: Steimatsky Ltd., 1993.

Alter, Robert. *The Five Books of Moses*. New York: W.W. Norton & Company, 2004.

"Ancient Law." Extract from *The Law Magazine and Review* in *The Albany Law Journal*, 1873, Vol. VI. Accessed from: http://books.google.com/books?id=OG6mAAAAIAAJ&dq=albany.

Angel, Gilda. *Sephardic Holiday Cooking: Recipes and Traditions*. New York: Decalogue Books, 1986.

Backon, Joshua. "Jacob and the Spotted Sheep: The Role of Prenatal Nutrition On Epigenetics of Fur Color." *Jewish Bible Quarterly*, pp. 263–264, 36:4, Oct.–Dec., 2008.

Ben Yehoshua, Shimshon. "Judean Balsam, in Hebrew 'Afarsemon' or 'Tzorey Gilead'-Balm of Gilead." Research paper, Bar Ilan University.

Berman, Adele and Marc Zvi Brettler, eds. *The Jewish Study Bible* (Jewish Publication Society TANAKH Translation). New York: Oxford University Press, Inc., 2004.

Berman, Joshua. "The Biblical Origins of Equality." *Azure*, Summer 2009, pp. 76–99.

The Book of Ruth, Megillas Ruth: A New Translation With A Commentary Anthologized From Talmudic, Midrashic And Rabbinic Sources. ArtScroll Tanach Series. New York: Mesorah Publications, Ltd., 1976.

Bown, Deni. *The Herb Society of America Encyclopedia of Herbs & Their Uses*. New York: Dorling Kindersley Publishing Inc., 1995.

Brownlow, Margaret E. *Herbs and The Fragrant Garden*. Kent, England: The Herb Farm Ltd., 1957.

Buchwald, Rabbi Ephraim. "The Lesson of the Fire-pans." Accessed at the National Jewish Outreach Program, http://rabbibuchwald.njop.org/2006/06/26/korach-5766-2006.

Campbell, Edward F. Jr. *Ruth: A New Translation with Introduction and Commentary.* Anchor Bible, Vol. 7. New York: Doubleday, 1975.

The Complete Jewish Bible, Judaica Press Hebrew and translation. Accessed from Chabad website: http://www.chabad.org/library/bible.

Chester, Steve. "From Heel to Toe." Parashat Ekev, Aug. 15, 1998. Torah Commentary, Union of American Hebrew Congregations. Accessed from: http://urj.org//learning/torah/archives/deuteronomy//?syspage =article&item_id=4904.

Creasy, Rosalind. *The Gardener's Handbook of Edible Plants.* San Francisco: Sierra Club Books, 1986.

Crowfoot, Grace Mary Hood and Louise Baldensperger. *From Cedar to Hyssop, A Study in the Folklore of Plants in Palestine.* London: Sheldon Press, 1932.

Danin, Avinoam. *Desert Vegetation of Israel & Sinai.* Jerusalem: Cana Publishing House, 1983.

Distribution Atlas of Plants in the Flora Palaestina Area. Jerusalem: Israel Academy of Sciences and Humanities, 2004.

"The Resourceful Caper." *Israel-Land and Nature,* Vol. 4, No. 4, Summer, 1980, pp. 138–141.

Danin, A. (ed.) 2006+, {continuously updated}, Flora of Israel online. The Hebrew University of Jerusalem, Jerusalem, Israel. Published at http://flora.huji.ac.il/browse.asp

Darom, David. *Beautiful Plants of the Bible: From the Hyssop to the Mighty Cedar Trees.* Israel: Palphot Ltd. nd.

Deen, Edith. *All of the Women of the Bible.* New York: Harper & Row, 1955.

Devoto, Bernard. *Across the Wide Missouri.* Boston: Houghton Mifflin, 1947.

Donin, Hayim Halevy. *To Be A Jew: A Guide to Jewish Observance in Contemporary Life.* New York: Basic Books, 1972.

Douglas, Mary. *Purity and Danger: An Analysis of Concepts of Pollution and Taboo.* London: Routledge and Keegan Paul, 1966.

Edelstein, Gershon and Mordechai Kislev. "Mevasseret Yerushalayim: The Ancient Settlement and its Agricultural Terraces." *Biblical Archeologist,* Winter, Vol. 44, pp. 53–56, 1981.

Encyclopedia Judaica. Vol. 2, 13. Jerusalem: Keter Publishing House Ltd., 1971.

Epstein, Isidore. (H. Freedman, translator). *Talmud, Tractate Pesahim.* London: Soncino, 1967.

Erlanger, Steven. "After a 2,000 year rest, a seed sprouts in Jerusalem." *The New York Times International.* June 12, 2008.

Facciola, Stephen. Cornucopia: *A Source Book of Edible Plants.* California: Kampong, 1990.

Feinbrun, Naomi. *Wild Plants in The Land of Israel,* drawn by Ruth Koppel. Israel: Hakibbutz Hameuchad Publishing House, 1960.

Feinbrun-Dothan, Avinoam Danin. *Analytical Flora of Eretz-Israel* (Hebrew). Jerusalem: Cana Publishing House Ltd., 1991.

Feliks, Yehuda. *Nature & Man in the Bible*. New York: Soncino Press, 1981.

Foggi, Bruno. *Flowers of Israel*. Italy: Bonechi & Steimatzky: 1999.

Foster, Steven. "Pomegranate: Fruit of Life." *Herb Companion*. Nov. 2008.

"Flowers in Israel." Accessed from: http://www.flowersinisrael.com.

Frazer, James. *The Golden Bough*. New York: Macmillian, 1923.

Frenkley, Helen and Beth Uval. "Self-guided Tour, Trail A." Israel: Neot Kedumim. nd.

Gardner, Jo Ann. "A Quest for the Bitter Herbs of Passover." *The Herbarist*, pp. 62–65, 2005.

"Za'atar and Hyssop: Everyday Spice and Ancient Herb." pp. 49–51, 2006.

"An Herbal Menorah. "The Herb Companion. Dec./Jan. 2003.

Gardner, Jo Ann and Karen Bussolini. *Elegant Silvers*. Portland, Oregon: Timber Press, 2005.

Gaster, Theodor H. *Festivals of the Jewish Year*. New York: William Morrow and Co., Inc., 1952.

Passover, Its History and Traditions. 1949.

Ginzburg, Louis. *Legends of the Bible*. Philadelphia: The Jewish Publication Society, 1956 (one volume edition).

Goor, Asaf and Max Nurock. *The Fruits of The Holy Land*. Jerusalem: Israel Universities Press, 1968.

Gray, Asa. *Gray's School and Field Book of Botany*. New York: Ivison, Blakeman & Company, 1887.

Gray, John. *Archeology and The Old Testament World*. New York: Harper Torchbooks, 1962.

Greenberg, Moshe. *Understanding Exodus*. New York: 1969.

Griffiths, Mark. *The New Royal Horticultural Society Index of Garden Plants*. Portland, Oregon: Timber Press, 1995.

Greenlee, John. *The Encyclopedia of Ornamental Grasses*. Emmaus, Pennsylvania. Rodale Press, 1992.

Grieve, Mrs. Maude. *A Modern Herbal*, 2 volumes. New York: Dover Publications, 1971 (reprint of original 1931 edition).

Grunfeld, Isidor. *Shemittah and Yobel: Laws referring to the Sabbatical Year in Israel and its produce*. New York: Soncino Press, 1972.

HaLevi, Ezra. "2,000-Year-Old Judean Date Seed Growing Successfully," Feb. 6, 2006. Accessed from http://israelnationalnews.com/News/News.aspx/97852.

Ha-Reubeni, Ephraim. *"Research in the Biblical Hyssop, History and Critique."* Jerusalem: Actes du Septième Congrès International d'Historie des Sciences, 1953, pp. 358–365.

Hareuveni, Nogah. *Desert and Shepherd in Our Biblical Heritage*. Israel: Neot Kedumim, 1991. "Flowers in the Land of the Bible," Part I. Guide to Filmstrip NKF-14. Neot Kedumim, 1972.

"Fruit in the Land of the Bible," Part 2. Guide to Filmstrip NKF -13B. Neot Kedumim, 1973.

"Mother of Wheat." *Neot Kedumim Newsletter,* Pesach 2007, p. 3.

Nature in Our Biblical Heritage. Israel: Neot Kedumim, 1980.

"Pesach." Guide to Filmstrip NKF-10. Neot Kedumim, nd.

"The Sabbatical Year." *Neot Kedumim News.* Winter, 1987, p. 1, 3.

"The Seventh Year." Fall, 2000, pp. 4–5.

Tree and Shrub in Our Biblical Heritage. Israel: Neot Kedumim, 1984.

Hepper, F. Nigel. *Illustrated Encylopedia of Bible Plants.* United Kingdom: Inter Varsity Press, 1992.

Planting A Bible Garden. Grand Rapids, Michigan: Fleming H. Revell, 1997.

Hertz, J. H., ed. *The Pentateuch and Haftorahs: Hebrew Text, English Translation and Commentary.* London: Soncino Press, 1963.

Hillel, Daniel. *The Natural History of the Bible.* New York: Columbia University Press, 2006.

The Holy Bible, Containing the Old and New Testaments. King James Version.

Holtz, Barry W., ed. *Back to the Sources: Reading the Classic Jewish Texts.* New York: Summit Books, 1984.

Huxley, Anthony. *Huxley's Encyclopedia of Gardening.* New York: Universe Books, 1981.

Jacob, Irene. *Biblical Plants: A Guide to the Rodef Shalom Biblical Botanical Garden.* Pittsburgh: Rodef Shalom Press, 1989.

Jastrow, Marcus. *A Dictionary of the Targumim, the Talmud Babli and Yerushalami, and the Midrashic Literature.* Accessed from: http://www.tyndalearchive.com/tabs/jastrow.

Jewish Encyclopedia, 1906 edition. Accessed from: http://www.jewishency-clopedia.com.

Jewish Virtual Library. Accessed from: http://www.jewishvirtuallibrary.org/jsource/judaica/ejud_0002_0020_0_19970.html.

Kadari, Tamar. "Daughters of Zelophehad.," 2005. Accessed from: Jewish Women's Archive: http://jwa.org/encyclopedia/article/daughters-of-zelophehad-midrash.

Kass, Leon R. *The Beginning of Wisdom: Reading Genesis.* Chicago: University of Chicago Press, 2003.

Kosofsky, Scott-Martin. *A Book of Customs: A Complete Handbook for the Jewish Year.* New York: HarperCollins, 2004.

Kugel, James L. *How to Read The Bible: A Guide to Scripture, Then and Now.* New York: Free Press, 2007.

Kushner, Lawrence. *The Book of Letters.* Woodstock, Vermont: Jewish Lights Publishing, 1990.

Lust, John. *The Herb Book.* New York: Bantam Books, 1974.

Lluz, David, Miri Hoffman, Nechama Gilboa-Garber and Zohar Amar. "Medicinal properties of *Comiphora gildeadensis.*" *African Journal of Pharmacy and Pharmacology,* Vol. 4(8), pp. 51–520, August 2010.

Manniche, Lisa. *An Ancient Egyptian Herbal.* Austin: University of Texas Press, 1989.

Mazar, Amihai, Dvory Namdar, Nava Panitz-Cohen, Ronny Neumann & Steve Weiner. "Iron Age beehives at Tel Rehov in the Jordan Valley." *Antiquity* 82, pp. 629–639, 2008.

Metzger, Bruce M. and Michael D. Coogan eds. *The Oxford Companion To The Bible*. New York: Oxford University Press, 1993.

Milgrom, Jacob. *Anchor Bible Series, Levitcus*, Vol. 2.

The Mishnah, Seder Zeraim Vol. V: Tractate Challah, Tractate Orlah, Tractate Bikkurim. A New Translation With An Anthologized Commentary. ArtScroll Mishnah Series. New York: Mesorah Publications, Ltd., 2004.

The Mishnah, Seder Zeraim Vol. IIa: Tractate Peah. A New Translation With A Commentary Anthologized From Talmudic, Midrashic, And Rabbinic Sources. ArtScroll Mishnah Series. New York: Mesorah Publication, Ltd., 1990.

Moldenke, Harold N. and Alma L. Moldenke. *Plants of the Bible*. New York: Dover Publications, Inc., 1986 (reprint of 1952 edition).

Morton, Julia F. *Fruits of Warm Climates*. Miami, Florida: Julia F. Morton, 1987.

Musselman, Lytton John. *Figs, Dates, Laurel, and Myrrh: Plants of the Bible and the Quran*. Portland, Oregon: Timber Press, 2007.

Palevitch, Dan and Zohara Yaniv. *Medicinal Plants of the Holy Land*. (Vol. I and II). The Agriculture Research Organization of Israel. Tel-Aviv: Modan Publishing House, 2000.

Phillips, Roger and Nicky Foy. *The Random House Book of Herbs*. New York: Random House, 1990.

Plaut, W. Gunther. *Torah: A Modern Commentary, Genesis,* Vol. 1. New York: Union of American Hebrew Congregations, 1974.

Plowden, C. Chicheley. *A Manual of Plant Names*. New York: Philosophical Library, 1968.

Podohretz, Norman. *The Prophets: Who They Were, What They Are*. New York: The Free Press, 2002.

Rabinowitz, Louis I. *Torah And Flora*. New York: Sanhedrin Press, 1977.

Riskin, Shlomo. "Menora is a tree of light." *The International Jerusalem Post*, March, 1990.

"The Science of Religion." June, 2005.

Roth, Cecil B. And Geoffrey D. Wigoder, eds. *The New Standard Jewish Encyclopedia*. New York: Doubleday & Company, Inc., 1970.

Sandison, George. *Wild Flowers of Palestine*. 1895.

Sarna, Nahum M. *Exploring Exodus: The Heritage of Biblical Israel*. New York: Schocken Books, 1986.

Saunders, E. P. *Judaism: Practice and Belief, 63 BCE–66 CE*. London: SCM Press, 1992.

Schaffer, Arthur. "The Agricultural and Ecological Symbolism of the Four Species of Sukkot." *Tradition*, 20 (2), Summer, 1982.

"The History of Horse-radish as the Bitter Herb of Passover."

Siegel, Judy. "Ancient date seed from Masada may yield 'medicinal' bounty." *The International Jerusalem Post*, June 20–26, 2008.

"Israeli pomegranates worth their weight in gold." Oct. 3–8, 2008.

Siegel-Itzkovich, Judy. "Medicinal date palm from oldest known seed plant." *The Jerusalem Post*, Nov. 25, 2011. Accessed from: http://www.jpost.com/Health/Article.aspx?id=246956.

Slotki, I. W. *Isaiah, Hebrew Text & English Translation With An Introduction And Commentary*. New York: Soncino Press, 1983 (rev. ed.).

Speiser, E. A. *Anchor Bible Series, Genesis : Introduction, Translation, and Notes*, Vol. 1. New York: Doubleday, 1964.

Steinsaltz, Adin. *Biblical Images: Men and Women of the Book*. New York: Basic Books, Inc., 1984.

The Essential Talmud. New York: Basic Books, Inc., 1976.

Stern, Yechiel Michel. *Halachos Of The Four Species*. Jerusalem: Feldheim, 1993.

Strong, James. *Strong's Exhaustive Concordance of the Bible*. Peabody, Massachusetts: Hendrickson Publishers, nd.

Tanakh: A New Translation of The Holy Scriptures According to the Traditional Hebrew Text. Philadelphia: The Jewish Publication Society, 1985.

Tigay, Jeffrey H. *The JPS Torah Commentary, Deuteronomy*. Philadelphia: The Jewish Publication Society, 1996.

Tristram, H. B. *Natural History of the Bible*. London: Society for Promoting Christian Knowledge, 1867.

Vamosh, Miriam Feinberg. *Food At The Time Of The Bible*. Herzlia, Israel: Palphot Ltd., 2007.

Wagner, Matthew. "'But in the seventh year...'" The International Jerusalem Post, Sept. 12–20, 2007.

"Weekly Torah (Parshah) with Rashi." Judaica Press translation, accessed from: http://www.chabad.org/parshah/default_cdo/jewish/Torah-Portion.htm.

Werblowsky, R. J. Zwi and Geoffrey Wigoder. *The Encyclopedia of the Jewish Religion*. New York: Holt, Rinehard and Winston, Inc., 1965.

"Wild Flowers of Israel." Accessed from: http://www.wildflowers.com.il.

Zohary, Daniel and Maria Hopf. *Domestication of Plants of the Old World*. New York: Oxford University Press, 1988.

Zohary, Michael. *Plants of the Bible*. Cambridge: Cambridge University Press, 1982.

COMMON NAMES CROSS-REFERENCE

Common name, Hebrew name, Latin name. Inevitably identification of some biblical names is not always certain.

acacia tree (*shittah*), *Acacia raddiana*, source of wood, *shittim*
almond tree (*shaked, luz*), *Amygdalus communis*
anemone, crown (*kalanit*), *Anemone coronaria*
apple of Sodom (*ptilat hamidbar*), *Calotropis procera*

balm of Gilead (*tzori*), *Commiphora gileadensis*, possible source of Judean
  balsam
barley (*seorah*), *Hordeum vulgare*
bitter herbs for the ritual of *maror* at the Passover Seder
    compass lettuce (*hazeret*), *Lactuca serriola*
    chicory (*olshin*), *Cichorium endivia*
    sow-thistle (*tamcha*), *Sonchus oleraceus*
    eryngo, *harhavina*, *Eryngium creticum*
    centary (*maror, dardar*), *Centaurea iberica*
broom bush, white (*rotem*), *Retama raetam*
bulrush (*agmon*), *Scirpus lacustris*
burning bush; holy bramble (*sneh*), *Rubus sanguineus, R. sanctus*

caper bush (*tzalaf kotsani*), *Capparis zoharyi*
carob tree (*haruv*), *Ceratonia siliqua*
cassia (*kez'iah*), *Cinnamomum cassia*
cattail, reed-mace, flag (*suf*), *Typha domingensis*
cedar of Lebanon (*erez*), *Cedrus libani*
cinnamon (*kinnamon*), derived from *Cinnamamon verum*
citron (*etrog*), *Citrus medica*
crowfoot, Persian, red buttercup (*nurit*), *Ranunculus asiaticus*

cucumbers (*kishuim*)
  muskmelon, *Cucumis melo*
  snake cucumber, *Cucumis melo* var. *flexuosus*
cypress, common (*gopher, brosh*), *Cupressus sempervirens*

date palm (*tamar*), *Phoenix dactylifera*

fig tree (*te'ena*), *Ficus carica*
  sycomore fig (*shikma*), *Ficus sycomorus*
flax (*pishtah*), *Linum usitatissimum*
frankincense (*levonah*), substance derived from *Boswellia* spp.

galbanum (*helbenah*), *Ferrula* sp.
garlic (*shumim*), *Allium sativum*
golden thistle (*hoah*), *Scolymus maculatus*
gourd, wild (*pakuot-sadeh*), *Citrullus colocynthis*
grapevine (*gefen*), *Vitis vinifera*
gum (*nekot*), substance derived from *Astragalus* spp.

henbane, golden (*shikaron zahav*), *Hyoscyamus aureus*
hyssop, Syrian hyssop (*ezov*), *Majorana syriaca*
  blue hyssop, *Lavandula stoechas*
  Greek hyssop, *Teucrium capitatum*
  Roman hyssop, *Satureja thymbra*
  wild or tea hyssop, *Micromeria fruticosa*

juniper tree, Phoenician (*arar*), *Juniperus phoenicea*

ladanum (*lot*) derived from *Cistus* spp.
  pink rockrose, *Cistus creticus*
  white rockrose, *Cistus salviifolius*
leeks (*hatzir*), *Allium porrum*
  salad leek, *Allium kurrat*
lentils (*adashim*), *Lens culinaris*

mandrakes (*dudaim*), *Mandragora autumnalis*
manna (*mahn*)
  Tamarix nilotica
  Haloxylon salicornicum
myrrh (*mor*), substance derived from *Commiphora myrrha* and other
  Commiphora species
myrtle (*hadas*), *Myrtus communis*

narcissus
  "lily among thorns," (*shoshanat hamakim*), *Narcissus tazetta*
nightshade, gray (*hahedek*), *Solanum incanum*

oak tree (*alon*)
  Tabor oak, *Quercus ithaburensis*
  common oak, Kermes oak, *Quercus calliprinos*
olive tree (*zayit*), *Olea europaea*
onions (*betzalim*), *Allium cepa*

papyrus (*gomeh*), *Cyperus papyrus*
plane tree, Oriental (*armon*), *Platanus orientalis*
poison hemlock (*rosh*), *Conium maculatum*
pomegranate (*rimmon*), *Punica granatum*
poplar
  white popular (*livneh*), *Populus alba*
  Euphrates poplar (*tzaftzafah*), *Populus euphratica*
poppy, field (*parag*), *Papaver umbanotum*
  opium poppy, *Papaver somniferum*

reed, common (*kaneh*), *Phragmites australis*

sage (*marvah, moriah*) candidates for models of the first menorah
  Jerusalem sage, *Salvia hierosolymitana*
  Judean sage, *Salvia judaica*
  Land of Israel sage, *Salvia palaestina*
  pungent sage, *Salvia dominica*
  three-leafed sage, *Salvia fruticosa*
squirting cucumber (*yeroket ha'hamor*), *Ecballium elaterium*
stacte, storax, styrax (*nataf*)
  Commiphora spp.
  Liquidambar orientalis

tamarisk tree (*eshel*), *Tamarix aphylla*
terebinth tree (*elah*)
  Atlantic terebinth, *Pistacia atlantica*
  Palestine terebinth, *Pistacia palaestina*
thorny burnet (*sirim*), *Sarcopoterium spinosum*
tulip, sharon, sun's eye
  "rose of Sharon," (*havatzelet hasharon*), *Tulipa agenensis*

watermelons (*avatihim*), *Citrullus lanatus*
wheat
  emmer wheat (*kussemet*), *Triticum dicoccum*

wild wheat (*khitta*), *Triticum dicoccoides*
willow (*arava*)
    common willow, *Salix acmophylla*
    poplar willow, *Populus euphratica*
    white willow, *Salix alba*
wormwood (*la'anah*)
    Artemisia absinthium
    Artemisia judaica
    Artemisia sieberi

INDEX OF LATIN PLANT NAMES

Common name references can be found under Latin names. Numbers in bold indicate a photograph.

GENERAL INDEX

Isaac, 27, 28–30, 32, 45, 47, 48, 75, 80, 81, 88, 89; binding-of, 26

Isaiah, prophet, 73, 127, 142, 241, 244, 245, 246, 267, 272, 274, 332; life and prophesies 261–264; parable of the vineyard, 73, 164, 242, 245

Ishmael, 12, 233; Ishmaelite, 52, 55, 146

Israel, Land of, 28, 67, 76, 100, 109, 133, 136, 152, 184, 273, 279, 288, 311, 330; agricultural realities in, 18, 106; thorny weeds in, 6, 10

Israelites, destiny of, 63, 71, 81; as farmers, 15, 287–288; grievances, 116, 204; journey, 77, 238; new culture, 106, 125; new moral vision, 47, 123, 128; origin of term, 192–193; pagan backsliding; rebellion, 214, 221; redeemed by God, 71, 77, 88, 101, 109, 170; rejection of God, 205; slave generation, 215, 219; sojourn in Egypt, 67; suffering in Egypt, 81, 95; tested, 239. See also Promised Land

Jabbock gorge, 46

Jacob, breeding flock, 39–43; deathbed blessings, 68–71; descendants of in Israel, 95; and Esau, 12, 27–30, 44, 75, 48; reconciling with, 32, 46; leader-shepherd, 22; love for Rachel, 34–36, 80; nurse, 45; sibling rivalry, 12; renamed Israel, 48

Jehoiakim, 135

Jeremiah, prophet, 57, 75, 119, 135, 240, 244; life and prophesies, 195–200

Jericho, 6, 98, 100, 163

Jerusalem, 71, 137, 167, 189, 261, 271, 279, 284, 305, 309, 311; burning of, 197, 278;

characterized as harlot, 263; unifying force, 101, 102, 130, 133, 138, 162, 166, 170, 301, 310; Zion, 264. See also Talmud

Jesse, 246

Jew, 152, 154, 177, 180, 184, 188, 190, 191, 219, 235, 247, 265, 272, 276, 288, 311; Jerusalem synonym for, 271; origin of name, 69, 193

Jewish law, 137, 179, 257, 313; tradition, 12, 15, 36, 38, 152, 187, 235, 257, 278, 279, 297, 301, 302, 311

Jewish War, Second, 154

Jezebel, 229, 231

Joseph, 36, 48, 52–56, 57, 61–63, 64, 66, 67, 69–71, 75, 80, 153, 289; and his brothers, 12, 146; ornamented tunic ("coat of many colors"), 53, 55, 58

Josephus, 37, 189, 319, 331

Joshua, 98, 163, 201, 214, 215, 216, 259, 271, 278, 286, 307, 315

Josiah, King, 196

Jubilee, Jubilee Year, 188, 192

Judah, 55, 68, 69, 75, 174, 175, 303; Tribe of, 71, 72, 193; See also Kingdoms, divided

Judea. See Kingdoms, divided

kashrut, 186

Kermes ilicis (karmil insect), 50, 102

Kimchi (family), 279

Kingdoms, divided, 290; Northern (Israel), 229, 262, 301; Southern (Judah, Judea), 15, 24, 49, 69, 132, 156, 164, 196, 261–262, 264, 271, 291, 295; destruction of, 278

Kohethite Levite, 221, 226

Korah, 210, 220, 221–223, 226–227, 249

Laban, 29, 34, 35, 36, 40–41, 45–46; in Passover Haggadah, 312

laws (*mitzvot*), 47, 53, 77, 97, 116, 128,188, 201, 220, 259, 263, 282, 305, 306, 307, 334; agricultural, 165, 166, 292, 293, 294; charity, 293, 295; dietary, 102, 167, 278–270; female inheritance, 250; love the stranger, 26, 162, 283, 293; Oral (Mishna), 257, 279, 301

Leah, 33, 34–36, 38, 46, 53, 54, 69

lekhet (gleanings), 165, 294, 296

Levi, 46, 47, 53; house of, 220, 223; Levites, 76, 167, 221, 222, 294, 309; Kohetite, 221, 226

levirate marriage (*yibbum*), 300, 303

locust bean (St. John's bread), 266, 267, 269

Lotz Cisterns landscape, *xvi*

Luria, Rabbi Isaac, 309, 312

Maccabees, 152, 157, 175

Maimonides (Rambam), 179, 247

Mamre, terebinths of, 19, 20, 22; oaks of, 24

manna, 115, 117–119; and Sabbath observances derived from gathering, 120

Manasseh, 249, 250, 325; meaning of, 63

maquis, 24, 49, 57, 176, 264, 276; described, 15; origin of term, 51

Marrah, bitter waters of, 116; sweeten, 119, 120

Masada, 252, 257

Massah and *Meribah*, 240. See also *Meribah*

matza, 100

Mendelian laws of heredity, 41, 43

menorah, 149–157, 224; Temple, 16

Meribah, 278; waters of, 211, 315

Mesopotamia, 5, 12, 13, 29, 45, 46, 289

Messiah, 164, 226, 235

mezuzah, *xix*

Midian, 80; Midianites, 55, 229, 238

midrash, 26, 91, 136, 136, 162–163, 236, 247, 251, 269; *midrashim* (pl.), 179, 310

milk and honey, land of, 88, 214, 283, 286, 305. *See also* Harueveni, Nogah

Miriam, 79, 210, 213, 219

Mishna, 8, 142, 174, 185, 187, 190, 193, 307, 308, 321; bitter herbs in, 197, 108, 113; defined, 107; different New Years in, 180, 279; Oral Tradition preserved in, 288, 301; Sages of Mishnaic period, 120, 251, 257; system of nomenclature, 138

mitzvot. See laws

mixed multitude, riff-raff, (*erev rav*), 204, 206, 238, 247

Moab (plains of), 201, 237, 297, 302; offspring of Lot, 303 ; Moabite, 238, 296, 298, 300, 301

Moreh, terebinth of, 19, 20, 26

Moses, biography, 79–81; Israelites' complaints to, 116, 239–240; last teaching, 259, 282–284, 293, 304–307, 314–316, 324, 328–329, 332; leader, 79, 104, 205, 259; name, 85; offense to God, 203, 325; plagues, 95–96, 104–105; rod, 89, 223, 226; shepherd, 22, 80, 87, 88, 89, 104, 116, 123, 187, 196, 315; and scouts, 6, 72–73, 213–214; unburdens to God, 205. *See also* shepherd's staff

nahal, defined, 73, 235; Kerit, 230, 235

Naomi, 296–301, 302

Nebo, Mount, 329, 332

Neot Kedumim, 138, 248, 280
New Testament, 265, 269, 278, 279
Nile, River, annual flooding, 52,
    61–62, 64, 66, 79, 81–84, 112,
    206, 284, 328; Delta, 82, 84, 208
Noah, 11, 13, 14, 17, 18, 20, 72, 80;
    Ark, 141
Noahide Laws, 120

Olives, Mount of, 15
omer, 100–101, 102, 106, 117, 294,
    302; counting of, 309–310
Oral Law. *See* laws
orla (forbidden fruit), 162, 165, 167,
    170, 186, 254, 306, 307

Passover (*Pesah*), 100, 170, 238,
    307; calendar adjusted to, 112;
    origin of, 105; Seder, 109. *See
    also* bitter herbs, Pilgrimage
    Festivals
Paradise. *See* Eden.
Patriarchs, 20, 34, 47, 53, 55, 187,
    293
pe'ah (uncut corner), 165, 186, 294,
    296, 302, 306
Pentateuch, 1, 257
Pharaoh, 70, 71, 238; concentration
    of power, 62, 66; daughter of,
    79; dreams, 60–62, 64, 65;
    Moses and Aaron confront,
    95–96, 104–105
Philistines, land of, 23, 238, 286
Philo, 313
Phineas (Pinhas, Pinchas), 229
Phoenicia, 173, 229
Pilgrimage Festivals (Harvest
    Festivals), 106, 133, 147, 169,
    309, 313
pitom, 172–173, 180
plagues, 95–97, 101, 104, 289; Ten,
    89
Pliny the Elder, 148, 164, 288, 319
Potiphar, 55; Potiphar's wife, 61

pottage, a mess of, xxi, 31
prayer for dew, 175; for rain, 175,
    178
Promised Land, journey to, 77, 79,
    80, 88, 119, 123, 130, 142, 201,
    203, 205, 213, 278, 328; farming
    in, 105, 165, 179, 306; features
    of, 282, 284–285; Israelites'
    settlement of, 291; temptations
    in, 316
prozbul, 90, 193

rabbinic Judaism, 190; literature,
    1, 59, 126, 142, 234, 251, 254,
    266, 267; interpretations, 264,
    302, 120, 179
rabbis, moral vision and the
    natural world, 107, 218, 253;
    status, 257–258; teachings, 91,
    108–109, 110, 136, 171, 172, 180,
    189, 226, 301, 310
Rachel, 33–36, 38, 45, 46, 48, 52,
    63, 80; Rachel's Tomb, 36
rain, early (*yoreh*), late (malkosh),
    56, 66, 108, 152, 229, 272, 273,
    275, 285, 309
Rashbam (Rabbi Samuel ben
    Meir), 289
Rashi (Rabbi Solomon ben Isaac),
    1, 17, 85, 86, 113, 120, 268, 289
Rebekah, 26, 27, 29–30, 34, 44, 45,
    49
rebellions, 203, 206, 210, 221, 222,
    240; Great Rebellion, 220, 221,
    222
Rechab family, 197
Red Sea, 79. *See also* Sea of Reeds
Rephidim, 240
Responsa literature, Jewish, 250
Reuben, 33, 35, 48, 53, 54, 55, 69,
    75; Reubenites, 221, 227, 325
Rosh Hashana, 180, 189, 218, 235,
    317, 325
Ruth, 76, 296–303

Saadiah Gaon, Rabbi, 136, 269
Sabbath (*Shabbat*), 74–75, 147;
    breaker and, 251; and divine
    time, 240; first, 117; imitation
    of God, 129, symbolism of table,
    75. *See also* Sabbatical Year
Sabbatical Year, Seventh Year, Year
    of Release (*Shmitta*), 10, 167,
    184–191, 192, 217
Sages (rabbis), 6, 25, 120, 150, 251,
    257
Samaria, capital Northern
    Kingdom, 230, 266
sanctuary (*mikdash*), 123–128,
    129, 130, 131, 133, 140, 159, 221,
    257
Sarah (Sarai), 28; name change,
    22
Sea of Reeds (*yam suf*), 79, 80, 84,
    85, 116, 238, 383
Sephardic, 109, 225, 227
Septuagint, 4
Seven, significance of number, 192
Seven Species (*Shivat Haminim*),
    among ancient artifacts, 163;
    as first fruits, 307; bounty, 6;
    bringing to Jerusalem, 310;
    important crops, 7; symbol of
    bounty, 6; of faith, *xix, xx,*
    308; vulnerable crops, 223,
    285–286, 307. *See also*
    Hareuveni, Nogah
Shatnez, 99
Shavuot (Feast of Weeks, *Matan
    Torah*, Pentecost), 105, 106, 133,
    147, 169, 170, 215, 285, 286, 296,
    302, 303, 307, 309–311.
Shechem, 19, 20, 53, 54; altar at,
    22; pagan city of, 49. *See also*
    Dinah
Sheol (Hell), 222, 226
shepherd, shepherding; culture,
    47, 48, 62, 64, 77, 125, 293; and
    farming, 69, 70–71, 73, 75, 132,

240, 287, 288, 328; leadership,
    12, 21, 22, 88, 89, 271; purity of
    vs. farming, 12, 187–188, 294;
    staff (crook, rod), 89, 92, 223,
    226; transformation of, 282,
    305–306, 334; values of, 47, 89
showbread, 144, 150, 151
shikhehah (forgotten grain sheaf),
    295, 296
shofar, 188, 235
Simeon, 46, 47, 53, 63; Tribe of,
    69, 91
Simon bar Yohai, Rabbi, 267
Sinai, Mount (Mount Horeb),
    covenant at, 169, 196, 229, 271,
    282, 306, 316, 328; journey to,
    77, 201, 204, 213; reach; 123,
    240; revelation at, 247
Socrates, 318
Sodom, 21, 329; and Gomorrah,
    199, 315, 327
Solomon, 69, 98, 125, 130–133,
    134–135, 137, 217, 253
Song of the Sea, 116
St. Catherine's Monastery, 91
sukka, (hut), 170, 171
Sukkot (Feast of Tabernacles), 152,
    166, 170–172, 175, 176, 180,
    182, 185, 215, 234, 311. *See also*
    Pilgrimage Festivals
synagogue, designs on, 74, 152,
    152, 164; origin of, 279

Tabernacle (*mishkan*), building of,
    77, 99, 124–127, 204; defined,
    128
Talmud, 1, 22, 88, 100, 107, 109,
    111, 137, 152, 154, 226, 242, 250,
    251, 252, 255, 275, 295, 309, 322;
    characterized, 66; Jerusalem,
    126, 172, 267; Order of Seeds,
    185. *See also* Babylonian
Tamar, 174
Temple, First, building of, 125, 130,

131, 132–135, 138; destruction
of, 188, 196, 226, 278; Second,
destruction of, 175, 189, 226;
rebuilding, 188; rededication
of, 152
Ten Commandments, 77, 123, 128,
222, 223, 249
Tent of Meeting (*ohel moed*), 124,
128, 222, 223, 249
Terah, 20
terraces (terrace farming; terraced
land), 15, 71, 73, 287, 290–291
Theophrastus, 141, 288
thorns and thistles, 88, 10, 187,
241, 244, 246, 248, 324
tikkun olam, 190, 193
Tisha b'Av, 261, 271
tithes, 266, 294; described, 167
Torah, 5, 9, 15, 77, 97, 119, 150, 157,
159, 170, 187, 188, 218, 227, 247,
250, 259, 263, 288, 293, 301, 302,
304; defined, 1; in the field, 109,
278; values of, 135, 137, 152, 334
Tree of Knowledge of Good and
Evil, 3–6
Tree of Life (*Etz Haim*), 3, 5, 150
Tu b'Shvat (*Tu Bishvat*), 181, 279.
See also Harevueni, Nogah
Tutankhamun, 252, 255
Tzalaf, 252, 255
Tzelafkhad; transliteration of, 256;
daughters' names (Mahlah,
Noah, Hoglah, Milcah,
Tirzah), 250, 256, 249; laws of
inheritance of, 249–251, 256,
257

Ur, 20

Varro, 288
Virgil, 288

wadi, definition, *xvii*, 212
Philistine Way, 238, 247

Western Wall, 252, 319
wilderness (*hamidbar*), circuitous
route in, 115; forty years in;
hazards of, 205; Israelites' sins
in, 237, 261; itinerary, 246; long
journey in, 201, 281, 284, 287;
of Paran, 213; of Sin, 237; 261;
terrain, 116, 204, 238. *See also*
Hareuveni, Nogah

Yom Kippur, 148, 188, 325

za'atar, 136–137, 138–139
Ziemba, Rabbi Mordechai, 309,
312
Zipporah, 87

LAND OF THE HEBREW BIBLE

(modern names in parentheses)

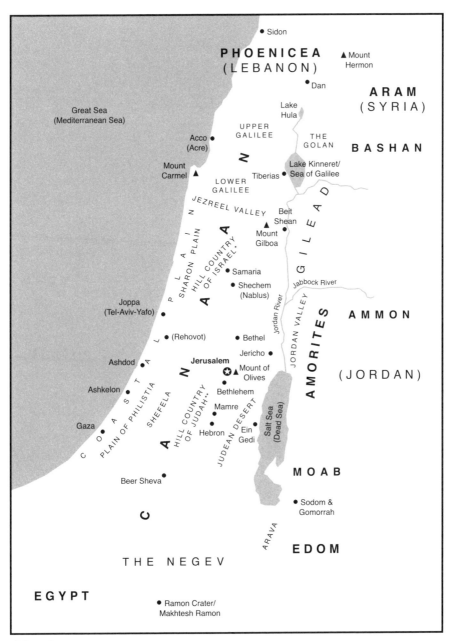

* Samaria
** Judea

EXODUS ROUTE FROM EGYPT TO THE PROMISED LAND

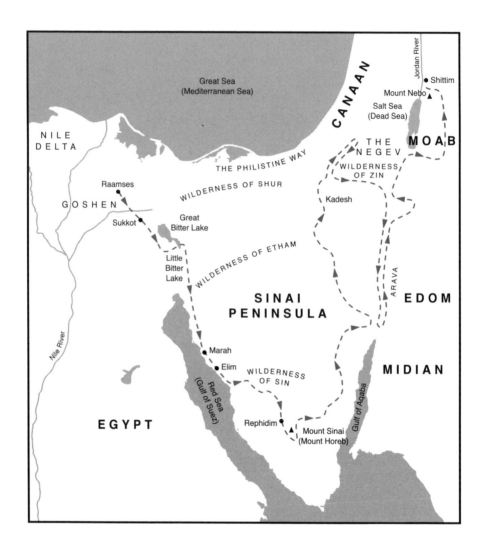